YOUNG
WINSTON'S WARS

YOUNG
WINSTON'S WARS

The Original Despatches of
WINSTON S. CHURCHILL
War Correspondent
1897–1900

Edited and with an
introduction and notes
by
FREDERICK WOODS

Leo Cooper Ltd
London

First Published in Great Britain, 1972 by
Leo Cooper Ltd
196 Shaftesbury Avenue
London WC2H 8JL
Copyright © Chartwell Trust 1972
This edition © Frederick Woods 1972

ISBN 0 85052 128 9

Text set in 11/12 pt. Monotype Ehrhardt, printed by letterpress,
and bound in Great Britain at The Pitman Press, Bath

To

WINSTON S. CHURCHILL

the other war correspondent of the same name

Contents

Illustrations

Maps

Acknowledgements

I would like to express my gratitude to the following for assistance: H. A. Cahn, Martin Gilbert, John McCracken; the staffs of the War Office Library, the Army Museum and the British Museum, Colindale.

I am also indebted to Heinemann Ltd for permission to quote from letters printed in the Companion Volume to Volume I of the official biography by Randolph S. Churchill; to the *Daily Telegraph* for permission to reprint the despatches from the North-west Frontier and Sudan; and to the Chartwell Trust for permission to reprint the Boer War despatches.

I must especially thank Winston S. Churchill for his interest and generous encouragement.

F.W.

Introduction

In spite of the demands of a full political life, Sir Winston Churchill found time to issue over 160 separate publications in book or pamphlet form, over sixty forewords or contributions to other books, and well over 800 press articles in media ranging from the *News of the World* and *Daily Mirror* to the *Journal of the Royal United Services Institution* and *Life*. Some of these articles have been reprinted in *Thoughts and Adventures* (1932), *Great Contemporaries* (1937), *Step by Step* (1939) and *Painting as a Pastime* (1948), but the majority remains ungathered. Many of them were unashamed potboilers dating from the wilderness thirties, when Churchill earned his living by writing articles that sometimes sank to the level of 'Are there men in the moon' and 'Life under the microscope.'[1] But among the newspaper articles that have not been reprinted are his war despatches from India (1897) and Sudan (1898); those from South Africa (1899–1900) were reprinted at the time in expanded form. These were among his best writings, often displaying a vividness and an economy not always present in later years, when he had turned to dictation as his method of writing and the practices of parliamentary rhetoric made themselves visible in his literary style.

*   *   *

Churchill's first publication came early, in the 19 December, 1891, issue of *The Harrovian*, a characteristically pugnacious letter of protest about the school gymnasium. Between then and the time he

---

[1] According to Lord Moran, Churchill claimed that he earned £20,000 a year from writing during this period. LORD MORAN *Churchill: The Struggle for Survival 1940–1965* (Constable, 1966), p. 420.

Introduction

left Harrow, several contributions appeared over various *noms de plume*, most of them merely childish but some displaying admirable brevity and wit; as, for instance, this sterling example of demolition by understatement on the subject of changing room facilities in the gymnasium.

'i. The room possesses two towels at present.
ii. These are changed once a week.
iii. They are used during that time by over 300 boys.
iv. Gymnastics is conducive to warmth.'[1]

This writing experience, slender though it was, was soon put to good use. Churchill received his commission in the 4th Hussars on 20 February, 1895, and immediately looked about him for a war with an eagerness that was not so much the result of bloodthirstiness as of professionalism: he was now a soldier and therefore needed military experience. The Queen was waging no war at that point but there was, however, at least an insurrection in Cuba, where insurgents had been harassing the Spanish army since 1894. Churchill, who felt that this would be more interesting and less expensive than 'a couple of months hunting at Leighton Buzzard', set off forthwith, accompanied by a fellow-subaltern, Reggie Barnes. To help finance the trip, he arranged to send letters back to the *Daily Graphic* for a fee of five guineas each, no mean fee in those days for a first assignment.[2]

In September, 1896, Churchill was posted to his regiment in Bangalore, but before his departure he made the acquaintance of General Sir Bindon Blood. Young and old soldier found a mutual respect and Blood willingly promised Churchill a position on his staff should he ever command another Indian expedition. The chance came in the following year when trouble flared once again on the North-west Frontier. Churchill was on leave, enjoying the sunshine of Goodwood, but he immediately cabled to remind Blood of his promise and set off for India. Unfortunately, all the staff positions were filled, so Churchill turned to journalism as a temporary expedient to get him to the front. But, although it later assumed

[1] 'Topics of the school', *The Harrovian*, 17 November, 1892.
[2] The letters appeared under the title 'The insurrection in Cuba' in the issues of 13, 17, 24 and 27 December, 1895; and 13 January, 1896. They have been reprinted in full, OBC pp. 604–18.

much greater importance in his life, writing at this time was only a means to an end.

Two motives were larger in Churchill's mind than the desire to write *per se*: the desire to experience war again by whatever means (and, if possible, to accumulate campaign medals); and the long-range plans for a political career that were already forming. On 5 September, 1895 he wrote to his mother:

'Herewith two letters for the *D.T.* [*Daily Telegraph*]. I do not know what terms you have made with them—but it should certainly not be less than £10 per letter. Having read please forward—and decide whether they should be signed or not. I am myself very much in favour of signing—as otherwise I get no credit for the letters. It may help me politically to come before the public in this way.'[1]

It was perhaps unwise of Churchill to leave the financial arrangements to Lady Randolph—never one to treat money with any high seriousness except when it was short—for she secured only £5 per letter. ('Haggling about the price,' she observed, 'would not have done.') To add insult to injury, she opted for anonymity as well. Churchill was incensed.

'I will not accept less than £10 a letter and I shall return any cheque for a less sum. I particularly asked for that amount *au moins* and when I think of the circumstances under wh those letters were written, on the ground in a tent temperature 115° or after a long days action or by a light which it was dangerous to use lest it drew fire—when I was tired and hustled and amid other adverse circumstances—I think they are cheap at the price. The £75 which the *D.T.* propose to give me will hardly pay my ticket for self & horses. The *D. Chronicle* offered me ten pounds a letter to go to Crete and I will not be defrauded in this way. As Dr Johnson says, "No one but a blockhead ever wrote except for money".'[2]

But for all his fury Churchill had to accept the offered amount, and continued to grumble at intervals thereafter. As late as January of the following year he was still muttering. 'Stingy pinchers' he

[1] Letter to Lady Randolph dated 5 September, 1897. OBC, p. 784.
[2] Letter to Lady Randolph dated 25 October, 1897. OBC, p. 812. However, it is worth noting that in a letter to the Duchess of Marlborough dated 8 February, 1898 Churchill asserted that 'though it is a poor thing to write for money, there is no harm in getting money for what you write.' OBC, p. 876.

growled in a brief return to the idiom of the classroom; and even later, 'I made it my business to lunch with the Editor of the *Pioneer* at Calcutta . . . he would not believe the *D.T.* had the conscience to pay me so little for the letters. He said they were a paper noted for their meanness.'[1]

Nevertheless, as he had to recognise, he had secured a national platform for his views and, if the letters were only by-lined 'By a young officer', Lady Randolph ensured that everyone of note—from the Prince of Wales down—knew the identity of the young officer.

His first professional despatches were conscientious and vivid, but he never forgot his political ambitions. Time and time again comments intrude which go far beyond the normal scope of war correspondence, and equally often rolling Churchillian perorations ring sonorously from the tightly-packed columns of type. Nor was he afraid of controversy. His attacks on the Indian Government and the Cabinet rankled in the higher echelons of the army and Parliament. Staff officers viewed with distaste the spectacle of a junior subaltern publicly criticising aspects of the military operations, particularly those relating to strategy and logistics; and the fact that he was unfailingly constructive was, presumably, merely a further source of irritation. And at home, members of the Government could hardly relish such phrases as 'the rapacity of Government' or, indeed, such statements as: 'It is fashionable in English politics to discredit the view of people on the spot. They are supposed to be excitable and prejudiced, to be unable to take the judicial and comprehensive views which can, it is believed, be adopted only in an atmosphere of ignorant indifference.'[2]

In other words, like it or not, the Cabinet—not to mention the War Office—was going to find itself out of step with Lieutenant Churchill.

Not surprisingly, perhaps, Churchill found himself the object of a certain amount of resentment from officers on Blood's staff which took the form of blocking any possible staff appointment. Churchill could hardly have expected much else; he clearly wanted to attract attention and, even at this early stage, had already lost interest in continuing his army career. Nevertheless, he reacted with characteristic truculence. 'I will invite you to consider what a contemptible position it is for high military officers to assume—to devote so

[1] Letter to Lady Randolph dated 21 October, 1897. OBC, p. 862.
[2] *Daily Telegraph*, 6 November, 1897.

much time and energy to harrying an insignificant subaltern.' And he added superbly: 'Talk to the Prince about it.'[1]

But although Churchill might adopt an air of injured innocence, he remained undeterred from his main purpose. While the despatches were still appearing in England, he started on a full history of the campaign. *The Story of the Malakand Field Force* (1898)—his first book—created an immediate impression among military and political circles, and even drew forth a delighted letter from the Prince of Wales.

'I cannot resist writing a few lines to congratulate you on the success of your book. I have read it with the greatest possible interest and I think the descriptions and the language generally excellent. Everybody is reading it, and I only hear it spoken of with praise.'[2]

Both despatches and book made friends, but they also made enemies—Kitchener included—who in the months to come would do their best to obstruct the outspoken and well-connected subaltern. None of the enmities was permanent, and as Churchill could call on the active assistance of such powerful allies as the Prince of Wales and the Prime Minister, they were scarcely more than irritations to him.

* * *

Two years previously, Kitchener's campaign to resubjugate the Sudan got under way. Progress was slow and affairs were just coming to a head in the spring of 1898, when a major action at Atbara heralded the commencement of the final stage. Churchill, watching from afar, pulled every string he could reach to secure an attachment. But the Malakand letters still rankled. Pressured by the Prince of Wales through General Sir Evelyn Wood, Kitchener brusquely replied, 'I would like . . . and Fincastle recommended by personage but do not want Churchill as no room.' Sir Evelyn persisted. 'Personage asked me personally desires you take Churchill.' Lady Jeune, a family friend of the Churchills, also cabled to Kitchener in terms which strongly suggest that Kitchener's excuse of lack of vacancies was not the reason he gave privately: 'Hope you will take Churchill. Guarantee he wont write.'[1]

Whether or not this promise was actually elicited from Churchill,

[1] Letter to Lady Randolph dated 21 October, 1897. OBC, p. 806.
[2] Letter from the Prince of Wales to Churchill dated 22 April, 1898. OBC, p. 930.

Introduction

the prospect still failed to seduce Kitchener, but Churchill was given a heaven-sent opportunity when the Prime Minister, Lord Salisbury, invited him to Downing Street to discuss his recently-published book. Again pressure was applied, and this time Kitchener gave in— but with ill grace. Churchill's letter of appointment was, to say the least, laconic.

'You have been attached as a supernumerary Lieutenant to the 21st Lancers for the Sudan campaign. You are to report at once at the Abassiyeh Barracks, Cairo, to the Regimental Headquarters. It is understood that you will proceed at your own expense and that in the event of your being killed or wounded in the impending operations, or for any other reason, no charge of any kind will fall on British Army Funds.'[2]

Churchill immediately proceeded to Cairo; if Kitchener had thought that the special conditions would deter Churchill he was sadly mistaken. Lady Jeune's guarantee notwithstanding, the intention to write was as strong as ever, though this time a subterfuge was necessary. Instead of a direct commission to act as official correspondent, Churchill chose to adopt the disguise of a combatant writing privately to a friend at home, not with any wish for publication but not dismayed if the recipient was so impressed that he sent the letters to a newspaper. So that the device gave maximum efficiency, it was arranged that the recipient should be the proprietor of the *Morning Post*, Oliver Borthwick. When printed, the letters were preceded by an editorial explanation of their 'provenance.'

Once this deception was under way, Churchill's attitude to it was ambivalent. On the one hand, he sought to preserve his anonymity— at least until such time as he was no longer dependent on his attachment; on the other hand, he was annoyed when what seemed to him to be unnecessarily stringent protection of his anonymity occurred. On 17 September, 1898 he wrote to his mother: 'There need be no secret about my having written the letters and the allusions to Cuba and the Frontier were deliberate.'[3] But a few days earlier he had written to Aylmer Haldane: 'If you look in the *Morning Post* it is

[1] Cable from Kitchener to Wood dated 9 July, 1898; cable from Wood to Kitchener dated 10 July, 1898; cable from Lady Jeune dated ? July, 1898. OBC, pp. 948-9.
[2] WINSTON S. CHURCHILL *My Early Life* (Thornton Butterworth, 1930), p. 182.
[3] Letter to Lady Randolph dated 17 September, 1898. OBC, p. 980.

xviii

possible that you will see that one of my friends has committed and continues to commit an unpardonable breach of confidence by publishing letters of mine. Don't give away the pious fraud as I do not want to be recalled. . . .'[1]

By this time, Churchill had finally made a firm decision to resign his commission, and once Omdurman was reduced he had no compunction about signing the last of the despatches. As he had observed to his mother about the Indian despatches, there was no point in not getting any credit. It was a calculated risk which, in the event, succeeded. But characteristically, he had pulled no punches, and reactions were understandably severe.

On 16 September, 1898, he wrote to Ian Hamilton: 'I am in great disfavour with the authorities here. Kitchener was furious with Sir E. Wood for sending me out and expressed himself freely. My remarks on the treatment of the wounded—again disgraceful—were repeated to him and generally things have been a little unpleasant. He is a great general but he has yet to be accused of being a great gentleman. It is hard to throw stones at the rising sun and my personal dislike may have warped my judgment, but if I am not blinded, he has been on a certainty from start to finish and has had the devil's luck to help him beside.'[2]

In fact, Churchill's attacks on Kitchener, particularly with regard to the desecration of the Mahdi's Tomb in Omdurman and the decapitation of the Mahdi's corpse, were fairly mild in the despatches, as Churchill had not had time to verify his information. They reached a peak in his campaign history, *The River War*, though it should be observed that in the abridged, one-volume edition that appeared only three years later, these criticisms were deleted. But by then Churchill was a Member of Parliament, and perhaps other considerations were more important.

But a more serious reprimand awaited Churchill. On 6 October the Prince of Wales wrote in heavily critical terms. 'I fear that in matters of discipline in the army I may be considered old fashioned— and I must say that I think an officer serving in a campaign should not write letters for the newspapers or express strong opinions of how the operations were carried out.

'If the Sirdar [Kitchener], as you say, viewed your joining his force with dislike—it is I am sure merely because he knows you write,

---

[1] Letter to Aylmer Haldane dated 11 August, 1898. OBC, p. 964.
[2] Letter to Ian Hamilton dated 16 September, 1898. OBC, pp. 979-80.

for which he has the greatest objection I understand—and I cannot help agreeing with him. . . .'[1]

But Churchill, once again, had made his point, and could afford to ignore such reactions. His despatches had created controversy, had demonstrated his total lack of fear or favour, and had created a considerable impact on the reading public—a portion of whom would soon meet him on the hustings.

For these despatches Churchill received £15 each—half as much again as he had demanded, and failed to get, only the year before. So he continued on his implacable way, achieving increasing success in terms of both his immediate financial returns and his long-range political plans.

As there was an overlap between the Indian and Sudanese campaigns, so there was an overlap between the Indian and South African campaigns. As long ago as late 1896 or early 1897 Churchill had written a memorandum entitled 'Our account with the Boers'. Still unpublished, it is an analysis of the situation immediately following the Jameson Raid of 1895, and it foreshadowed with astonishing consistency some of the attitudes and beliefs that Churchill expressed in his Boer War despatches. 'Imperial aid must redress the wrongs of the Outlanders; Imperial troops must curb the insolence of the Boers. There must be no half-measures. The forces employed must be strong enough to bear down all opposition from the Transvaal and the Free State; and at the same time to overawe all sympathisers in Cape Colony. There will not be wanting those who will call such a policy unscrupulous. If it is unscrupulous for the people of Great Britain to defend their most vital interests, to extend their protection to their fellow-countrymen in distress and to maintain the integrity of their Empire, "unscrupulous" is a word we shall have to face.'[2]

Here, encapsulated three years before the 'second' Boer War are the main points hammered home time and again in the despatches: protection and state aid for the settlers; a strong enough army in the field, with the implication that the Boer strength should not be underestimated; the strength and vitality of the Empire; the necessity for force motivated by benevolence.

As before, Churchill's criticisms of the political, military—and, in

[1] Letter from the Prince of Wales to Churchill dated 6 October, 1898. OBC, p. 984.
[2] OB, p. 449.

xx

one instance, religious—handling of the campaign were trenchant and biting. By now his attitudes towards the High Command were notorious. There is a delicious description of him haranguing Sir Charles Warren at the height of Spion Kop with impassioned references to 'Majuba' and 'the great British public'; and a masterly miniature appeared in a regimental paper of the time.

> 'On the stricken field
> See:—With wallets
> stuffed with ointments
> Balm'd 1st field dressings—
> ever accompanied by his
> faithful Vulture—gently
> chiding erring generals,
> heartening disheartened
> Brigade Majors—the
> prematurely bent figure
> of the late Candidate for
> Oldham, the one lodestone
> of hope to the weary
> soldier.'[1]

On 17 September, 1899, Churchill received a telegram from Alfred Harmsworth, founder of the *Daily Mail*, inviting him to become the *Mail's* correspondent in South Africa. Churchill immediately contacted Oliver Borthwick and offered to write for the *Morning Post* 'for my expenses, copyright of work, and one thousand pounds—for four months shore to shore—two hundred a month afterwards.' He also retained freedom of movement and opinion.

Churchill afterwards described this remuneration as 'higher, I think, than any previously paid in British journalism to war correspondents.'[2] In the context of the turn of the century, the payment was considerable, but Borthwick secured a major series of despatches that transformed Churchill from a precocious young subaltern into one of the greatest of the Victorian war correspondents, worthy of comparison with William Howard Russell and G. W. Steevens (who eventually covered the war for the *Daily Mail* and died of enteric fever in beleaguered Ladysmith).

For Churchill, too, the bargain was satisfactory. In *My Early*

[1] OBC, p. 1153.
[2] WINSTON S. CHURCHILL, op. cit, p. 244.

Life (1930) he recorded that 'the sales of *The River War* and of my two books of war correspondence from South Africa, together with the ten months' salary amounting to £2500 from the *Morning Post*, had left me in possession of more than £4000.'[1] Closer to the event, but after his first American lecture tour in 1900, he wrote to his mother: 'I am very proud of the fact that there is not one person in a million who at my age could have earned £10,000 without any capital in less than two years.'[2]

In the event, Churchill saw a great deal of action.[3] He observed or took part in the major actions of Spion Kop, Dewetsdorp, Vaal Krantz, Pieters, Johannesburg and Pretoria; was a member of the first party to enter Ladysmith; and was given the unexpected but priceless bonus of his capture and escape, which instantly established him as a national figure, a glamorous and daring hero, a subject even for popular music hall songs.[4] All this was to prove invaluable when he came to stand for Parliament for the second time.

In the sphere of military action, the Boer War eclipsed anything that Churchill had so far experienced; and in political—and indeed in ethical and personal—terms, he was considerably moved. In the midst of a plethora of jingoistic and propaganda-ridden journalism from the front, he could honestly write, 'I have not been afraid to write the truth as I see it.' As might be expected, this in itself led to criticism, for the general public did not want to be told of the Boers'

[1] Ibid, p. 374.

[2] Letter to Lady Randolph dated 1 January, 1901. OBC, p. 1225.

[3] It seems probable that, at the outset, Churchill did not anticipate such close involvement for he set off for South Africa with, among other things:

> 6 bottles Vin d'Ay Sec
> 18 bottles St Emilion
> 6 bottles light port
> 6 bottles French vermouth
> 18 bottles Scotch whisky (10 years old)
> 6 bottles Very Old Eau de Vie landed 1886
> 12 Rose's cordial lime juice

OBC, p. 1052.

[4] 'You've heard of Winston Churchill—
This is all I have to say—
He's the latest and the greatest
Correspondent of the day.'

Sung by T. E. Dunville, Lancashire music hall comedian.

virtues, or of their justifications, or their courage and humanity. But Churchill always respected an honourable foe, and his ability (at that time, at least) to see two sides of a question led to further misunderstandings, culminating in the controversy caused by the statement in his maiden speech in the House of Commons (18 February 1901): 'If I were a Boer I hope I should be fighting in the field.'

The Boer War despatches are a major landmark in the field of war journalism. With them Churchill reached both the climax and the end of his brief but incandescent career as a correspondent. With far less experience he had achieved both Steevens' immediacy and Russell's humanity. He had made a mark both as a writer and as some-one—as yet untried—who was potentially a major political force. At that point he could have asked for little more. In the summer of 1900 he could look back with satisfaction on his achievements during the previous three years, and could look forward, at the age of twenty-five, with reasonable certainty to the successful beginning of a political career that owed at least as much to his own efforts as to the memory of his father.

In 1893, just before Churchill entered Sandhurst, his father described him, in a letter to the Duchess of Marlborough, as having 'little [claim] to cleverness, to knowledge or any capacity for settled work. . . . Nothing has been spared on him; the best coaches every kind of amusement and kindness especially from you and more than any boy of his position is entitled to. The whole result of this has been either at Harrow or Eton[1] to prove his total worthlessness as a scholar or as a conscientious worker.' To young Winston himself, Lord Randolph wrote: 'you will become a mere social wastrel one of the hundreds of public school failures, and you will degenerate into a shabby unhappy and futile existence.'[2]

Lord Randolph had died in 1895, so Churchill was denied the satisfaction of reminding him of those cruel statements. But he must

[1] At this point, Lord Randolph was already suffering from the progressive mental paralysis which finally killed him. The Spencer-Churchills had been Etonians for six generations, and Lord Randolph was under the delusion that Churchill had been at both schools. Churchill was, in fact, sent to Harrow as it was felt that its high position would be healthier for the sickly child than low-lying Eton.

[2] Letter from Lord Randolph to the Duchess of Marlborough dated 5 August 1893, OBC, pp. 385-7; letter from Lord Randolph to Churchill dated 11 August, 1893, OBC, pp. 390-1.

have remembered the latter at least, and if he did so with an ironic relish it would have been only just.

Henceforth, journalism always loomed large in Churchill's life but from now on the major impetus was political. Professional journalism had served its purpose for the time being. But in so doing, it had started one of the twentieth century's greatest writers on one of his several careers. And if Churchill's literary verve succumbed in time to the extended purple patches of rhetoric, at least it started—and succeeded—in the toughest sphere of all.

*   *   *

In many respects, Churchill's war despatches were very much of their time. He wrote passionately of the Queen, the Empire and the Flag; yet he rarely wrote jingoistically. His writing was informed with humanity and charity (except when he was attacking hypocrisy or what he considered to be official ineptitude), and he displayed that respect—even admiration—for a good enemy that characterised the days when chivalry and cavalry were synonymous, an attitude that saw its last flickering expression during the Battle of Britain. After the battle of Omdurman he visited the field and saw the thousands of Dervish dead. While relishing the victory over what he saw as feudal tyranny, he nevertheless paid tribute to the twisted corpses.

'When a soldier of a civilised power is killed his limbs are composed and his body is borne by friendly arms reverently to the grave. The wail of the fifes, the roll of the drums, the triumphant words of the funeral service, all divest the act of its squalour, and the spectator sympathises with, perhaps almost envies, the comrade who has found this honourable exit. But there was nothing *dulce et decorum* about the Dervish dead. Nothing of the dignity of unconquerable manhood. All was filthy corruption. Yet these were as brave men as ever walked the earth. The conviction was borne in on me that their claim beyond the grave in respect of a valiant death was as good as that which any of our countrymen could make. . . . There they lie, those valiant warriors of a false faith and of a fallen domination, their only history preserved by their conquerors, their only monument their bones—and these the drifting sand of the desert will bury in a few short years. Three days before I had seen them rise eager, confident, resolved. The roar of their shouting had swelled like the surf on a rocky shore. The flashing of their blades and points had displayed their numbers, their vitality, their ferocity. They were confident in their strength, in the justice of their cause, in the support of their religion. Now only the heaps of corruption on the plain and fugitives dispersed and scattered in the wilderness remained. The terrible machinery of scientific war had done its work. The Dervish host was scattered and destroyed. Their end, however, only anticipates that of the victors, for Time, which laughs at Science, as Science laughs at Valour, will in due course contemptuously brush both combatants away.'[1]

This is as moving an obituary as might be expected from any enemy, moving both in its own terms and in the context of the conventional British attitudes of the period to primitive enemies. Similarly, Churchill could extend great sympathy and almost affection to a fallen Boer. Reminded of the death of Field-Cornet de Mentz in the action at Acton Homes, he wrote:

'De Mentz! The name recalled a vivid scene—the old field-cornet lying forward, grey and grim, in a pool of blood and a litter of empty cartridge cases, with his wife's letter clasped firmly in his stiffening fingers. He had "gone down fighting", and had had no doubts what course to steer. I knew when I saw his face that he had thought the whole thing out. . . . He himself was killed with the responsibility on his shoulders of leading his men into an ambush which, with ordinary precautions, might have been avoided. His widow, a very poor woman, lived next door to the hotel, nursing her son who had been shot through the lungs in the same action. Let us hope he will recover, for he had a gallant sire.'[2]

It has often been said that Churchill glorified war. He did not; he relished the excitement of war as a personal experience, but no-one saw more clearly than he the futility of war—perhaps not so much in terms of the loss of human life in the generality as in terms of the death of this or that valiant protagonist. The attitude is almost Arthurian, for surely Churchill was one of the last survivors of the chivalric age (indeed, he survived it to the extent of having to accept responsibility for the bombing of Dresden and other acts that were far from being chivalric). He mourned the fact that 'golden lads and girls all must, as chimney-sweepers, come to dust,' but if the death was honourable, or in an honourable cause, he could also celebrate that death. When Lord Ava was fatally wounded he could write, in

[1] *Morning Post*, 6 October, 1898.
[2] *Morning Post*, 12 July, 1900.

Introduction

terms that are probably aversive to many of us today, 'Lord Ava is seriously wounded, a sad item, for which the only consolation is that the Empire is worth the blood of its noblest citizens.[1]

This, even if the sentiments now seem artificial, is by no means glorification of war, but merely the expression of an attitude that was as acceptable to Victorians as disenchantment and flat realism are to the present generations.

Social attitudes apart, Churchill's descriptions of war are sharp and economical. Technically, perhaps, the structure is often contrived: short, staccato, often verbless sentences used in a most academic way. And yet the result is undeniably effective; the textbook method yields a result that goes beyond mere theory. There is genuine excitement in Churchill's descriptions of fighting, an excitement that reflects Churchill's own relish of the hazards without in any way revealing any taste for death or destruction for its own sake. The short, brittle sentences take in the tiny details sharply and efficiently, and contrast admirably with the more sonorous phrases that he uses for more general narration.

The Victorian era saw many campaigns and even more war correspondents who competed in the flourishing popular press for attention. Some were conventional and dull, some were mere propagandists, some were brilliant, involved and fluent. Among the last category were Russell, Steevens and Churchill.

War is an imperialist symptom, and it is no coincidence that the greatest period of British imperial rule also fathered the three greatest war correspondents in the history of English-language journalism. In this triumvirate, Churchill has some claim to be considered *primus inter pares*. Emotions about Churchill can still run high, and many will reject the claim; but on an objective basis, it must be conceded that his war despatches during this limited period rank among his greatest writings. When it is considered that he was still in his early twenties when he wrote them, the achievement should be seen in true perspective.

FREDERICK WOODS
Richmond, 1972

[1] *Morning Post*, 6 February, 1900.

The abbreviations OB and OBC used throughout these footnotes refer to the following: OB = RANDOLPH S. CHURCHILL *Winston S. Churchill*, Volume I (Heinemann, 1966); OBC = RANDOLPH S. CHURCHILL *Winston S. Churchill*, Companion Volume to Volume I (Heinemann, 1967).

xxvi

Editorial Note

Churchill used these despatches as the bases of his four campaign books: *The Story of the Malakand Field Force* (1898), *The River War* (1899), *London to Ladysmith* and *Ian Hamilton's March* (1900).

The first two books were largely rewritten, using both subsequently acquired knowledge and hindsight. As he put it in the Preface to *The Story of the Malakand Field Force*, 'I have freely availed myself of all passages, phrases and facts which seemed appropriate.' There are, therefore, occasional passages that appear in both the despatches and the books.

London to Ladysmith and *Ian Hamilton's March* are virtually reprints of the original despatches, though, particularly in the latter, there are major additions. I have chosen, therefore, to provide a selection of these despatches, covering about two-thirds of the total. The newspaper text has been followed throughout.

Like all journalists, Churchill was at the mercy of the sub-editor. These editing processes cannot now be precisely identified, but certain areas present no problems. Headlines and crossheads, for instance, were clearly added in London (though in a few of the Boer War despatches there are indications that Churchill offered headlines of his own); these have been eliminated. Similarly, as newspaper column-widths necessitate compromises in paragraphing, I have taken the liberty of reparagraphing where it seems clear that this is stylistically and structurally valid.

In the Sudan campaign, Churchill came up against a sub-editor with a positively Teutonic passion for capitalisation; I have de-capitalised wherever possible throughout so that capitalisation, where used, contributes to an intended rhetorical effect or has a specific point. (In military terms, for example, 'an army' is not necessarily the same as 'an Army'.) I have also brought the punctuation more into line with contemporary usage, and have corrected certain obvious misprints and some grammatical errors that would have been dealt with by Churchill himself had he had the opportunity for revision. And finally, I have added brief notes on the senior officers and major protagonists mentioned in the text except where the context makes this unnecessary.

The despatches are printed in their order of writing, which was not always their order of appearance. Publication dates are given at the end of each despatch.

The maps printed with the original despatches from South Africa were based on sketches supplied by the author. They have been redrawn for this edition and, where necessary, clarified, When maps appeared in more than one despatch, they have been repeated here. There being no map with the Sudan despatches, I have inserted a map on page 77 to assist the reader.

'*I have only cared to write what I thought was the truth about everybody.*'

❋

'*War, disguise it as you may, is but a dirty, shoddy business, which only a fool would play at.*'

The North-West Frontier

1897

The Daily Telegraph

6 October–6 December, 1897

MALAKAND, 3 September

As the correspondent approaches the theatre of war he will naturally endeavour to observe every sign along the line of communications which indicates an unusual state of affairs. The first incident that suggested the great mobilisation on the frontier happened as I was leaving Bangalore. The 6th Madras Infantry were going to the front. It was a striking and, in some ways, a moving spectacle. The Madras Army is a very much-married army. The Madras sepoy is a domesticated person. Women of every age and class hung, weeping, to the departing soldiers, their husbands or sons, who were going to some distant and mysterious danger, perhaps never to return. But the sadness was relieved by a striking and—if I may use an epithet adapted to the sentiment of the year—an Imperial thought. For hundreds of years the waves of conquest have swept across India from the north. Now the tale was to be different. The despised and often-conquered Madrassi, under his white officers, would be carried by the railway to teach the sons of those who had made his fathers slaves that at last there were fighting men in the South.

At the station I was confronted by a fact which brings home with striking force the size of the Indian Empire. On asking the booking clerk—a sleek Babu—how far it was to Nowshera, he replied, with composure, that it was 2,027 miles. I rejoiced to think of the disgust with which a Little Englander would contemplate this fact. And then followed five weary days of train, the monotony of the journey only partially relieved by the changing scenes which the window presents. Northwards, through the arid tracts that lie between Guntahal and Wadi Junction, through the green and fertile slopes of the Central Provinces, to more dry and unpropitious country at the foot of the great mountains, with the never-ceasing rattle of the railway irritating the nerves and its odious food cloying the palate, I am swiftly carried. At Umballa a wing of the Dorsetshire Regiment is waiting,

3

deterred from moving to Peshawar by several cholera cases; a few rest-camps near the line, a few officers hurrying to join their regiments, half-a-dozen nursing sisters travelling north on an errand of mercy, are the only signs so far of the war. But as Rawalpindi is neared the scene displays more significant features. Long trains of transport show the incessant passage of supplies to the front. One, in particular, of camels presents a striking picture. Six or seven of these animals are crowded into an open truck. Their knees are bound to prevent them moving on the journey, and their long necks, which rise in a cluster in the middle, have a strange and ridiculous aspect. Sometimes, I am told, curiosity, or ambition, or restlessness, or some other cause induces a camel to break his bonds and stand up, and as there are several tunnels on the line, the spectacle of a headless 'oont' is sometimes to be seen when the train arrives at Rawalpindi.

This great northern cantonment usually contains a large garrison, but now most of its occupants are at Peshawar or Kohat, and those who remain are anxiously and eagerly expecting their orders. Situated at the junction of two strategic railways, Rawalpindi must necessarily attract the attention of all who take an intelligent interest in the defences of the British Empire—of whatever nationality they may be. It is defended by a strong permanent fort, and the railways enable troops to be thrown either on the Kohat or Peshawar lines, as circumstances may decide. But when I recall the dusty roads, the burnt-up grass, the intense heat, and the deserted barracks, I am unable to recommend it as a resting-place for either the sybarite, the invalid or the artist.

Six hours' rail from 'Pindi' brings one to Nowshera, the base of the operations of the Malakand field force. Here the train is left, with a feeling of relief which is, however, soon dispelled by the jolting of the tonga. A large and well-filled field hospital here presents the unpleasing and sombre side of a campaign. Fever, dysentery and bullets have accumulated more than three hundred poor fellows in the different wards, and the daily deaths mark the progress of what tacticians and strategists have called 'the waste of war'.

It is fifty miles from Nowshera to the Malakand Pass, and the journey occupies seven hours in a tonga and involves much beating of galled and dilapidated ponies. Everywhere are the tracks of an army. A gang of prisoners chained hand to hand, escorted by a few Sikhs, marched sullenly by in the blazing heat. Suspicious characters,

4

I am informed, being deported across the frontier into British territory until things are more settled. Some dead transport animals lay by the roadside, their throats hurriedly cut. The different stages—Mardom, Jelala, Dargai—are marked by rest camps and small mud forts, while droves of slaughter cattle and camels and scores of mules attest the necessary but unpicturesque business of the Commissariat.

After Dargai the Malakand Pass is reached, and henceforth the road winds upwards, until a two hours' climb brings the tonga to rest beneath the hill on which the fort stands. The ground is as broken and confused as can be imagined. On every side steep and often precipitous hills, covered with boulders and stunted trees, rise in confused irregularity. A hollow in the middle—the crater—is the camp of the West Kent Regiment. The slopes are dotted with white tents, perched on platforms cut in the side of the hill. On one of these platforms my own is now pitched, and its situation commands a view of the ground on which, a month ago, the fighting took place. In front is the signal station—a strong tower held by a picket—from which all day long the heliograph is flickering and blinking its messages to Nowshera, India, and on to the tape machines at the London clubs. To the left is Guides Hill, stormed in '95 by the corps who have given it its name, and who are now at Khar, four miles down the valley. To the right is the point from which Sir Bindon Blood[1], a month ago, delivered that turning and flanking movement—one of those obvious moves that everybody thinks of afterwards—which cleared the valley at one stroke from the tribesmen, and opened the way to the relief of Chakdara. Soldiers of many kinds are moving among the trees and tents. The tall Sikh, the red in his turban relieving the businesslike brown of the khaki; the British infantryman, with his white pouches and belts, none the whiter for six weeks' service; an occasional Lancer of the General's escort, and crowds of followers in every conceivable costume, beginning at nothing but a rag and often ending abruptly, combine to produce a picture full of interest and animation.

Since the return of the column from the Upper Swat a period of waiting has supervened. Naturally, there is much discussion in the camp as to future movements. A reconnaissance has displayed the whole of the Boner valley—a valley containing large numbers of rebellious tribesmen—and naturally everyone has been eager to

[1] Bindon Blood (1842–1940). Major-General commanding the Malakand Field Force, 1897. KCB, 1896; GCB, 1909. Retired as General 1907.

invade so promising a country. But from Simla an order has arrived that the Bonerwals are to be spared. Great disappointment has been succeeded by trenchant criticism. Forbearance is construed by the natives as fear, and Boner's successful defiance of the Government will ring along the frontier, and find an echo in every bazaar in India. The 'home authorities', generally called 'politicians', the House of Commons, the Secretary of State, are successively arraigned. 'Is India,' it is indignantly asked, 'to be governed for its own good or to harmonise with party politics in England?' And the reply that the British public, having acquired by luck and pluck a valuable property in the East, intend to manage it as they please meets with no approval.

In so vexed a controversy I do not venture to express a decided opinion, but it is possible to compromise. India has a right to be governed only for its own good. Great Britain has a right to govern India as it sees fit. The only solution which will reconcile these two statements is to instil into the minds of the British people correct ideas on the subject, and then duty and inclination will combine to produce a wise and salutary policy.

Meanwhile rumours run through the camp of movements here and marches there, all ultimately pointing to a move against the Mohmands. It should be remembered that this powerful tribe deliberately made an unprovoked attack on a British post and, without cause or warning, committed a violation of the Imperial territory. I rejoice to be able to end this letter with the news that such audacity is no longer to remain unchastised, and that movements are now contemplated which indicate the adoption of a policy agreeable to expert opinion and suited to the dignity of the Empire. Of the progress of these movements, of the resistance that may be encountered, of the incidents that occur, I hope to give some account in my subsequent letters and, if possible, to draw for the everyday reader, at his breakfast table in 'comfortable England', something of a picture of the vivid open-air scenes which are presented by the war in the Indian Highlands.

6 October, 1897

2

KHAR, 6 September

The first turning to the right, after crossing the Malakand Pass,
leads to Khar. The road winds round the sides of the hills—is sometimes embanked and at others scarped out of the steep slopes—until,
by a gradual descent, the fertile plain of the Lower Swat is reached.
The distance is about four miles, but in spite of the shortness of the
way, and of the cowed and humble attitude of the natives in this
valley, the regulations as to traversing it are strict. Individuals must
be accompanied by an escort. Whenever possible they will arrange to
go in couples, and in every case arms must be carried. Isolated instances of fanaticism have to be guarded against, and it is only
through the precautions observed that no accident has so far occurred.
   Riding along this road with an officer who took part in the recent
operations, I learned many details of the fight. Every rock, every hill,
every nullah had its story. Here their 'snipers' lay for two days
firing into the Guides' camp. There was the ravine up which they
crawled; here was 'where we charged and chased them right up to
those hills over there'; and, again, 'there is where poor So-and-So
was killed'. On the left a square mud fort, its walls partly destroyed,
and pierced by several ragged round holes, marked the spot where
the picket of the 31st were rushed, and nearly all killed or wounded.
The tribesmen made the holes in the wall, and broke in. The soldiers
ran first to one hole and then to another to repel the attack; but it
was like caulking a sieve, and they were overwhelmed.
   At length a turn of the road displayed the Swat Valley—a broad,
level plain, terminated by the hills on which the fort of Chakdara
stands. The camp of the 2nd Brigade filled the foreground. Rows and
rows of tents and lines of horses marked the streets of the canvas
town. A few standards, captured from the enemy, and the smoke of
many fires, lighted to cook the evening meal, showed that it was
occupied by soldiers. A group of khaki-clad figures playing desultory

7

football on one side, and the smooth grass of the polo ground on the other, attested the nationality of its occupants. As we progressed we caught up long lines of camels, five or six on a string, returning ungracefully from being watered to their pickets for the night. They walked silently on their padded feet. Whatever may be the beauties of the wild camels of the desert, they are not shared by the transport variety of the species. The air of sad disgust which their faces wear seems to show that the 'oont' appreciates his ugliness.

Within the camp everything was clean and orderly. The pipeclay of peace was gone, but in its place was the practical and businesslike regularity of service—a regularity which sometimes admits of a judicious irregularity. We found our way to a mess and, dismounting, accepted a glass—a pewter glass—of the beverage of the British officer—whisky and soda; alas! without the ice which in India can alone make life worth living and drinks worth drinking. As we sat and chatted the day drew to a close. Gradually the sun sank below the mountains, and the valley became plunged in shadows. A grey mist rising at either end obscured and contracted the view. The rugged tops of the hills still caught the sunlight for a little, but minute by minute the shadows rose, and presently it was quite dark.

The early stage in this letter at which night has come on might favour the supposition that the arrival of darkness was unexpected and inadvertent. I hasten to correct so erroneous an impression. It is when the curtain of night has descended upon the scene and when the actors and properties are removed from view that the spectator may amuse himself by considering the morality, the objects and performance of the drama.

Let us, then, begin as we hope to end, with the enemy. In the examination of a people it is always best to take their virtues first. This clears the ground and leaves sufficient time for the investigation of the predominant characteristics. The Swatis, Bonerwals, Mohmands and other frontier tribes with whom the Malakand Field Force is at present engaged are brave and warlike. Their courage has been abundantly displayed in the present campaign. They charge home, and nothing but a bullet stops their career. Their swordsmanship—neglecting guards—concerns itself only with cuts and, careless of what injury they may receive, they devote themselves to the destruction of their opponents. In the selection of positions they exhibit considerable military skill, and as skirmishers their use of cover and preservation of order entitle them to much praise. It is mournful to be compelled to close the catalogue of their virtues thus early, but the closest scrutiny of the facts which have been placed before me has resulted in no further discovery in this direction. From year to year their life is one of feud and strife. They plough with a sword at their sides. Every field has its protecting tower, to which the agriculturist can hurry at the approach of a stranger. Successful murder—whether by open force or treachery—is the surest road to distinction among them. A recent writer has ascribed to these people those high family virtues which simple races so often possess. The consideration of one pregnant fact compels me reluctantly to abandon even this hope. Their principal article of commerce is their women—wives and daughters—who are exchanged for rifles. This degradation of mind is unrelieved by a single elevated sentiment. Their religion is the most miserable fanaticism, in which cruelty, credulity and immorality are equally represented. Their holy men—the Mullahs—prize as their chief privilege a sort of 'droit de seigneur'. It is impossible to imagine a lower type of beings or a more dreadful state of barbarism.

I am aware of the powerful influence of climate upon character. But the hill men cannot even plead the excuse of a cold and barren land for their barbarism. The valleys they inhabit are fertile and often beautiful. Once the spots where their squalid huts now stand were occupied by thriving cities, and the stone 'sangars' from which they defy their foes are built on the terraces which nourished the crops of a long forgotten civilisation. Everywhere are the relics of the old Buddhists on whom these fierce tribes, thrown out of that birthplace of nations, Central Asia, descended. Their roads, their temples, and their ruins have alone survived. All else has been destroyed in that darkness which surrounds those races whose type is hardly on the fringe of humanity. But it may be urged, 'However degraded and barbarous these people may be, they have a right to live unmolested on the soil that their fathers conquered.' 'They have attacked your posts,' says the Little Englander, carefully disassociating himself from anything British, 'but why did you ever put your posts there?' To answer this question it is necessary to consider the whole matter from a wider point of view than the Swat Valley affords.

Starting with the assumption that our Empire in India is worth holding, and admitting the possibility that others besides ourselves might wish to possess it, it obviously becomes our duty to adopt measures for its safety. It is a question of a line of defence. The Indus is now recognised by all strategists as being useless for this purpose.

The most natural way of preventing an enemy from entering a house is to hold the door and windows; and the general consensus of opinion is that to secure India it is necessary to hold the passes of the mountains. With this view small military posts have been built along the frontier. The tribes whose territories adjoin have not been interfered with. Their independence has been respected, and their degradation undisturbed. More than this, the influence of the flag that flies from the fort on the hill has stimulated the trade of the valley, and increased the wealth of its inhabitants. Were the latter amenable to logical reasoning, the improvement in their condition and the strength of their adversaries would have convinced them of the folly of an outbreak. But in a land of fanatics common sense does not exist.

The defeat of the Greeks sent an electric thrill through Islam. The Ameer[1]—a negative conductor—is said to have communicated it to the 'Mullahs', and they generated the disturbance among the frontier tribes. The ensuing flash has kindled a widespread conflagration. This must now be dealt with courageously and intelligently. It is useless, and often dangerous, to argue with an Afghan. Not because he is degraded, not because we covet his valleys, but because his actions interfere with the safety of our Empire, he must be crushed. There are many in Europe, though they live amid the prosaic surroundings of a highly developed country, where economics and finance reign supreme, who yet regard, with pleasure and with pride, the wide dominions of which they are the trustees.

These, when they read that savages have been killed for attacking British posts and menacing the security of our possessions, will not hesitate to say, with firmness and without reserve, 'So perish all who do the like again'.

7 October, 1897

[1] Hadda Mullah, Mohammedan priest. Published an inflammatory book in Delhi during 1896, and had particular influence with the Mohmands.

3

KOTKAI, 9 September

Major-General Sir Bindon Blood and his staff left the Malakand camp on the afternoon of the 6th, and riding through Khar reached Chakdara before night. The road lies through the valley of the Swat. The distance is about ten miles, and the day was fine and cool. I cannot recall any incident that occurred. I am indeed becoming painfully conscious that this correspondence is now so far advanced that a battle or some other exciting affair is necessary, or at least desirable, in order to make it acceptable to your readers. In these days of telegraphs and newspapers, however, it is impossible to appeal to imagination to supply the deficiencies of fact. But it should be remembered that battles—though a most important item—fill but a very small part of the time of a campaign; and the reader who would obtain a clear idea of a soldier's life on service must mentally share the fatigues of the march and the monotony of the camp. The fine deeds and the thrilling moments of war are but the highlights on a picture, of which the background is routine, hard work and discomfort.

The Fort of Chakdara guards the bridge across the Swat—a rapid, and at this time of year, a considerable river. It stands on and around a rocky knoll, which rises from the plain, at about two hundred yards from the surrounding hills. Against the assault of an enemy unprovided with artillery it should be secure, but the fact that it is commanded from the adjacent heights makes its defence dangerous and painful to the garrison, and might, through the gradual diminution of their numbers, ultimately endanger its safety. From the moment when Lieutenant Rattray[1] galloped in from the Khar polo-ground to take command of the post till it was relieved by the Malakand Field Force, a ceaseless and pitiless fire harassed the defenders. The bullets buried into the stone walls or kicked spurts of dust in the

[1] Haldane Burney Rattray (1870–c1922). Serving with 45th Sikhs. Received DSO in 1898 and retired as Lieutenant-Colonel.

courtyard of the fort. The interior communication of the garrison
was impeded. Many of the ramparts could only be occupied to repel
an attack by soldiers exposed to an enfilade fire from the hills. But in
spite of these defects of construction the place was held against the
determined attacks of 6,000 tribesmen.

When the heights overlooking the fort have been protected—as I
understand they are to be—by small works, the fort will become
impregnable, as far as the natives are concerned.

During the night we spent at Chakdara definite orders arrived from
Simla respecting the movements of this force, which it is now
necessary I should describe. I approach the task with trepidation. It
is difficult to explain military manoeuvres without the aid of a map.
Maps are always unpopular. Besides distracting attention from the
letterpress, it may be said of them that when they are simple they are
misleading, and when they are complicated they are tiresome. The
map being rejected, an approximate description must suffice. The
three great military points on the frontier, where troops are now
concentrated or from which they are operating, are Kohat, Peshawar,
and Malakand. These form a line facing north-north-west, of which
Malakand is the northern extremity. The arc of a circle drawn from
Malakand to Peshawar passes through the country of the Mohmands.
It is by this route that two brigades, under Sir Bindon Blood, have
been directed to march in order to effect a junction with an equal
force, which, under Brigadier-General Elles,[1] will move from
Peshawar to meet and, if necessary, to help them.

The Mohmands, through whose territories the line of march lies,
are the tribe which attacked the British posts at Shabkadar a month
ago, and who have been mentioned in these letters as being among
the most audacious of the savages of the border. Their valleys have
never hitherto been traversed by a British force; indeed, for more
than two thousand years it is probable no white man has penetrated
these obscure and mysterious recesses. Had the Mohmands extended
to others that freedom from interference which they themselves have
so long enjoyed, they might have continued in that state of degraded
barbarism which appeals so strongly to certain philanthropic persons
in England. But, without cause or warning, unprovoked and
unexpected, they assailed the great Power which lies to the south, and

[1] Edmond Roche Elles (1848–1934). Brigadier-General commanding
the Mohmand Field Force. KCB, 1898. Retired as Lieutenant-General
1908.

that Power, which, as Daniel Webster once said, 'for the purposes of military conquest and subjugation, not even Imperial Rome, at the summit of its power, could rival,' has extended a long arm in chastisement.

As part of the arm, which part I will not strain the metaphor by specifying, the 2nd Brigade marched on the 7th from Chakdara to Sarai. Meanwhile, Brigadier-General Wodehouse,[1] still further in advance, with the 3rd Brigade, had seized the bridge across the Panjkora river, by which the entrance to Bajaur is gained. On the 9th the 2nd Brigade, with whom was Sir Bindon Blood and the Divisional Staff, again broke camp and, effecting the passage of the river, under the protection of General Wodehouse's artillery, marched past his brigade and arrived safely here.

The Divisional Staff, with whom I had the pleasure of riding, started early from Sarai, the stars still shining when the column moved off. Perhaps it is by contrast with the other hours that the dawn in India seems so delicious. The chills of the night are gone; the heat of the day has not yet begun. It is a cool and refreshing time. I repress with an effort the impulse to describe, or try to describe, the sunrise over the mountains. All the available and suitable words have, doubtless, been used before by several writers and skipped by many readers. Indeed, I am inclined to think that descriptions of this kind, however good, convey nothing to those who have not seen the lovely spectacle, and are unnecessary to those who have. Nature will not be admired by proxy.

After marching for a couple of hours we halted for breakfast near some trees which threw long shadows to the slanting beams of the early sun, watching the column as it defiled along the road. There was the soldier as he appears on service. The tinsel and polish of parade had vanished. The marching figures slouched heavily along, their rifles carried at every conceivable angle, smoking and talking. Their travel-stained khaki was a study in neutral tints, hardly relieved by the warm colours of the native turbans. A motley crowd of followers hung on the flanks and rear of the battalions. The superfine soldier of London or Aldershot would find much to sneer at. The barrack-square martinet might be scandalised. And yet, beneath this appearance of ease was the iron framework of discipline and

[1] Joscelin Heneage Wodehouse (1852–1930). Brigadier-General commanding 3rd Brigade Malakand Field Force. CB, 1889; CMG, 1890; KCB, 1908; GCB, 1913.

training. The cavalry had already passed, but, as the advanced party of the infantry approached and perceived the general, I was surprised—my ideas drawn from recollections of Cuba—by the precision with which they shouldered arms in salute.

There were the Guides Infantry—renowned for marching and fighting along the length and breadth of the Indian frontier, who have recently shown that their reputation is not undeserved. More of them followed, the different types of Dogras and Pathans distinguishing the companies. Then a mountain battery passed—a long string of variously laden mules, each of which carried some portion of a field gun. They looked insignificant and disordered. But let some hostile tribesman appear on that distant ridge, and in a moment the mules will have disappeared and the six little guns will be discharging their seven-pound Ring shell[1] with accuracy, rapidity, and effect. The 35th Sikhs and 38th Dogras followed the battery, and then came what is after all the peg on which all the others hang—a British infantry battalion. Those brown-clad men, with their belts, packs, and rifles, have made as fine a picture on the pages of history as the Legions of Caesar, the Janissaries of the Sultans, or the Old Guard of Napoleon. Interminable lines of mules and camels followed with supplies.

I had watched the passage of one of the brigades of an army which, in proportion to its numbers, is probably the most powerful military machine the world has ever seen. English modesty forbids me to say more. Nor was there more to say, for, breakfast being ended, we remounted and trotted on. The bridge across the Panjkora river is a light and unsubstantial structure of wire ropes, which oscillate violently when even one man walks over. The passage of the 2nd Brigade and its supplies occupied the whole day. The 3rd Brigade are to cross tomorrow, and possibly the 1st Brigade on the 11th, though this is uncertain. The crossing is covered by the guns of the 10th Field Battery, which occupies a commanding position to the right of the road. It has been a matter of considerable astonishment here that these large guns have been got over the execrable tracks which alone are available. But the perseverance of troops to get to the front overcomes many obstacles which the books would classify as 'unpassable'. We camp and march with all the precautions of war, and in the hope that these precautions will not have been taken in vain.

8 October, 1897

[1] Ring shell consisted of a cast-iron on a core of rings, weakened to break up on explosion. It was still being used in the First World War.

4

NAWAGAI, 12 September

In my last letter to you I gave some account of the march of a column of troops in service in India. Since then we have been continuously moving, at a rate varying from eight to fourteen miles a day, and we have now arrived at the entrance of the passes which give access to the country of the Mohmands. The two brigades which compose the force Sir Bindon Blood intends to employ against this tribe move separately under their own brigadiers, but keep within four or five miles of each other, so as to be able to concentrate at the shortest possible notice. Starting by starlight, a halt is made at about eight o'clock for breakfast, and the troops usually reach the camping-ground at midday. Many people have read of the sufferings of the British soldiers in the Indian Mutiny, through being compelled to march and fight in the hot weather. August and September in these parts are as hot as it is agreeable to imagine or elegant to express, and the exposure to the sun is undoubtedly a very severe trial to the European troops. Of course, since 1857 sweeping changes have been made in the dress of the soldier. The pith helmet, with its long covering shade, shields the head and face. A padded spine-protector is buttoned on to the back, and a loose and cosy khaki uniform is substituted for the stocks and tunics of former days. But the sun remains the same, and all precautions can only modify without preventing the evil effects. What those effects are, the hospital returns will tell with more force than many words.

The men are so cheery and good-humoured, so anxious to get on, so eager to find the enemy, so pleased at being on active service, that it is only right that their endurance of severe hardships should be recorded. On the march the British and native regiments mutually inspire each other to exertions. The soldiers of India naturally feel the effects of the climate less than those from cooler lands. This, of course, the British infantryman will not admit. The dominant race resent the slightest suggestion of inferiority. When we arrived at the camping-ground this morning the camel transport was far behind, and it was necessary to wait on the bare and dusty plateau for a couple of hours, in the blaze of the sun, until the baggage should arrive. I talked to some of the Queen's Regiment—which is the English regiment with the 3rd Brigade. The men had just marched fourteen miles with arms and ammunition, and not one had fallen out by the way. They looked strained and weary, but nothing would induce them to admit it. 'An easy march,' they said. 'Should have been here long ago if the native troops had not kept halting.' This is the material for empire-building. Nor should the sepoy be forgotten. There are few troops in the world would do what the 35th Sikhs did on 1 August. When a regiment marches till eighteen of its men die on the road rather than leave the ranks, it must be admitted that they are animated by that very high courage which not only dares but endures.

It is difficult to convey the impression that these splendid Indian troops make on an impartial spectator. Their strength, their patience, their skill with the weapons are shown by a thousand incidents of march, camp, and picket. Their bravery has been attested on many occasions. Their discipline may be gauged by anyone who takes the trouble to watch them. It has been said that they would not face European troops. On this point I will not presume to express an opinion, but if ever the opportunity of deciding the question should occur, I would, in confidence, recommend the readers of these letters to hedge any bets they may have made in favour of Germans or Russians.

Nothing is so remarkable as the ascendancy which the British officer maintains over the native soldier. The dark sowars follow the young English subaltern who commands them with a strange devotion. He is their 'butcha'—the best in the regiment—as brave as a lion. None rides so straight as he; no one is so confident. Things seem to be going wrong; men and horses are rolling over. But looking to him they feel it is all right. He is 'in the know', and will pull them out of any difficulty. To save his life they will sacrifice their own. Nor could a squadron face its comrades if their officer's body had been left in the hands of the enemy. The military history of England—a long and diverse volume—does not record an instance of their confidence being misplaced.

And this brings me to a case of gallantry which has occurred in this campaign, and of which I have been intending to send some account since the full facts came to light. It is getting rather ancient history now—but good stories bear repetition. At the engagement of Lundaki, on 17 August, the cavalry were pursuing the flying tribesmen, and as a squadron was emerging from difficult ground two of its officers, who had pressed forward, impelled by that spirit which loses us lives and gains us battles, were wounded. They lay in a re-entrant angle at the foot of a hill. On the hill were large numbers of the enemy, a few of whom ran forward to cut up the wounded men in approved Afghan fashion, while the others continued firing. Meanwhile, three other officers had come up and, regardless of the fire, immediately proceeded to try and carry away the wounded men. After being for some four minutes in a situation in which it seemed impossible that anyone could live, the two survivors, Colonel Adams[1] and Lord Fincastle,[2] succeeded in carrying away the bodies of their comrades. Of the five officers who had ventured into this death-trap two were killed and two were wounded, and all the horses were killed.

It is an excellent instance of the actions by which the ascendancy of the British officer is maintained over the gallant Asiatics he commands. The example of these men calmly endeavouring to rescue their brother officers within fifty yards of a hundred rifles, and surrounded by a ferocious mob of swordsmen, probably does more to preserve the loyalty of the Indian soldier than all the speeches of Westminster and all the experiments of Simla.

While I have been writing all this the camels have arrived, and the brigade is now camped, as far as it is possible to camp without tents; a luxury of which the 40lb scale does not admit. Shelters are improvised from blankets and waterproof sheets. Beneath these scanty coverings, where the thermometer marks anything up to 110 degrees, the soldiers wait for evening. The time is long; the heat trembles over the dusty plain as over the funnel of an engine; the wind is hot, and

[1] Robert Bellew Adams (1856–1918). Serving with the Queen's Own Corps of Guides. Victoria Cross, 1897. CB, 1898; KCB, 1912. Retired as Major-General, 1911.

[2] Alexander Edward, Viscount Fincastle (1871–1962). Served with the Malakand Field Force as Blood's ADC during which period he received the Victoria Cross and was mentioned three times in despatches. Also acted as special correspondent to *The Times*. In the Boer War he raised and led Fincastle's Horse. During the First World War, he was wounded twice, received the DSO, and was mentioned four times in despatches.

the water tepid; but presently the shadows lengthen and the glare diminishes. At sunset everyone revives. Even the animals seem to share the feeling of relief. The sun has gone, and with him the sentiments of hatred he inspires, and we strive to forget that tomorrow morning he will be ready to begin again at the usual hour.

I am sensible that in this letter I have recorded little but the heat. It is a matter of great regret to all here that the heat is at present the greatest daily event. The opposition which had been expected between Panjkora and Nawagai has collapsed. The Government of India have mobilised such enormous forces that the enemy have either fled to the hills, or burying their weapons have decided to wait for a more favourable opportunity. It is possible that the Mohmands may fight a little 'for their honour', but all the smaller tribes have sent in 'jirgas' and expressed their regret at having been so thoughtless as to attack the British posts and kill British subjects. After this 'amende honorable' it would be discourteous to think further of the matter, and the Indian Government having displayed, in the concentration of enormous armies, that disregard of expense so frequently manifested by those who do not have to pay will now proceed to show that Christian spirit which takes the form of forgiving other people's injuries.

The present state of affairs on the frontier raises several serious questions, and as the column is halted for a few days I shall devote a couple of letters to submitting to the Englishmen at home the opinion of some of his countrymen abroad on matters that affect their common interests and possessions.

9 October, 1897

5

CAMP INAYAT KILA, 17 September

I had intended to devote this letter to a consideration of the frontier question from a local point of view. But a succession of exciting events has forcibly reminded me that the duty of the war correspondent is primarily to chronicle incident. The night that my last letter was despatched from Shumshuk was marked by the firing of the first shot I have had to record since joining the Malakand Field Force. A 'sniper', as they are called in the Anglo-Indian army, had pensively fired a few bullets into camp. As is usual on these occasions, the result was only to wake a few of those who had been least busy during the day. Next evening a cavalry reconnaissance, up the Watelai Valley, was followed home by a score of tribesmen, firing Martini rifles[1] and, as we sat at dinner, half-a-dozen shots invested what had hitherto been an agreeable picnic with something of the reality of war. On the 14th Sir Bindon Blood and the 3rd Brigade marched to Nawagai, and the 2nd Brigade, coming up from Khar, camped near the former resting place. The march to Nawagai was undisturbed, and the night I passed there was profoundly peaceful. But meanwhile, twelve miles away the 2nd Brigade was getting the benefit of the hornet swarm our passage had raised. The tribesmen had hurriedly collected and, taking advantage of broken ground, attacked the camp with vigour and effect. In the morning we were breakfasting at Nawagai when everyone was surprised by the arrival of a native officer with an escort of 11th Bengal Lancers who had ridden 'trot and gallop' with the news of the night's fighting. 'Three British officers and twelve native soldiers killed and wounded—six hours' action—and a cavalry pursuit', such were the outlines of the message. All this has, of course, been telegraphed to England, and I am sensible that I should not fill this letter with details of what

[1] Martini and Martini-Henry rifles. .45 calibre magazine rifles, capable of an effective range of 1450 yards.

has already been recorded while so many vivid incidents remain untold.

Permission having been granted me to accompany the returning escort and join the 2nd Brigade for the impending engagement, I selected a scanty but judicious outfit—of which the most important items were chocolate, a waterproof, and a toothbrush—and started. The road lay at first through deep watercourses—nullahs they are called—which might have afforded cover to an enemy, and through which the cavalry picked their way with care and caution, but presently we emerged into the broad plains of Khar and Nawagai, and looked around for signs of the camp. Right across the spacious plateau lay a long brown string of marching men and mules. The brigade was moving into the Watelai Valley to a convenient camping ground from which to direct the punitive operations against their assailants of the night before. The blazing thatch of three or four fortified villages sent a high column of smoke into the air—blue against the mountains, brown against the sky. The troops were halted on the site of their resting-place for the night, and as the small party with which I was riding arrived, the cavalry came back from the pursuit and began to look to their horses. The bright steel of the lance-points was here and there dulled by red streaks and blotches. A sowar displayed his with pride. 'How many altogether?' was the question asked on all sides. 'Twenty-one; but they are still game; there will be another attack tonight,' answered an officer.

Everyone was eager to talk of the events of the night before. How they had had no sleep. How they had lain prone while the bullets whistled in from all quarters. Of the daring of the enemy. Of the composure of the troops. Of the general discomfort and danger. The 'doolies' of the field hospital passed, each with its pale, stricken occupant. One contained poor Harington,[1] so dangerously wounded that while I write his life is despaired of. The tents showed many bullet-holes, and everyone looked tired and drawn. 'You were lucky to be out of it last night,' they said; 'but there's plenty more coming.' The camp showed that this belief was general. Everyone was digging a hole—a kind of soup-plate—in the earth in which to sleep. The shelter trench thrown up all round the sides was higher than usual. The hospital was protected by flour bags and boxes. It was not difficult to realise what all this meant.

[1] HenryAndrewHarington(1869–1897).Diedofwoundsreceived during the action of 14 September while serving with the 26th Punjab Regiment.

But the expected attack did not come off, and only the 'snipers' displayed energy and vigour. At ten o'clock there began a brisk fire, which necessitated all the tents being taken down lest they should form a target, and for some similar reason all the lights went out very soon. Desultory firing continued at intervals throughout the night—some 200 or 300 shots were fired—without injuring anyone, and without awakening those who had been up the previous night. The camp was full of noise. The challenges of the sentries, the squeaking of the mules, the firing of the pickets, divested the night of all solemnity. Here was no place for reflection, for speculation on the chances of the morning, or recollection of the dangers of the day. It displayed a life lived only in the present. There might be fighting tomorrow. Some people might be killed or wounded. It was sufficient to be alive for the moment; and the camp—if those varied items that compose one can be said to have a collective identity—shrugged its shoulders, and, regarding the past without regret, contemplated the future without alarm.

I realise that if I have to attempt to give you any account of the action of the Mohmand Valley, which occurred next day, this letter would be expanded to unwieldy dimensions. Hence I must leave the reader with the picture of a sleeping camp, where the moonlight displays the dark figures of soldiery in every attitude of weariness, and glints brightly from the bayonetted rifles that lie along the shelter trench, where mules and horses shift uneasily in their pickets, and where, perhaps, inscrutable Fate is calmly selecting the victims of the morrow.

14 October, 1897

6

INAYAT KILA, 18 September

I have now to describe the action of the Mohmand Valley, which occurred on Thursday last, and which, as far as loss of life is concerned, exceeds in importance any Indian engagement since the Afghan War. In pursuance of the intention to inflict necessary chastisement on the assailants of the camp at Markhanai, the 2nd Brigade marched on 16 September to destroy some fortified villages at the head of the Mohmand Valley. I do not propose to write an official account of the engagement that ensued. That is a duty which properly devolves on the historian. All I shall endeavour to do is to convey a picture of some of the scenes and incidents which I witnessed, to the readers of a daily paper in matter-of-fact, law-abiding London. It is necessary, however, that they should be asked to testify that in the narrative which follows I have rigidly adhered to my role of an interested spectator. If in these letters an expression can be detected which appears antagonistic to this idea, I shall submit to all the evil things that the ingenuity of malice can suggest.

As the squadron of the 11th Bengal Lancers approached the head of the valley it was possible to distinguish the figures of a numerous force of tribesmen on the terraced hillsides. Through a telescope they appeared seated in long lines, each with his weapon upright beside him. At first they took no notice of the gradual advance and deployment of the troops which was developing in the plain below, but as formed bodies of infantry drew nearer they began to ascend the hills slowly. At about half-past seven the cavalry, trotting to within range, dismounted, and, running a hundred yards forward, opened fire with their carbines. It was immediately answered. From behind rocks and slopes of ground, on spurs, and from stone houses, little puffs of smoke darted. A brisk skirmish began. A good many bullets whistled about, but small damage was done to either side. After half an hour most of the enemy had gone out of range, and the Lancers, mounting, went in search of more congenial work with the cavalry-man's weapon. Four companies of the 35th Sikhs now came up, and moved up to the spur at the top of which the village stood. This spur will be more fully described as the account proceeds. Little opposition was offered to the advance. A few 'snipers' fired steadily from among rocks and trees, but were driven from place to place by well-aimed volleys. By half-past ten the village had been occupied, and many of the loopholed hovels—dignified by the name of houses—of which it was composed were in flames.

Hardly an enemy was to be seen. With the exception of an occasional volley from the troops, and a dropping fire from a few daring marksmen on the hillsides, all was quiet and peaceful. Everyone expressed regret at the pusillanimity of the enemy in going off without making any resistance and, as the camp was eight miles away, a retirement was ordered, to get the men back as soon as possible. The regiment was to retire by alternate half-companies, in the prescribed fashion. This movement accordingly began. But as soon as the first body of infantry was seen to be departing an extraordinary change took place.

From far up the hillsides men came running down, darting from rock to rock, and cover to cover. The firing immediately became heavy. With the greatest boldness individual tribesmen advanced to within a hundred yards of the covering half-company and, unde-terred by their fire, began to make accurate practice. A chorus of shouts and yells rose from among the hills. Here and there, behind ridges and rocks, sword-blades flashed menacingly. In a few moments both flanks were turned, and the last half-company was ordered to retire, lest it should be cut off.

A short digression is now necessary to describe the configuration of the ground at this point. The spur along which the retirement was taking place consisted of three knolls, the nearest the main hill being the highest. In section it resembled a switchback railway. As soon as the first and highest knoll had been left the enemy ran forward and occupied it. As the Sikhs retired across the dip of ground, or 'col', which leads to the second knoll, they were exposed to a close-range fire from the first. I think a couple of sepoys fell here, and were safely carried away to the rear.

At the top of this second little hillock a stand was made, and for a moment the enemy were checked. Then they again began to turn the flanks. Again it was necessary to fall back. Up to this moment the situation had been one which might provide material for the moralist —adventure for the soldier, excitement for the neuropath, and copy for the journalist. Now, suddenly, grim tragedy burst upon the scene. As the soldiers rose from the shelter of the rocks behind which they had been firing, an officer turned quickly round, his face covered with blood. He put his hands to his head and fell on the ground. Two of the men ran to help him away. One fell shot through the leg. A sepoy who was still firing sprang into the air and, falling, began to bleed terribly. Another fell close to him. Everyone began to pull those men along, dragging them roughly over the rocky ground in spite of their groans. Another officer was immediately shot. Several Sikhs ran forward to his help. Thirty yards away was the crest of the spur. From this a score of tribesmen were now firing with deadly effect. Over it ran a crowd of swordsmen, throwing pieces of rock and yelling. It became impossible to remain an impassive spectator. The two officers who were left used their revolvers. The men fired wildly. One officer and two wounded sepoys were dropped on the ground. The officer lay on his back. A tall man in dirty-white linen pounced on him with a sword. It was a horrible sight.

The retreat continued. The ground favoured the enemy, who both commanded and turned the troops. Most of the wounded were, however, carried off. The bullets struck dust-spurts all round. Others passed in the air with a sound like that produced by sucking through the lips. At length the bottom of the hill was reached. Then somebody sounded the charge. The men halted. Bayonets were fixed. It was a supreme moment. The officers ran forward and waved their swords. Everyone began to shout. Then the forward movement began—slowly at first, but gaining momentum rapidly. As the enemy fled back to their hills many dropped under the fire of the Sikhs.

A subaltern with a dozen British infantry now came up—the most welcome sight I had seen for half an hour. Reinforcements continued to arrive. The Brigadier ordered the Buffs to retake the spur and completely destroy the village. Covered by the fire of the mountain battery, this regiment now advanced, and occupied the hill and village. There was some firing, and several men were wounded, but the enemy again awaited the moment of retreat to attack. At three o'clock this was ordered. The Buffs, however, were well handled, and held everything at a distance with their Lee-Metford rifles.[1] By half-past four the withdrawal was completed. But the enemy still pressed the regiment strongly. It was not till this second retirement was over that I realised that other things had been happening in other parts of the field. The dressing stations were crowded with wounded. The cavalry had delivered a fine charge. A company of the 35th Sikhs, high on a hill to the right, was being hard pressed by the enemy. Two companies of the Guides had been sent to extricate it. Through the glasses it was possible to distinguish the figures of the combatants against the skyline. Every one had been fully occupied in different directions. The events I have described so fully were merely an incident in the engagement. Indeed, a battle is a scene of which the spectator cannot study the detail without losing the proportions or the proportions without missing the detail. But, perhaps, that is true of many other things besides.

In order that the isolated company of the 35th Sikhs should not be cut off, it was necessary that the homeward march should be very slow. The Guides, who had gone to the relief, were themselves hard pressed, and they in turn had to be covered by the guns and the Buffs. Gradually darkness came on, intensified by a thunderstorm and broken by vivid flashes of lightning, which assisted the enemy to fire at the columns. The smoke puffs of the day were replaced by spurts of fire. The men were tired out, having had nothing to eat all day and having made great exertions. The Buffs, however, covered the retreat with the greatest steadiness. Their fire was accurate and effective. The men were determined and the officers cheery. Though individual 'snipers' often advanced to within fifty yards of the regiment perfect order was preserved, and they were received with careful volleys. The consequence was that the rearguard reached camp at 8.30 without much loss.

In the expectation of an attack, the camp had been reduced to half its size. Tents and baggage lay in confused heaps. The pack animals were crowded together. Now that the storm had passed the night was pitch dark. It was difficult to find anything or anybody. Gradually the fact became known that all the troops were not in camp. The Brigadier, two companies and the battery were still in the plain. Then the sound of guns firing could be heard. They were being attacked. Four companies of the Dogras were ordered to parade

[1] .303 magazine rifles capable of an effective range of 2900 yards when fitted with dial sights (1800 yards with barleycorn sight). A cavalry carbine version, dating from 1894, had a range of 2000 yards.

to go to their assistance, but the order was countermanded. Indeed, considering the darkness, the broken nature of the ground, and the exhaustion of the troops, it is doubtful whether it would have arrived in time, if at all. It was an anxious night; perhaps, the fitting close to an exciting day.

15 October, 1897

SHUMSHUK, 21 September

I avail myself of an uneventful day—when the troops are resting beneath such scanty shelters as can be improvised from waterproof sheets and blankets; when everyone who can find a covering from the perpendicular rays of the midday sun has disappeared from view, and only the sentries pace the cracked and dusty soil; when there is no news to write of, and plenty of time to write it in—to give you some account of the political aspect of the frontier, and of the causes and influences which have worked to produce the present situation. It is fashionable in English politics to discredit the opinion of people on the spot. They are supposed to be excited and prejudiced, to be unable to take the judicial and comprehensive views which can, it is believed, be adopted only in an atmosphere of ignorant indifference. But I feel that the reader who has persevered thus far with these letters has already said the worst that he intends of their author, and I shall, therefore, make no apology for writing of the frontier question, while the mountains of Afghanistan frown from the westward, and the cousin of Umra Khan is salaaming to the political officer in the opposite tent.

I must revert to a period when the British power, having conquered the plains of India and subdued its sovereigns, paused at the foot of the Himalayas and turned its tireless energy to internal progress and development. The 'line of the mountains' formed a frontier as plain and intelligible as the cliffs which define the limits of the sea. To the south lay the British Empire in India; to the north were warlike tribes, barbarous, unapproachable, irreclaimable; and far beyond these lay the other great Power of Asia. It was long the wisdom of Anglo-Indian statesmen to preserve a situation which contained so many elements of finality and so many guarantees of peace. When the northern savages, impelled by fanaticism or allured by plunder, descended from their mountains and invaded the plains, they were met by equal courage and superior discipline and driven in disorder to their confines. But this was found to be an inadequate deterrent, and the purely defensive principle had to be modified in favour of that system of punitive expeditions which has been derided as the policy of 'Butcher and bolt'.

Gradually, as the circumstances altered, the methods of dealing with them changed. The punitive expeditions had awakened an intense hostility among the tribesmen. The intrigues of Russia had for some time been watched with alarm by the Indian Government. As long as the border could remain a no-man's land—a kind of great gulf fixed—all was well; but if any Power was to be supreme there, that Power must not be Russia. The predominance of Russian influence in these territories would give them the power to invade India at their discretion, with what chances of success need not be here discussed. A change of policy became inevitable.

The climax was reached after the termination of Lord Ripon's[1] Vice-Royalty. The open aggression which had characterised the Russian frontier policy of '84 and '85 had been met by a supine apathy to the interests of the State which deserved, and which, had the issue been less important, might have received, actual punishment. It was natural that his immediate successors should strive to dissociate themselves from the follies and blunders of those years. The spirit of reaction led to the final abandonment of the venerable policy of non-intervention. Instead of the 'line of the mountains' it was now maintained that the passes through them must be held. This is the so-called 'Forward Policy'. It is a policy which aims at obtaining the frontier Gilgit-Chitral-Jellalabad-Kandahar.

There were many who were opposed to the view. There are many who oppose it now. Nor is there any difficulty in finding arguments against it. But it is very doubtful whether it was ever possible to avoid it. The frontier policy makes itself, and is dictated by circumstances rather than by men. At any rate, it is certain that this forward movement is now beyond recall. Successive Indian Administrations have urged, successive English Cabinets have admitted, the necessity of finding a definite and defensible frontier. The old line has been left. The new is not yet attained. To retreat is impossible, and the more rapid the advance the sooner will the troubles of a transition stage be over. The rulers of India, whether here or at home, while recognising the facts, shrink from the legitimate conclusions. Dynamite in

[1] Viceroy of India, 1880–1884.

the hands of a child is not more dangerous than a strong policy weakly carried out. Until the men in power are bold enough to lay their case frankly and fairly before the country, and trust to the courage and good sense of an ancient democracy, the present vacillation will continue, and the current disorders will recur.

The most marked incident in the 'Forward Policy' has been the retention of Chitral. Since that step was taken, strenuous efforts have been made by the 'Mullahs' to foment a general rising of the tribes against the British. It is not difficult to see the cause that excites the hostility of the priesthood. Contact with civilisation destroys the superstition and credulity on which the wealth and influence of the 'Mullah' depends. A combination of the religious forces of India against that civilising, educating rule which unconsciously destroys the faith in idols of brass and stone is one of the dangers of the near future. Here it is Mohammedanism that is threatened, and resists. To produce the present revolt many forces have been at work, and the outbreak of fanaticism in Dir, Swat and Chitral, and its communication to the rest of the North-West Frontier, has been inspired and promoted by more astute brains than these wild valleys produce. Secret encouragement has come from the south—from India itself. Actual support and assistance has been given from Kabul. But it is worth noting that the reputation of the Anglo-Indian army is held so high by those who have faced it that for a long time all the efforts of the ordinary 'Mullahs' failed. This year, however, a combination of influences has occurred. The victory of the Turks over the Greeks; the publication of the Ameer's book on 'Jehad'; his assumption of the position of a Caliph of Islam; and much indiscreet writing in the Anglo-Indian press have united to produce a boom in Mohammedanism.

The moment was propitious; nor was the man wanting. What Peter the Hermit was to the regular bishops and cardinals of the Church, the 'Mad Mullah' has been to the ordinary priesthood of the Afghan border. A wild enthusiast, convinced of his divine mission, he preached a crusade, here called Jehad, against the infidel. This fired the mine. The Mullah Powindah and the Mullah Adda—crafty politicians, hitherto powerless—seized the opportunity and fanned the flame.

The extraordinary credulity of the people is hardly conceivable. Had the 'Mad Mullah' called on them to follow him to attack Malakand and Chakdara they would have refused. Instead he worked miracles. He sat at his house and all who came to visit him brought him a small offering of food or money, in return for which he gave them a little rice. As his stores were continually replenished he might claim to have fed thousands. He asserted that he was invisible at nights. Looking into his room they saw no one. At these things they marvelled. Finally he declared that he would destroy the infidel. He wanted no help. No one should share the honours. The heavens would open and an army would descend. The more he protested he did not want them the more exceedingly they came. Incidentally he mentioned that they would be invulnerable. Other agents added arguments. I have been shown a captured scroll upon which the tomb of the Ghazi—he who has killed an infidel—is depicted in heaven as no fewer than seven degrees above the Caada itself. Even after the fighting—when the tribesmen reeled back from the terrible army they had assailed, leaving a quarter of their number on the field—the faith of the survivors was unshaken. Only those who had doubted had perished, said the Mullah, and displayed a bruise which was, he informed them, the sole effect of a twelve-pound shrapnel shell on his weird person.

The rising of 1897 is the most successful attempt hitherto made to combine the frontier tribes. It will not be the last. It is marked by several peculiar features which distinguish it from all former outbreaks. The strange treachery at Maizar marks the influence of a guiding hand. The simultaneous revolt of distant tribes is an evidence of secret workings. These features will be more pronounced in the future. Civilisation is face to face with militant Mohammedanism. When we reflect on the moral and material forces arrayed, there need be no fear of the ultimate issue, but the longer the policy of half measures is adhered to the more distant the end of the struggle will be.

An interference more galling than complete control, a timidity more rash than recklessness, a clemency more cruel than the utmost severity, mark our present dealings with the frontier tribes. To terminate this sorry state of affairs it is necessary to carry a recognised and admitted policy to its logical and inevitable conclusion: to obtain the Gilgit-Chitral-Jellalabad-Kandahar frontier, and reduce to law and order everything south of that line.

6 November, 1897

8

THE CAMP, INAYAT KILA, 23 September

Remembering that the narration of incident must always be the first duty of the war correspondent, I will begin this letter where my last ended, and give an account of the events and operations that followed the action of the Mohmand Valley on 16 September. As soon as it became light the single squadron of Bengal Lancers attached to the force started to the relief of the missing troops. Their guns had been heard during the night, and from time to time even volleys of musketry had been noticed; but their whereabouts, their condition, and their fortunes were unknown. After trotting for about three miles the figures of men could be distinguished moving about the walls of the village of Deremdullah. Soon the glint of a bayonet showed that these figures were the soldiers for whose safety there had been so much anxious suspense. The sowars, actuated by a common impulse, rose in their stirrups and began to cheer, but there was no response.

Nor was this strange. The village was a shambles. In an angle of the outside wall, protected on the third side by a shallow trench, were the survivors of the fight. All around lay the corpses of men and mules. The bodies of five or six native soldiers were being buried in a hurriedly-dug grave. It was thought that, as they were Mohammedans, their resting-place would be respected by the tribesmen. Sixteen wounded men lay side by side in a roofless hut, and their faces, drawn by pain and anxiety, looked ghastly in the pale light of the early morning. Two officers, one with his left hand smashed, the other shot through both legs, were patiently waiting for the moment when the improvised tourniquet could be removed, and some relief afforded to their sufferings. The Brigadier, his khaki coat stained with the blood from a wound on his head, was talking to his only staff-officer, whose helmet displayed a bullet hole. The most ardent lover of realism would have been satisfied. Food, doolies, and doctors soon arrived. The wounded were brought to the field hospitals to be attended to; the unwounded hurried back to camp to get breakfast and a bath. In half an hour the ill-omened spot was occupied only by the few sowars engaged in shooting the wounded mules, and the vultures, who watched the proceedings with an expectant interest.

The story of the night is soon told. In the darkness of the storm the General, anxious for the safety of the two companies of Guides Infantry which had been sent to the assistance of the extreme right, had halted at the village. An accurate fire had been their welcome. Men and mules had been shot. To go on was now impossible; either the guns or the wounded must have been left. This was, of course, not to be thought of. To remain was the only alternative. A dozen soldiers of the Buffs, who had been escorting a dooly and were separated from their regiment, and a few native sappers, led by Lieutenant Watson, attempted to clear the village with the bayonet; but they were too few. The officer was wounded; several men were killed. They tried again. Once more the officer was wounded, this time so seriously that he could no longer stand. After that the little garrison was confined to the defensive. Sheltering themselves behind the carcasses of mules and the bodies of the killed they held out against all attacks, until, at two o'clock, the two companies of Guides for whom they had waited arrived, and cleared the village of the enemy.

No operations took place on the 17th. The soldiers rested; casualties were counted; wounds were dressed; confidence was restored; the funerals of the British officers and men killed the day before took place at noon. Everyone who could attended; but all the pomp of military obsequies was omitted, and there were no Union Jacks to cover the bodies, nor were volleys fired over the graves lest the wounded should be disturbed. Somewhere in the camp—exactly where is now purposely forgotten—the remains of those who had been lost in fighting for their country—all that men can be sure of—were silently interred. No monument marked the spot. The only assurance that it should be undisturbed is that it remains unknown. Nevertheless, the funerals were impressive. To some the game of war brings prizes—honour, advancement, or experience; to some the consciousness of duty well discharged, and to others the excitement of the play, and the knowledge of men and things. But here were those who had drawn the evil numbers—who had lost their all and gained only a soldier's grave. Looking at those shapeless forms, confined in a regulation blanket, the pride of race, the pomp of Empire, the glory of war appeared the faint and unsubstantial fabrics of a dream, and I could not help realising with Burke, 'what shadows we are and what shadows we pursue'.

The situation with which Sir Bindon Blood, at Nawagai, was confronted on the 17th was as follows: In his front was the Hadda Mullah with several thousand tribesmen—holding the Bedmanai Pass. In his rear the whole of the Mohmand Valley was in a blaze. General Elles was still four marches distant, and the Panjkora brigade had not sufficient transport to move. He was thus between two fires. More than this, the Khan of Nawagai, a chief of great importance in these parts, was only kept loyal by the presence of the 3rd Brigade. If the 3rd Brigade had moved from Nawagai—either to assist General Jeffreys[1] with the Mohmands or to meet General Elles from Shab-kadar—the Khan would have thrown his weight against the British. The flame in the Mohmand Valley, joining the flame on the Bedmanai, would have produced a mighty conflagration. Sir Bindon Blood, therefore, decided to stop at Nawagai, to keep the Khan loyal and the pass clear at all costs, and to divide the Hadda Mullah's forces from the tribesmen in the Mohmand Valley. Nawagai was the key to the situation. That key could not be held without difficulty and danger; but the General was confident in his ability to maintain himself against all attacks. He sent General Jeffreys orders to vigorously continue operations against the Mohmands, entrenched his camp, and waited.

The tribesmen—whose tactical instincts have been evolved by centuries of ceaseless war—were not slow to realise that the presence of the 3rd Brigade at Nawagai was fatal to their chances, and they accordingly resolved to attack it. On the night of the 20th a most determined assault was made by more than 4,000 men on Sir Bindon Blood's camp. That assault was repulsed with great slaughter, the fire of the British infantry being particularly crushing. Not a single man got into the entrenchment, though their bodies lying within a yard of the ditch attested the valour and vigour of their charge. Thus the situation was saved. The next day General Elles arrived in the valley with his leading brigade. Sir Bindon Blood, placing the 3rd Brigade of the Malakand Field Force at his disposal, and leaving him to clear the Bedmanai Pass from the now disheartened and dispersing

[1] Patrick Douglas Jeffreys (1848–1922). Commanded 2nd Brigade of the Malakand Field Force, his last command.

tribesmen, joined General Jeffreys at Inayat Kila, and turned his attention to the Mohmand Valley.

In spite of the fact that no reinforcements could be sent to the 2nd Brigade, of the high fighting qualities that the tribesmen had shown, and of the large number of sick and wounded whose protection still further reduced the fighting force, the situation had greatly improved since the 16th. General Jeffreys had prosecuted his task with stubborn perseverance, and as I write the tribesmen are talking of terms and submission. Though I have now anticipated the result of the actions of the 2nd Brigade on the 18th, 20th, 22nd and 23rd, in the Mohmand Valley, I do not propose to leave them unrecorded, and my next letter will give an account of them.

The situation here need cause no anxiety at home. There are difficulties and dangers on the Indian frontier, as in many parts of the British Empire. These difficulties and dangers are being faced with skill, courage, and composure. Unfortunately all fighting must be attended with loss of life. But the ultimate issue is certain, and Continental Powers who watch with jealous elation the obstacles with which England is confronted in India may be assured that the strong and vigorous spirit that conquered an Empire in the past will be sufficient to maintain it in the future.

2 November, 1897

9

INAYAT KILA, 28 September

I realise that I have fallen into considerable arrears in this correspondence. This letter—in which it was my intention to describe the actions of the 18th, 20th, 22nd and 23rd in the Mohmand Valley—should have been written several days ago. But the reader must remember that while an active life, full of incident and adventure, provides much material to write about, it also leaves but little time for the actual labour of composition. Amid the labours of the day, the clamours of the camp, or the alarms of the night there is small opportunity and often small inclination for that judicious reflection which should properly precede a letter to a newspaper. One vivid scene succeeds another. A strong impression is effaced before it can be recorded, and many events worthy of note are either lost in the perspective of the past, or become old and uninteresting on the long journey to London.

I shall therefore be very brief in the description of the four punitive engagements which occupied the 2nd Brigade of the Malakand Field Force last week. On 18 September, two days after the important action which I have previously recorded, Brigadier General Jeffreys marched to attack the fortified village of Domodoloh. As the troops approached the hills the field-glasses displayed the figures of armed tribesmen thickly clustered on the different spurs which commanded the line of advance, and as soon as the leading infantry came within range a brisk fire was opened from many points. The Guides Infantry attacked the centre, the 35th Sikhs the right, and the 38th Dogras the left of the position. Musketry fire became general. The mountain battery—reduced by its losses in men and mules on the 16th to only four guns—came into action and began shelling the summits, from which the smoke-puffs were most frequent and continuous. Covered by their fire the infantry advanced and, driving the enemy to the tops of the highest peaks, occupied the village. So far there had been

35

no difficulty and very little danger. The sappers accomplished the destruction of the towers and other fortifications and, at 11.30, the order for withdrawal was given. The moment when it is necessary to retire before an Asiatic foe is the moment of danger. Immediately the firing increased. Everywhere on the hillsides men appeared, shouting, shooting, waving their swords. But the troops who formed the centre, and against whom their counter-attack was directed, were versed in every phase of frontier warfare. Instead of the misfortune which I had witnessed in the retreat of the 35th Sikhs on the 16th, a beautiful exposition of tactical skill was presented by the Guides Infantry. Every attempt to rush was checked by a steady and crushing volley. Each half company retired protected by the flanking fire of other units. A few men were left behind on each position to mask the withdrawal of the rest. Not a single precaution was forgotten; not a single opportunity was afforded to the enemy. The result was that a small loss was the cost of a most important operation.

At the bottom of the hill the Buffs took up the duty of rearguard, and the deliberate care with which the fire of that terrible weapon the Lee-Metford, with its more terrible dum-dum bullets,[1] was directed effectually checked any pursuit. The whole affair was conducted with a loss of only two men killed and five wounded; this in spite of the fact that firing had been continuous for nearly four hours. Such are the lessons of war! As long as things are going on all right, as long as Fortune smiles and discipline prevails, few people are killed. But a slip, an omission, an accident swiftly expands the casualty list to a very different proportion. The action of 20 September presented similar features to those just described. The enemy showed in greater strength and counter-attacked with greater vigour, but

[1] The dum-dum bullet was named after the Indian town near Calcutta, where they were made. The rounded nose was left uncovered by the cupro-nickel jacket. Used with Lee-Metford rifles and fatally effective up to 2000 yards. The dum-dum was internationally outlawed on 29 July, 1899, though Britain did not ratify the agreement until later, which may explain Churchill's indignation at their use by the Boers, contrasting oddly with his approval here.

The Mark II Special dum-dum was brought into use in 1898. The Mark I was therefore still in use at the time covered by these despatches, and this is presumably the explanation of the Hindustani phrase 'ek dum', 'ek' being the Hindustani for 'one'.

were again met with equal discipline and staunchness. The Buffs—who cleared the hills to the right—bore the brunt of the opposition, and I was afforded the opportunity of observing that formidable machine—a British battalion in action. Again the advance was practically unopposed; again the withdrawal was pressed with vigour. But the fire of calm, determined men, led by officers whose composure was only disturbed by their elation, held everything at a distance.

A somewhat interesting example of the skill with the rifle to which these tribesmen attain occurred. Lieutenant J. Hasler's[1] company was a little to the left of the crest of the spur, along which the retirement was being executed. Bullets continually passed overhead from the far side, and the Lieutenant walked to the crest to see from what direction these were coming. The half-company on this side were having quite a lively time. Far away up the mountain was a peak, and from this thirty or forty riflemen were firing. Their bullets whistled about or struck the rocks and stones all round. In a few moments two officers and three or four men were hit. After much careful sighting and observation with the Lee-Metford rifle the distance was found to be nearly 1,500 yards. Those who know the range and power of the Martini-Henry rifle—with which the enemy were firing—will appreciate the skill which can inflict loss at so great a distance.

The retirement of the Buffs was a fine display of discipline and courage. As soon as the troops got clear of the hill, the enemy began firing from the shelter of the burning village. The ground was level, and afforded no cover to the soldiers. The bullets whistled overhead, or cut, with a curious sucking noise, into the ground, which was wet with the night's rain. Yet a distant spectator might have imagined that this was some parade movement—so slowly did the lines of skirmishers retire, and so perfect was their dressing. The only circumstances that seemed to oppose the idea of a drill-ground were the little knots of men carrying off the wounded, or an occasional group around one who had just fallen. Although the affair was a small one, an acute observer might get some glimpse of what Napier has called 'the strength and majesty with which the British soldier fights'. The Buffs' casualties were three officers and eleven men, while the total casualties of the brigade were sixteen.

[1] Julian Hasler, (1868– ?). Served with the East Kent Regiment.

At this action the cavalry again—in defiance of the views of all theoretical tacticians—displayed their value in frontier warfare. The single squadron of the 'useless arm' attached to the Second Brigade had been so much employed during the week that it was reduced to barely forty lances. These were, nevertheless, sufficient to protect the left flank of the brigade from a dangerous attack. Over 600 tribesmen, who had collected in an adjoining valley, endeavoured to come to the assistance of their countrymen in the village. To do this it was necessary that they should cross a little open ground. Each time they attempted to do so the Lancers trotted forward ominously. The terror of these hillmen for cavalry is extreme. Many of them had been chased from Khar to Chakdara two months ago by these same fierce horsemen, and they had no desire to repeat the experience. Finally they decided to make a wide detour by the hills, and arrived, of course, long after the action was over. But for this the losses must have been very much heavier and the withdrawal of the troops a matter of greatly increased difficulty.

The actions of the 22nd and 23rd were in many respects similar to those I have just described, and as the resistance of the enemy was not so well sustained, I will not become tedious by relating their details. One incident must, however, be recorded. The line of march on the 22nd lay past the village of Desemdullah or Bibot, in which the severe fighting of the night of the 16th had taken place. In company with several officers I rode to look again at the ill-fated spot. It will be remembered that the bodies of Mohammedan native soldiers killed in the fighting had been buried there. The sight which was presented to our gaze was horrible and revolting. The remains had been disinterred and mutilated. Remembering that a morning journal is read to a large extent at the breakfast table, I do not intend to describe the condition in which these poor fragments of humanity were found.

I must, however, invite the reader to consider the degradation of mind and body which can alone inspire so foul an act. These tribesmen are among the most miserable and brutal creatures of the earth. Their intelligence only enables them to be more cruel, more dangerous, more destructive than the wild beasts. Their religion—fanatic though they are—is only respected when it incites to bloodshed and murder. Their habits are filthy; their morals cannot be alluded to. With every feeling of respect for that wide sentiment of human sympathy which characterises a Christian civilisation, I find it impossible to come to any other conclusion than that, in proportion as these valleys are purged from the pernicious vermin that infest them, so will the happiness of humanity be increased, and the progress of mankind accelerated.

9 November, 1897

10

INAYAT KILA, 2 October

Although I have already written twice this week, I feel that some account of the important action of Agrah on 30 September should reach the English papers with as little delay as possible, and I therefore add this letter to the homeward mail. The village of Agrah lies in a re-entrant of the mountains at the western end of the Mohmand Valley, and is about two miles south of Zagai. From this camp it is a march of nine miles. Behind the village, still further to the west, tower the peaks of the Hindu Raj range, along the summits of which lies our boundary with the Ameer—the Durand line. Close to the frontier, Gholam Hyder, the Afghan Commander-in-Chief, is encamped with a powerful army. I do not desire in these letters to meddle in high politics, or to raise questions of a wider importance than can fairly be solved by irresponsible opinion, but I cannot refrain from suggesting that the proximity of the Afghan frontier and of this Afghan army may perhaps explain how it was that the defenders of an obscure village were numbered by thousands, and that the weapons of a poverty-stricken tribe were excellent Martini-Henry rifles.

It was evident, as the Guides cavalry approached the hills, that resistance was contemplated. Several red standards were visible to the naked eye, and the field-glasses disclosed numerous figures lining the various ridges and spurs. The squadrons, advancing as far as the scrub would allow them, soon drew the fire of isolated skirmishers. Several troops dismounted and returned the salute with their carbines, and at 8.45 a dropping musketry fire began. The brigade now came into action in the following formation: the cavalry on the extreme left covered the head of a considerable valley, from which our flank was threatened; the Guides Infantry and the Royal West Kent Regiment prolonged the line to the centre of the attack; the 31st Punjab Infantry moved against the spurs to the right of the village;

and 38th Dogras were in reserve. The action was begun by the Guides Infantry storming the ridges to the left of the enemy's position. These were strongly held and fortified by stone walls—called sangars —behind which the defenders were sheltered. The Guides advanced at a brisk pace, and without much firing, across the open ground to the foot of the hills. The tribesmen, shooting from excellent cover, maintained a hot fire. The bullets kicked up the dust in all directions, or whistled viciously through the air; but the distance was short, and it was soon apparent that the enemy did not mean to abide the assault. When the troops got within 100 yards and fixed bayonets a dozen determined men were still firing from the sangars. The Afridi and Pathan companies of the Guides—uttering shrill cries of ex- ultation, culminating in an extraordinary yell—dashed forward, climbing the hill as only hillmen can climb, and cleared the crest. On the side of the next hill the figures of the retreating tribesmen were visible, and many of them were shot down before they could find shelter.

It was a strange thing to watch those conspicuous forms toiling up the hillside, dodging this way and that as the bullets cut into the earth around them; but with the experience of the previous ten minutes fresh in the memory, pity was not one of the emotions it aroused. A good many fell, subsiding peacefully, and lying quite still, and their fall was greeted by strange little yelps of pleasure from the native soldiers. These Afridi and Pathan companies of the Guides Infantry suggest nothing so much as a well-trained pack of hounds, for their cries, their movements, their natures are similar.

The West Kents had now come into line on the Guides' right, and while the latter held the long ridge the British regiment moved upon the village. Here the resistance became very severe. The tangled, broken nature of the ground, rising in terraces, sometimes 10ft high, and covered with high crops, led to fighting at close quarters, with heavy loss on both sides. Loud and continuous grew the musketry fire. The 31st Punjab Infantry, who had ascended the spurs on the right, soon joined hands with the West Kents, and both regiments became hotly engaged. Meantime the mountain battery, which had come into action near the centre, began to throw its shells over the heads of the infantry on to the higher slopes, from which the enemy were firing.

It soon became evident that the troops were too few for the work. On the left the Guides' Infantry were unable to leave the ridge they had captured lest it should be re-occupied by the enemy, who were showing in considerable strength. A great gap arose, in consequence, between the Guides and the Royal West Kents, and this enabled the tribesmen to get around the left flank of the British Regiment, while the 31st Punjab Infantry, on the right, were also turned by the enveloping enemy. It is to these circumstances that most of the losses were due.

The village was carried with the bayonet and partially destroyed. But the pressure of the enemy now became so strong that the brigadier, fearing the troops might get seriously involved, ordered the retirement to commence. As usual, the enemy pressed the withdrawal, but with less vigour than on former occasions. This close fighting leads to heavy loss, but it tells equally on both sides. The battery, now advancing to within 800 yards of the enemy's line, opened a rapid fire of shrapnel, and this cleared the spurs which commanded the line of retirement. The bursting shells were a remarkable sight. A little puff of smoke in the air, where the explosion took place, and a great cloud of dust where the bullets and splinters struck the ground.

A continuous stream of doolies and stretchers now began to flow from the fighting line. Soon all available conveyances were exhausted, and the bodies of the killed and wounded had to be carried over the rough ground in the arms of their comrades—a very painful process, which drew forth many groans from the suffering men. At length the withdrawal was completed, and the brigade ventured to camp. The cavalry covered the rear, and their presence deterred the enemy from leaving the hill.

The loss in killed and wounded was four officers and fifty-six men. It may be thought that this list of casualties does not justify the employment of such expressions as 'severe fighting', 'heavy loss', etc. But all things are relative, and the severity of an action should be judged by the proportion which the casualties bear to the numbers engaged. Few people who have not accompanied an army in the field can have any idea of the rapidity with which the fighting strength diminishes. Sickness alone is responsible for nearly a quarter of the whole force. Then there are duties of all kinds to be discharged in camp, and on the line of communications. Signallers, escorts, orderlies, grain-collecting parties, water pickets, and a host of other details have to be deducted. Finally, each battalion has to leave two companies to protect the camp. The result of all this is that the available fighting strength of the brigade is reduced to about 1,300 men. On the 30th about 1,000 were engaged, and in this number the loss of sixty is severe. Anyone who disputes this assertion should compare these figures with those of some of the famous Egyptian battles. Consider, for instance, the battle of Firket. Here the casualties amounted to fifty out of a total of nearly 10,000 men engaged.

Riding back to camp, I observed a gruesome sight. At the head of the column of doolies and stretchers were the bodies of the killed, each roped on to a mule. Their heads hung down on one side, their legs on the other. There was no other way, and it was better than leaving their remains to be insulted and defiled by the savages with whom we are fighting. At the entrance to the camp a group of surgeons were awaiting the wounded. Two large operating-tables, made of medical boxes and covered with waterproof sheets, were also prepared. These things make one realise that there is a side to warfare browner than khaki. I have taken advantage of a morning when I am compelled to remain in camp to describe to you the action of Agrah. While I write I can hear the guns of the skirmish which is in progress four or five miles away, and can see the smoke of the burning huts rising in the still air. It is, however, quite a small affair, and is probably unattended by any loss of life. But this is a strange war, and the more I see and the further these letters progress the more do I realise the difficulty of conveying a true picture to the Englishman at home.

Here, at the mouth of the Mohmand Valley, is the entrenched camp of Inayat Kila. Originally it was surrounded only by a small shelter trench, but as the night firing has been frequent and the possibility of attack continual the trench has grown in the three weeks we have been here until it is quite a formidable defence; and the interior of the camp is honeycombed with holes and pits. The whole valley is displayed. The clear atmosphere and the strong light make the mountains which surround it seem much nearer than they really are. It is possible to distinguish not only the scenes of the recent action, but also of those which have still to be fought. Over all is a cloudless sky of the deepest blue, in which the sun blazes mercilessly.

26 October, 1897

II

INAYAT KILA, 6 October

I write to you again from the same address—from the great entrenched camp which stands at the mouth of that wide bay in the mountains which people in England must be getting to know familiarly as the Mohmand Valley. But since my last letter the camp has doubled in size, and now contains a division instead of a brigade. As soon as Sir Bindon Blood received the news of the action of 30 September he marched here from Panjkora with every available man and gun. A powerful force is now concentrated, and fourteen guns and 2,000 rifles will be in line at the next engagement.

In the meanwhile another smaller action has taken place, of which —though it presented similar features to those already described— it is, nevertheless, desirable you should receive some account. I cannot, however, write as an eye-witness, for it may, perhaps, be remembered that the guns were firing in the distance while I was finishing my last letter. The village of Badalai was the cause of the fight. Its inhabitants were clearly proved to have taken part in the night attack of 14 September on the camp of the 2nd Brigade, and they admitted having sent their fighting men to the attack on Chakdara and the Malakand. When they refused to surrender the rifles which were demanded by the Government officers, they knew that they would be punished, and took precautions accordingly. As usual, there was little opposition to the advance, and the village was occupied, its towers and fortifications demolished, and the houses fired. Then the troops began their homeward march. Very large numbers of the enemy now appeared. It is calculated by many officers that no fewer than 3,000 men were visible. Spreading out in a crescent nearly four miles from end to end, they advanced firing. A severe combat ensued. The guns shelled every group that afforded a target, and the two batteries between them fired nearly 180 shrapnel shell with considerable effect. The infantry also opened a heavy fire.

44

The enemy, who declined to leave the broken ground, suffered severely, and eventually drew off. The firing was throughout at long range—probably never less than 700 yards; but in spite of this, the skirmish cost us nearly twenty men killed and wounded. This was 3 October.

Since then there has been a little cavalry work but no serious fighting. Some of this I have had opportunities of witnessing, and an account may interest those who are not so foolish as to imagine that the day of cavalry is over. The task which is usually confided to the cavalry in these mountain actions is to protect one of the flanks. The ground hardly ever admits of charging in any formation, and it is necessary for the men to use their carbines. On 30 September the cavalry were so employed. On the left of the hostile position was a wide valley, full of scrubby trees and stone walls, and occupied by large numbers of the enemy. Had these tribesmen been able to debouch from this valley they would have fallen on the flank of the brigade, and the situation would have become one of danger. For five hours two weak squadrons of the Guides Cavalry were sufficient to hold them in check. The methods they employed are worth noticing. Little groups of six or seven men were dismounted, and those, with their carbines, replied to the enemy's fire. Other little groups of mounted men remained concealed in nullahs, hollows, or behind obstacles. Whenever the enemy tried to rush one of the dismounted parties, and to do so advanced from the bad ground, the mounted patrols galloped forward and chased them back to cover. The terror which these tribesmen have of cavalry is out of keeping with their general character. It was a beautiful display of cavalry tactics in this kind of warfare and, considering the enormous numbers of the enemy who were thus kept from participating in the main action, it demonstrated the power and value of the mounted arm with convincing force.

I, yesterday, saw some very similar work, though on a smaller scale. A squadron was engaged in covering the operations of a foraging party. A line of patrols moving rapidly about presented difficult targets to the enemy's sharpshooters. I found the remainder of the squadron dismounted in rear of a large bank of stones. Twenty sowars, with their carbines, were engaged in firing at the enemy, who had occupied a morcha—a small stone fort—some 300 yards away. Desultory firing continued for some time, shots being fired from the hills, which were half a mile away, as well as from the morcha.

Bullets kept falling near the bank, but the cover it afforded was good and no one was hit. At length word was brought that the foraging party was finished, and that the squadron was to retire under cover of the infantry. Now came a moment of some excitement. The officer in command knew well that the instant his men were mounted they would be fired at from every point which the enemy held. He ordered the first troop to mount and the second to cover the retirement. The men scrambled into their saddles and, spreading out into an extended line, cantered away towards a hollow about 300 yards distant. Immediately there was an outburst of firing. The dust rose in spurts near the horsemen, and the bullets whistled about their ears. No one, however, was hit. Meanwhile, the remaining troop had been keeping up a rapid fire on the enemy to cover their retirement. It now became their turn to go. Firing a parting volley, the men ran to their horses, mounted, and followed the first troop at a hand gallop, extending into a long line as they did so. Again the enemy opened fire, and again the dusty ground showed that their bullets were well directed. Again, however, no one was hurt, and the sowars reached the hollow, laughing and talking in high glee. The morning's skirmishing had, however, cost the squadron a man and a horse, both severely wounded. Such affairs as these are of daily occurrence here, and are of the greatest value in training the soldiers. Of course, the Guides Cavalry know all there is to know of frontier war. But there are many other regiments who would be immensely benefited, and who would be made infinitely more powerful fighting organisations, if they were afforded the opportunity for such experience.

I had intended to defer criticism of the military aspect of the campaign till a later stage in this correspondence, but since I have devoted so much of this letter to the cavalry I may as well deal with their affairs, 'whiles I am in the way with them'. The great feature which the war on the Indian frontier of 1897 has hitherto displayed is the extraordinary value of cavalry. At Shabkadar a charge of the 13th Bengal Lancers was more than successful. In the Swat Valley, during the relief of Chakdara, the Guides Cavalry and 11th Bengal Lancers inflicted the most terrible loss on the enemy. To quote the words of Sir Bindon Blood's official report to the Adjutant-General, these regiments, 'eager for vengeance, pursued, cut up and speared them in every direction, leaving their bodies thickly strewn over the fields'. Again, after the action of Landakai the cavalry made a most vigorous pursuit, and killed large numbers of the flying enemy.

Since I have been with this force I have been a witness of the constant employment of the cavalry, and I have frequently been informed by general officers that they would be very glad to have a larger number at their disposal. On the morning of 16 September it was the cavalry who were able to catch up the enemy before they could reach the hills and take some revenge for the losses of the night. And since then in every action they have been the first in and the last out.

There has been a boom in cavalry. But one section, and that the most important, has been deprived of its share in the good fortune. The authorities have steadily refused to allow any British cavalry to cross the frontier. Of course, this is defended on the ground of expense. 'British cavalry costs so much,' it is said, 'and natives do the work just as well.' 'Better,' say some. But it is a poor kind of economy to cause professional disheartenment to a most expensive and important branch of the service. The ambition that a young officer entering the Army ought to set before him is to lead his own men in action. This ought to inspire his life and animate all his efforts. 'Stables' will no longer be dull when he realises that on the fitness of his horse his life and honour may one day depend. If he thinks his men may soon be asked to stand by him at a pinch he will no longer be bored by their interests and business. But when he realises that all is empty display, and that his regiment is a sword too costly to be drawn, he naturally loses keenness, and betakes himself to polo as a consolation.

I have met up here many young men in frontier regiments, both in the cavalry and the infantry, who have already served in three or even four campaigns. Daring, intelligent and capable, they are proofs of the value of their training, and are fit to lead their men under any conditions and in any country. We subalterns in British cavalry regiments do occasionally manage to see a little active service in strange and various capacities—as transport officers or on the staff; but to lead in the field the men we have trained in peace is a possibility which is never worth contemplating. To the young man who wants to enjoy himself—to spend a few years agreeably in a military companionship, to have an occupation—the British cavalry will be suited. But to the youth who means to make himself a professional soldier, an expert in war, a specialist in practical tactics, who desires a hard life of adventure and a true comradeship in arms, I would recommend the choice of some regiment on the frontier, like those fine ones I have seen—the Guides and the 11th Bengal Lancers.

I am aware that those who criticise an existing state of things ought to be prepared with some constructive legislation which would remedy the evils they denounce. Though it is unlikely that the Government of India will take my advice, either wholly or in part, I hereby exhort them to quit the folly of a 'penny wise' policy, and to adhere consistently to the principle of employing British and native troops in India in a regular proportion. That is to say, that when two native cavalry regiments have been sent on service across the frontier, the third cavalry regiment so sent shall be British.

Besides this, in order to give cavalry subalterns as many opportunities of seeing active service as possible, subaltern officers should be allowed to volunteer for emergency employment with native cavalry. I have talked to several officers who command cavalry regiments up here, and they tell me that such an arrangement would work excellently, and that as they are always short of officers it would supply a want.

I would suggest that the subalterns should, with the approval of their Colonel, be attached to the native regiment and, after passing in Hindustani and being reported as qualified to serve with native troops, be considered available for employment as described. I shall be told there are financial difficulties. I do not believe this. There are plenty of cavalry subalterns whose eagerness to see service is so strong that to have an extra chance they would submit to any arrangement that the rapacity of Government might impose.

To be technical is a grave offence, and I realise keenly that if these letters ever obtained so evil a reputation they would be shunned as the House of Commons is shunned on a service night. I have strayed far away from the camp in the Mohmand Valley—into the tangled paths of military controversy—and I cannot better conclude than by asking the reader to forgive—as he will surely forget—all that has been said.

13 November, 1897

12

INAYAT KILA, 8 October

We have entered upon a period of comparative peace. The Mohmands have expressed a wish to sue for terms, and negotiations are
now going on between the political officers and the tribal jirgahs.
The khans of Jar and Khar, who have been, from interested motives,
very loyal and useful to the British Government during the stay of
the brigades in this valley, are also endeavouring to promote a settlement. It would be rash to predict what the outcome will be. The
peculiar position of this tribe—astride the frontier line—enables them
to assume a very different attitude towards the Sirkar than could be
maintained by tribes of equal strength otherwise situated. Not only
do they receive assistance from Afghanistan in arms and men, but it
is a refuge to which they can withdraw, and in which they have
already placed their families, their flocks and their herds. The
independent demeanour which they display takes the form during
the negotiations of shooting at our grass-cutters and foraging parties,
and of firing into camp from time to time. The troops, of course, feel
it incumbent on them to reply, so I am justified in qualifying the
peace we are enjoying by the epithet 'comparative'.

A second convoy of sick and wounded leaves the camp tomorrow,
and, travelling slowly down the line of communications, should
reach Nowshera in about a week. There the hospital is, I hear, full
but room for the latest arrivals will be made by drafting the less
serious cases to the large new base for wounded which has been
established at Rawalpindi, and which contains accommodation for
500 men. It is a long and a tedious journey for invalids, and they will
be very weary of the jolting doolies before the comfortable beds of
Nowshera are reached. The cheeriness and patience of the wounded
men exceeds belief. Perhaps it is due to a realisation of the proximity
in which they have stood to death; perhaps partly to that feeling of
relief with which a man returns for a spell from war to peace. In any

case, it is remarkable. A poor fellow—a private in the Buffs—was hit at Zagai, and had his arm amputated at the shoulder. I expressed my sympathy, and he replied, philosophically, 'You can't make omelettes without breaking eggs,' and, after a pause, added, with much satisfaction, 'The regiment did well that day.' He came of a fighting stock, but I could not help speculating on the possible future which awaited him. Discharge from the service as medically unfit, some miserable pension insufficient to command any pleasures in life except those of drink, a loafer's life, and a pauper's death. Perhaps 'the regiment'—the officers, that is to say—would succeed in getting him work, and would, from their own resources, supplement his pension. But what a poor system it is by which the richest people in the world neglects the soldiers who have served it well, and which leaves to newspaper philanthropy, to local institutions, and to private charity a burden which ought to be proudly borne by the nation.

Most of the officers and men wounded in this valley have been hit by bullets from Martini-Henry rifles, and it may be of some interest to consider the source from which the tribesmen have obtained these arms. The perpetual state of intestine war in which they live creates a naturally keen demand for deadly weapons. A good Martini-Henry rifle will always command a price in these parts of Rs400, or about £25. As the actual value of such a rifle does not exceed Rs50, it is evident that a very large margin of profit would accrue to the enterprising trader. All along the frontier, and from far down into India, rifles are stolen by expert and cunning thieves. One tribe—the Ut Khels—who live in the Khyber Pass, have made the traffic in arms their especial business. Their thieves are the most daring. Their agents are the most remote. Some of their methods are highly ingenious. One story, which may not yet have reached the English Press, is worth repeating. A coffin was presented for railway transport. The relatives of the deceased accompanied it. The dead man, they said, had desired to be buried across the frontier. The smell proclaimed the corpse to be in an advanced state of decomposition. The railway officials afforded every facility to the passage of so unpleasant an object. No one impeded its progress. It was unapproachable. It was only when coffin and mourners were safe across the frontier that the police were informed that a dozen rifles had been concealed in the coffin, and that the body was represented by a piece of well-hung beef.

I regret to state that theft is not the only means by which the frontier tribes obtain weapons. At the camp near Manda I had an opportunity of inspecting a hundred rifles which had been surrendered by the local tribesmen. Of these rifles nearly a third were condemned Government Martinis, and displayed the Government stamp. Now no such rifles are supposed to exist. As soon as they are condemned, the arsenal authorities are responsible that they are destroyed, and this is in every case carried out under European supervision. The fact that such rifles are not destroyed and are found in the possession of transfrontier tribesmen points to a very grave instance of dishonest and illegal traffic which is being carried on by some person or persons connected with the Arsenal. It need hardly be said that a searching inquiry has been instituted.

Another point connected with these rifles is that even when they have been officially destroyed—by cutting them in three pieces—the fractions have a market value. Several were shown to me which had been rejoined and mended by the tribesmen. These were, of course, very dangerous weapons indeed. The rest of the hundred had strange tales to tell. Two or three were Russian military rifles, stolen probably from the distant posts in Central Asia. One was a Snider—taken at Maiwand—and bearing the number of the ill-fated regiment to whom it had belonged. Some had come from Europe, perhaps through Persia; others from the arms factory at Cabul. It was a strange instance of the tireless efforts of supply to meet demand.

We have now been nearly a month in the Mohmand Valley, and every spur and re-entrant of the mountains that surround it have acquired significance and importance from the numerous actions and reconnaissances. It now appears that the end is in sight, and that this episode in the story of the Malakand Field Force is soon to be concluded. At such a time it may not be inappropriate to consider the question of profit and loss. The tribesmen are reduced to submission. Their villages have been punished. Their grain and fodder have been requisitioned. The towers and forts from which they carry on their feuds and wars have been blown up by dynamite and are now in ruins. A severe lesson has been given. An example has been made. The power of the Empire has been asserted. But the cost has been heavy. Twenty-three officers and 245 men have been killed and wounded.

The whole question of the armament of the frontier tribes is of the greatest importance. The natives of these hills display a surprising aptitude with the rifle. Whatever frontier policy be pursued it is well that it should be pursued rapidly. The difficulties of dealing with these tribesmen will naturally increase as they obtain possession of more and better weapons. In this country transport is the life and soul of any force. At night it is necessary to pack the animals into the small area of an entrenched camp. A night attack by long-range fire on such a target must inevitably be attended with many casualties among the mules and camels. At Markhanai, on 14 September, eighty were killed, and in the severe attack on Sir Bindon Blood's camp at Nawagai, on 20 September, no fewer than a hundred and twenty were destroyed. Such losses would soon impair the mobility of any brigade. Nor is there any way by which in such a country they can be prevented. It is impossible to find camping grounds which are not commanded by some hill or assailable from some nullah. The more general adoption of such tactics as I have alluded to would soon paralyse military operations in these valleys, and reduce to immobility any force that might be employed. And so by this road I have come to the old conclusion that whatever is to be done on the frontier should be done quickly and completely.

It must seem strange to many people in England that the casualties in this valley should be in so different a proportion to those which have occurred elsewhere. While other generals have been gaining comparatively bloodless victories in various quarters, it is fallen to the lot of a single brigade to meet with stubborn and severe resistance and to sustain losses which exceed the accumulated losses of all the great armies now mobilised on the Indian frontier. The main cause is, as I have already stated, the proximity of the Afghan border. But it would be unjust to deny to the people of the Mohmand Valley the reputation for courage, tactical skill, and marksmanship which they have so well deserved. During uncounted years they have brawled and fought in the unpenetrated gloom of barbarism. At length they struck a blow at civilisation, and civilisation, though compelled to record the odious vices that the fierce light of scientific war has exposed, will yet ungrudgingly admit that they are a brave and warlike race. Their name will live in the minds of all men for some months, even in this busy century, and there are many families in England who will never forget it. The Valley and its people have become historic. But perhaps they do not realise all this, or if they do it may not alter the regret they feel for having tried conclusions with the British Raj. Their game has cost them dear. Indeed, as we have already been told, 'Nothing is so expensive as glory.'
16 November, 1897

13

NOWSHERA, 14 October

When, in my last letter, I wrote that a convoy was starting for the base, I did not anticipate that I should accompany it myself. Nothing happens but the unexpected, and very little but the unwelcome. Yet the moment of departure might have been more inopportune. The operations in the Mohmand Valley have terminated, the tribesmen have submitted, and the Malakand Field Force will turn its attention to other quarters. I have therefore been able to witness a complete episode in the frontier war. Whether the patience of the reader would have tolerated a continuation of these letters is a question which will remain unanswered, for the conclusion of hostilities against the Mohmands and the expiration of my leave equally mark a period when the correspondence should cease. It would, however, be inconsiderate to offend the superstitious by making the thirteenth letter the last, nor do I care to tell a tale without attempting to point the moral at the end.

The convoy of sick and wounded was to be escorted as far as the Panjkora river by the Royal West Kents, who were themselves in need of some recuperation. To campaign in India without tents is always a trial to a British regiment; and when it is moved to the front from some unhealthy station like Peshawar or Delhi, and the men are saturated with fever and weakened by the summer heats, the sick list becomes long and serious. Typhoid, from drinking surface-water, and the various other kinds of fever which follow exposure to the heat of the day or the chills of the night soon take 100 men from the fighting strength, and the general of an Indian frontier force has to watch with equal care the movements of the enemy and the fluctuation of the hospital returns. As soon, therefore, as Sir Bindon Blood saw that the Mohmands were desirous of peace, and that no further operations against them were probable, he sent one of his British regiments to their tents near the Panjkora.

About sixty wounded men from the actions of 30 September and 3 October and the same number of sick formed the bulk of the convoy. The slight cases are carried on camels, in cradles made by cutting a native bedstead in two, and called 'cacolays'. The more serious lie in doolies or litters, protected from the sun by white curtains, and borne by four natives. Those who are well enough ride on mules. The infantry escort is disposed along the line with every precaution that can be suggested, but the danger of an attack on the long straggling line of doolies and animals on difficult and broken ground is a very real and terrible one.

Starting at six the column reached Jar, a march of eight miles, at about ten o'clock. Here we were joined by a wing of the 24th Punjab Infantry, which was coming up to relieve the Royal West Kent. The camp at Jar has the disadvantage of being commanded from a hill to the north, and the Salarzais—another pestilent tribe, whose name alone is an affliction—delight to show their valour by firing at the troops during the night. Of course, this could be prevented by moving the camp out of range of this hill. But then, unfortunately, it would be commanded by another hill to the south, from which the Shumozai section of the Utman Khel—to whom my former remarks also apply—would be able to amuse themselves. The inconvenience of the situation has therefore to be faced.

We had not been long in camp before the oldest son of the Khan of Jar, who has been comparatively loyal during the operations, came to inform the colonel in command that there would be 'sniping' that night. Certain evil men, he said, had declared their intention of destroying the force, but he, the heir-apparent to the Khanate of Jar and the ally of the Empress, would protect us. Four pickets of his own regular army should watch the camp—that our slumbers might not be disturbed—and when challenged by the sentries they would reply 'Chokidar' (watchman). This all seemed very satisfactory, but we entrenched ourselves as usual, not, as was explained, because we doubted our protector's powers or inclinations, but merely as a matter of form.

At midnight precisely the camp was awakened by a dozen shots in rapid succession. The Khan's pickets could be heard expostulating with the enemy, who replied by jeers and bitter remarks. The firing continued for an hour, when the 'snipers', having satisfied their honour, relieved their feelings and expended their cartridges, went away rejoicing. The troops throughout remained silent and vouchsafed no reply.

54

It may seem difficult to believe that fifty bullets could fall in a camp only a hundred yards square—crowded with animals and men—without any other result than to hit a single mule in the tail. Such was, however, the fact. This shows of what value a little active service is to the soldier. The first time he is under fire he imagines himself to be in very great danger. He thinks that every bullet is going to hit him, and that every shot is being aimed at him. Assuredly he will be killed in a moment. If he goes through this ordeal once or twice he begins to get some idea of the odds in his favour. He has heard lots of bullets and they have not hurt him. He will get home safely to his tea this evening, just as he did the last time. He becomes a very much more effective fighting machine. From a military point of view the perpetual frontier wars in one corner or other of the Empire are of the greatest value. This fact may one of these days be proved when our soldiers are brought into contact with some peace-trained conscript army.

Though the firing produces very little effect on the troops—most of whom have been through the experience several times before—it was a severe trial to the wounded, whose nerves, shattered by pain and weakness, were unable to bear the strain. The surgeon in charge told me that the poor fellows quivered at every shot as if in the anticipation of a blow. A bullet in the leg will make a brave man a coward. A blow on the head makes a wise man a fool. Indeed, I have read that a sufficiency of absinthe can make a good man a knave. The triumph of mind over matter does not seem to be quite complete as yet. I saw a strange thing happen while the firing was going on, which may amuse those who take an interest in the habits and development of animals. Just in front of my tent, which was open, was a clear space, occupied by a flock of goats and sheep. The brilliant moonlight made everything plainly visible. Every time that a bullet whistled over them or struck the ground near them they ducked and bobbed in evident terror. An officer, who also noticed this, told me it was the first time they had been under fire; and I have been wondering ever since whether this explains their fear or makes it more inexplicable.

Nearly the whole of this letter has been about the 'sniping' at Jar, on the night of 10 October, and I can very well understand a critic asking why so much should be written about so common an incident. It is, however, because this night firing is so common a feature that I feel that no picture of the war on the Indian frontier would be complete without some account of it.

The next day we crossed the Panjkora river, and I started to ride down the line of communication to the base at Nowshera. At each stage some of the comforts of civilisation and peace reappeared. At Panjkora we touched the telegraph wire; at Savai were fresh potatoes; ice was to be had at Chakdara; a comfortable bed at the Malakand; and, at length, at Nowshera, the railway. But how little these things matter, after all. When they are at hand they seem indispensable, but when they cannot be obtained they are hardly missed. A little plain food and a philosophic temperament are the only necessities of life.

I do not intend to ask the reader to accompany me any further from the scene of action. He is free, and his imagination may lead him back to the wide valleys, the rugged mountains, and the waving crops of the Afghan Highlands. If he will, he may continue among camps and men in a glorious and active life, compared to which all other pursuits and occupations are dull and unreal. I return to the monotony of melancholy Madras, but before doing so I shall venture to offer some remarks on those military and political features which strike a spectator most forcibly. These will form the subject of two more letters.

19 November, 1897

14

Nowshera, 15 October

It may at first seem that a letter wholly devoted to military considerations is inappropriate to a newspaper the vast majority of whose readers are unconnected with the Army. But in these days it is necessary for everyone who means to be well-informed to have a superficial knowledge of everyone else's business. Nor should it be forgotten that the English are essentially a warlike, though not a military, people; that is to say, they are always ready to fight, though not always prepared to do so. Encouraged also by what Mr Gladstone has called 'the growing militarism of the times', I hope that, avoiding technicalities, it may be of some general interest to glance for a moment at the frontier war from a purely professional point of view. The observations which follow must be taken as applying to the operations in the Mohmand Valley, which have been described in this correspondence; but I do not doubt that they are also applicable to the whole frontier.

The first and most important consideration is transport. Nobody who has not seen for himself can realise what a great matter this is. I well recall my amazement when watching a camel convoy more than a mile and a half long, and escorted by half a battalion of infantry. I was informed that it contained only two days' supplies for one brigade. People talk lightly of moving columns hither and thither as if they were mobile groups of men who had only to march about the country and fight the enemy wherever found, and very few understand that an army is a ponderous mass which drags painfully after it a long chain of advanced depots, stages, rest camps, and communications, by which it is securely fastened to a stationary base. In these valleys—where wheeled traffic is impossible—the difficulties and cost of moving supplies are enormous; and as none, or very few, are to be obtained from the country the consideration is paramount. Mule transport is for many reasons superior to camel transport. The mule moves faster, and can traverse more difficult ground. He is also more hardy, and keeps in better condition. When Sir Bindon Blood began his advance against the Mohmands he equipped his 2nd Brigade entirely with mules. It was thus far more mobile, and was available for any rapid movement that might become necessary. To mix the two—camels and mules—appears to combine the disadvantages of both, and destroy the superiority of either.

I have in a former letter described the usual nightly 'sniping', which is so common a feature of this kind of warfare. As this is sometimes varied by more serious attacks, and even actual assaults, the camps are, or should be, always entrenched. It is thought advisable to have the ditch towards the enemy as, modern weapons notwithstanding, the ultimate appeal is to the bayonet, and the advantage of being on higher ground is then considerable. The infantry always sleep behind the trench, all round the camp, one section of each company usually with their accoutrements on, so as to be instantly ready. Sentries are posted every twenty-five yards, and the rifles, with the bayonets fixed, should be left lying on the parapet of the shelter-trench. One other point is worth noticing. When a battery forms part of the line round a camp, infantry soldiers should be placed between the guns. Artillery officers do not like this; but, though they are very good fellows, there are some things in which it is not well to give way to them. Everyone is prone to over-estimate the power of his arm.

In the Mohmand Valley all the fighting occurred in capturing villages which lay in rocky and broken ground in the re-entrants of the mountains. The lesson learnt there by all who participated in the operations was that in every case the spurs on either side must be occupied before the village is attacked, and held until after it has been burnt and the centre has safely retired. Of course, it will be said that this is an obvious and well-known principle of war. Nevertheless, I have thought it worth mentioning because much of our loss on 16 September was caused by the 35th Sikhs advancing without having their flanks protected, and on 30 September most of the casualties in the 31st Punjab Infantry were due to the fact that no troops were available to occupy the high ground to their right.

After the capture and destruction of the village, the troops had always to return to camp, and a retirement became necessary. The difficulty of executing such an operation in the face of an active and numerous enemy, armed with modern rifles, was great. I had the opportunity of witnessing six of these retirements from the rear companies. Five were fortunate and one was disastrous, but all were attended with loss and, as experienced officers have informed me, with danger. As long as no one is hit everything is successful, but as soon as a few men are wounded the difficulties begin. No sooner has a point been left—a knoll, a patch of corn, some rocks, or any other incident of ground—than it is seized by the enemy. With their excellent rifles they kill or wound two or three of the retiring company, whose somewhat close formation makes them a good target. Now, in civilised war these wounded would be left on the ground and matters arranged next day by parley. But on the frontier, where no quarter is asked or given, to carry away the wounded is a sacred duty. It is also the strenuous endeavour of every regiment to carry away their dead. The vile and horrid mutilations which the tribesmen inflict on all bodies that fall into their hands, and the insults to which they expose them add, to unphilosophic minds, another terror to death. Now, it takes at least four men, and very often more, to carry away a body. Observe the result. Every man hit means five rifles withdrawn from the firing line. Ten men hit puts a company out of action as far as fighting power is concerned. The watchful enemy presses. The groups of men bearing the injured are excellent targets. Presently the rearguard is encumbered with wounded. Then a vigorous charge with swords is pushed home. Thus, a disaster occurs.

Watching the progress of events, sometimes from one regiment, sometimes from another, I observe several ways by which these difficulties could be avoided. The Guides, long skilled in frontier war, were the most valuable instructors. As the enemy seize every point as soon as it is left, all retirements should be masked by leaving two or three men behind from each company. These keep up a vigorous fire, and after the whole company has taken up a new position, or has nearly done so, these men run back and join them. Besides this, the fire of one company in retiring should always be arranged to cover another, and at no moment should the firing ever cease. The covering company should be actually in position before the rear company begins to move, and should open fire at once. I was particularly struck on 18 September by the retirement of the Guides Infantry. These principles were carried out with such skill and thoroughness that, though the enemy pressed severely, only one man was wounded. The way in which Major Campbell, the commanding officer, availed himself of all the advantages of retiring down two spurs and bringing a cross fire to bear to cover the alternate retirements resembled some intricate chess problem rather than a military evolution. The enemy were completely outmanoeuvred, or, as I should say were I not your correspondent, 'Never got a look in.'

The power of the Lee-Metford rifle with the new dum-dum bullet—it is called, though officially, the 'ek dum' bullet—is tremendous. The soldiers who have used it have the utmost confidence in their weapon. Up to 500 yards there is no difficulty about judging the range, as it shoots quite straight, or, technically speaking, has a flat trajectory. This is of the greatest value. During the retirement at Zagai, on 20 September, the Buffs were the most severely pressed by the enemy and had had several men hit. A lieutenant—Lieutenant Reeves[1]—remained behind with a section of ten men, in the hope of bringing some effective fire to bear upon the enemy. He invited me to watch the event. The tribesmen were collecting about 250 yards away behind some rocks, and preparing to run down the nullah on our left, so as to outflank and, perhaps, cut off this small body. But the fire was extremely good, and for some time none dared advance from the rocks. Then one man ran into the open, waving his sword. The section fired, and he fell, lying very still, a patch of white. Four others immediately rushed from cover to his help. A second volley killed all four. After this display of marksmanship we continued our retreat unmolested for some time. The men had a good rifle, and they were cool. Against such a combination it is well to be careful. The necessity of having the officers in the same dress as the men was apparent to all who watched the operation. The conspicuous figure which a British officer in his helmet presented in contrast to the native soldiers in their turbans drew a well-aimed fire in his direction. Of course, in British regiments the difference is not nearly so marked. Nevertheless, at close quarters, the keen-eyed tribesmen always made an especial mark of the officers, as the following story may show.

When the Buffs were marching down to Panjkora, they passed the Royal West Kent coming up to relieve them at Inayat Kila. A private in the up-going regiment asked a friend in the Buffs what it was like at the front. 'Oh,' replied the latter, 'you'll be all right so long as you don't go near no officers nor no white stones.' Whether the advice was taken is not recorded, but it is certainly sound, for three days

[1] Frederick Spencer Reeves (1872–?). Served with the East Kent Regiment.

later—on 30 September—in those companies of the Royal West Kent Regiment that were engaged in the village of Agrah eight of eleven officers were hit or grazed by bullets.

Signalling by heliograph was throughout the operations of the greatest value. I had always realised the advantages of a semi-permanent line of signal stations along the communications to the telegraph, but I had doubted the practicability of using such complicated arrangements in action. In this torrid country, where the sun is always shining, the heliograph is always useful. As soon as any hill was taken communication was established with the Brigadier, and no difficulty seemed to be met with, even while the attack was in progress, in sending messages quickly and clearly. In a country intersected by frequent ravines, over which a horse can move but slowly and painfully, it is the surest, the quickest, and indeed the only means of inter-communication. I am delighted to testify these things, because I had formerly been a scoffer.

The principle of concentrating artillery has long been admitted in Europe. Sir Bindon Blood is the first General who has applied it to mountain warfare in India. It had formerly been the custom to use the guns by twos and threes. At the action of Landakai in August the Malakand field force had eighteen guns in action, of which twelve were in one line. The fire of this artillery drove the enemy, who were in great strength and an excellent position, from the ground. The infantry attack was accomplished with hardly any loss, and a success was obtained at the cost of a dozen lives which would have been cheap at a hundred.

After this, it may seem strange if I say that the artillery fire in the Mohmand Valley did very little execution. It is nevertheless a fact. The Mohmands are a puny tribe, but they build their houses in the rocks; and against sharpshooters among rocks guns can do little. Through field-glasses it was possible to see the enemy dodging behind their rocks whenever the puffs of smoke from the guns told them that a shell was on its way. Perhaps smokeless powder would have put a stop to this. But in any case, the targets presented to the artillery were extremely bad.

Where they really were of great service was not so much in killing the enemy, but in keeping them from occupying certain spurs and knolls. On 30 September, when the Royal West Kent and the 31st Punjab Infantry were retiring under considerable pressure, the British Mountain Battery moved to within 700 yards of the enemy and opened a rapid fire of shrapnel on the high ground which commanded the line of retreat, killing such of the tribesmen as were there, and absolutely forbidding the hill to their companions. I happened to be with the infantry at the time, and it was an extraordinary experience to hear the shells screaming overhead, and to watch them cutting the whole crest of the ridge into a cloud of dust by the hundreds of bullets they contained.

I have touched on infantry and artillery and, though a previous letter has been almost wholly devoted to the cavalry, I cannot resist getting back to the horses and the lances again. The question of sword or lance as the cavalryman's weapon has long been argued, and it may be of interest to know what are the views of those whose experience is the most recent. Though I have had no opportunity of witnessing the use of the lance, I have heard the opinions of many officers both of the Guides and the 11th Bengal Lancers. All admit, or assert, that the lance is in this warfare the better weapon. It kills with more certainty and convenience, and there is less danger of the horseman being cut down. As to length, the general opinion seems to be in favour of a shorter spear. This, with a corrected poise at the butt, gives as good a reach, and is much more useful for close quarters. Major Beatson,[1] one of the most distinguished cavalry officers on the frontier, is a strong advocate of this. Either the pennon should be knotted, or a boss of some sort affixed about eighteen inches below the point. Unless this is done there is a danger of the lance penetrating too far, when it either gets broken or allows the enemy to wriggle up and strike the lancer. This last actually happened on several occasions.

Now, in considering the question to what extent a squadron should be armed with lances, the system adopted by the Guides may be of interest. In this warfare it is very often necessary for the cavalryman to dismount and use his carbine. The lance then gets in the way and has to be tied to the saddle. This takes time, and there is usually not much time to spare in cavalry skirmishing. The Guides compromise matters by giving one man in every four a lance. This man, when the others dismount, stays in the saddle and holds their horses. They also give the outer sections of each squadron lances,

[1] Stuart Brownlow Beatson (1854–1914). Commanded 11th Bengal Lancers. Mentioned in despatches three times during this campaign, and received the CB. KCSI, 1906; KCB, 1910; KCVO, 1912. Retired as Major-General, 1905.

and these, too, remain mounted, as the drill-book enjoins. But I become technical. Yet the reader will forgive me if he has ever seen the lance point covered with blood and glittering redly in the sunlight. It will recall a vivid impression.

I have thus reviewed most of the military features which have attracted my attention. The concluding impression is that in mountain war the spectator will be struck more by the weakness than the power of modern weapons.

This has been, perhaps, a cold-blooded letter. We have considered men as targets. Tribesmen fighting for their homes and hills have been regarded only as the objective of an attack; killed and wounded human beings merely as the waste of war. The philosopher may observe with pity, and the philanthropist deplore with pain that the attention of so many minds should be directed to the scientific destruction of the human species; but practical people in a business like age will remember that they live in a world of men—not angels—and rule their conduct accordingly.

3 December, 1897

15

NOWSHERA, 16 October

I am conscious of a certain undefined feeling of solemnity in beginning the last letter of this long correspondence—a feeling which the
reader may not share, but with which he may, perhaps, amiably
sympathise. For the conclusion marks the end of the most vivid and
valuable experience fortune has yet accorded me. The moment and
the mood are not unsuited to the consideration of the more general
aspect of the Frontier Question.

It is with regret that I do not see any sign of permanency in the
settlements that have been made with the tribesmen in Dir, Swat
and Bajaur. They have been punished, not subdued; rendered
hostile, but not harmless. Their fanaticism remains unshaken.
Their barbarism is unrelieved. Some have been killed, but these
fertile valleys will in a few years replace the waste of war. The riddle
of the frontier is still unsolved. It is not possible to sum up questions
of such magnitude in ten terse lines of prose. Still less can they be
settled, as many people appear to imagine, by a phrase, an epigram,
or a proverb. The frontier policy must be looked at from many
standpoints, moral, political, military, and economic. When I consider the vast accumulations of diverse and often conflicting facts
which can be assembled under each of these heads, and reflect on the
extraordinary volume of technical and specialised knowledge necessary for the proper appreciation, I feel that to take a comprehensive
grasp of the whole question is a task beyond the mind and memory
of man. It is not possible to generalise indefinitely on every subject.
A point is reached when all relation between detail and proportion is
destroyed—as in a picture of such great size that to see the whole it is
necessary to stand so far away that the forms and colours are alike
indistinguishable.

I do not, therefore, desire to be dogmatic. The old frontier policy—
the policy of holding the line of the mountains—contained many

elements of finality. We have left that line; and between it and an advanced line, conterminous with the Afghan frontier, and south of which all shall be reduced to law and order, I do not see any hopes of a permanent settlement. We are in midstream. Regarded economically, the outlook is extremely bad. The trade of the highland valleys will never pay a shilling in the pound on the military expenditure; and, morally, it is unfortunate for the tribesmen that our spheres of influence clash with their sphere of existence. But those best acquainted with the question are unanimous in saying that it is impossible to go back. Indeed, bearing in mind the unrest in India, the hostility in Afghanistan, the irritation of the frontier tribes, and the possibility of further Russian encroachments, it seems that retrocession is made impossible by the sheer force of solid, concrete, materialised facts. We must therefore go on.

At this point the arms question comes in. Every year the tribesmen will have better weapons, and the difficulties of dealing with them will be increased; therefore we must go on as quickly as possible. It is Hobson's choice.

The responsibility for the situation rests with those who first forsook the old policy of the line of the mountains. They have accepted that responsibility, and have defended their action; but I am inclined to think that the rulers of India ten years ago, or a hundred years ago, were in great matters as much the sport of circumstances as their successors are today.

The prospect is adverse. I have, however, several times noticed in the last few weeks that many of the Afghan valleys seem to be completely surrounded by mountains, and to have no outlet. But as the column advances a break in the hills becomes visible, and presently a pass appears. Sometimes it is difficult and tortuous; sometimes it is occupied by the enemy, and must be forced. But I do not recall having seen any valley which has not a way out.

That way we shall ultimately find if we march with the firm step of an Imperial people, who recognise the dangers and the obstacles, but who, remembering what has been achieved in the past, are prepared to encounter whatever the future may contain.

These letters have now reached a conclusion. I have consistently adhered to their original object—to present a picture of the frontier war—and I shall indulge the hope that in some small degree they may stimulate the growing interest which the proud democracy of England is beginning to take in those great estates beyond the sea of which they are the proprietors.

6 December, 1897

Sudan

1898

The Morning Post

31 August–13 October, 1898

I

Korosko, 8 August

You would rightly call me faithless, my dear . . ., if I were to make no effort to carry out my promise to give you some account of the features and the fortunes of the war on the Nile. I cannot, indeed, engage to write to you with a complete and detailed account of the considerable operations in progress. You will recognise the difficulties of such correspondence. The duties of a soldier, the vicissitudes of war, and the heat of the sun consume alike time and energy. The news itself, the rough material of letters, comes to hand in uncertain quantities and by fits and starts, so that one day there will be much to write of and scarcely any opportunity of putting pen to paper, and another will see abundance of leisure, but nothing to tell. And beside all this, a great effort is needed to write a letter which is to go a long distance, in the same way that it is a matter of much exertion to throw a stone far. But in spite of these difficulties, I shall try in this and following letters to paint you a picture of the war, and shall hope to raise in your mind a lively impression of the scenes and characters of the last act in the great drama of Khartoum.

During the last fortnight the 2nd British Brigade has been moving steadily up the Nile towards the camp on the Atbara, where the whole division will be concentrated, and where the zone of actual operations may be said to begin. Steamers and dahabeahs dot the reaches of the brown river, toiling up in the teeth of the current, now nearly six miles an hour, coming down again empty and swift, as if lighthearted as well as lightly laden, but always on the move. But I shall not attempt to describe the order and arrangement of the various regiments or the halts and stages of their journey, for you would hardly thank me for copying out pages of a time-table. It will be sufficient if I sketch the progress of the particular unit of which I am a fraction.

The entraining of troops is ever a long and wearying affair. The soldiers, arrayed in what they call 'Christmas Tree Order,' and dangling with water bottles, haversacks, canteen straps, cloaks, swords, and carbines from every part of their bodies, clank awkwardly into the carriages. Then the baggage has to be loaded, kitbags must be stowed, and provision made for food and filtered water. With infantry it is a laborious affair. But with cavalry the difficulties are more than doubled. Saddlery, forage, and above all horses have to be packed into the trucks. When I tell you that the horses are stallion Arabs you will easily realise what a kicking and a squealing the stowage of this last item caused. But perseverance overcomes everything, even the vivacity of the little Arab horse, though at times he seems almost to be infected with the fanaticism of the human inhabitants of the land of his birth. At length all things are accomplished. The band strikes up 'Auld Lang Syne.' For a moment the train is linked to the platform by the handshaking of those who go and those who stay. Then it slowly moves off, gaining pace and increasing the distance gradually until its growing rattle drowns the cheering and the fitful strains of the band. We are off. Whither? Southward to Khartoum, and perhaps beyond for all—perhaps very far beyond for some.

The journey from Cairo to the Atbara camp divides itself naturally into four stages, through all of which the troops must toil, but through which I do not intend to tediously drag you. You shall fly airily along the miles of road, rail, and river, and shall pause merely where there is something to look at or something to discuss. Twenty-four hours from Cairo by train the first halt is reached—Khizam. Here we are on the Nile. The railway is left, and we proceed by steamers. One was already waiting for the squadron. The versatile and ubiquitous Cook had undertaken the arrangements, as his name painted on everything clearly showed. The horses had to be moved from the trucks, and persuaded, in spite of their protests, to enter two great barges. On these they were tightly packed—so tightly, indeed, that they could not kick, and biting was the sole expression they could give to their feelings. The baggage was then shipped, and when this task was finished the steamer took the barges in tow, and pushing out into the stream began its journey to Aswan. The barges were heavy, the currents adverse and strong, hence the progress was slow and tedious. At times, getting into slack water, we made nearly four miles an hour; at others the speed diminished to about two, and on one occasion, in a narrow place, the steamer had only about half a mile an hour the best of it. A little stronger stream and progress would have ceased altogether. Still, the steamer was comfortable and the nights cool. Indeed, even the days were not oppressive. The horrors of war were represented merely by the food, whose original plainness was not improved by the misdirected efforts of the cook. But I know you care nothing for such matters, and would not sympathise were I to dilate on them. For four days and nights the steamer plodded up the Nile, up to Aswan, perhaps even up to Wadi Halfa. I am in the domain of Baedeker, and I will not do him or you an unkindness by transcribing his words nor by poaching on his preserves. Besides, surely you have 'done' the Nile yourself? Everyone 'does' it nowadays: you must not be eccentric.

At Luxor we stopped for a couple of hours, moored almost to the temple. I paid it a flying visit, and was reminded of Rider Haggard's *Cleopatra*—perhaps the most popular book on Egyptology on the market. Something in the strange shapes of the great pillars appeals to that love of the mystic which all human beings possess. It takes no effort of imagination to roof the temple and fill its great hall with the awestruck worshippers, or to people the odd, nameless chambers at the far end with the powerful priests who crushed the body and soul out of ancient Egypt, and tyrannically prescribed the thoughts as well as the actions of its people and its sovereigns. Now that the roof is off and the sun shines into all the nooks and corners we may admire the beauty of the work without fearing its evil purposes. It is also a favourite place of tourists to be photographed in. The science and triumph of the living century is displayed in vivid contrast with the art and repose of that long dead. We are reminded of the bright butterfly on the tomb. The truth of the simile, however, vanishes when the photographs of the tourists are proudly shown by the local photographer. We were not without philistines on board.

'Have you been to the temple?' I asked an officer.

'No, certainly not; supposing I am killed, I shall have dragged all round there for nothing.'

But Baedeker pricks my conscience. I must write no more about Luxor, for is it not appropriately described in 'Route B, Cairo to Aswan'? The days pass slowly on the steamer. The scenery is monotonous, the sky an unclouded blue, the weather set fair. But one idea grows steadily in the mind until it fills it altogether—the Nile. It is everything. It is all there is. On either side of the broad brown stream there is but a tiny strip of cultivation, and then the desert. I am told that a man might journey due west and never see a house or the smoke of a cooking pot until he reached the American Continent. Or he might go east and find nothing but waste and desolation until he came to the shores of India. There is nothing but the Nile. *Aut Nilis aut nihil.* But it is sufficient, this wonderful river, whose geographical, no less than its historical, origin is shrouded in uncertainty, and fable fills my mind, and if I mistake not you will hear more of it in these letters.

It is the great waterway of Africa. It is the life and soul of Egypt. It is Egypt, since without it there is only desert. We shall drink its waters, duly filtered. We shall continue to wash in it, charged as it is with the magic mud which can make the wilderness a garden and raise cities from the desolate sand. On its waters we shall be carried southwards to the war and on to Khartoum. It is the cause of the war. It is the means by which we fight. It is the end at which we aim. Through every page which I write to you about the campaign your imagination must make the Nile flow. It must glisten through the palm trees during the actions. You must think of the lines of animals, camels, horses and slaughter cattle, that march from camps every evening to be watered. Without the river we should never have started. Without it we could not exist, Without it we can never return. You may also be amused by the reflection that the great river has befriended all ages, and with an impartial smile has borne the stately barges of the Pharaohs and the unpretentious stern-wheel steamers of Messrs Cook and Sons (Egypt) (Limited). It has seen war with the balista and the short Roman sword, and is now witnessing the military employment of 6 in quickfiring guns and lyddite shells.[1] It has supported through all history the lives of a nation. It will presently carry this letter to you. And between these extremes it has seen and done everything. But I recognise that you will regard its achievements as incomplete unless it brings the steamer quickly to more vivid scenes than those that have filled this letter.

We reached Aswan at last, and there began again the business of disembarkation. The first cataract of the Nile opposed the further passage of the original steamer. But above the cataract another waited. From Aswan to Shellal is a march of six miles. The horses, delighted to stretch their limbs, enjoyed themselves immensely.

[1] Lyddite shells used a picric acid explodant. Because of the erosion caused to gun barrels, TNT superseded lyddite fairly rapidly, though the latter was still being used in 1914.

The heat and the dust moderated the enthusiasm of their riders. The baggage went by train, with a sufficient escort. For my part I felt no desire to remain at Aswan. I have heard that there are people who visit this place for the purposes of pleasure. Such people would probably enjoy a summer at Jacobabad, the hottest town in India, or delight in taking a small house in Aden for a year or two. *De gustibus . . .!* They would, of course, advance the temple of Philae as an excuse. I confess I viewed this celebrated ruin with a keen feeling of hostility. The great dam across the Nile, which will increase the area and the fertility of Egypt and improve the condition of her people, is to be built six or seven feet lower, so as to preserve the temple. The storage of millions of gallons of water, the addition of thousand of acres to the Egyptian territory, the augmentation of Egyptian revenues by thousands of pounds, the happiness and welfare of thousands of patient peasants—these, and all these, are to be thrown away to save the temple. Was ever such sacrifice offered on the altar of false religion? Was ever such a piece of idiocy perpetrated in a utilitarian and rational age? I heard a whisper, indeed—only a whisper—that the engineers might make some slip in their calculations and smother Philae after all. I am, therefore, glad to have seen it.

The scene when we arrived at Shellal was a strange one indeed. In the foreground, under the shade of the palm trees, whose sombre tints were brightened by the glow of the evening sun, were the fresh steamers which were to carry us to Wadi Halfa. The shore was lined with barges and dahabeahs. On the bank piles of military stores were accumulated. Great stacks of shovels, of small arm ammunition, of medical stores, of all the varied necessaries of a modern army, rose on every side. The train which had conveyed us from Aswan drew up in the midst of this. An array of coolies and of convicts—the same as the coolies, only with heavy chains on their legs—was drawn up to assist the soldiers in unloading the trucks and loading the boats. The work began. The spectacle, as far as the foreground was concerned, was one of singular animation. Blue-clothed natives and khaki-clad soldiers bustled about in a busy whirlpool. Whistles blew, trumpets sounded, the horses fought and squealed, and occasionally people swore. And behind, among the dark rocks of river gorge—these heaps of gigantic pebbles, signs of the Nile's fury in the past—the broken pillars and walls of the temple of Philae were silhouetted against the sunset sky. The past looked down on the present and,

73

offended by its exuberant vitality, seemed grimly to repeat the last taunt that age can fling at youth: 'You will be as I am one of these days'. At dusk we started. But I must not take you too long a stage or hurry you on as we are hurrying. I will try and write to you again from Wadi Halfa. I think there will be time there, though it would seem that matters are developing with unexpected rapidity 'up the river.'

31 August, 1898

2

WADI HALFA, 10 August

Nothing of any importance has occurred, to my knowledge, since last I wrote to you, my dear . . ., But you would be unjust as well as unkind were you to observe that this letter is therefore wholly unnecessary. Until there are battles to describe I cannot give you any account of battles. And, on the other hand, you would really have cause to complain if I were suddenly to confront you with war's alarms without having made you in some way acquainted with the aspect of the country or prepared you for the sight of the enemy. In any case, I feel bound to show you the way to the theatre of war, if only in order that you may be able to find your way back should the event prove unfortunate, or should I myself be unable to guide you. I told you of our re-embarkation at Shellal under the shadow of the temple of Philae. I will now carry you on towards Wadi Halfa, if, that is, the progress does not weary you. The steamers on this reach of the river are much smaller than those lower down. To convey the squadron of cavalry two were provided. Two dahabeahs and a barge all full of horses were lashed to the sides of each of these, and thus, four boats abreast, we started slowly up the river. The white steamer between the boats and barges suggested a tall soldier with three somewhat disorderly women hanging on his arms. The effect was increased when one or two of the dahabeahs put up a great white sail like an enormous feather sticking out of a bonnet.

The steamers themselves are worth looking at. They draw only a few inches of water. Their boilers are in the bows and a steam pipe carries the power to a cylinder on either side of the quarter. The pistons from these cylinders turn a great paddle-wheel which protrudes from the stern. The appearance is peculiar. The red blades of the wheel only dip about eight inches in the water, and splash it brown and thick over the whole of the stern. The machinery—wheels, cranks, pistons, everything—is exposed, and is so drenched with spray that I marvel that it does not all become rusty. On the roof is an awning, and beneath this the officers lie during the heat of the day and the warmth of the night. It is from this coign of vantage that I write to you this morning. Above Aswan the character of the river is changed. The belt of cultivation which bordered the lower reach has dwindled to a mere strip of green, varying from ten to a hundred yards in breadth, and often broken by long intervals of barrenness. The river itself is narrower and consequently deeper. Few sandbanks are to be seen. Rock, indeed, is the characteristic of this stage of our journey. The gorge which the great river has labouriously cut is dark and deep. The walls of black rock on either side are heaped with stone debris and marked clearly by the action of the water. Their sombre appearance harmonises with the bad colour of the muddy water, and is relieved merely by the bright buff-coloured sand which has silted all over them in exactly the same way that snow lies about the summits of the Alps. It is impossible not to be conscious of a feeling of desolation. Not a blade of grass, not a shrub, not a tree brightens the ragged, amorphous summits of the hills, and he would soon be a hot and a hungry man who should wander on these forsaken peaks.

The mind reverts to the river, and clings to it with a feeling of relief and of security, as to an old and trusted friend. Here and there along the banks are villages hardly distinguishable from the rocks on and of which their poor miserable houses are built. Still they show the presence of life. Little black, naked children run down to the water's edge to wail 'backsheesh' at the passing steamers, mournfully as if they knew beforehand they would get nothing. Their elders stand in blue and white clothes further off, or sit on donkeys gazing dully at the crowded boats. I marvel how these people live. Their apparent property consists of forty or fifty date palms, perhaps an acre of doura, a kind of Indian corn, and a water-wheel, without which nothing would be possible. As the banks here are higher than those below, this is of more elaborate construction than the simple lever and counterpoise arrangement which punctuates the miles from Cairo to Aswan. There is a sort of stone tower in which two lean bullocks circle slowly and unwillingly, turning a horizontal wheel. This wheel, by means of a cog, turns a vertical wheel, the bottom of which dips in the river. Round this wheel is an endless chain of earthenware pots. When the oxen march forward the wheels revolve, the pots dip in the water, are filled, are carried upwards and

The Nile from Aswan to Khartoum

around, and empty their contents into a wooden pipe. Thus a continual stream of water flows to the thirsty sand, and such is the power of this wonderful water that the sand forthwith bursts into a crop. The device is ingenious, its aspect not unpicturesque. For to complete the scene we must add the date palms which cluster thickly round the vivifying wheel. These palms are tall, white-stemmed, with beautiful, bushy tops and spreading foliage. Among their dark green leaves there is a dash of red and yellow which promises a bountiful crop of dates ere the month be out. Such are the villages and vegetation.

There is one other sign of life, and it is a sign of that busy life that belongs to a civilised age. Along the bank of the river runs the telegraph wire. Looking at the slender poles and white insulators—for the wire itself is invisible against the background of the rock—it is impossible not to experience a glow of confidence in the power of science which can thus link the most desolate regions of the earth with its greatest city and keep the modern pioneer ever within hail of home. We may also wonder as we look what news that wire will presently carry back to Great Britain, whether of success or failure, of peace or war, or whose names it will flash homeward as being of no more account to living men. You will perhaps think that I have given a somewhat pessimistic description of the scenery. But what would you expect? The banks of this part of the Nile display an abundance of barrenness. Their characteristic is monotony. Their attraction is their sadness. Yet there is one hour when all is changed. Just before the sun sets towards the western rocks a delicious flash brightens and enlivens the landscape. It is as though some titanic artist in the hour of inspiration was retouching the picture, painting in dark purple shadows among the rocks, strengthening the lights on the sand, gilding and beautifying everything, and making the whole scene live. The river, whose windings give the impression of a lake, turns from muddy brown to silver grey. The sky from a dull blue deepens into violet in the west. Everything under that magic touch becomes vivid and alive. And then the sun sinks altogether behind the rocks, the colours fade out of the sky, the flush off the sands, and gradually everything darkens and grows grey like a man's cheek when he is bleeding to death. We are left sad and sorrowful in the dark, until the stars light up and remind us that there is always something beyond.

But I must not waste paper and time in describing such beautiful scenes. I know you want to hear about war and bloodshed. Of course, you will come and see the sunset on the Nile for yourself—if, indeed, you have not seen it already. If we are not yet in the province of war, we are at least among its rumours. We hear tales of gunboats shelling Omdurman, of one with a funnel shot away, and of the advances of General Hunter with two Egyptian brigades to Shabluka. Besides this we have been telegraphed orders to hurry on with all speed, which looks as if events were also marching at the double. I hope to tell you something of all this in my next letter—probably from the Atbara. In the meanwhile you must write to me. Remember that, however you may be entertained by the news from the great river, your interest is but faint compared to that which I and many others here feel in the politics and gossip of the Great City.

2 September, 1898

3

A T B A R A, 15 August

I began this letter, my dear . . ., nearly a week ago, but instead of finishing it I have only succeeded—such has been the hurry and hard work of the last few days—in losing what little I had written. The original letter began somewhat differently, and in it I had intended to give you a detailed account of the Sudan Military Railway and of our journey along it. I then hoped to send you another letter describing the great entrenched camp at Atbara. The time, and indeed the energy, to write two such letters are now lacking, and I must compress the abundant material into one. I do not expect you will complain. I daresay you are as impatient as I am to have done with the journey and to arrive on the scene of action—perhaps of actions. Yet I should have liked to have written more about the country, because to understand the peculiar features of this war it is essential to have a lively realisation of the enormous length of the lines of communication, of the great scale of the ground, and above all of the wonderful river, without which no military operations would be possible—or necessary. If, in reading the telegrams and correspondence from this country you will always think of the Nile, you will find the explanation of much that might otherwise appear obscure. The river is the key to the whole conundrum of the military operations. Every movement has the closest reference to it. Every soldier, every follower, every animal depends on it for daily water.

You will remember the long journey up the Nile from Khizarm to Wadi Halfa, which I described in my last letters, and which occupied nearly ten days and ten nights. All this time the steamer was toiling up the strong stream and making at the best three miles an hour, and on some occasions scarcely able to hold its own against the current. But though our progress was slow it was continuous, and on the 13th we disembarked at Wadi Halfa and packed the horse and baggage into the trucks of the military railway. The distance from Halfa to the Railhead at Atbara is nearly four hundred miles. The train accomplishes this in about thirty-six hours. It is an unpretentious-looking train, but though neither paint nor padding adorns its carriages, it is not uncomfortable. A long horse truck was provided for the officers, and others for the men. A roof of odd pieces of board protects the occupants from the sun. A canvas blind hanging all round excludes some of the dust. In the middle of the carriage stands a large earthenware filter full of water, agreeably cooled by the evaporation. The railway is the youngest in the world. It has grown faster than iron rails have ever been laid before: 'Nearly a mile and a quarter a day,' say those who shared the labour and the credit of its construction. It is not only a young railway, but a young man's railway. Lieutenant Girouard and a few subalterns of Engineers projected and executed the whole work easily, rapidly, and thoroughly.

One of the subalterns, the Traffic Manager, a keen, alert young gentleman, met us at the 'quay' or mud bank whence the railway starts. In England or in India he might have divided the responsibility of looking after a few detonators or some pioneer equipment with some majors and a colonel. Here he had a wider scope. Everything, he said, was ready. The baggage would be moved by a fatigue party, the train could start as soon as it was loaded, there was an 'angarib' or native bed, a 'charpoy,' as it would be called in India, for every officer and, incidentally, dinner was prepared at the Egyptian army mess for everyone. The agreeable anticipations which this news aroused were fully justified by the event, and over some cool soda water, suitably coloured, the subaltern explained to me many things about the railway—its length, its gauge, the number of trains that had run over it, the daily average, the amount of supplies in tons that had been hauled to the front, the difficulties, and above all the cheapness, of the construction. I marvelled, and I would willingly set all these details down in this letter but that there are two good reasons for not doing so: first, because you might not be interested by statistics; and, secondly, because I have forgotten them.

We started the same night that we landed, and when it became daylight were in the middle of the desert. The full force of that abomination of desolation smote one when the landscape was viewed from the window. Not a living thing, animal or plant, was to be seen. Great wastes of smooth sand, a little rosier than buff, a little paler than salmon, stretched in all directions to the far horizon. Occasional rocky hillocks rose from this fiery ocean, black and barren. Over all the heat began, as the sun rose, to glitter and to dance. The line of railway and the telegraph wires run in a long-drawn perspective into the distance. The mirages alone give relief to the picture—the relief that salt water would give to a thirsty castaway. I was chiefly impressed with their number. Never was optical illusion so cheap, so common. Wherever the eye might wander the mocking shimmer of unreal waters deceived and tantalised. The traveller turns with eagerness to the earthenware filter, and, drinking deep, thanks Heaven that nature is not often swayed by the spiteful, mischievous imp who prompted such a grim joke.

All day long we travelled in these unpropitious lands, without a sample of which no well-regulated inferno would be complete, and with the evening reached Abu Hamed. A year ago an armed patrol mounted on swift camels might have approached the walls only to turn and gallop away amid the whistle of pursuing bullets. Now the train steams into the station, and the engine, uncoupling, moves off towards an engine-house, whence a fresh locomotive is already approaching. Civilised man can accomplish a great deal in a very short time if he takes off his coat to the work. We paid the tribute of recollection to the gallant officers whose white crosses in the burying-ground attest at once their conquest and their death, and then slept while the train, during the hot hours of the night, hurried through Berber and Darmali to the camp at Atbara. As soon as the squadron arrived at Railhead the horses and baggage were taken across the Nile, and we bivouacked on the western bank of the river, along which we are now advancing, and shall, if all's well, continue to advance until Omdurman is reached and pursuit dies away in the desert beyond. The business of transporting horses, men, and kits across the river was long, hot, and tedious. I shall not ask you to share the experience. The camp and fort will interest you more.

The railway runs right to the end of the tongue of land which lies between the north side of the Atbara river and the east bank of the Nile. At the end of the line is a huge depot. Great piles of biscuit-boxes, of ammunition boxes, and of stores of all kinds fill a space of many acres. Three months' supplies for all troops south of this point have been accumulated. The great reserve secures the Expeditionary Army against the most unlikely contingencies. Suppose a repulse should be sustained in front of Omdurman, suppose that the Arab tribes all along the attenuated line of communication were to rise, suppose even that a foreign force occupied Egypt, the army on the

Upper Nile would still be a factor to be reckoned with, might return to the north, might strike east to the Red Sea and Suakin, or south-east to Kassala, would in any case have time to look about for an object of attack or a loophole of escape. The whole advanced base, except where protected by the river, is surrounded by a strong entrenchment, whose profile rises at least ten feet above the ground, and against which it was hoped in the spring that the Emir Mahmoud[1] would dash himself. Within this fortified place the army had waited for some weeks looking watchfully up the river, while the Dervishes, concentrating at Metemmeh and Shendy, proclaimed that they would capture Berber. There followed the flank march to Umdabia, when Mahmoud tried to circumvent what he could not overcome: the breakdown of his caravans of supplies; his fatal halt on the Atbara river, 'formed to a flank', and unable to maintain the offensive; and then the swift merciless counter-stroke which destroyed his army and sent him a prisoner, to the gaol at Wadi Halfa. But, of course, you know all this.

Outside the entrenchment are the camps of the 2nd British Brigade. The 1st, or 'Fighting Brigade,' as the men call themselves, have already moved on in steamers to the point of concentration before Shabluka. There are, however, the Rifles, the Grenadier Guards, the Lancashire and Northumberland Fusiliers, the two squadrons of the 21st Lancers, several Egyptian battalions, numerous details, some Maxim[2] guns, and General and Staff—altogether a considerable population, all of whom will move south in the next few days, and leave Atbara Camp deserted. The whole place is under the shadow of the Egyptian flag, whose red colour and white crescent and star are everywhere conspicuous. It is only over the Headquarter Office of the British division that a small Union Jack proclaims the substance.

The cavalry camp is across the river, and communication is maintained by the unceasing toil of a small steamer called the *Tahra*, which, translated, means 'The Virgin.' I crossed several times in this little boat. Its history may amuse you. It was originally one of General Gordon's steamers, and was captured in sections—for it had never been put together—when Khartoum fell. The Dervishes

---

[1] Mahmoud Wad Ahmed, a Dervish leader captured and jailed after the battle of Atbara.

[2] Maxim guns were first used by British troops on the North-west Frontier during 1890. They were .303 calibre, belt-fed, and capable of 600 rounds per minute.

assembled it, and since no infidel had ever defiled it they proudly christened it *El Tahra*. But the *Tahra* began a career of usefulness after the action at Mafir in 1896, where she was recaptured by the Egyptian troops. As soon as we had crossed the Nile we received orders to move south. On the eastern bank of the river is the transport of the whole of the British division, mustering fourteen or fifteen hundred mules, donkeys, and camels. Besides this there are the horses of two field batteries, whose guns have been taken up by steamer and some remounts for the Egyptian cavalry. All these are to proceed to the point of concentration before Shabluka by a march of eight days along the banks of the Nile. The two squadrons of the 21st Lancers and two Maxim guns will form their escort. We are to start tomorrow, 16 August. I do not myself think that there will be any opposition to our march as there are three Egyptian brigades and their cavalry two hundred miles in front of us; but, as you know, it is not wise in war to trust to such assumptions, and we are to take all precautions. Whatever force the Dervishes might bring against us, two squadrons and two machine guns could easily extricate themselves, but of course a mounted force, having practically no defensive power, can do nothing for a convoy except to prevent the villagers pilfering. We shall see, and I shall hope to write you some account of our march and of the country through which it lies in my next letter, which I will send, if possible, from Metemmeh.

Meanwhile, as I said, you must think of the Nile. The river grows on me day by day. It colours all one's thoughts. It is a sort of subdued *motif* that recurs throughout the whole opera. We had been travelling on and along the Nile for hundreds of miles when we disembarked at Wadi Halfa. Then we cut across nearly four hundred miles of desert by rail, and yet here at Atbara we strike the river again, broader than ever, nearly one thousand five hundred yards from bank to bank, with a six-mile current, swishing along a tremendous volume of brown, muddy water whose surface, disturbed by upheavals and eddies, resembles that of a deep lock when it is being filled. If I had not an hereditary shrinking from publicity of all kinds, and were to write a book about this campaign, I should call it *The War for the Waterway*.[1] Perhaps you would like to do so. I make you a present of the title, and you may use such facts as these letters contain, provided, of course, that you arrange the wording differently.

24 September, 1898

[1] The eventual title was *The River War*.

4

BIVOUAC MAGYRICH (Near Metemmeh), 20 August

I told you, my dear . . ., that I would try and write to you from Metemmeh, and I am better than my word for we are still one march away from that town. We are halted for the day, however, and I were foolish as well as faithless were I to miss so good an opportunity of keeping my promise. Indeed, if I do not write now, I shall perhaps fall sadly behindhand in this correspondence; for we are going to march continuously from here to Wad Habeshi, in front of Shabluka, and really when I come into camp after eight hours of this sun I feel but little inclination to write even to you and, had I sufficient inclination, the time would be lacking. I should be sorry if these letters were to cease, or to be broken by so long an interval that the continuity of the story I am trying to tell was destroyed, for it is a great pleasure for me to write to you.

I am going to begin this letter with a personal reference, which I hope will not be as unpleasant for you to read as it was for me to undergo. The cavalry escort and the convoy started in the early morning of the 16th from Atbara on their march to Shabluka. I remained behind, and intended to catch up the column in the evening at the first camp, about fifteen miles away. The business I had on hand took me much longer than I had anticipated, and it was not until the sun was on the horizon that the little ferry steamer *Tahra* landed me on the west bank. I made inquiries about the road. 'It is perfectly simple,' they said. 'You just go due south until you see the camp fires and then turn towards the river.' This I proceeded to do. I had gone about a mile when the sun sank and the world went into darkness. The bushes by the Nile were thick and thorny, and to avoid these I struck into the desert, steering due south by the polar star. I rode on at a trot for nearly two hours thinking all the time that it would be a welcome moment when I sat down to dinner, and above all to a drink. Suddenly, to my dismay the sky began to cloud over, and my guiding star and the pointers of the Great Bear faded and became invisible. For another hour I endeavoured to pursue my old direction, but the realisation that I was out of my bearings grew stronger every moment. At last the truth could be no longer disguised. I was lost: no dinner, no drink, nothing for the pony, nothing to do but wait for daylight.

One thing seemed clear in the obscurity. It was futile to go on at random and to exhaust the animal on whom alone depended my chance of catching up the troops. So I selected a sandy spot behind a rock, and passing the reins round my wrist endeavoured to sleep. Thirst and the fidgetting of the pony effectually prevented this, and philosophic meditation was the sole, and an altogether insufficient, consolation. The sky remained clouded, but the night was hot. The view in every direction was concealed by the darkness, but the bareness of the desert was none the less apparent. The consciousness of its utter waste and desolation grew. A hot, restless, weary wind blew continuously with a mournful sound over the miles and miles of sand and rock, as if conscious of its own uselessness: a rainless wind over a sterile soil. In the distance there was a noise like the rattle of a train. It was more wind blowing over more desert. The possibility of Dervishes was too remote to be considered, but as the night wore on the annoyance at missing a needed dinner and the discomfort of my position were intensified by another sensation—a horrible sensation of powerlessness, just like that which a man feels when his horse bolts and will not be stopped. Supposing morning should reveal nothing but desert, and the trees by the Nile should be hidden by the ground and by the low hills and knolls which rose on all sides. Of course, by riding towards the rising sun I must strike the Nile sooner or later. But how far was I from it? The idea that the distance might be beyond the powers of my horse jarred unpleasantly. Reason coming to the rescue checked such imaginings with the comfortable reflection that twenty miles was the most I could have ridden altogether. Meanwhile the hours passed without hurrying.

About half past three in the morning the clouds cleared from one part of the sky, and the beautiful constellation of Orion came into view. Never did the giant look more splendid. Forthwith I mounted and rode in his direction, for at this season of the year he lies along the Nile before dawn with his head to the north. After two hours' riding the desert scrub rose into higher bushes, and these becoming more frequent and denser showed that the Nile was not far off.

Meanwhile the sky in the east began to pale, and against it there drew out in silhouette the tracery of the foliage and palm trees by the river's brink. The thirsty pony pricked up his ears. In the gloom we brushed through the thorny bushes, spurred by a common desire. Suddenly the undergrowth parted, and at our feet, immense and mysterious in the growing light, the Nile was revealed. I have told you of the great river before. Here it thrusts itself on you. Jumping off my horse I walked into the Nile till it rose above my knees, and began easily to drink its waters, as many a thirsty man has done before; while the pony, plunging his nose deep into the stream gulped and gulped in pleasure and relief as if he could never swallow enough. Water had been found. It remained to discover the column.

After much riding I reached their camping ground, only to find it deserted. They had already marched. There was a village near by. Once it had consisted of many houses and had supported a large population. Now only a few miserable people moved about the mud walls. Famine and worse than famine, the curse of the Khalifa,[1] had destroyed nine-tenths of the inhabitants. I selected one of the remainder, whose 'tarboush' or fez proclaimed him a man of some self-respect and, perhaps, even of some local importance, and applied to him for breakfast and a guide. He spoke nothing but Arabic: I only one word of the language. Still we conversed fluently. Opening and shutting my mouth and pointing to my stomach, I excited his curiosity, if not his wonder. Then I employed the one indispensable Arabic word 'backsheesh.' After that all difficulties melted. From a corner of the mud house in which he lived he produced a clean white cloth full of dates. From another corner some dhurra satisfied the pony. From an inner apartment, which smelt stale and acrid, three women and several children appeared. The women smiled amiably and began to wait on me, handing me the dates one by one in fingers whose dark skin alone protected them from the reproach of dirt. The children regarded the strangely-garbed stranger with large eyes which seemed full of reflection but without intelligent result. Meanwhile the lord of these splendours had departed with a wooden bowl. Presently he returned bearing it filled with fresh, sweet, but dirty, milk. This completed a repast which, if it will not gratify the palate of the epicure, will yet sustain the stomach of the traveller. Dates are almost the only food the people eat: perhaps they add a

[1] Abdullahi Ibn Sayed Mohammed (c1843–1899). Nominated First Khalifa (literally 'successor') by the Mahdi.

little Indian corn or, as a special luxury, some milk; and yet on this simple fare they wax strong, and occasionally vicious.

I next proceeded to ask for information as to the column. With the point of my sword I drew on the red mud wall the image of a Lancer—grotesque, disproportionate, yet, as the event proved, not unrecognisable. The women laughed, the man talked and gesticulated with energy. Even the children became excited. Yes, it was true. Such a one had passed through the village early that morning. He pointed at the sun and then to the eastern horizon. But not one—many. He began to make scratches on the wall to show how many. They had watered their horses in the river—he lapped vigorously from his hand—and had gone on swiftly. He pointed southwards, and made the motion of running. Then he gazed at me hard and, with an expression of ferocious satisfaction, pronounced the word 'Omdurman.' He was a Jaalin—one of the almost exterminated tribe—and looking at the ruins and the desolation I could not wonder that he rejoiced that the strong and implacable arm of civilisation was raised to chastise his merciless enemies. I replied to his speech by repeating with considerable solemnity the word 'backsheesh,' and at this without more ado he put on his boots and a dirtier blue shirt, picked up his broad-bladed sword, and started. But I will not weary you with the further account of my wanderings in the riparian bush, or of the other meals of dates and milk I was forced, and indeed fain, to eat. In the evening I caught up with the column at its camp, and washed away the taste and recollection of native food and native life with one of the most popular drinks of the modern world. I said I would begin this letter with a personal experience. I have begun, continued, and ended it without departing from the subject. Yet you may forgive me, for you must admit that personal matters are suited to such letters, and you may, from the account I have given, fill in with some touches of local colour the picture which I trust your imagination is gradually painting of the people, the scenery, and the war along the banks and on the waters of the Nile.

27 September, 1894

5

CAMP BEFORE SHABLUKA, 24 August

I devoted my last letter, my dear . . ., exclusively to my own experiences, and you would rightly blame me if I were not to make some amends for indulging my vanity, by writing forthwith some account of the military movements. The cavalry convoy started from Atbara on 16 August on its march to this camp—a total distance in a straight line of a hundred and fifteen miles, but probably with the windings of the road not less than a hundred and forty. This was accomplished successfully in seven days' march, averaging twenty miles a day, and one day's halt on the 20th. The fact that we were escorting camels and mules added to the severity of the marches, for though twenty miles a day is not excessive for cavalry, it makes a great deal of difference when the troops have continually to halt and wait for the slow pack animals. Throughout the sun was very hot, and we had in the two squadrons nearly a dozen cases of heat apoplexy, only one of which, however, up to date, has terminated fatally. The Arab horses stood the hard work well, and not more than twenty had to be shot or left behind out of about three hundred.

Our march lay partly in the desert and partly along the strip of vegetation by the Nile to which we returned every evening to water, and by which we camped each night. I have already described to you the desert scenery, and, though by describing it again I might impress you with its monotony, you would hardly thank me for a barren letter on a barren subject. The strip of bushes and trees by the river is in places more than a mile wide, and the numerous hollows becoming flooded by the rising waters necessitate wide detours, though they afford convenient drinking places. At times the generous flood even reaches the desert itself, and the hot mud swallows the water as if it were consumed, like all other things, with a dreadful thirst. Except at the very brink of the river only plants of deep roots survive. The most frequent is a kind of thorn bush—indeed, a very effective kind of thorn bush—which is used for making zarebas. It has white thorns and pale green leaves, and looks very pretty. Yet the traveller whose clothes have been torn, and whose flesh has been pricked, will find its beauty an altogether insufficient 'apologia pro vita sua'. There are also leafy bushes which bear large and luscious-looking fruits. They are little more than bladders of air, however, containing nothing but a milky liquid which produces blindness if injected into the eyes. Such is the riparian flora. But I must not forget the palm tree whose groves and clusters, here and there rising above and superior to the inhospitable undergrowth, alone remind the wayfarer that nature is not always cruel and mocking.

Of animals—birds and beasts—there are few. An occasional herd of gazelle gallops across the path. Here and there the track of hares, whose long tails drag along the ground and leave a continuous line among their footprints, are to be seen. Convoys of sand grouse and perhaps a great bustard are flushed by the advanced patrols, and near the villages the trees are occupied by pigeons. The villages themselves are full of significance. The whole bank of the river is dotted with them, and their extent and number show clearly that human industry could easily in the future, as in the past, raise from the soil the livelihood of a great population. But the villages are empty and in ruins. Hardly an inhabitant is to be seen. Yet riding in the woods we may learn the explanation. Under the trees, behind a broken wall, in a hollow of the ground, among the rocks, the skeleton makes its silent accusation, and imagination swiftly fills in the picture of the flying peasants hunted hither and thither in the scrub, only to fall one by one into the clutches of their pursuers and learn what the mercy of the Khalifa means. And the British soldier, seeing these things, reflects with pleasure on the sharpness of his lance and the really beautiful effects which the new expanding bullets produce on flesh and bone.

On the fourth day we halted in a shady grove of palm trees on the edge of the Nile and rested ourselves and our horses. The broad river was by no means deserted. Steamboats, gunboats, tugs, dahabeahs, natives floating swiftly downstream on inflated skins, filled the great waterway with life and the affairs of men. One by one I watched seven steamers, each with four barges lashed to its sides, beating their way up the Nile towards Khartoum. From end to end, from top to bottom, they were crowded with the khaki-clad Infantry of the 2nd British Brigade. All came near enough to our bivouac among the palm trees for the soldiers to shout jokes and friendly chaff at one another. Several times we had to stop to put on board such sick as could no longer march. The Grenadiers, the Rifles, and the two Fusilier battalions all passed us that day, and so did General Gatacre[1] and his aide-de-camp Captain Brooke.

The next day our march was resumed, and after twenty miles of hot and dusty scrub we reached the plain of Metemmeh and bivouacked about a mile south of the town on the very spot where the Desert Column had reached the hard-won water thirteen years ago. Several officers rode over the field of Abu Kru, or Gubat, as it is sometimes called. The trenches which the British soldiers dug when they waited before Metemmeh in 1885 are still visible, as are also the graves of the officers and men who perished there. It was with a strange emotion that we looked at the scene of the end of that historic march, and reflected on the mournful news that the gunboats brought back from Khartoum to those who had dared and done so much that their efforts were in vain—that they were too late. With the ground before me I could easily imagine the Desert Column, weak, exhausted, encumbered with wounded, yet spurred by a maddening thirst, toiling with their wounded General painfully towards the river. They clear the low sand hills, and the green bushes by the bank encourage them to a last effort. Suddenly the square halts. The savage enemy, infuriated at the prospect of his quarry escaping, has determined to make one more charge and finish the business, for surely Allah will support so good a chance. The low scrub is alive with nimble figures of spearmen. On horseback the Emirs direct the attack. The swarm of men burst into the open ground at a swift run. But the stubbornness of the weary soldiers is strengthened by the stimulus of exasperation. Never have they shot better before or since. The whole attack withers away at five hundred yards. The ground is littered with the bodies of the assailants. It was a knockdown blow. Back troop the survivors, Emirs and spearmen, sick of it, and then the discipline of the soldiers gives way with a snap, and the whole force—officers, men and animals —breaks rank and rushes madly without order to the river, and drink, and drink, and drink again of the soft, sweet water. And I am told that had the enemy made a second attack they would have destroyed them all. But this they were in no condition to do for several days.

[1] William Forbes Gatacre (1843–1906). Created KCB after Omdurman, but two years later relieved of his command and sent home after losing five companies of his division at Reddersburg, during the Boer War. Nicknamed 'Backacher' by his troops.

The town of Metemmeh is a large, struggling labyrinth of mud houses. It is a study in sepia, nor would the artist who should paint it require any other colour. Before it stretches the plain where Mahmoud and his army of nearly twenty thousand men were encamped for several weeks at the beginning of the year. The whole place is covered with the bones of animals, and not always of animals. Carcasses of camels, donkeys, mules, the hide hanging in strips from their ribs, and revealing dark cavities within, dot the ground. Every kind of filth and garbage is strewn about. There is a sickly smell. Fat bald-headed vultures circle lazily overhead, or waddle composedly up to the cavalry, as if speculating on the value of their reversions. Metemmeh was a great stronghold of the Jaalins, and when Mahmoud took it last year he put all the men and children to the sword. He also paraded all the women and, selecting forty for even greater horrors, had the others decapitated. This paladin is now in Wadi Halfa Gaol, and will probably soon become the object of sympathy among certain classes in England. The correct procedure in his case would be to try him by the ordinary law for any one of these numerous murders, and if he should be found guilty to hang him prosaically and by the neck. It would, of course, be urged on his behalf that he had only acted according to his nature, and that he should not be judged by our standards. Some people will perhaps admit the plea. I do not think, my dear . . ., that you will be of that number, for I remember that you have several times asserted in my hearing your belief in an eternal standard of right and wrong independent of and superior to climate, custom, and caprice.

After three more long days of marching, unmarked by incident, we reached this great camp, where all the army is now concentrated, and whence we move almost immediately southward towards our goal. I dare say a description of this place and of the Expeditionary Force will interest you, but I must reserve it for another letter, or you will think my correspondence as wearying to read as it appears to be to answer. The postal arrangements here are very bad and I will charitably conclude that the fact that I have received no letters from you is due to this cause. But I need scarcely say how much I look forward to hearing all your news. It is a symptom of the contrariness of life that we always want to be informed of some place other than that in which we are.

28 September, 1898

92

6

CAMP WAD HABESHI (before Shabluka), 25 August

The halt of three days which we are making here before the final advance is, my dear . . ., very favourable to correspondence. There is no lack of material, for I am sure you will be interested by an account of this great camp—the greatest I have ever seen; and by a lucky and rare coincidence there is also plenty of time for writing. I told you in my last letter of the march of the cavalry convoy from Atbara to this place. We arrived at noon on the 23rd, and were hospitably and courteously received by the officers of the Egyptian cavalry, who provided entertainment for the men as well as for the officers, and sent fatigue parties from their squadrons to help in laying out the lines and in watering, feeding, and picketing the horses. But it is not with these matters that I shall fill this letter.

The camp of Wad Habeshi, a little to the north of the Shabluka cataract, is of great extent. With two small exceptions, the whole of the Nile Expeditionary Force was yesterday concentrated here. To-day many troops have marched south, but at a great review on the 23rd no fewer than twenty-two thousand bayonets and lances were in line. This powerful force is composed as follows: 1st and 2nd British Infantry Brigades (eight strong battalions); 1st and 2nd Sudanese Brigades, 3rd and 4th Egyptian Brigades. In all, three infantry divisions. Besides a battery of Maxim guns, the 37th British Field Battery, two great 40 pounders for breaching, one battery of Egyptian Horse Artillery, and four batteries of quick-firing $12\frac{1}{2}$ pounders—a total of forty-six guns. There are also details of all kinds, hospital, telegraph, &c, and a due proportion of engineers and Army Service Corps. Such is the force on the banks of the Nile which has been massed for the capture of Omdurman and the expulsion of the Baggara tribesmen from the Khedivial territories. It may be conveniently spoken of as an Army Corps. I must not forget the flotilla of gunboats, which is by no means the least important or remarkable feature in the operations. There are three large new boats mounting 12-pounder quick-firing guns and Maxims. These look very imposing with their white loopholed sides and fighting galleries. They rise high above the bank of the river, and seem in contrast to the tents great battleships. Besides this, there are three gunboats of the 1896 class, and four of the older armed steamers —a total of ten war vessels, mounting over twenty guns and numerous maxims.

As you may easily imagine, the whole scene is one of busy animation. The great camp lies lengthways along the river bank, and is nearly two miles from end to end. The Nile secures it from attack towards the east. On the western and southern sides are strong lines of thorn bushes staked down and forming a zareba, and the north face is protected by a deep artificial watercourse which allows the waters of the river to make a considerable inundation. Standing on the bank of this work the observer sees the whole camp displayed. Far away to the southward are the white tents of the British division. A little nearer rows and rows of grass huts and blanket shelters mark the bivouacs of the Egyptian and Sudanese brigades. On a small eminence is the Sirdar's[1] large white tent with the red flag of Egypt flying from a high staff. To the right a small grove of palm trees serves as the mess of the officers of the Egyptian cavalry. The whole riverside is filled by a forest of masts. Crowds of dahabeahs, barges, and steamers are moored closely together, and while looking at the tall funnels it seems hard to believe that this is not the docks of some populous city in a well-developed and civilised land. The foreground of the picture is filled by the cavalry lines, which occupy a large area of ground, and the spectacle of successive rows of horses' backs is remarkable, if not imposing.

But the significance of the picture grows when the mind, outstripping the eye, passes beyond the long, low heights which mark the gorge and cataract of Shabluka and contemplates the ruins of Khartoum and the city of Omdurman. There are known to be over thirty thousand fighting men collected there in their best stronghold.

[1] Horatio Herbert Kitchener (1850–1916). Sirdar of Egyptian army 1893–9. Chief of Staff to Lord Roberts, South Africa 1899–1900; Commander in chief 1900–1902. Commander in chief, India 1902–9. British Agent and Consul-General, Egypt, 1911–14. Secretary of State for War 1914–15. KCMG, 1894; KCB, 1896; Baron, 1898; Viscount and OM, 1902; Earl, 1914; KG, 1915.

The Khalifa has declared his intentions to destroy the impudent invaders. Allah is said to have fully approved of his plan. Loud is the boasting and many are the oaths which are taken as to what treatment the infidel dogs shall have when they are come to the city walls. The streets swarm with men and resound with their voices. Everywhere is preparation and defiance. And yet over all hangs the dark shadow of fear. Nearer and nearer comes this great serpent of an army, moving so slowly and with such terrible deliberation, but always moving. A week ago it was sixty miles away. Now it is but fifty. Next week only twenty short miles will intervene, and then the creep of the serpent will cease, and, without argument or parley, there will be a swift and sudden dart and the end will come.

Perhaps to these savages with their vile customs and brutal ideas we appear as barbarous aggressors. The British subaltern, with his jokes, his cigarettes and his soda water, may seem to them a more ferocious creature than any Emir or fanatic in Omdurman. The Highlanders in their kilts, the white loop-holed gunboats, the brown-clad soldiery and the lyddite shells are all elements of destruction which must look ugly when viewed from the opposite side. And yet there is no way out. No terms but flight or death are offered. The quarrel is *à l'outrance*. The red light of retribution plays on the bayonets and the lances, and civilisation, elsewhere sympathetic, merciful, tolerant, ready to discuss or to argue, eager to avoid violence, to submit to law, to effect a compromise, here advances with an expression of inexorable sterness, and rejecting all other courses offers only the arbitrament of the sword.

The Shabluka position is unoccupied by the enemy. Until a few days ago a small hostile cavalry force remained in observation. Their intention was to prevent any steamers and gunboats from coming through the cataract and interfering with the Dervish preparations before the actual advance took place. The opinion here is that the enemy have acted wisely in not attempting to defend the heights of Shabluka, as these positions though strong can be easily turned, and had they attempted to hold them they would have been defeated with heavy loss. They are now all concentrated in and around Omdurman, and the expectation is that Kerreri, six miles from the city, will be the scene of the general engagement. Whether this will terminate the war is uncertain. Should the Dervishes continue to cling to Omdurman it is possible that the street fighting which may

95

follow the storm of that place will involve heavy loss. But I am foolish to speculate, for you will know the facts before this letter reaches you. It were idiotic to make a prophecy which may be falsified, even before it is proclaimed. All we know is this—the enemy are in Omdurman, and we are going there to find them.

The camp here is now breaking up. Two Egyptian brigades, two Sudanese brigades, with three British battalions of the 2nd Brigade—the Grenadiers and the Northumberland and Lancashire Fusiliers—march south this morning to Wad Bishara, eleven miles away. The rest of the infantry follow to-morrow. The cavalry and some of the artillery move on the 27th, and the whole force will be concentrated again at Hagir at the head of the cataract, twenty-one miles south of this and thirty-two miles from Khartoum on the 28th. The next march will bring the cavalry screen into contact, and a collision will then be imminent. While these movements are taking place on the west bank, Major Stuart-Wortley[1] with 3,500 Jaalin Irregulars will move down the east bank and occupy the attention of the enemy in that quarter. I will try to write to you again from the next camp, south of Shabluka. But you know what the vicissitudes of war are. It is, indeed, possible that my next letter may tell you of the capture of Khartoum. For my part I should prefer to have an opportunity of describing several minor operations first, and not have the whole affair settled in one big rush. Unfortunately, I am not consulted.

It is a strange war, my dear . . ., in every way different to the operations I witnessed in Cuba and on the Indian Frontier. Usually the game gets warmer by degrees. One day comes the news that a patrol of the enemy has been seen—perhaps fired on. The next there is some skirmishing at the outposts, and a few wounded men are brought into camp. Then there is a little 'sniping' or a dashing reconnaissance. Gradually the forces close and the more serious operations develop. But this is different. There are no enemy within thirty miles of us at this moment. Not a shot has been fired since the action on the Atbara in April. The camp is as peaceful as Aldershot or Bisley. And yet we can guess that one morning the guns will begin to fire and a big battle will be fought. Looking further ahead—let us say to this time next month—the camp will again be pitched in this convenient spot. We shall be looking northwards towards

[1] Edward James Montagu-Stuart-Wortley (1857–1934). Awarded DSO after Omdurman, and later CMG. Retired as Major-General.

home. The boats will be moored to the bank. The horses will stand quietly in their lines. The moving city will be full of life. Yet remember this, there are two squadrons of the 21st Lancers, nine squadrons of Egyptian cavalry; in all, fifteen hundred cavalry; some will be missing, some will have remained further south. It is a little strange writing to you of such thoughts, for when you receive this letter you will know who are these absentees. It almost seems that you know already whether you will receive another letter from the camp at Wad Hamid. But if you did know I would not let you tell me. The great story of life is spoiled if we skip the pages and look on ahead or to the end. I will do nothing so unphilosophic.

3 October, 1898

7

KHARTOUM, 5 September

You see the address, my dear . . ., It is with a feeling of exultation that I write it big and black at the top of the page. The fact that a European can again in safety and confidence post a letter from such a situation has alone a deep significance. I am sure you will want to know how it all happened. Yet there is so much to tell that I hesitate where to begin. I told you in my last letter from Wad Habeshi Camp that I should probably have no opportunity of writing until after the event. Nor was I wrong. I should have liked to make your imagination march with the cavalry screen from Shabluka to Kerreri all through the thick scrub by the banks of the Nile, and peering cautiously for Dervishes under every bush. I should have liked to have described the reconnaissance and patrolling by day and the high zarebas and closely-packed camps at night, where each man slept booted and belted with his weapon ready to his hand.

I would have tried to draw you some picture of the advance of the army. A long row of great brown masses of infantry with a fringe of cavalry dotting the plain for miles in front, with the Camel Corps—chocolate-coloured men on cream-coloured camels—stretching into the desert on the right and the gunboats stealing silently up river on the left, scrutinising the banks with their guns; while far behind the transport and baggage trailed away into the mirage, and far in front the telescope might discover the watching Dervish patrols. I would have written some account of our first contact with the enemy and of the expectations of war which we draw from that affair; but for all this you would not thank me, for the telegraph has already told you that tremendous events have taken place, and it is of these that you would have me write. Let me, then, begin at the 1st of September and describe the reconnaissance of Kerreri and the Battle of Khartoum which followed on the next day.

The whole army broke camp on the morning of the 1st and marched

98

slowly towards the Kerreri position, which consisted of a line of low rocky hills at right angles to the river. In front were the cavalry and the Camel Corps, and these, pushing rapidly forward, soon interposed a distance of perhaps eight miles between them and the main force. The 21st Lancers were on the left nearest the Nile. The nine Egyptian squadrons curved backwards in a wide half-moon to protect the right flank.

We had not accomplished more than a mile when about a hundred enormous vultures joined us, and henceforth they accompanied the squadrons, flying or waddling lazily from bush to bush and always looking back at the horsemen. Officers and men alike were struck by this strange and unusual occurrence, and it was freely asserted that these birds of prey knew that two armies were approaching each other, and that this meant a battle and hence a feast. It would be difficult to assign limitations to the possibilities of instinct. The sceptic must at least admit that the vultures guessed right, even if they did not know. Yet we thought them wrong when we found the strong Kerreri Hills abandoned and the little Dervish camp, which had been shelled the day before, deserted and solitary.

The squadron of the 21st to which I have the pleasure of being attached halted at the foot of the hill. Colonel Martin and a few other officers ascended it, taking signallers with them. We waited. Then presently a message was sent down which filled us all with curiosity to look over the crest. The signal flag wagged tirelessly, and we spelt out the following words: 'Khartoum in sight.' More than thirteen years had passed since an Englishman could have said that with truth.

After a short halt the advance was resumed, and turning a shoulder of the hill I saw in the distance a yellow-brown pointed dome rising above the blurred horizon. It was the Mahdi's Tomb,[1] which stands in the very heart of Omdurman. From the high ground the field glass disclosed rows and rows of mud houses, making a dark patch on the brown of the plain. To the left, the river, steel-grey in the morning light, forked into two channels, and on the tongue of land between them the gleam of a white house showed among the trees. Then we knew that before us was Khartoum and the confluence of the Blue and White Niles.

A black, solitary hill rose between the Kerreri position and Omdurman. A long, low ridge running from it concealed the ground beyond. For the rest there was a wide, rolling, sandy plain of great

[1] Mohammed Ahmed (1848–1885).

99

extent, and patched with coarse, starveling grass. The river—the inevitable river—framed the picture on the left, and by its banks a straggling mud village stood. This, though we did not know it, was to be the field of Khartoum.

It was deserted. Not a living soul could be seen. And there were many who said at once that there would be no fight, for here we were arrived at the very walls of Omdurman and never any enemy to bar our path. Then, with our four squadrons looking very tiny on the broad expanse of ground, we moved steadily forward.

It was about three miles to the hill and ridge of which I have written—the last ridge which lay between us and the city. If there was a Dervish army, if there was to be a battle, if the Khalifa would maintain his boast and accept the arbitrament of war, much must be visible from that ridge. We looked over. At first nothing was apparent except the walls and houses of Omdurman and the sandy plain sloping up from the river to the distant hills. Then four miles away, on our right front, I perceived a long black line with white spots. It was the enemy. It seemed to me as we looked that there might be three thousand men behind a high dense zareba of thorn bushes. That, said the officers, was better than nothing. There would in any case be a skirmish.

I will not weary you with describing our tortuous movements towards the Dervish position. Looking at it, now from one point of view, now from another, but always edging nearer, the cavalry slowly approached it, and halted in the plain about two miles away, three great serpents of men—the light-coloured one, the 21st Lancers; a much longer and blacker one, the Egyptian squadrons; a mottled one, the Camel Corps and Horse Artillery.

From this distance a clearer view was possible, and we distinguished many horsemen riding about the flanks and front of the great dark line which crowned the crest of the slope. A few of these rode forward carelessly towards the watching squadrons to look at them. They were not apparently acquainted with the long range of the Lee-Metford carbine. Several troops were dismounted, and at eight hundred yards fire was made on them. Two were shot and fell to the ground. Their companions, dismounting, examined them, picked up one, let the other lie, and resumed their ride without acknowledging the bullets by even an increase of pace.

While this little incident passed so did the time. It was now nearly eleven o'clock. Suddenly the whole black line, which seemed to be zareba, began to move. It was made of men not bushes. Behind it other immense masses and lines of men appeared over the crest, and while we watched, amazed by the wonder of the sight, the whole face of the slope became black with swarming savages. Four miles from end to end, and in five great divisions, this mighty army advanced, and swiftly. The whole side of the hill seemed to move. Between the masses horsemen galloped continually. Before them many patrols dotted the plain, above them waved hundreds of banners, and the sun, glinting on perhaps forty thousand hostile spear-points, spread a sparkling cloud. It was, perhaps, the impression of a lifetime, nor do I expect ever again to see such an awe-inspiring and formidable sight. We estimated their number at not less than forty thousand men, and it is now certain fifty thousand would have been nearer the truth.

The steady and continuous advance of the great army compelled us to mount our horses and trot off to some safer point of view, while our patrols and two detached troops, engaging the Dervish scouts, opened a dropping fusillade. I was sent back to describe the state of affairs to the Sirdar, but as had he already witnessed the spectacle from the top of the black hill—Heliograph Hill I shall call it in future—you are the first to receive my account.

From the summit the scene was extraordinary. The great army of Dervishes was dwarfed by the size of the landscape to mere dark smears and smudges on the brown sand of the plain. Looking east another army was now visible—the British and Egyptian army. All three divisions had crossed the Kerreri position and now stood drawn up in formation for attack in a crescent, with their backs to the Nile. The transport and the houses of the village filled the enclosed space. I looked from one array to the other. That of the enemy was without doubt denser and longer. Yet there seemed a superior strength in the solid battalions, whose lines were so straight that they might have been drawn with a ruler. Neither force could see the other, though but five miles divided them.

At a quarter to two the Dervish army halted. Their drill appeared excellent, and they all stopped as by a single command. The nearest troops to them were the 21st Lancers, who were about a mile and a half away. We watched them anxiously, for if they continued to advance the action would have been brought on at once. No sooner had they halted than their riflemen discharged their rifles in the air with a great roar—a barbaric *feu-de-joie*. Then they all lay down on the ground, and it became evident that the matter would not be settled till the morrow.

We remained in our position among the sand hills of the ridge until the approach of darkness, and during the afternoon various petty encounters took place between our patrols and those of the enemy, resulting in a loss to them of about a dozen killed and wounded and to us of one man wounded and one horse killed. Then, as the light failed, we returned to the river to water and encamp, passing into the zareba through the ranks of the British division, whose officers and men, looking out steadfastly over the fading plain, asked us whether the enemy were coming and, if so, when. And it was with confidence and satisfaction that we replied and they heard: 'Probably at daylight.'

I have told you of one sight which I witnessed on the 1st of September, and I were but a poor chronicler if I were to forget or omit the other. At about eleven o'clock the gunboats had ascended the Nile and engaged the enemy's batteries on the river face of Omdurman. Throughout the day the loud reports of their guns could be heard, and looking from our position on the ridge we could see the white vessels steaming slowly forward against the current under clouds of black smoke from their furnaces, and amid other clouds of white smoke from their artillery. The forts replied vigorously, but the British aim was accurate and their fire crushing. The embrasures were smashed to bits, and many of the Dervish guns dismounted. Then the gunboats began to shell the Mahdi's Tomb. This part of the proceedings was so interesting that it distracted my attention at intervals from the advancing army.

The dome of the Tomb rose high and prominent above the mud houses of the city. A lyddite shell burst over it—a great flash, a white ball of smoke, and, after a pause, the dull thud of the distant explosion. Another and another followed. Presently, instead of the white smoke there was a prodigious cloud of red dust, and the whole Tomb disappeared. When this cleared away we saw that instead of being pointed it was now flat topped. Our shells continue to strike it with like effect, some breaking holes in the dome, others smashing off the cupolas, all enveloping it in dust, until I marvelled alike at the admirable precision and the wasteful folly of the practice. I feel inclined to write a little bitterly to you on this subject, because the mania to destroy this building cost me on the next day a good and gallant friend, and very nearly cost the country a skilful general.

When the gunboats had completed their bombardment, had sunk

a Dervish steamer, had silenced all the hostile batteries, and had sorely battered the Mahdi's Tomb, they returned leisurely to the camp and lay moored close to the bank to lend the assistance of their guns in case of attack. And as the darkness became complete they threw their powerful searchlights over the plain and on to the distant hills, and all night long these dazzling beams disturbed, though they protected, the slumbers of the army.

The consciousness of the limitless possibilities of the morrow delayed the sleep which physical weariness invited, and a desire to inspect the precautions for defence led me around the perimeter of the zareba. The army had not formed a quadrilateral camp as on other nights, but lay down to rest in the formation for attack they had assumed in the afternoon. Every fifty yards behind the thorn bushes were double sentries. Every hundred yards a patrol with an officer was to be met. Fifty yards in rear of this line lay the battalions, the men in all their ranks, armed and accoutred, but sprawled into every conceivable attitude which utter weariness could suggest or dictate. The full moon rising early displayed the whole scene. Imagination was stimulated, and I would set down some of my impressions for your private eye, did I not know you were a cynic, and would observe that others had thought the same on similar occasions before. So I shall end this letter here and now, and leave you, if I can, with some realisation of the solemnity and the significance of a night when two armies, one of fifty thousand, one of twenty-five thousand, both equally confident, and both equally brave, are waiting at five miles' distance for the coming of the morning and the settlement of their quarrel.

4 October, 1898

8

KHARTOUM, 6 September

The bugles all over the camp by the river began to sound at half-past four. The cavalry trumpets and the drums and fifes of the British division joined the chorus, and everyone awoke amid a confusion of merry or defiant notes. The moon was full, and by its light and that of lanterns we dressed ourselves—many with special care. Those who were callous, who had seen much war, or who were practical, set themselves to deliberately eat a substantial meal of such delicacies as 'porrig', 'sausig', ration biscuits, and 'bully' beef. Then it grew gradually lighter, and the cavalry mounted their horses, the infantry stood to arms, and the gunners went to their batteries, while the sun rising over the Nile displayed the wide plain, the dark rocky hills, and the waiting army. It was as if all the preliminaries were settled, the arena cleared, and nothing remained but the final act and the rigour of the game.

As soon as it was light enough to move, several squadrons of British and Egyptian cavalry were pushed swiftly forward to feign contact with the enemy and to learn his intentions. It was my fortune to be sent with an advanced patrol of the 21st Lancers, and though I know that it is of the battle that you wish to hear, and not of my personal experiences, I must describe events from my own stand-point. At half-past five the British and Egyptian army was drawn up in line, with its back to the river. Its flanks were secured by the gunboats, which were moored in the stream. Before it was the rolling sandy plain. To the right were the rocky hills of the Kerreri portion, near which the nine squadrons of Egyptian cavalry were massed. On the left the 21st Lancers were trotting towards Heliograph Hill, with their advanced patrols already cantering up its lower slopes. My patrol was, I think, the first to reach the top of the ridge and to look into the plain beyond. I had expected that the Dervish army would have retired to their original position, and could not believe

104

that they would advance to the attack in daylight across open ground. Indeed, it seemed more probable that their hearts might have failed them in the night and that they had melted away into the deserts of Kordofan. But these anticipations were immediately dispelled by the scene which was visible from the crest of the ridge.

It was a quarter to six. The light was dim, but growing stronger every minute. There in the plain lay the enemy, their numbers unaltered, their confidence and intentions apparently unshaken. Their front was nearly five miles long, and composed of great masses of men joined together by thinner lines. Behind and to the flanks were large reserves. They looked from where I stood dark blurs and streaks, relieved and diversified with odd-looking gleams of light from the spear points. After making the necessary reports I continued to watch the strange and impressive spectacle. As it became broad daylight, that is to say about ten minutes to six, I suddenly realised that all the masses were in motion and advancing swiftly. Their Emirs galloped about, among and before their ranks scouts and patrols began to scatter themselves all over the front. Then they began to cheer. They were still a mile away from the hill when a tremendous roar came up in waves of intense sound, like the tumult of the rising wind and sea before a storm.

The advance continued. The Dervish left began to stretch out across the Kerreri Plain—as I thought to turn to our right flank. Their centre, over which the black flag of the Khalifa floated high and remarkable, moved directly towards the hill. Their right pursued a line of advance south of Heliograph Hill, and would, I saw, pass over the ground on which I stood. This mass of men was the most striking of all. They could not have mustered less than seven thousand. Their array was perfect. They displayed a great number of flags— perhaps five hundred—which looked at the distance white, though they were really covered with texts from the Koran, which by their admirable alignment made the divisions of the Khalifa's army look like the old representations of the Crusaders in the Bayeux Tapestry. I called them at the moment 'the white flagmen' to distinguish them from the other masses, and that name will do as well as any other.

The attack developed. The left, under a famous Emir, appeared to have mistaken the squadrons of the Egyptian Cavalry for our main position. Ten thousand strong they toiled right up to the Kerreri hills, and did not come into action until later in the day. The centre deployed across the plain and marched straight towards the zareba.

One small brigade of their great force—perhaps about two thousand strong—halted five hundred yards from my patrol, and perceiving the Lancers paid us the compliment of detaching a dozen riflemen to drive us from our point of observation. After a while these began to shoot so straight that it became expedient as well as desirable to move round the hill out of their fire. From this new position the centre was no longer visible, but the 'white flagmen' were of sufficient interest and importance to occupy the attention.

As the whole Dervish army continued to advance this division, which had until now been echeloned in rear of their right, moved up into the general line, and began to climb the southern slopes of Heliograph Hill. They, too, saluted us with musketry, but as the hill was within good artillery range of the zareba I knew that they would have something else to occupy their attention when they and their banners appeared over the shoulder and crest of the ridge, and we remained spectators, sheltering among the rocks about three hundred yards to their right flank.

Meanwhile yet another body of the enemy, who had been drawn up behind the 'white flagmen', was moving slowly towards the Nile, echeloned still further behind their right, and not far from the suburbs of Omdurman. These men had evidently been posted to prevent the Dervish army being cut off from the city, and it was these that the 21st Lancers charged and drove back about two hours later. My attention was distracted from their movements by the loud explosion of artillery. The Dervish centre had come into range, and the batteries opened on them. Above the heads of the moving masses shells began to burst, dotting the air with smoke balls and the ground with bodies. But they were nearly two miles away, and the distance rendered me unsympathetic.

I looked back to the 'white flagmen'. They were very nearly over the crest. In another minute they would become visible to the batteries. Did they realise what would come to meet them? They were in a dense mass scarcely two thousand yards from the 32nd Field Battery and the gunboats. The ranges were known. It was a matter of machinery. The more distant cannonade passed unnoticed as the mind concentrated on the impending horror. I could see it coming. It was a matter of seconds, and then swift destruction would rush on these brave men.

They topped the crest and drew out into full view of the whole army. Their white flags made them conspicuous above all. As they saw the camp of their enemies they discharged their rifles with a great roar of musketry and quickened their pace, and I was alarmed to see a solitary British officer, Lieutenant Conolly of the Greys, attached to the 21st, galloping across their front at only a hundred yards distance. He had been sent out to take a final look behind the hill. Fortunately he returned safely, and with the necessary information. For a moment the white flags advanced in regular order, and the whole division crossed the crest and were exposed.

Forthwith the gunboats, and the 32nd Battery, and other guns from the zareba opened on them. I was but three hundred yards away, and with excellent glasses could almost see the faces of the Dervishes who met the fearful fire. About twenty shells struck them in the first minute. Some burst high in the air, others exactly in their faces. Others again plunged into the sand and exploding, dashed clouds of red dust, splinters, and bullets amid their ranks. The white flags toppled over in all directions. Yet they rose again immediately, as other men pressed forward to die for Allah's sacred cause and in the defence of the successor of the True Prophet of The Only God. It was a terrible sight, for as yet they had not hurt us at all, and it seemed an unfair advantage to strike thus cruelly when they could not reply.

From the purely military point of view I was not impressed with the effects of the shells. I had looked to see fifty men drop to each projectile. You read of these things in the text books on war, and you hear them stated every time you talk to an artillery officer. What soldier has not heard of the results of target practice? Eighty per cent of hits, &c. I watched most carefully, and from a close and excellent position. About five men on the average fell to each shell. Still, there were many shells. Under their influence the mass of the 'white flagmen' dissolved into thin lines of spearmen and skirmishers, and came on in altered formation and diminished numbers, but with unabated enthusiasm.

And now, the whole attack being thoroughly exposed, it became the duty of the cavalry to clear the front as quickly as possible and leave the further conduct of the debate to the infantry and the Maxim guns. We therefore retired into the zareba, and, taking advantage of the river bank, watered and fed our horses, while all the time the fusillade grew louder and more intense, and we wondered what progress the attack was making.

Of this I saw nothing, but it appears that the *debris* of the 'white flagmen' joined the centre, and that these continued their advance against the zareba gradually, spreading out and abandoning their dense formations, and gradually slowing down. At about eight hundred yards range of the British division the advance ceased, and they could make no further headway. Unable to advance, they were unwilling to retire, and their riflemen, taking advantage of the folds of the ground, opened and maintained an unequal combat. By 8.30 it was evident that the attack had been repulsed. The loss in the zareba did not exceed sixty killed and wounded. That of the enemy was not less than two thousand. Colonel F. Rhodes,[1] the *Times* correspondent, was unfortunately among the wounded, being shot through the shoulder as he sat on his horse near the Maxim guns.

The second phase of the action, or, as an excitable correspondent called it, 'the second battle,' now began. Disregarding the presence of the Dervish left on and among the Kerreri Hills, the Sirdar gave the order for the army to march on towards Omdurman. The 21st Lancers moved out of the zareba and trotted over the ridge near Heliograph Hill. The whole of the British division made a left wheel, and faced south, their left on the river at right angles to the enemy's centre, and to their former front. The Egyptian and Sudanese divisions were echeloned on the right by brigades. Thus the army presented its flank to the Dervish centre, and its right rear to the Dervish left. Probably Sir Herbert Kitchener was anxious above all things to gain a moral advantage, and realised that if he could enter Omdurman the resistance of the enemy would collapse. Events, however, proved the movement to be premature. The Dervish left, who had started out in the morning confident of victory, and who had vainly toiled after the elusive cavalry and Camel Corps among the Kerreri Hills, now returned an exasperated but undefeated ten thousand. Infusing into the centre the encouragement of a reinforcement, they fell on General MacDonald's Sudanese Brigade, which was the rearmost of the echelon. That officer, who by personal prowess and military conduct has passed from the rank of private to that of general, faced about, and met the attack with a skill and determination which excited the admiration of all. General Lewis, with the Egyptian Brigade, also swung round, and thus the army assumed an A-shaped formation, the apex pointing west and away

[1] Francis William Rhodes (1851–1905). Elder brother of Cecil Rhodes. Acted as special correspondent for *The Times* during the Sudan campaign, and afterwards edited *The River War* for Churchill.

from the Nile, four brigades looking north-west towards the Dervish attack.

This was the critical moment of the engagement. The Sirdar, not the least disconcerted by the discovery of his mistake, immediately proceeded to rectify it. The movement of bringing up the right shoulders of the army ceased. Pivoting on the two brigades who were now hotly engaged, the British division and the whole south front of the A swung round until it became a straight line facing nearly west. Advancing in that direction the army steadily drove the Dervishes before them, away from the river, and as the left began to come up more and more threatened to cut their line of retreat.

Of this and all this I had but fleeting glances, for an event was taking place on the southern slopes of Heliograph Hill which absorbed my whole attention, and may perhaps invite yours. I will describe it at length and in detail, because I write as an eye witness, perhaps even as more, and you may read with interest. Everyone describes an action from his own point of view. Indeed, it is thence that we look at most things, human or divine. Why should I be or make an exception?

At about a quarter past eight the 21st Lancers moved out of the zareba, and occupied a position on the ridge of Heliograph Hill, whence a view of the ground right up to the walls of Omdurman was obtainable. Here we waited, dismounting a few troops to fire at the Dervish skirmishers on the higher slopes. At 8.40 orders reached us to advance, harass the enemy's right, and endeavour to cut him off from Omdurman. In pursuance of these orders Colonel Martin[1] advanced his regiment in line of squadron columns slowly down the southern slopes of the ridge and hill, and continued across the plain in a south-westerly direction. In the distance large numbers of the enemy could be seen retreating into Omdurman. The whole plain was crossed by a continual stream of fugitives.

In the foreground about two hundred Dervishes were crouching in what appeared to be a small khor or crease in the plain. The duty of the cavalry to brush these away and proceed at once to the more numerous bodies in rear was plain. With a view to outflanking them the squadrons wheeled to the left into columns of troops, and, breaking into a trot, began to defile across their front. We thought them spearmen, for we were within three hundred yards and they

[1] Rowland Hill Martin (1848–1919). Commanding officer 21st Lancers 1892–8. Mentioned in despatches and awarded CB after Omdurman.

had fired no shot. Suddenly, as the regiment began to trot, they opened a heavy, severe, and dangerous fire. Only one course was now possible. The trumpets sounded 'right-wheel into line,' and on the instant the regiment began to gallop in excellent order towards the riflemen. The distance was short, but before it was half covered it was evident that the riflemen were but a trifle compared to what lay behind. In a deep fold of the ground—completely concealed by its peculiar formation—a long, dense, white mass of men became visible. In length they were nearly equal to our front. They were about twelve deep. It was undoubtedly a complete surprise for us. What followed probably astonished them as much. I do not myself believe that they ever expected the cavalry to come on. The Lancers acknowledged the unexpected sight only by an increase of pace. A desire to have the necessary momentum to drive through so solid a line animated each man. But the whole affair was a matter of seconds.

At full gallop and in the closest order the squadron struck the Dervish mass. The riflemen, who fired bravely to the last, were brushed head over heel in the khor. And with them the Lancers jumped actually on to the spears of the enemy, whose heads were scarcely level with the horses' knees.

It is very rarely that stubborn and unshaken infantry meet equally stubborn and unshaken cavalry. Usually, either the infantry run away and are cut down in flight, or they keep their heads and destroy nearly all the horsemen by their musketry. In this case the two living walls crashed together with a mighty collision. The Dervishes stood their ground manfully. They tried to hamstring the horses. They fired their rifles, pressing their muzzles into the very bodies of their opponents. They cut bridle-reins and stirrup-leathers. They would not budge till they were knocked over. They stabbed and hacked with savage pertinacity. In fact, they tried every device of cool determined men practised in war and familiar in cavalry. Many horses pecked on landing and stumbled in the press, and the man that fell was pounced on by a dozen merciless foes.

The regiment broke completely through the line everywhere, leaving sixty Dervishes dead and many wounded in their track. A hundred and fifty yards away they halted, rallied, and in less than five minutes were reformed and ready for a second charge. The men were anxious to cut their way back through their enemies. But some realisation of the cost of that wild ride began to come to all of us. Riderless horses galloped across the plain. Men, clinging on to their saddles, lurched hopelessly about, covered with blood from perhaps a dozen wounds. Horses streaming from tremendous gashes limped and staggered with their riders. In one hundred and twenty seconds five officers, sixty-six men, and one hundred and nineteen horses out of less than three hundred had been killed or wounded.

The Dervish line, broken and shattered by the charge, began to reform at once. They closed up, shook themselves together, and prepared with constancy and courage for another shock. The 21st, now again drawn up in line of squadron columns, wheeled and, galloping round the Dervish flank, dismounted and opened a heavy fire with their magazine carbines. Under the pressure of this fire the enemy changed front to meet the new attack, so that both sides were formed at right angles to their original lines. When the Dervish change of front was completed they began to advance against the dismounted men. But the fire was accurate, and there can be little doubt that the moral effect of the charge had been very great, and that these brave enemy were no longer unshaken. Be this as it may, the fact remains that they retreated swiftly, though in good order, towards the ridge of Heliograph Hill, where the Khalifa's black flag still waved, and the 21st Lancers remained in possession of the ground—and of their dead.

I have told you the story of the charge, but you will perhaps care to hear a few incidents. Colonel Martin, busy with the direction of his regiment, drew neither sword nor revolver, and rode through the press unarmed and uninjured. Major Crole Wyndham had his horse shot from under him by a Dervish who pressed his muzzle into the very hide. From out of the middle of that savage crowd the officer fought his way on foot and escaped in safety. Lieutenant Wormald, of the 7th Hussars, thrust at a man with his sword, and that weapon, by a well-known London maker, bent double and remained thus.

I saw myself Sergeant Freeman trying to collect his troops after the charge. His face was cut to pieces, and as he called on his men to rally, the whole of his nose, cheeks, and lips flapped amid red bubbles. Surely some place may be found in any roll of honour for such a man.

Lieutenant Nesham, of the 21st Lancers, had an even more extra-ordinary escape. Amid a crowd of men slashing and stabbing he remained in his saddle throughout. His left hand was nearly severed from his body by single stroke. He managed to twist the reins round his right wrist. The near bridle rein and the off stirrup-leather were both cut. The wounded officer reeled. His enemies closed around him. He received another deep cut in his right leg and a slighter one in his right arm. Yet his horse, pressing forward, carried him through the Dervishes to fall fainting among the rallying Squadrons.

I have written thus of others. You would ask me of my own experiences. You know my luck in these things. As on another occasion in the Indian Frontier, I came safe through—one of the very few officers whose saddlery, clothes, or horse were untouched, and without any incident that is worth while putting down here.

One impression only I will record. I remember no sound. The whole event seemed to pass in absolute silence. The yells of the enemy, the shouts of the soldiers, the firing of many shots, the clashing of sword and spear were unnoticed by the senses, unregistered by the brain. Others say the same. Perhaps it is possible for the whole of a man's faculties to be concentrated in eye, bridle-hand, and trigger-finger, and withdrawn from all other parts of the body.

It was not until after the squadrons had reformed that I heard of the death of Lieutenant Grenfell, of the 12th Lancers. This young officer, who to great personal charm and high courage added talents and industry which gave promise of a successful and even a famous military carreer, and who had earlier in the day reconnoitred the enemy, riding close up to their ranks under a hot fire in a manner that excited general admiration, had been cut down and killed. And at this shocking news the exhilaration of the gallop, the excitement of the moment, the joy and triumph of successful combat faded from the mind, and the realisation came home with awful force that war, disguise it as you may, is but a dirty, shoddy business, which only a fool would play at. Nor was it until the night when I saw Charles Neufeld[1] released from thirteen years of suffering and degradation that I again recognised that there are some things that have to be done, no matter what the cost may be. With this reflection, and with the knowledge that he felt probably little pain, certainly no fear, Robert Grenfell's friends, among whom I am sorrowfully proud to count myself, may—indeed must—be content.

[1] Charles (Karl) Neufeld (1856–1918). A Prussian explorer captured by the Khalifa in 1887 and kept in chains until he was found by Bennet Burleigh, special correspondent of the *Daily Telegraph*, and released after Omdurman.

The Lancers remained in possession of the dearly-bought ground. There was not much to show that there had been a desperate fight. A quarter of a mile away nothing would have been noticed. Close to, the scene looked like a place where rubbish is thrown, or where a fair has recently been held. White objects, like dirty bits of newspaper, lay scattered here and there—the bodies of the enemy. Brown objects almost the colour of the earth, like bundles of dead grass or heaps of manure, were also dotted about—the bodies of soldiers. Among these were goat-skin water bottles, broken weapons, torn and draggled flags, cartridge cases. In the foreground lay a group of dead horses and several dead or dying donkeys. It was all litter.

We gathered reverently the poor remains of what had but a quarter of an hour before been the soldiers of a great and civilised Empire, and, horrified at their frightful wounds, laid them in a row. The wounded were sent with a small escort towards the river and hospitals. Then we remounted, and I observed, looking at my watch, that it was half-past-nine—only breakfast-time, that is to say, in distant, comfortable England. I daresay it occurred to others who were unhurt that there was yet plenty of time. At any rate, I deferred my thanks until a later hour.

I will not prolong this letter. If I am tired of writing, it reminds me that you may be weary of reading. Were I to continue I could not do justice to the subject, nor you to my efforts. Of the end of the battle, of the entry into Omdurman, and of the fight of the Khalifa I will write to-morrow. If this has amused your leisure, read further; if not, send my letter back unopened.

29 September, 1898

9

Camp Omdurman, 8 September

Let me continue my account, my dear . . ., from the point where I was yesterday reminded that there are limits to your patience and my perseverance. By half-past nine the 21st Lancers were again trotting across the Plain of Omdurman towards the long lines of fugitives who streamed across it. With the experience of the past half-hour in our minds, and with the great numbers of the enemy in our front, it seemed to many that a bloody day lay before us. But we had not gone far when individual Dervishes began to walk towards the advancing squadrons, throwing down their weapons, holding up their hands and imploring mercy. It is doubtful what claim these had to clemency. The laws of war do not admit the right of a beaten enemy to quarter. The victor is not obliged to accept his surrender. Of his charity he may do so, but there is no obligation, provided of course that he make it clear to the suppliant that he must continue to fight. These were savages who had for many years afflicted the Sudan and cumbered the earth. We well knew the mercy they would have offered us had the fortunes of the day been reversed. The soldiers had seen their dead comrades hacked out of all semblance of humanity by the unimaginable ferocity of this same enemy who now asked for quarter, and consequent feeding and medical attendance. And there were some who would have said, 'Take up your arms and fight, for there is no mercy here.'

Yet it seems that those who use the powerful weapons of civilisation—the shrapnel shell, the magazine rifle, and the Maxim gun—can afford to bear all that the wild spearman may do without descending to retaliation. At any rate, I rejoice for the honour of the British cavalry when I reflect that they held their heads very high, and that the regiment that suffered by far the greatest loss took also the greatest number of prisoners.

As soon as it was apparent that the surrender of individuals was accepted the Dervishes began to come in and lay down their arms, at first by twos and threes, then by dozens and finally by scores. Meanwhile, those who were still intent on flight made a wide detour to avoid the cavalry, and streamed past our front at a mile's distance in uninterrupted succession. 'It looked,' to quote an officer's description, 'just like the people hurrying into Newmarket town after the Cambridgeshire.' The disarming and escorting of the prisoners delayed our advance, and many thousands of Dervishes escaped into Omdurman. To harry and annoy the fugitives a few troops were dismounted with carbines, and a constant fire was made on such as did not attempt to come in and surrender. Yet the crowds continued to run the gauntlet, and I myself saw at least twenty thousand men make good their escape from the field. Many of these were still ready to fight, and replied to our fire with bullets, fortunately at very long range. It would have been madness for two hundred Lancers to have galloped in among such masses, and we had to be content with the results of the carbine fire. The need of a fresh cavalry brigade was apparent. I could not help thinking of my Frontier friends, and of the effect which three smart regiments of Bengal Lancers would have produced. I write from the military and technical point of view. From any other it was evident that there had been enough killing that day.

Meanwhile the Sirdar, having made his army face nearly west, and having repulsed the attack of the Dervish left under Osman Sheikh-ud-Din, continued to advance away from the river, driving the Dervishes before him. But at about twelve o'clock he shut up his glasses and, remarking that the enemy had had 'a good dusting', reverted to his previous intention of marching on Omdurman. This second attempt was in every way successful. The Dervishes were now thoroughly beaten. Their whole army had suffered great loss. All had been engaged. All had been defeated. To explain the movement briefly and clearly rather than correctly—the army which was advancing in line westwards suddenly went fours left and marched south in column, leaving the enemy to continue their flight at their pleasure and discretion.

At about two o'clock, and three miles from Omdurman, the whole force halted to rest by the banks of a khor. You will ask me to explain what a khor is. It is simply a hollow. When these hollows lie close to the flood Nile the waters of the river flow up them and give them the appearance of tributaries, whereas they are just the reverse. They are, indeed, similar to the subsidiary canals of an irrigation system. In the Punjab and in other parts of India the result is produced by artificial means. But the Nile is a natural irrigation system, and has found out all the engineering devices for itself. Whatever your idea of the khors may be, I can assure you that they are cool and convenient drinking-places.

To this khor the Lancers also made their way, and the thirsty horses plunged their noses in the water. The scene was a strange one. You must imagine a five hundred yards stretch of the Suez Canal. On the banks are crowds of men and animals. The whole of the British Infantry Division fills one side. Multitudes of khaki-clad men are sitting in rows on the slopes. Hundreds are standing by the brim or actually in the red, muddy water, drinking deeply. Two or three dead animals lying in the shallows show that the men must be thirsty rather than particular. Everywhere waterbottles are being filled. It is the Nile that has come into the desert to refresh the tired animals and weary men—the Nile, which is the soul of the whole story, the spirit of the Sudan drama.

At four o'clock the march on Omdurman was resumed. The Egyptian cavalry, the 21st Lancers and the Camel Corps moved round the outskirts of the city, everywhere obstructed and delayed by the surrender of hundreds of prisoners. The infantry, the Sudanese in front, and the Sirdar at their head, entered the town. At first the route lay through the suburbs. A few shots were fired at the troops as they marched through the maze of mud houses, but no resistance was encountered. All the city was deserted and silent; not a Dervish was to be seen. Presently three men advanced slowly to meet the victorious General. They knelt in the roadway and presented him with the keys of the city itself and of the various public buildings —the prison and the arsenal. He accepted their surrender and spoke words of peace. Rising swiftly, they shouted out the good news, and thereupon from every house men, women and children appeared in the joy of relief from fear.

The march continued. Arrived at the great wall which divides the city proper from its suburbs the advance was checked. Though the wall had been breached in many places by the gunboats there were signs of resistance and many armed Dervishes were gathered on the parapets. It became necessary for the Maxim guns and a battalion of Sudanese to clear these defenders from the wall. But there was very little spirit in them, and a few minutes' firing sufficed.

Then the Sirdar rode towards the prison. The key would not fit the great door. The General, first and almost alone, rode through a narrow passage among the houses to a smaller entrance. This he was able to open, and the prisoners, over one hundred in number, were set at liberty. Of their names and conditions I will not write, because you will read these things in the newspapers. But the whole incident was intensely dramatic, and those who saw it carried away with them an impression which will live fresh and vivid in their minds for some years.

Meanwhile, behind the General came the army. On a broad front they entered the city and fired occasional volleys and, receiving occasional shots in return, they marched through Omdurman from end to end and returned to the suburbs to camp for the night.

Thus the occupation of Omdurman was accomplished, and only one sad and terrible accident marred the triumph. While the Sirdar with four guns with a battalion of infantry was taking possession of the ruins of the Mahdi's Tomb the red flag of the Headquarters Staff attracted the attention and drew the fire of two guns which had been left outside the town. I am told that their orders justify their action, and that they only carried out the intructions which the Sirdar had given. At any rate these facts are clear. Three shells burst in quick succession over the Staff and soldiers in the square in front of the Tomb. Another screamed overhead. Immediately everyone hurried from the spot in astonishment and alarm. But Mr Hubert Howard, one of the correspondents of *The Times* newspaper, who was in the upper room of the Khalifa's house, which adjoined the Tomb, was killed by a fifth shell before he could follow.

Mr Hubert Howard was a man of some reputation, and of much greater promise. The love of adventure had already led him several times to scenes of war and tumult. In 1895 he passed the Spanish lines in Cuba, and for six weeks fought and was hunted with the Cuban insurgents, whose privations and dangers he shared, and whose cause he afterwards pleaded warmly. At this time I was, as you know, with the Spanish forces witnessing their operations, and the fact that we had been on opposite sides proved a bond of union. Thereafter I saw him frequently. His profession—that of the Law—gave him more opportunities for travelling than fall to the lot of a subaltern of horse. On the outbreak of the Matabele War he hurried to South Africa, and in the attack on Sekombo's Kraal in the autumn of 1896 he acted as adjutant of Robertson's Cape Boys, and displayed military qualities which left no doubt in the minds of those who saw that he should have been a soldier, not only for his own sake, but for that of the army. Having, on his own initiative, captured a steep and nearly precipitous hill, which proved of considerable tactical value, he was severely wounded in the ankle. He refused to leave the field, and continued till the end of the day to drag himself about, directing and inspiriting his men. His services on this occasion, not less than his known abilities, obtained for him the position of Secretary to Lord Grey. The recrudescence of trouble in Mashona-land and Matabeleland in 1897 led him again to the field, and in many minor engagements—those unheeded skirmishes by which unknown men build up our Empire—he added to his reputation as a soldier and as a man.

On his return to England he passed without difficulty the needful examinations for admission to the Bar, and had been duly called. But war was in his blood. The great military expedition preparing on the Nile fascinated his imagination. His literary powers were known. He proceeded to Egypt a month ago—only a month ago—as joint correspondent of *The Times* with Colonel Rhodes.

I need not tell you how pleasant it was to ride with him on our long march up from the Atbara river, of the arguments and discussions which arose, of the plans for the future which were formed. You know how many times a week energetic and virile youth conquers the world in anticipation. You are familiar with the good fellowship of a camp, and know that the best of friends are made in the open air and when peril of life impends or exists.

A close and warm acquaintance was formed between him and the officers of the 21st Lancers. With their squadrons he witnessed the reconnaissance of Kerreri on the 1st of September. With all of us he rode out the charge on the morning of the 2nd. One of the first to force his way through the enemy's lines, he was the first to ride up and offer his congratulations to the colonel. But the firing behind the ridge attracted him, and as he aspired to share all the dangers he rode off in search of new adventure.

Of the occupation of Omdurman I saw nothing, for the cavalry hung on the flanks of the city until the night was far advanced, nor was it until eleven o'clock that we returned, hungry ourselves, and with weary horses, to bivouac near the 2nd British Brigade. There it was I heard the news. At first it seemed incredible. But there are no limits to the devilish ingenuity of malicious fortune, and the truth became certain that the man who had passed through many dangers, and who had that morning escaped unhurt from a charge where the casualties reached twenty-five per cent, had been killed by a British shell, the victim of an accident.

I would pay some tribute to his memory if words were of any avail. He was so brave a man that pity seems almost an insult, and the feeling grows that he will not have minded, whatever may lie beyond this world. It is of the type that I write. He was representative of those young men who, with famous names, and belonging to the only true aristocracy the world can now show, carry their brains and enthusiasm to the farthest corners of our wide Empire and infuse into the whole body the energy and vigour of progress. That force which in the national life of France and Germany is directed solely to military, and in the United States solely to commercial, enterprises animates in our fortunate state all parts of the public service. Seeking for roads by which to advance the commonweal, men like Howard spread to our farthest provinces. Their graves, too, are scattered. His lies in the desert near the city of Omdurman. Thither his brother correspondents carried his body on the morning after the action, and General Hunter, passing at the moment, halted a Sudanese brigade to pay a last compliment to courage and resolution.

The complete destruction and dispersal of the Dervish army and the capture of their capital was accomplished with the loss of under five hundred soldiers. The great host which had risen in the morning confident of victory and nothing doubting were scattered in flight or death before night. Many thousand bodies lay about the plain and all along the line of retreat. The Khalifa, fearing the retribution which he was conscious of having deserved, fled on a swift camel, and with a small following made good his escape, using a route where the wells were small and far between. And the Sirdar, thoroughly satisfied with the issue of the event and wearied by the anxieties of the day, went to sleep in peace and security in the city of Omdurman.

I will write to you tomorrow if time allows, and tell you of the hoisting of the British flag, and of the scenes which the field of battle displayed. But I will not tell you all the horrors, as the taste for realism is one which should not be greatly encouraged. The desire to hear about dreadful things and the desire to see them are, after all, akin. Who shall say that the desire to do them is not also in the relationship? There will, however, be horrors enough.

29 September, 1898

10

Camp Omdurman, 9 September

My dear . . ., there has been such a rush of facts lately that my pen has proved a very insufficient channel to convey them to you. The Nile at flood time overflows its banks, and millions of tons of red, magic water that might have made the sandy, barren desert green and lively are lost and wasted in purposeless outlets, or pour forgotten to the sea. I do not venture to make the similitude 'march on all fours' to compare your mind to the desert, my facts to the vivifying mud. Permit me only to observe that much has happened which I have been unable to see, and that I have seen much that I cannot for various reasons set down here. You must not look on this correspondence as an attempt to tell the story, much less record the history of the campaign. I only write you letters which, because they contain the impressions of the moment, may characterise with some dashes of local colour the picture which the telegrams have created in your brain.

The last two letters I wrote you were about the battle of Khartoum. They contained mainly what I saw myself. Much that was worthy of study and attention you will not find therein. For a clear account of the brilliant manoeuvres of General Macdonald's brigade, of the capture of the Khalifa's black flag, of the skilful handling of the Egyptian cavalry on the extreme right, and of the wonderful charges of the Baggara Horse when they realised that 'all was lost except honour', you must read the reports of the five and twenty distinguished journalists who accompanied the army. But I think my account had carried you in some fashion safely through the day to the bivouac of the very weary but victorious army in the outskirts of Omdurman.

At about ten o'clock at night the 21st Lancers picketed their horses near the 2nd British Brigade, and being too tired to go to sleep at once I prowled off in search of information. The headquarters camp was very silent. On a native bed, his slumbers ensured and protected by a sentry, lay the Sirdar in well-deserved repose. A few yards away Colonel Wingate was stretched on the ground busily writing by an uncertain light the telegram announcing the victory.

In the background stood a strange figure—a pale-faced man with a ragged red beard and whiskers, clad in a blue-and-white Dervish jibba or smock. He spoke continuously in a weak voice and indifferent English. A native sergeant was busy about his feet with a hammer. There was an occasional clink. The clink explained matters. This was Charles Neufeld, thirteen years the Khalifa's prioner, having his fetters knocked off. There were two sets of leg-irons. The smaller—with links about an inch each way—he had worn ever since he was captured in 1885. The larger—I could just lift the shackle with one hand—he had worn for two years only. Three enormous iron rings were about each ankle. They could break the coupling chains, but the rings had to remain till the morning. He talked volubly. The remark that seems most worthy to record was this: 'I have forgotten how to walk.' I thought of the Bastille prisoner in *A Tale of Two Cities*.

The news obtainable on the night of 2 September at headquarters—after all the fount of knowledge—was briefly this. The troops had marched through Omdurman from end to end. They would occupy it in the morning. The Khalifa and the remains of his army had fled, leaving about ten thousand dead on the field. The survivors of various factions were fighting among themselves in the city, and would be 'dealt with' at daylight. Our loss was under five hundred officers and men. All this seeming satisfactory I returned to my squadron, and having supped agreeably on sausages and jam, made the fitting acknowledgments to Providence and went to bed, or rather to ground.

Early the next morning orders reached the 21st Lancers to move round to the south side of Omdurman and remain there in observation during the day. It fell to my lot to be sent to make inquiries as to the condition and wants of the officers and men, wounded the day before, and whom we had not seen since they rode or were carried bleeding and in pain from the scene of the charge. After some searching I found the barges which contained the wounded. In spite of circumstances they were all in good spirits. Colonel Rhodes was there, propped up against the railing of a barge with a bullet through his shoulder, but brave and cheery as ever, the life and soul of the hospital as formerly of the camp. Sentenced to death by the Boers, he had been shot by the Dervishes. Truly he has suffered many things at the hands of the low-grade races of Africa. But he has laughed and lived through all his misfortune.

We had heard that Lieutenant Nesham had lost his left hand, and it was with relief that I learned that it might be saved. He told me of his return to camp from the field. He was bleeding terribly. Brinton, himself in like plight, had seen him, had managed, though his arm was useless, to get a tourniquet from his pocket, and had made a soldier put it on Nesham's arm, explaining the method to the man. This had saved Nesham's life. Otherwise, said the doctors, he would probably have bled to death. These are the sort of facts that brighten the picture of war with beautiful colours, till from a distance it looks almost magnificent, and the dark background and dirty brown canvas are scarcely seen.

Nothing of historic importance happened on 3 September. You know the tidying-up that follows an action. There were, of course, funerals, chiefly of soldiers who had died of their wounds. The others had already been interred. The long wail of the Dead March sounded, not for the first time, by the banks of the Nile, and a silent column of slow-pacing British soldiers accompanied a yet more silent row of bodies—to their last resting-place. On an eminence that overlooks the hazy desert, the green trees of Khartoum, and the mud labyrinth of Omdurman, and before which the majestic river sweeps with the cool sound of waters, a new churchyard appeared. The piles of reddish stones, and the protecting crosses which the living raised as a last tribute to those who had paid the bill for all the fun and glory of the game, will not, I think, be their only or their most enduring monument. The destruction of a state of society which had long become an anachronism—an insult as well as a danger to civilisation; the liberation of the great waterway; perhaps the foundation of an African India; certainly the settlement of a long account; these are cenotaphs which will excite the interest and the wonder of a not ungrateful posterity.

The 4th of September—the anniversary of the French Republic—may become memorable for another great event. Detachments of officers and men from every regiment, British and Egyptian, were convoyed across the Nile in the gunboats and steamers to take part in the Gordon Memorial Service, and to witness the hoisting of the British flag amid the ruins of Khartoum. You will have read full accounts of what happened, and I need not describe how the little red flag of the Khedive and a great Union Jack—four times as big—

were run up the staffs while the officers saluted and the men presented arms; how the band played the Egyptian national anthem and 'God save the Queen'; and how the Sirdar called for three cheers for Her Majesty and for the occasion. We are a sober and phlegmatic stock, yet the dramatic appeals to most of us at times, and you may well believe that the response was earnest and hearty. And some there were who cheered because of a victory over men; some in the exultation of the conquest of territory; some that a heavy debt had been heavily paid; and others that the war was over, and they would presently return home. But, for my part, I raised my voice and helmet in honour of that persevering British people who, often affronted, often checked, often delayed, usually get their own way in the end.

The memorial service followed, and the solemn words of the English Prayer Book were read in that distant yet historic garden. A great man, a Christian and a soldier, a gentleman as well as a General, had perished in former days. Now here were his country-men, who had travelled far and through many dangers, come to do him honour, to complete his work, and over his unknown grave, on the scene of his famous death, to pay the only tributes of affection and respect which lie in human power. The ceremony was duly fulfilled. And now the British people may, through their Ministers and agreeably with the wishes of the Sovereign, tell some stone-mason to bring his hammer and chisel and cut on the pedestal of Gordon's statue in Trafalgar Square the significant, the sinister, yet the not unsatisfactory word, 'Avenged.'

Would you have me write more today? I think I will assume that you have read enough. The battlefield will keep—despite its occu-pants—till tomorrow. Thither I will then conduct you. But you must not forget to bring a bottle of eucalyptus oil.

6 October, 1898

II

CAMP OMDURMAN, 10 September

I suppose it will interest you, as it did me, to learn about the appearance of the battlefield after all the fighting was over. I feel certain that any attempt I may make to depict the horrible sights it presented will differ from the reality as a shadow does from the substance. Besides, however accurately and vividly I were able to portray the scene, I can not—thank Heaven—recall the smell, and your impressions must needs be imperfect without that dreadful accessory. So that while I am not desirous of making a second visit myself I need not shrink from inflicting on you some account of my first.

First of all, let me explain roughly the shape of the field. The Nile lies north and south. Around a mud village by its left bank, and facing mainly west, was the zareba of the British and Egyptian armies. About a mile on the right of this, the Kerreri Ridge ran from the river and at right angles to it. About a mile to the left was another similar ridge, which I have hitherto called Heliograph Hill, but which in future will be known as Lancer's Hill. The river and the two ridges frame three sides of the picture. On the fourth side the plain trails away into the mirage and towards distant hills which do not concern us. Within this wide tract of country there lie, perhaps, eleven thousand bodies. Without this tract there are a few scattered hundreds—the victims of the cavalry charge, of chance bullets, or of the pursuit.

On 5 September, three days after the action, I rode with Lord Tullibardine,[1] of the Egyptian cavalry, to examine the scene. Our road lay by the khor, whereat the victorious army had watered in the afternoon of the 2nd. Thence across the sandy-rock-strewn plain to the southern slopes of Heliograph Hill. And so we came at once on to

[1] John George Murray, Marquess of Tullibardine (1871–1942). Served as a Lieutenant in the Royal Horse Guards 1898. Awarded DSO, 1898.

the ground over which the 21st Lancers had charged. Its peculiar formation was the more apparent at a second view. Looking from the spot where we had wheeled into line and begun to gallop, it was scarcely possible to believe that a deep khor or nullah, to use the Indian expression, ran right across what appeared to be smooth and unobstructed plain. An advance of a hundred yards revealed the trap, and displayed a long ditch with rocky sides, steeply sloping, about 5 ft in depth and perhaps 20 ft wide. In this trench lay about a dozen bodies of Dervishes, half-a-dozen dead donkeys, and a litter of goatskin water-bottles, Dervish saddles and broken weapons. The level ground beyond was spotted with corpses. Some had been buried where they fell by their friends in the city, and their places were indicated by little mounds of lighter-coloured earth. Half-a-dozen horses, stripped of saddles and bridles, made a brown jumble in the background. In the centre a red and white lance pennon flying from a stick marked the grave of the fallen Lancers. And that was all. Yet the place may be remarkable. At any rate, a great many officers of all regiments and arms had been to visit it.

We rode on. We climbed the ridge of Heliograph Hill, following almost the same route as that of the 'white flagmen' three days previously. At the crest of the ridge the village and the outline of the zareba came into sight, and it was evident that we had now reached the spot where the Dervish column had come into the artillery fire. All over the ground—on the average three yards apart—were dead men, clad in the white and patched smocks of faithful Dervishes. Three days of burning sun had done their work. The bodies were swollen to almost gigantic proportions. Twice as large as living men, they appeared in every sense monstrous. The more advanced hardly resembled human beings, but rather great bladders such as natives use to float down the Nile on. Frightful gashes scarred their limbs, and great black stains, once crimson, covered their garments. The smell redoubled the horror.

We galloped on. A strong hot wind blew from the west across the great plain and hurried, foul and tainted, to the river. Keeping to windward of the thickest clusters, we picked our way, and the story of the fight unfolded itself. Here was where the artillery had opened on the swarming masses. Men had fallen in little groups of five or six to each shell. Nearer to the zareba—about eight hundred yards— the musketry had begun to tell, and the dead lay evenly scattered about—one every ten yards. Two hundred yards further the full force of the fire, artillery, Maxims and rifles, had burst on them. In places desperate rushes to get on at all costs had been made by devoted, fearless men. In such places the bodies lay so thickly as to hide the ground. Occasionally there were double layers of this hideous covering. Once I saw them lying three deep. In a space not exceeding a hundred yards square more than four hundred corpses lay festering. Can you imagine the postures in which man, once created in the image of his Maker, had been twisted? Do not try, for were you to succeed you would ask yourself, with me: 'Can I ever forget?'

I have tried to gild war, and to solace myself for the loss of dear and gallant friends, with the thought that a soldier's death for a cause that he believes in will count for much, whatever may be beyond this world. When the soldier of a civilised power is killed in action his limbs are composed and his body is borne by friendly arms reverently to the grave. The wail of the fifes, the roll of the drums, the triumphant words of the Funeral Service, all divest the act of its squalour, and the spectator sympathises with, perhaps almost envies, the comrade who has found this honourable exit. But there was nothing *dulce et decorum* about the Dervish dead. Nothing of the dignity of unconquerable manhood. All was filthy corruption. Yet these were as brave men as ever walked the earth. The conviction was borne in on me that their claim beyond the grave in respect of a valiant death was as good as that which any of our countrymen could make. The thought may not be original. It may happily be untrue. It was certainly most unwelcome.

The incidents of the battle might be traced by the lines and patches of the slain. Here was where Macdonald's brigade, three artillery batteries and several Maxim guns had repulsed the Khalifa's attack. A great heap of corpses lay round the spot where the black flag had been captured. There was where the brigade had faced about to meet Ali Wad Holu and his ten thousand warriors. There again was where the Baggara Cavalry had made their last splendid charge to certain death. The white-clad bodies of the men were intermingled with the brown and bay horses, so that this piece of the field looked less white-speckled than the rest. They had ridden straight at the solid line of bayonets and in the teeth of a storm of projectiles. Every man had galloped at full speed, and when he fell he shot many lengths in front of his horse, rolling over and over—destroyed, not conquered by machinery. At such sights the triumph of victory faded on the mind and a mournful feeling of disgust grew stronger. All this was bad to see, but worse remains behind; after the dead, the wounded. The officer or soldier who escapes from the field with a wound has a claim on his country. To the private it may mean a pension. To the officer a gratuity, perhaps a 'mention in despatches', certainly advancement in his profession. The scar may even,when the sting has departed, be a source of pride—an excuse to retell the story. To soothe the pain there are anaesthetics. To heal the injury the resources of science are at hand. It was otherwise with the Dervish wounded.

There may have been wounded Dervish among the heaps of slain. The atmosphere forbade approach. There certainly were many scattered about the plain. We approached these cautiously, and pistol in hand examined their condition. Lord Tullibardine had a large water-bottle. He dismounted and gave a few drops to each till all was exhausted. You must remember that this was three days after the fight, and that the sun had beaten down mercilessly all the time. Some of the wounded were very thirsty. It would have been a grateful sight to see a large bucket of clear, cool water placed before each shaking feverish figure. That, or a nameless man with a revolver and a big bag of cartridges, would have seemed merciful. The scenes were pathetic. Where there was a shady bush four men had crawled to die. Someone had spread a rag on the thorns to increase the shade. Three of the unfortunate creatures had attained their object. The fourth survived. He was shot through both legs. The bullet—a Martini-Henry bullet—had lodged in the right knee-cap. The whole limb was stiffened. We gave him a drink. You would not think such joy could come from a small cup of water. Tullibardine examined his injury. Presently he pulled out his knife, and after much probing and cutting extracted the bullet—with the button-hook. I have seen, and shall see perhaps again, a man with a famous name worse employed.

Would you be further sickened with the horrors of the field? There was a man that had crawled a mile in three days, but was yet two miles from the river. He had one foot. The other remained behind. I wonder if he ever reached the water he had struggled so hard to attain. There was a man with both legs shattered. He had dragged himself along in a sitting posture, making perhaps four hundred yards a day. The extraordinary vitality of these poor wretches only prolonged their torments. Another had reached the water and had died at its brim. Let us hope he had his drink first. All this was three days after the action. Yet on 9 September, when a week had passed, there were still a few wounded who had neither died nor crawled away, but continued to suffer. How had they lived? It is not possible that they could have existed so long without food and water. The women and the disarmed population of Omdurman had been busy. Many hundreds not quite helpless had dragged themselves off and died all along the line of retreat. Those who were from the country round Omdurman had succour from their relations or neighbours. But it was bad for the man who had come from afar and had no friends. The women would, perhaps, spare him a few drops of water— enough to help him through the day—but if he were a stranger they would do no more. Thus it was that these painful and shocking cases occurred.

Let us get back to camp. There is nothing to be gained by dallying on the field—unless you are anxious to become quite callous, so that no imaginable misery which can come to flesh will ever move you again. I have writ somewhat in these letters to you of vengeance and of the paying of a debt. It has been said that the Gods forbade vengeance to mankind because they reserved for themselves so delicious and intoxicating a drink, and it may well be that vengeance is sweet. But one should not drain the cup quite to the bottom. The dregs are sometimes filthy tasting. In any case a surfeit should be avoided.

So, as the haze of the desert deepened into the gloom of the night and the blurred outlines of the distant hills faded altogether from the view, we rode back to camp—'home to Omdurman', and left the field of battle to its silent occupants. There they lie, those valiant warriors of a false faith and of a fallen domination, their only history preserved by their conquerors, their only monument their bones— and these the drifting sand of the desert will bury in a few short years. Three days before I had seen them rise eager, confident, resolved. The roar of their shouting had swelled like the surf on a rocky shore. The flashing of their blades and points had displayed their numbers, their vitality, their ferocity. They were confident in their strength, in the justice of their cause, in the support of their religion. Now only the heaps of corruption in the plain and fugitives dispersed and scattered in the wilderness remained. The terrible machinery of scientific war had done its work. The Dervish host was scattered and destroyed. Their end, however, only anticipates that of the victors, for Time, which laughs at Science, as Science laughs at Valour, will in due course contemptuously brush both combatants away. Yet it may happen in some distant age, when a mighty system of irrigation has changed the desolate plain of Omdurman into a fertile garden, and the mud hovels of the town have given place to the houses, the schools and the theatres of a great metropolis, that the husbandman, turning up a skull amid the luxuriant crop, will sapiently remark: 'There was aforetime a battle here.' Thus the event will be remembered.

6 October, 1898

Camp Omdurman, 11 September

This place is rapidly becoming unfashionable, my dear. . ., All the *élite* have departed with remarkable swiftness to more comfortable, if less historic, scenes. The battalions of the British division are despatched daily, dropping down the swift stream of the Nile in the great sailing barges called gyassas. The distinguished personages who gathered, like vultures, for the battle, have dispersed themselves to digest their glory and anticipate their decorations. The September shooting season is over at Omdurman. The Nile yachting week is now in full swing. Everyone is dispersing. The words 'Khalifa' and 'Khartoum' may now be handed over to the historian and the politician, the army 'having no further need of their services'.

The Sirdar himself has gone further south to Fashoda with two battalions, two Maxims and a battery on board his gunboat flotilla, leaving his congratulations, which are pouring along the telegraph, to accumulate at 'Wire Head'. There are many rumours about Fashoda at which, should I record them, your superior wisdom would be amused. The only fact appears to be that the Dervish gunboat *Bordaine* was sent recently by the Khalifa to reconnoitre towards Fashoda and returned from its quest with nearly a hundred men wounded by the small-bore bullets of a civilised force which was in occupation. Whether this force be French or Belgian, and whether they will go peaceably or protest violently, I do not know, so will not predict. But of this I think you may be certain that the Battle of Fashoda will be fought in Westminster, that tempers rather than lives will be lost, and ink rather than blood expended.

The 21st Lancers started on their return march on the 6th and, remembering the tediousness of the journey up, you may rejoice that you are not compelled to toil down the weary miles to the Atbara. I, being detailed for transport work, remain behind and propose to keep your imagination, if you will allow me, as a companion. Then,

130

1. A group of War Correspondents on board a Nile steamer heading south, 1898. WSC is second from the left, middle row

2. WSC as a prisoner of war, Pretoria, 1899

3. WSC as Tory candidate for Oldham, 1899

when everything is satisfactorily wound up, we can go down the river together, and shall doubtless reach civilisation in time for the Autumn Handicaps.

The Sirdar paid the Lancers the compliment of coming to see them off. Colonel Martin formed up his regiment in mass and made the prescribed salutes. The Sirdar rode forward. I give you the verbatim report of his speech, which will show you that he is a man of deeds. He said:

'Colonel Martin, officers and men of the 21st Lancers, I am very proud to have had you under my command. The fine charge you made the other day will long go down to history in the annals of your regiment. I will not keep you any longer, but I hope you will have a pleasant march down to the Atbara.'

Whereupon the Lancers gave three cheers for a victorious general and retired in column of troops from the right. I watched the regiment ride away across the plain—a brown moving column of men, with a cloud of dust drifting towards the river. Before them the outline of Heliograph Hill—they say it will be called Lancer's Hill for the future—was silhouetted black against the evening sky. Their road led them across the scene of their charge, and perhaps you will allow me to revert for a space to that memorable event.

The glamour of a cavalry charge impresses a wide public. Thousands of people who care little, and know less, of the more intricate and delicate operations of war are attracted by the dramatic aspect which such an incident presents. This keen interest will perhaps call forth a great deal of unmeasured eulogy and of extravagant expression. It is not fitting that those sentiments of duty and patriotism which rise from the altar and the hearth should descend to the music hall and the pothouse. Once praise oversteps the strict line of truth it becomes fulsome and ridiculous. It may be worthwhile for a moment to consider dispassionately what the Lancers dared and what they did. I may claim to write with both knowledge and impartiality since, as you know, I was myself a participant in the charge without being a member of the regiment.

First of all, let us consider whether the charge was necessary. Colonel Martin's orders were to clear the ground between the army and Omdurman, and to endeavour to cut off the flying Dervishes from that city. As he advanced to carry out these orders he found his path barred by a formed body of the enemy. These suddenly opened an intense fire. I shall submit that there was no choice but to charge or gallop away. The definite orders excluded the latter alternative. In any case there was no time to argue. At that close range it was impossible so heavy a fire could be ineffective.

He ordered the regiment to charge. Immediately it became apparent that the enemy's force was unexpectedly great—indeed, that it was ten times as great as had been believed. It was then quite impossible to turn back. It was not even desirable to do so. The event proved that the two thousand five hundred Dervishes were not a force beyond the powers of the cavalry. The charge was pushed home. In this I see nothing splendid, nothing magnificent, nothing that the disciplined cavalry of any European nation might not reasonably be expected to perform.

Now for the achievement. If the number of the enemy was ten times as great as was expected, the results were proportionately increased. Two thousand five hundred unshaken and formed infantry, famous for the use of their weapons, famous for their valour and contemptuous of cavalry, were overthrown, ridden through and finally driven from the ground. This was due, I most firmly believe, to the excellence of the drill, which enabled the regiment to strike the enemy in a solid wall of men and horses. And the excellence of the drill was due to the excellent individual qualities of the troopers. I do not think that it required any high order of courage merely to charge, but the manner in which the charge was delivered is worthy of the highest praise, and proved conclusively that the soldiers were men of great calmness, determination and capacity. The fact that they rode through an enemy whose closely packed line was more than twelve deep attests that they were also men of considerable physical strength.

It was afterwards that the heroic element began to appear. The extraordinary celerity with which the squadrons reformed, the soldierly eagerness of the troopers to charge again, their steady and effective musketry when they were presently dismounted, showed that a loss of nearly 25 per cent had not in the least impaired their *morale* or disturbed their equanimity. The observer might realise 'that strength and majesty with which the British soldier fights'. No savagery disgraced their victory. No excitement ruffled their serenity. After the charge they remained what they had been before it—simply good and gallant men, well trained to war, ready and willing to obey any orders they might receive. Their numbers, indeed, were weakened, but the strength of the regiment, since it had become more terrible by its experience, was unaltered. And what is the material from which such soldiers are made? They were specimens of the warlike Briton at his best—the six-year-old British soldier. These were no boys following their officers in blind ignorance. They were no conscripts marched in a row to their death. Every man was an intelligent human being who thought for himself, acted for himself, took pride in himself and knew his own mind. Spontaneity, not mere passive obedience, was the characteristic of their charge. They exhibited the discipline of a pack of hounds, not that of a flock of sheep.

We may now discern the reason why this charge—which did not greatly influence the fortunes of the battle—was of perhaps as great value to the Empire as the victory itself. You may have heard of— I may perhaps have seen—occasions when a young, raw British regiment, broken with fever and rotten with disease, has not shown those intrinsic fighting virtues without which no race can long continue to rule. Perhaps there have been moments when we have doubted whether those qualities which enabled us to conquer are unimpaired; whether the blood of the race circulates as healthy and as free as in days gone by. All great empires have been destroyed by success and triumph. No empire of the past has enjoyed so great a measure of that fatal glory as the British. The patriot who boasts his faith in our destiny may often anxiously look back, fearing, almost expecting, to discover signs of degeneration and decay. From the study of the men—I mean the troopers—who charged on 2 September 'the weary Titan' may rise refreshed and, contemplating the past with calmness, may feel confidence in the present and high hope in the future. We can still produce soldiers worthy of their officers—and there has hitherto been no complaint about the officers. It was with such satisfying, if self-satisfied, reflections that I watched the Lancers trail away towards the fateful hill, watched them climb the ridge and disappear in the reeking plain beyond. It was the regiment's baptism of fire and steel. They have no long list of battles on their appointments and their crests. They have no proud traditions handed down from wars in France, in Spain and in the Low Countries. But they will now inscribe the word 'Khartoum' as the first honour on the regimental arms. And there will be many who will be quite contented with that. I had meant, my dear . . ., to pass away the afternoon with a visit to the city of Omdurman, but I have kept you so long moralising on cavalry charges and such-like bloody events that we must postpone the expedition till tomorrow.

7 October, 1898

13

Camp Omdurman, 12 September

If this letter fails to amuse you, my dear . . ., it will be another proof that thirteen is an unlucky number. For my part I am so well satisfied at this correspondence having grown so lengthy that I may perhaps be careless of what may happen to its tail. I can easily understand the impatience with which you brook your imagination being detained at Omdurman while great events are taking place elsewhere, and the mud city is no longer the centre of the world's interest. Yet it would not be fair if you were to hurry away after you have tasted the excitement of the battle without in some way sharing the fatigues and monotonies of the war. For that is what the medal hunter does. I would invite you to wait just a little longer, until at least the first rush of neuropathic sybarites is over, and the boats and trains are less crowded. In the meantime we may find something to attract the eye and stir the brain even in this abode of flies, filth and effluvia. Besides, you have not yet become acquainted with the city of Omdurman.

The victorious army lies straggled along the river from the muddy waters of Khor Sambat to the suburbs of the city, a distance of nearly three miles. The southern end of the camp is already among the mud houses. Yet it is a ride of twenty minutes to the Great Wall. The road is as broad as Piccadilly and beaten level by much traffic. On both sides are mud houses. At the end the dome of the Mahdi's Tomb, sorely battered, is conspicuous. About a quarter of a mile from this we reach, on the left, as Baedeker would say, the wall of the city itself. As an obstacle the wall appears most formidable. The stones are well laid in regular courses and the thickness is great. The officers who had toiled with the big forty-pounder guns all the way from London eyed it with disappointed appetite. They had hoped to smash it to pieces. Unfortunately, the foolish people had opened the gates and prevented the fun. It was possible, however, to see the effect of the artillery on the waterside. Here the gunboats had been at work at close and effective range. The results were remarkable. The wall was perhaps 8 ft thick. Great round holes had been made in it. They were as neat and clean as if they had been punched in leather. There was no *debris*. A storming party would not have had to stumble over ruins of bricks and mortar. The impact of the shell had removed everything—disintegrated everything. The wind had blown the powder that remained away. Where there had been an obstacle there was now an open doorway.

Within the wall were many horrible sights. Much killing and the paying-off of old scores had followed the downfall of the Khalifa's power, and preceded the organisation of the new government. It had been a stormy interregnum. Dead bodies of men and women lay about in the streets and in the narrow alleys. Some were the victims of the bombardment, some of the Maxim guns which had been used to clear the walls, but the greater number were a silent statement of the results of the intermittent firing we had listened to on the night of 2 September. The meaning of the recurring rifle shots and occasional volleys that had disturbed, though they could not prevent, our slumbers was now plain.

Outside the wall the houses had been built of mud. Within the wall they were also built of mud. The style of Sudan architecture, though it may boast a pure simplicity, is monotonous and unpleasing. It is an unprofitable land. There are cities, and there are plains, but the cities are cities of mud, and the plains are plains of sand. Desolation, squalor and sterility are the characteristics of the Sudan. It is all worthless. There is only the river—the great waterway. Some thousands of miserable savages may eke out a degraded existence in the riparian belts and the oases. The wise man will keep to his boats. Trade may in time grow up with the desert peoples, and thus the sandy wastes may be 'developed' and their populations 'elevated'. But the operations will be very gradual. Commerce is a plant of slow growth even in the most generous soils, and it never grows more slowly than when the unwise husbandman has tried to fertilise with corpses. Yet it may be said of the Sudan—as of most places—that its future lies before it. Time is a busy workman, and has always some new trick. Who shall say that some day stronger hands than ours shall not spread the river water over the barren plains and make the confluence of the Blue and White Niles the seat of man's happiness and dignity? But of this we may assure ourselves, that the physical must precede the moral, that there must be some wealth before there is any wisdom, and that the time has not yet come when the Khartoum College—with perhaps a chair of Philosophy or Political Economy—need be established in the desert at the expense of the British people. We must irrigate before we educate, and it will be a long time before it is economically worthwhile to do either in the Sudan.

There is, however, my dear . . ., an excellent field for missionary enterprise. The people are ignorant and passionate. They do not love their conquerors. Every unpleasant circumstance will enhance the merit of the action. The flies, the smells, the heat, the bad water, the insufficient food, all the accessories of martyrdom are present. Doubtless we shall soon witness the spectacle of the missionary, regardless alike of ridicule, discomfort and danger, striving in this distant land to preach the Gospel of Peace to the survivors of the war, and to tell them the good tidings the army marched so far to bring.

The Khalifa's house, the Mahdi's Tomb and the arsenal, or 'Beit-el-Amana', as it is called, are situated outside the great Wall of Omdurman. The first is a building of some pretensions. It is conveniently close to the Tomb, and we may imagine the Khalifa repairing thither at frequent intervals for celestial guidance and retailing the results of his visions and prayers to his deluded or sceptical subjects. The house itself was one-storied, but there was an annex which attained to the dignity of two rows of windows. I visited this first, climbing up a narrow but solid staircase, which gave access to the upper room—an apartment about 20 ft square. What its contents may originally have been it is impossible to say. The whole place was picked clean, and nothing had escaped the vigilant eye of the Sudanese plunderer. There was a hole in one of the walls, and the floor and ceiling were spotted with scars. The shell which had caused the damage lay in splinters on the ground. The yellow sublimate of the lyddite shell furred the interior surfaces of the pieces of iron with an evil-smelling powder. For the rest the room was bare.

From the window a view might be obtained of the city. The whole prospect was displayed. Row after row and line on line of mud houses extended on every side. The sight was not inspiring. The ugliness and universal squalor jarred unpleasantly on the eye and fancy. Yet we may imagine the Khalifa, only a week before, standing at this very window and looking over the homes of the thousands he ruled, proud of their numbers, confident in their strength, ignorant of their degradation. It was true Mahmoud was prisoner and his army scattered. It was true the accursed infidels had crawled with their host to the south of Shabluka, so that they were but thirty miles away. It was true that their steamers and cavalry would be at the gates before many hours had passed. Of this and all this there was no doubt. But the battle was not fought yet. There were fifty thousand faithful Dervishes ready to die or conquer for their dread Lord and for the Prophet of the One God. Surely they should prevail against the Unbeliever, despite his big guns, his little guns, and all his iniquitous contrivances. Surely Allah would not let the True Faith perish, or the Holy Shrine of his Mahdi be defiled. They would be victorious. They would kill these rabble Egyptians—he thought of ways and means—whose backs they had seen so often, and they would roll back to Cairo, as they had done before, the pestilent white man who had come from out of the unknown to annoy them and disturb their peace. And the Khalifa, soothed by such comfortable reflections, remembered that he had that day married a new wife, and turned his thoughts to the house he would build for her when the bricks should be floated across from the Khartoum ruins.

The rest of the Khalifa's house was practically uninjured by the shell fire. It was an extremely good dwelling. The doorway gave access to a central hall paved with black stone, and with rooms and offices opening out on each side. One of these contained a fine large bath, with brass taps for hot and cold water. The other chambers may have been used for sleeping or eating or study, but as they had been stripped of every stick of furniture it was impossible to know. The house had been, at any rate, the abode of one who must have possessed civilised qualities, since he was cleanly and showed some appreciation of the decencies of life. It should never be forgotten that the accounts of the Khalifa and his crimes depend for their truth on the testimony of those who had the strongest motives for compassing his destruction.

From the Khalifa's house I repaired to the Mahdi's Tomb. Your mind will probably be familiar with its shape and architecture. It was much damaged by the shells. The apex of the conical dome had been cut off. Two of the small cupolas were completely destroyed. The dome itself had one enormous and several smaller holes smashed in it. The bright sunlight streamed through these and displayed the interior. Everything was wrecked. Still it was possible to distinguish the railings round the actual sarcophagus and the stone beneath which the body presumably lay. This place had been for more than ten years the most sacred and holy thing that the people of Sudan knew of. Their miserable lives had perhaps been brightened, perhaps in some way ennobled, by the contemplation of something which they did not quite understand, but which they believed exerted some protecting influence. It had gratified that instinctive desire for the mystic which all human creatures possess, and which is perhaps the strongest reason for believing in a progressive destiny and a future state. And we had deliberately destroyed and profaned it. Was this a worthy or a dignified revenge? Of course you will say that the Mahdi was a false prophet. But that only means, my dear . . ., that *you* do not believe him. 'False' is the epithet which all religious sects have applied to all others since the beginning of all things. I have even heard a darker story concerning this Tomb. It is rumoured that the body has since been exhumed and decapitated. But we must not believe this. The civilisation which can direct the shrapnel shell must not war with the dead, or strike at the living through their super-natural beliefs.[1]

The road from the Tomb to the arsenal was crowded with Sudanese soldiers dragging captured cannon from the river batteries to a convenient storage place. The arsenal itself consisted of a large and strongly-built square house standing in a courtyard, surrounded by a high stone wall. Military material of all kinds and of all periods were heaped and littered about. Gatling and Nordenfeldt guns,[2] taken perhaps at the destruction of Hicks Pasha's army, stood near suits of chain armour which a Crusader may once have worn. Spears of all sorts and patterns were piled into great stacks. Here were heaps of Remington rifles.[3] There were battle-axes and javelins. The Krupp and the war drum lay side by side. Among all, and carelessly scattered about, was gunpowder in bags, in barrels, or lying in little black heaps on the ground.

I do not purpose to set down an inventory. Yet the enumeration

[1] The Mahdi's Tomb was desecrated and the corpse decapitated on Kitchener's orders. Churchill is here circumspect, but when he had confirmed his information he was open in his attacks on Kitchener in *The River War*. 'To destroy what was sacred and holy to them was a wicked act. . . .' Churchill was also outraged by the slaughter of Dervish wounded after Omdurman, for which he also blamed Kitchener.

[2] By this time, both Nordenfeldt and Gatling guns were belt-fed, but the earlier models referred to here were probably 'organ-guns', consisting of a row of rifle-barrels fixed side by side, and gravity-fed.

[3] Presumably the 11 mm single-shot version.

of six items may interest you, and may show you how diverse was the collection which years of rapine had gathered into this curious storehouse.

There was a fine Drum-major's staff ornamented with gold and surmounted by the Lion of Abyssinia. This was presumably captured from King John's ill-fated army. There was a wooden provision box containing sardines and other potted meats, which were wrapped up in a sheet of the *Etoile Belge* newspaper bearing the date 24 March, 1894. This had come evidently from the Congo. Perhaps it had belonged to the gay Lothaire. There was an excellent chronometer by a well-known London maker in perfect order, and probably taken from some wrecked ship in the Red Sea. General Gordon's telescope, as bright and clean as the day it was purchased, stood in one of the rooms. On the floor of another lay the bell of the Khartoum Church. Last of all I would notice the Khalifa's carriage.

This vehicle, which may one day grace Madame Tussaud's halls, stood in the courtyard. It was shaped like a victoria, with a prolonged hood which extended over the box-seat and was there supported by two iron bars. It was by a French maker—Erler, Paris—and may or may not have been a present to the Khedive Ismail. The whole turn-out was now covered with gaudily-coloured cloths of various hues. The hood was red outside and flame-coloured yellow inside. The floor was carpeted with puce. The steps and interior seat were lined with violet. The box-seat was cobalt blue. It had evidently been covered with the end of a piece of cloth for across it, in broad white embroidered letters two inches high, the following legend was prominently displayed: '*Superfine broadcloth, made in Germany.*'

The calm assurance of the statement, not less than its incongruity, might well, as Gibbon would say, 'provoke a smile amid the horrors of war.' But other reflections lie behind.

Consider, my dear . . ., how strange and varied are the diversions of an Imperial people. Year after year, and stretching back to an indefinite horizon, we see the figures of the odd and bizarre potentates against whom the British arms continually are turned. They pass in a long procession. The Akhund of Swat, Cetewayo brandishing an assegai as naked as himself, Kruger singing a Psalm of Victory, Osman Digna, the Immortal and the Irrepressible, Theebaw with his umbrella, the Mahdi with his banner, Lobengula gazing fondly at the pages of *Truth*, Prompeh abasing himself in the dust, the Mad Mullah on his white ass and, latest of all, the Khalifa in his Coach of

State. It is like a pantomime scene at Drury Lane. These extraordinary foreign figures, each with his complete set of crimes, horrible customs and 'minor peculiarities' march one by one from the dark wings of Barbarism up to the bright footlights of Civilisation. For a space their names are on the wires of the world and the tongues of men. The Sovereign on his Throne, the Minister in his Cabinet, the General in his tent pronounce or mispronounce their styles and titles. A thousand compositors make the same combination of letters. The unusual syllables become household words. The street-boy bellows them in our ears. The artisan laughs over them at night in his cottage. The child in the nursery is cajoled into virtue or silence by the repetition of the dread accents. And the world audience clap their hands, amused yet impatient, and the Potentates and their trains pass on, some to exile, some to prison, some to death—for it is a grim jest for them—and their conquerors, taking their possessions, forget even their names. Nor will history record such trash.

Perhaps the time will come when the supply will be exhausted and there will be no more royal freaks to conquer. In that gloomy period there will be no more of these nice little expeditions—'the image of European war without its guilt and only twenty-five per cent of its danger'; no more medals for the soldiers, no more peerages for the generals, no more copy for the journalists. The good old times will have passed away, and the most cynical philosopher will be forced to admit that though the world may not be much more prosperous it can scarcely be so merry.

8 October, 1898

14

ATBARA FORT, 16 September

I told you we should get down the river in good time, my dear . . .,
Nor was I wrong. My transport duties collapsed unexpectedly—
indeed, as we have seen all there is to see at Omdurman, I may almost
say conveniently. We are arrived at Atbara, whence you may perhaps
remember the cavalry convoy started exactly a month ago. Much
has happened since then, and there have been some who have not
witnessed the end of the event. We are fortunate. Your imagination,
riding like dull care—the absurdity of the similitude is its own excuse
—behind the horseman, has passed safely through the midst of war,
and I shall shortly return it in as good condition as when I first claimed
it of you. But since you marched up by land some description of
the river journey may not bore you, especially as the voyage down
the Nile in a gyassa is characterised by other features than the scenery.

First of all I must write of a feat of arms which the newspapers in
their exuberance have overlooked. It is only about a private soldier,
who did not know any of the war correspondents, and perhaps, since
he could not tell them, that is the reason his act has passed un-
chronicled, and he himself might have remained 'an unknown man
of valour.' Since I am sure of my facts I am careless to whom you
repeat the story.

As the charging squadrons of the 21st Lancers closed with the
enemy in the action of the 2nd of September, Private Byrne was
struck by a bullet, which passed through his right arm and inflicted
a severe wound. His lance fell from his hand, but he succeeded in
drawing his sword. This delayed him, and he was one of the last men
to get clear of the stabbing and hacking mass of Dervishes alive.
Safety was then in sight. Lieutenant R. F. Molyneux,[1] of the Blues,

[1] Richard Frederick Molyneux (1873-1954). Served in the Sudan
campaign as a Lieutenant in the Royal Horse Guards. Groom-in-waiting
to HM King George V 1919-1936. KCVO, 1935.

141

had however been wounded. Dismounted, disarmed, and streaming with blood, this officer was still endeavouring to make his way through the enemy, and to follow the line of the charge. He was beset on all sides. He perceived Private Byrne, and called on him for help. Whereupon, without a moment's hesitation, Byrne replied, 'All right, sir,' and turning, rode at four Dervishes who were about to kill his officer. His wound, which had partly paralysed his arm, prevented him from grasping his sword, and at the first ineffectual blow it fell from his hand, and he received another wound from a spear in the chest. But his solitary charge had checked the pursuing Dervishes. Lieutenant Molyneux regained his squadron alive, and the trooper, seeing that his object was attained, galloped away, reeling in his saddle. Arrived at his troop his desperate condition was noticed and he was told to fall out. But this he refused for some time to do, urging that he was entitled to remain on duty and have 'another go at them.' At length he was assisted from the field fainting from loss of blood.

When the whole facts of this case are dispassionately considered there will be few who can recall an act of greater devotion or can imagine a braver man than Byrne. The spectacle of this soldier, crippled, practically helpless, riding single-handed to the attack of four Dervishes and back into the hell from which he had once escaped to save his officer will not pale before the finest stories of Antiquity or of Romance. Official recommendations have been made, and we may await with interest their result.[1]

I accompanied the Grenadier Guards down the river. Every night that week had witnessed the departure of one or other of the British battalions. All day long the flotilla of gyassas—great broad-bottomed sailing boats pushed into the middle of the stream. The flowing white canvas was hoisted, and like a flight of enormous birds the whole fleet started for home and comfort with the warm south wind in the shoulder of the sails and the flood Nile pressing six miles an hour at the keel. The pace was swift, yet the current was barely outstripped. Looking at the water the boats seemed motionless. Only the banks slipped past. How easily all the weary miles of march were covered. The strong river was impatient to be rid of the invaders who had disturbed its waters. The farewell cheers of the remaining regiments grew faint and broken. The strains of the Sudanese Band playing 'The British Grenadiers' died away. The mud houses and the

[1] Private Byrne was subsequently awarded the Victoria Cross.

bivouacs on the bank were lost in the distance and in the twilight, and men turned their minds and faces towards a cooler, kinder land wither they would presently return.

It was very strange, going down the river in this pleasant fashion, to watch the camping grounds and watering places pass in quick succession. Already we were near the scene of action. Here was the khor where all had drunk on the day itself. A little lower down, the old zareba we had defended was displayed. The scarlet glint of a lance pennon over Robert Grenfell's grave, and we paid the only tribute in our power—a mournful thought—to the memory of that gallant young officer, of whom as of Young Siward, it may be said:

> 'He only lived but till he was a man;
> The which no sooner had his prowess confirmed
> In the unshrinking station where he fought,
> But like a man he died.'

And so onwards, northwards, homeward, while the night grew dark above the boats and hid them from each other, and the little fires which twinkled on the stern to cook the evening meal alone showed that we drifted in company. Presently the stars came out, and by their light intensified the blackness of the moving lines of bushes on the banks, and increased the glitter of the disturbed waters of the river.

The philosophical reflections which such scenes and surroundings cannot fail to raise in the speculative mind were dispelled by the wind shifting to the east and blowing harder every minute. The sails were pulled down hastily, and none too soon, and the boats were hurriedly brought to rest on the western bank. But the storm was on us. Clouds of dust began to drive across the river, making night hideous and existence hateful. The mouth, nostrils, eyes, and ears were choked with this abominable gravel. It penetrated the clothing, and an odious feeling of grit prevented sleep and strained patience. This, however, was but a prelude. The wind increased. Gradually rain drops began to mingle with the dust. Presently they predominated. Then the rain broke, everything and everybody were speedily drenched. The rain, modifying the dust, covered the soldiers with a coat of mud. Meanwhile the waves of the Nile began to dash over the moored boats, driving their occupants to take shelter among the thorn bushes of the bank. At about twelve o'clock the mast of one of the largest gyassas, an enormous pole nearly 50 ft long, fell with a resounding crash on the ground. Luckily no one obstructed it.

Shouts of unpitied distress were whirled away with clothing and other articles by the fierce tempest. At length towards morning the storm died away, and we prepared to resume our voyage. But the damage was considerable. Besides the dismasted boat two others had sunk near the shore, swamped by the waves, one was struck on a sandbank helpless and hopeless higher up the stream, two had their rudders smashed, and one, the one containing all the regimental trophies—flags, spears, shields, a piece of cannon—had foundered in midstream and was irretrievably lost. Nobody was, however, drowned or injured, so there was much to be thankful for. But it was hard to realise that the river which had caressed us so tenderly in the evening had behaved thus rudely when the lights were out.

It was necessary first of all to raise the two boats which had sunk in shallow water. A strong rope was fastened on to the bows and passed through a block at the masthead of a more fortunate consort. To the end of this rope the muscular energy of a company of stalwart Guardsmen was then applied. I watched the mast anxiously. It bent. For a moment is seemed that it would break, and that we should have but thrown good gyassas after bad. Then the sunken hull began to move, and in a moment the rim of its bulwarks appeared above the waters. As soon as the water inside was thus cut off from the water of the river half a dozen men, black and white, jumped into the swamped boat, naked and shivering in the grey of the morning, and began to bale with tin biscuit boxes. Meanwhile the sunken gyassa was kept at the surface by the tackle fastened on to our mast. (I write 'our' because Lieutenant Crichton's gyassa in which I had the pleasure to voyage was the one entrusted with these salvage operations.) For some time the baling operations appeared to produce but little result other than splashing and rough chaff, but gradually the level of the water inside the boat began to sink below that of the river and the strain on our mast lessened. Presently the wreck began to float of its own buoyancy. At length our assistance became superfluous. Finally all the water was baled out, and the half company whose clothes and stores were thus rescued were invited to get on board again, take possession of their effects—a little damped—and try again the hazards of water transport.

Two or three hours of wind and current brought us to Royan Island. We ought to have reached this place the night before, and should have done so but for the gale. Colonel Hatton and the leading boat had indeed accomplished the passage, and had continued on

144

through the Shabluka cataract. The rest of the fleet tied up for an hour or so to breakfast and to dry their clothes.

Royan Island was the advanced depot of the army at Omdurman. Besides the stores there was considerable hospital accommodation. Rows of big square tents, 'E.P. tents,' as they are called in India—I know not why—had been set up near the palm-trees by the bank. The Red Cross flag was conspicuous. There were a good many sick. I inquired the local death rate. 'Average about two deaths a day' was the answer. Another cemetery was growing by the banks of the Nile. More British soldiers were being 'sunk in Egyptians'. I thought of Rudyard Kipling, and realised that what is true of the ocean may also be applied to the Nile:

> 'If blood be the price of Admiralty
> Lord God we ha' paid it in.'

Our gyassa was among the first to arrive. I watched the landing of the next. It was a difficult and delicate operation. The great boat came down stream with wind and current helping her, and making perhaps ten miles an hour. Suddenly her helm went over, and she headed for the bank. It seemed that a mighty crash impended, but the mud acted as a buffer. There was a padded shock. Two natives sprang out with a rope, twenty Grenadiers seized hold of it. The boat, caught by the force of the river, was swirled off into midstream again. The strain grew. Gradually the pulling men triumphed, and the vessel was drawn into shore and moored securely. So it was with all the others.

At midday the Guards re-embarked, and the fleet began to drift through the Shabluka Pass. You may remember that when the Army came up towards Khartoum this strong position was turned, and as the cavalry participated in the movement I had no opportunity of seeing the gorge of the Shabluka. It is well worth seeing. The Nile, which above the gorge is perhaps a mile across, here narrows to a bare 300 yards. The pace of the streams becomes more rapid. Great swirls and eddies disturb its surface. On either side rise black, broken, and precipitous cliffs. They look like piles of stones thrown carelessly on a roadway. Among them the river winds. Between the barren heights and the water is strip of green bushes and grass. The bright colour seems the more brilliant by contrast with the muddy water and the sombre rocks. It is a forbidding passage. A few hundred riflemen scattered Afridi-wise among the tops of the hills, a few field guns in mud forts by the bank—and the door would be shut. Luckily the Shabluka position can easily be turned—a detour of ten miles will enable troops to avoid the hills. What seems really wonderful is that the Nile has not discovered this too. Why a river should charge a range of mountains and force a way through their rocks when the circle of a few miles would have given a sand bed and an unobstructed channel is difficult to explain. I can only conclude that the gorge of the Shabluka is igneous, not aqueous, and that the Nile found its bed already made by an even mightier hand. The gyassas accomplished the passage of this cataract without misfortune, but not without adventure. At times we grazed a sharp and dangerous rock by a few yards; at others the swirl of the river swept the boat into the bushes of the bank. Once for nearly an hour we circled aimlessly in a whirlpool, enduring—not in silence—the taunts of the more fortunate voyagers who passed swiftly by in great elation. Time brought its revenges, and we enjoyed the satisfaction of seeing them only a little later caught in an eddy, which carried them back far up the gorge.

At length the walls of rock separated and the green strip broadened into the regular Nile belt with the desert behind. At this northern end of the Shabluka Gorge are four Dervish forts. They are well built and form nearly a straight line—three on one bank and one on the other. Each fort has three embrasures, and may, when occupied, have been a formidable defence to the cataract. The embrasures are badly designed and allow no sweep of fire to the guns. Some tactical knowledge was, however, displayed in the construction of the works. They could combine their fire, and the gorge was held on strict tactical principles at the enemy's end. Much care had been devoted to the building of these defences, and we may imagine the doubt and the suspicion of their garrisons when the Khalifa ordered their abandonment. The great guns by which such store was set must be hoisted out and towed back to Omdurman. The forts which had taken so many weeks to build were to be relinquished. Surely all was not well. Yet the Khalifa had said that he would destroy the 'infidel pigs' on the Kerreri Plain, and had he not the counsels of the Mahdi, who stands before the Throne of the True God amid the choicest *houris* of Paradise? It were impious to question. Perchance it was a trap—a stratagem.

After the passage of the Shabluka we drifted uneventfully with the stream. The camp of the 21st Lancers was passed on the morning of the third day. They were still on their long march back to Atbara. Six hours later Metemmeh came into view, and with the evening the boats tied up at the palm grove below Nasri Island, whence I wrote you my third letter on the way up. I will not make you drag out the voyage—for the days were oppressively hot and the sun beat pitilessly down on the scanty coverings which the soldiers might improvise from blankets and waterproof sheets. At daylight on the fifth day we reached the confluence of the Atbara and the Nile, and, landing, camped again on familiar ground.

I would take leave of you here, my dear . . ., were it not that you might think me unceremonious. The journey from Atbara to Cairo I have already described, but as you might find the hours in the train and steamer tedious and dull, I shall try to employ your fancy with some discussion of the meanings which underlie those grave affairs; and this will form the subject of the final letter of this long and varied correspondence.

11 October, 1898

15

Assiout, 20 September

Only one incident, my dear . . ., marked our return journey from the camp at Atbara to civilisation. In great heat and choking dust we again were carried by the Sudan military railway across the desert. Again we reclined, covered with grit and perspiration, on angaribs. Again I marvelled at the courage of the Engineers who could plan and construct a railway through such abominable solitudes.

The whole countenance of the land is terrible. As wide and extensive as the sea, it is less hospitable, and has all its barrenness without any of its beauty. The train plods wearily, making about ten miles an hour, along an apparently endless track. Nothing varies the monotony of the scene. The telegraph posts are the most enlivening feature. Mile after mile slips by—and they are all the same. Hour after hour passes, and all are hot. At intervals we stop at stations, distinguished only by numbers, and consisting of a wooden hut and a signal post.

It was one of these stations—'No 6'—that the incident occurred. And since any incident in the desert is always rare and sometimes welcome, I will set it down. The engine, which had been working more jerkily every minute of the preceding hour, stopped with an ominous and alarming suddenness. Every one got out. Something was wrong. The awful thought that we might perhaps have to wait some twenty hours or so at this attractive spot arose in many minds. Then the worst was known. The engine had broken down. It was in a thoroughly bad condition. Hard work had worn it out. I will not commit myself to technical language. It appeared that everything was loose. The native engine-driver was appalled and perfectly hopeless. It would not work and go forward, he said, whereas before it had worked and gone forward. Undoubtedly there was an accident. But who should say Allah had not some wise purpose? There would not be much delay. Another engine might come, perhaps tomorrow—this last hopefully. And we were all going home.

How dreadful are the curses which Mahommedanism lays on its votaries! Besides that fanatical frenzy, which is as rational and as dangerous in a man as hydrophobia in a dog, there is this fearful fatalistic apathy. The effects are apparent in many countries. Improvident habits, slovenly systems of agriculture, sluggish methods of commerce, insecurity in property exist wherever the followers of Mahomet rule or live. A degraded sensualism deprives this life of its grace and refinement; the next of its dignity and sanctity. Individuals may show splendid qualities, but the influences of the religion is paralysing. It does, indeed, teach men how to die. It should rather teach them how to live. Dying is a trick very few people have been unable to pick up.

To return to No 6. The versatility of a British officer saved us a most unwelcome delay. Lieutenant F. Bathurst, of the Grenadier Guards, proceeded to the locomotive—stimulated the driver's energy—patched up the engine, and getting into the cab himself succeeded in 'coaxing her' along the odd two hundred miles that separated us from Wadi Halfa. It appeared that he had made a practice in England of driving engines and was most fully acquainted with all the details of the work. When I reflect on the delightful aspect of No 6 Station, and realise how much longer we might have contemplated its beauties, I cannot control my admiration of this most desirable accomplishment.

At Wadi Halfa were letters, but none from you. You are very faithless. Perhaps when I return you will assure me that you have written many times in answer to these that I send you so regularly. You will assert that your correspondence has gone astray, or has pursued me to Omdurman, or you will make some other excuse. I shall accept none. This is the last letter I shall write you from the Sudan. By a fortunate coincidence my patience and the material news come to a simultaneous end. But perhaps you will consider yourself less punished by the cessation than by the continuance of this correspondence.

On the way up the journey from Shellal to Halfa took five days. Going down it occupies but one. The difference is due to the Nile, whose current may be said to count two votes on a division. At Shellal the Grenadier Guards were delayed for some hours pending the arrival of troop trains. With several officers I had myself rowed across the river, and examined the temple of Philae. I fear you must have thought me somewhat of a vandal because I wrote you that I was prepared to see it for ever submerged in order that Egypt might become more prosperous. It is certainly a very beautiful and interesting ruin. Yet I cannot alter my opinion. Surely if a small model were made, the Egyptologists might be content. We might also erect a pillar overlooking the waters beneath which the temple would lie with an inscription in a classic tongue: 'Here stood the temple of Philae, sacrificed in 1899 to the welfare of the world.'

I bade farewell to the Nile at Shellal—a most unnecessary proceeding. Before the train had journeyed for an hour the eternal river reappeared among the palm trees, and presently the line passed along an embankment lapped on all sides by the flood waters. Few more extraordinary spectacles can be seen by the tourist than that which submerged Egypt presents. On every side a vast sheet of water dotted with village-covered islands stretches away to the distant mountain boundaries of the Nile Valley. Right through the broadest part of this great expanse and for several hundred miles the railway runs along its low, narrow embankment—a turnpike road across an ocean. It is not until the light-house tower of Alexandria has sunk below the horizon that the traveller may rightly say good-bye to the river which is the life of Egypt and the soul of the Sudan. And he who has voyaged many days on its stream, who has drunk deeply of its soft, sweet, but deadly water, who has followed its majestic course for near two thousand miles will not readily dissociate from the memory of the Nile a strange, almost mystic, feeling of reverence.

Here, then, my dear . . ., we are to part. Together we have toiled up the stream, have marched by its banks amid the palms and the thorn bushes, have fought and destroyed the people with whom there was cause of quarrel. Together we have drifted homeward until we are so near to civilisation that you need my escort no more. Were I to take your imagination further it might be thought that I was not truly writing this letter from the address at the top of the page. Yet, before we separate, it may be worth while to reflect on diverse matters.

There will be few who will deny the justice of the war which has at last been brought to a conclusion. Certain savage men had invaded the Egyptian territories, had killed their inhabitants and their guardians, and had possessed themselves of the land. In due course it has become convenient, as well as desirable, to expel these savages and reoccupy these territories. The Khedive enjoys his own again, by proxy. The Dervishes are slain or scattered. They lived by the sword. Why should they not perish by the magazine rifle!

The quarrel was embittered by the element of revenge. I may have mentioned the word to you several times as we approached by daily marches the ruins of Khartoum. But now vengeance is glutted, and I for one have had enough of such talk. A short ride over the field of Omdurman would have satisfied the most unrelenting. It is not an incentive to which General Gordon would often have appealed. It is not—whatever the German Emperor may say—a dignified passion for a great nation to indulge in. His Imperial Majesty would scarce admire it as much in the French people. Let us have done with it. It is sufficient that we have reconquered the Sudan because it was right and necessary that we should do so.

Of the people of the Upper Nile with whom we have warred you have doubtless read much. They possess the usual Mahommedan vices, and the inseparable Mahommedan virtue—contempt of death. Their Heaven is to them a Heaven of intelligible bliss. When we reflect on the squalour, degradation, poverty, and discomfort with which they are afflicted on earth it is not difficult to understand why they do not fear or even object to take the Great Plunge. It has been freely stated that the Khalifa was a cruel tyrant, and that the British and Egyptian Armies entered Omdurman to free the people from his yoke. Never were rescuers more unwelcome. The thousands that advanced on the zareba on 2 September or who stood unflinching against the cavalry charge were not pressed men. They fought for a cause to which they were devoted and for a ruler in whose reign they acquiesed. I know not how a man can better prove the sincerity of his opinions than by dying for them. It gives him at least a claim to be believed.

Of the Khalifa himself it is difficult for me to write, since he gave us no opportunity of discussing matters. His house exhibited several signs of cleanliness and refinement, and the loyalty of his people—unquestionably displayed—gives him some claims to be considered a fair ruler according to his light and theirs. He did not, even in the crash of his authority, massacre his prisoners, and when found they did not look ill-fed. It has been said that he was cruel. If that be so, he may yet find companions in other and more scientific nations. Still, he is gone, 'bag and baggage;' his power is forever shattered; his followers are destroyed or dispersed; and the philanthropist need have no doubts that what has happened in the Sudan is for the good of the world and of our country.

The tactics and the general conduct of the campaign must rightly excite admiration and win applause, since they ended in complete success. There are, indeed, discordant notes. Some reaction is of course inevitable after the indiscriminate eulogy which has been bestowed on every action of every department throughout this expedition. It is as natural as it is inevitable. After the deluge of praise there will come the recoiling undercurrent of criticism and abuse. Then the tides of public opinion will assume their proper level. We shall arrive at an accurate measure of the truth, and when all has been said and sifted the truth will remain very brilliant and glorious—all the more glorious because it is sober and judicial.

Since in these letters I have tried to write only what is fair and true, and because no man should write that of which he is either ashamed or afraid, I shall venture in conclusion to subscribe myself—

Yours truly,

WINSTON SPENCER CHURCHILL

13 October, 1898

South Africa

1899–1900

The Morning Post

27 November, 1899–25 July, 1900

I

EAST LONDON, 5 November

We have left headquarters busy with matters that concern as yet no one but themselves in the Mount Nelson Hotel at Capetown—a most excellent and well-appointed establishment, which may be thoroughly appreciated after a sea voyage, and which, since many of the leading Uitlanders have taken up their abode there during the war, is nick-named 'The Helot's Rest.' Last night I started by rail for East London whence a small ship carries the weekly English mail to Natal, and so by this circuitous route I hope to reach Ladysmith on Sunday morning. We have thus gained three days on our friends who proceed by the *Dunottar Castle*, and who were mightily concerned when they heard—too late to follow—of our intentions. But though it is true in this case that the longest way round is the shortest way, there were possiblities of our journey being interrupted, because the line from De Aar Junction to Naauwpoort runs parallel to the southern frontier of the Free State, and though hostile enterprises have not yet been attempted against this section of the railways they must always be expected.

Railway travelling in South Africa is more expensive but just as comfortable as in India. Lying-down accommodation is provided for all, and meals can be obtained at convenient stopping-places. The train, which is built on the corridor system, runs smoothly over the rails, so smoothly, indeed, that I have no difficulty in writing. The sun is warm and the air keen and delicious. But the scenery would depress the most buoyant spirit. We climbed up the mountains during the night, and with the daylight the train was in the middle of the great karroo. Wherefore was this miserable land of stone and scrub created? Huge mounds of crumbling rock, fashioned by the rains into the most curious and unexpected shapes, rise from the gloomy desert of the plain. Yet, though the karroo looks like a hopeless wilderness, flocks of sheep at distant intervals—one sheep requires six hundred acres of this scrappy pasture for nourishment—manage to subsist; and in consequence now and again the traveller sees some far-off farm.

We look about eagerly for signs of war. Little is as yet to be seen, and the karroo remains unsympathetic. But all along the southern frontier of the Free State the expectation of early collision grows. The first sign after leaving Capetown is the proclamation against treason published by Sir Alfred Milner. The notice-boards of the railway stations are freely placarded with the full text in English and Dutch, beginning with 'Whereas a state of war exists between the Government of Her Majesty and the Governments of the South African Republic and of the Orange Free State . . .' continuing to enjoin good and loyal behaviour on all, detailing the pains and penalties for disobedience, and ending with 'God save the Queen'. Both races have recorded their opinions on their respective versions: the British by underlining the penalties, the Dutch by crossing out the first word of 'God save the Queen'. It is signed 'A. Milner', and below, in bitter irony, 'W. P. Schreiner'.[1]

Beyond Matjesfontein every bridge, and even every culvert, is watched by a Kaffir with a flag, so that the train runs no risk of coming on unexpected demolitions. On the road to De Aar we passed the second half of the brigade division of artillery, which sailed so long ago from the Mersey in the notorious transports *Zibengla* and *Zayathla*. The gunners were hurrying to the front in three long trains, each taking half a battery complete with guns, horses and men. All were light-hearted and confident, as soldiers always are going off to the wars, and in this case their satisfaction at being on land after five weeks of uncomfortable voyage in antiquated ships was easily to be understood. But this is no time for reproaches.

At Beaufort West grave news awaited the mail, and we learned of the capitulation of twelve hundred troops near Ladysmith. It is generally believed that this will precipitate a rising of the Dutch throughout this part of the Colony and an invasion by the commandos now gathered along the Orange River. How far that belief is well-founded you will be able to judge before this letter reaches London. The Dutch farmers talk loudly and confidently of 'our victories', meaning those of the Boers, and the racial feeling runs high. But the British colonists have an implicit faith—marvellous when the past is

[1] W. P. Schreiner, Prime Minister of Cape Colony, 1898–9.

remembered—in the resolve of the Imperial Government and of the nation never to abandon them again.

At De Aar the stage of our journey which may be said to have been uncertain began. Armoured trains patrol the line; small parties of armed police guard the bridges; infantry and artillery detachments occupy the towns. De Aar, Colesberg and Storbmerg are garrisoned as strongly as the present limited means allow, and all the forces, regulars and volunteers alike, are full of enthusiasm. But, on the other hand, the reports of Boer movements seem to indicate that a hostile advance is imminent. The Colesberg bridge across the Orange River has been seized by the enemy, the line between Bethulie and Colesberg has just been cut, and each train from De Aar to Stormberg is expected to be the last to pass unassailed. We, however, slept peacefully through the night and, passing Colesberg safely, arrived at Stormberg, beyond which all is again secure.

Stormberg Junction stands at the southern end of a wide expanse of rolling grass country, and though the numerous rocky hills, or kopjes as they are called, which rise inconveniently on all sides make its defence by a small force difficult, a large force occupying an extended position would be secure. Here we found the confirmation of many rumours. The news of a Boer advance on Burghersdorp, 25 miles away, is, it seems, well-founded, and when our train arrived the evacuation of Stormberg by its garrison of a half battalion of the Berkshire Regiment, 350 men of the Naval Brigade, a company of mounted infantry and a few guns, was busily proceeding.

The sailors were already in their train, and only prevented from starting by the want of an engine. The infantry and artillery were to start in a few hours. It is rather an unsatisfactory business, though the arrival of more powerful forces will soon restore the situation. Stormberg is itself an important railway junction. For more than a week the troops have been working night and day to put it in a state of defence. Little redoubts have been built on the kopjes, entrenchments have been dug, and the few houses near the station are already strongly fortified. I was shown one of these by the young officer in charge. The approaches were cleared of everything except wire fences and entanglements; the massive walls were loopholed, the windows barricaded with sandbags, the rooms inside broken one into the other for convenience in moving about.

Its garrison of twenty-five men and its youthful commander surveyed the work with pride. They had laid in stores of all kinds for ten days, and none doubted that Fort Chabrol, as they called it, would stand a gallant siege. Then suddenly had come the message to evacuate and retreat. So it was with the others. The train with the naval detachment and its guns steamed off, and we gave it a feeble cheer. Another train awaited the Berkshires. The mounted infantry were already on the march. 'Mayn't we even blow up this lot?' said a soldier, pointing to the house he had helped to fortify. But there were no such orders; only this one which seemed to pervade the air: 'The enemy are coming. Retreat—retreat—retreat.' The station-master—one of the best types of Englishmen to be found on a long journey—was calm and cheerful.

'No more traffic north of this,' he said. 'Yours was the last train through from De Aar. I shall send away all my men by the special tonight. And that's the end as far as Stormberg goes.'

'And you?'

'Oh, I shall stay. I have lived here for twelve years, and am well known. Perhaps I may be able to protect the company's property.'

While we waited the armoured train returned from patrolling—an engine between two carriages cloaked from end to end with thick plates and slabs of blue-grey iron. It had seen nothing of the advancing Boers, but, like us and like the troops, it had to retire southwards. There were fifty Uitlanders from Johannesburg on the platform. They had been employed entrenching; now they were bundled back again towards East London. I talked with some of them and heard the fullest confirmation of the horrible barbarities perpetrated by the Boers on the trainloads of refugees. A British officer on special service was also explicit. He had been at Stormberg while the exodus from the Republics was going on. The Boers plundered the flying folk mercilessly, and had insulted or assaulted men and women. The chief sufferers were the Basuto fugitives. They had been brutally flogged with sjamboks, and came across the frontier bleeding from the wounds. Moreover, their little store of money had been stolen by the 'simple pastoral people' and they were in many cases starving. 'One woman', said the officer, 'had been flogged across the breasts, and was much lacerated.' Such is the Boer—gross, fierce and horrid—doing the deeds of the devil with the name of the Lord on his lips. It is quite true that he is brave, but so are many savage tribes.

So we left Stormberg in much anger and some humiliation, and jolted away towards the open sea, where British supremacy is not yet contested by the Boer. At Molteno we picked up a hundred volunteers

—fine-looking fellows all eager to encounter the enemy, but much surprised at the turn events had taken. They, too, were ordered to fall back. The Boers were advancing, and to despondent minds even the rattle of the train seemed to urge 'Retreat, retreat, retreat'.

I do not desire to invest this wise and prudent though discouraging move with more than its proper importance. Anything is better than to leave small garrisons to be overwhelmed. Until the army corps comes the situation will continue to be unsatisfactory and the ground to be recovered thereafter will increase in extent. But with the arrival of powerful and well-equipped forces the tide of war will surely turn.

27 November, 1899

2

ESTCOURT, 6 November

The title[1] of this letter derives its justification and propriety from the fact that it explains where I would like to be if not where I am. The reader may remember that we started post haste from Capetown and, having the good fortune to pass along the southern frontier from De Aar to Stormberg by the last train before the interruption of traffic, had every hope of reaching Ladysmith while its investment was incomplete. I had looked forward to writing an account of our voyage from East London to Durban while on board the vessel; but the weather was so tempestuous and the little steamer of scarcely 100 tons burthen so buffeted by the waves that I lay prostrate in all the anguish of sea-sickness, and had no thought for anything else. Moreover, we were delayed some twenty hours by contrary winds; nor was it until we had passed St John's that the gale, as if repenting, veered suddenly to the south-west and added as much to our speed as it had formerly delayed us. With the change of the wind the violence of the waves to some degree abated, and though unable to then record them on paper I had opportunity of gaining some impressions of the general aspect of the coasts of Pondoland and Natal. These beautiful countries stretch down to the ocean in smooth slopes of the richest verdure, broken only at intervals by lofty bluffs crowned with forests. The many rivulets to which the pasture owes its life and the land its richness glide to the shore through deepset creeks and chines, or plunge over the cliffs in cascades which the strong winds scatter into clouds of spray.

These are regions of possibility, and as we drove along before our now friendly wind I could not but speculate on the future. Here are wide tracts of fertile soil watered by abundant rains. The temperate sun warms the life within the soil. The cooling breeze refreshes the inhabitant. The delicious climate stimulates the vigour of the

[1] One of the headlines to this despatch was 'With Headquarters.'

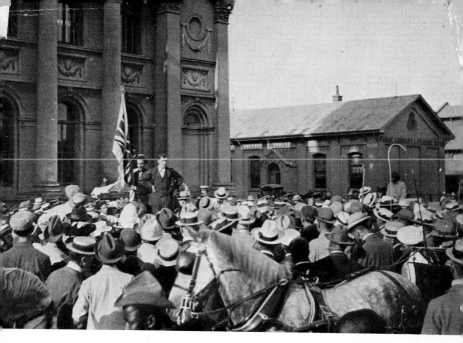

4. WSC addressing the crowd in Durban after his escape

5. WSC, war correspondent, South Africa, 1899

6. WSC as a Lieutenant in the South African Light Horse, 1900

European. The highway of the sea awaits the produce of his labour. All nature smiles, and here at last is a land where white men may rule and prosper. As yet only the indolent Kaffir enjoys its bounty and, according to the antiquated philosophy of Liberalism, it is to such that it should for ever belong. But while Englishmen choke and fester in crowded cities, while thousands of babies are born every month who are never to have a fair chance in life, there will be those who will dream another dream of a brave system of state-aided—almost state-compelled—emigration, a scheme of old age pensions that shall anticipate old age, and by preventing paupers terminate itself; a system that shall remove the excess of the old land to provide the deficiency of the new, and shall offer even to the most unfortunate citizen of the Empire fresh air and open opportunity. And as I pondered on all these things the face of the country seemed changed. Thriving ports and townships rose up along the shore, and inland towers, spires and tall chimneys attested the wealth and industry of men. Here in front of us was New Brighton; the long shelving ledge of rock was a sea-wall already made, rows of stately buildings covered the grassy slopes; the shipping of many nations lay in the roadstead; above the whole scene waved The Flag, and in the foreground on the sandy beach the great-grand-children of the crossing-sweeper and the sandwich-man sported by the waves that beat by the Southern Pole, or sang aloud for joy in the beauty of their home and the pride of their race. And then with a lurch—for the motion was still considerable—I came back from the land of dreams to reality and the hideous fact that Natal is invaded and assailed by the Boer.

The little steamer reached Durban safely at midnight on 4 November, and we passed an impatient six hours in a sleeping town waiting for daylight and news. Both came in their turn. The sun rose, and we learned that Ladysmith was cut off. Still, 'as far as you can as quickly as you can' must be the motto of the war correspondent, and seven o'clock found us speeding inland in the extra coach of a special train carrying the mails. The hours I passed in Durban were not without occupation. The hospital ship *Sumatra* lay close to our moorings, and as soon as it was light I visited her to look for friends, and found, alas! several in a sorry plight. All seemed to be as well as the tenderest care and the most lavish expenditure of money could make them. All told much the same tale—the pluck and spirit of the troops, the stubborn unpretentious valour of the Boer, the searching musketry. Everyone predicted a prolonged struggle.

'All those colonials tell you,' said an officer severely wounded at Elandslaagte, 'that the Boers only want one good thrashing to satisfy them. Don't you believe it. They mean going through with this to the end. What about our Government?'

And the answer that all were united at home, and that Boer constancy would be met with equal perseverance and greater resources lighted the pain-drawn features with a hopeful smile.

'Well, I never felt quite safe with those politicians. I can't get about for two months' (he was shot through the thigh) 'but I hope to be in at the death. It's our blood against theirs.'

Pietermaritzburg is sixty miles from Durban, but as the railway zigzags up and down hill and contorts itself into curves that would horrify the domestic engineer the journey occupies four hours. The town looks more like Ootacamund than any place I have seen. To those who do not know the delightful hill station of Southern India let me explain that Pietermaritzburg stands in a basin of smooth rolling downs, broken frequently by forests of fir and blue gum trees. It is a sleepy, dead-alive place. Even the fact that Colonel Knowle, the military engineer, was busily putting it into a state of defence, digging up its hills, piercing its walls, and encircling it with wire obstructions did not break its apathy. The *Times of Natal* struggled to rouse the excitement, and placarded its office with the latest telegrams from the front, some of which had reached Pietermaritzburg via London. But the composure of the civil population is a useful factor in war, and I wish it were within the scope of my poor pen to bring home to the people of England how excellently the colonists of Natal have deserved of the State.

There are several points to be remembered in this connection. Firstly, the colonists have had many dealings with the Boers. They knew their strength; they feared their animosity. But they have never, for one moment, lost sight of their obligations as a British colony. Their loyalty has been splendid. From the very first they warned the Imperial Government that their territories would be invaded. Throughout the course of the long negotiations they knew that if war should come, on them would fall the first of the fury of the storm. Nevertheless, they courageously supported and acclaimed the action of the ministry. Now at last there is war—bitter war. It means a good deal to all of us, but more than to any it comes home to the Natalian. He is invaded; his cattle have been seized by the Boer; his towns are shelled or captured; the most powerful force on which he relied for protection is isolated in Ladysmith; his capital is being loopholed and entrenched; Newcastle has been abandoned, Colenso has fallen, Estcourt is threatened; the possibility that the whole province will be overrun stares him in the face. From the beginning he asked for protection. From the beginning he was promised complete protection; but scarcely a word of complaint is heard. The townsfolk are calm and orderly, the press dignified and sober. The men capable of bearing arms have responded nobly. Boys of sixteen march with men of fifty to war—to no light easy war. The Imperial Light Infantry is eagerly filled. The Imperial Light Horse can find no more vacancies, not even for those who will serve without pay. The Volunteers and Town Guards bear their parts like men.

Nor is this merely while the danger impends. I talked with a wounded Gordon Highlander—one of those who dashed across the famous causeway of Dargai and breasted the still more glorious slope of Elandslaagte.

'We had the Imperial Horse with us,' he said. 'They're the best I've ever seen.'

And the casualty lists tell the same tale. To storm the hill the regiment dismounted less than two hundred men. They reached the top unchecked, their colonel, their adjutant, Lieutenant Barnes, seven other officers and upwards of sixty men killed or wounded—nearly 30 per cent. Many of this corps came from Johannesburg. After this who will dare call Uitlanders cowards? Not that it will ever matter again.

Viewed in quieter days, the patient, trustful attitude of this colony of Natal will impress the historian. The devotion of its people to their sovereign and to their motherland should endear them to all good Englishmen and win them general respect and sympathy; and full indemnity to all individual colonists who have suffered loss must stand as an Imperial debt of honour.

6 December, 1899

3

PRETORIA, 19 November

Now I perceive that I was foolish to choose in advance a definite title[1] for these letters and to think that it could continue to be appropriate for any length of time. In the strong stream of war the swimmer is swirled helplessly about hither and thither by the waves, and he can by no means tell where he will come to land or, indeed, that he may not be overwhelmed in the flood. A week ago I described to you a reconnoitring expedition in the Estcourt armoured train, and I pointed out the many defects in the construction and the great dangers in the employment of that forlorn military machine. So potent were these to all who concerned themselves in the matter that the train was nicknamed in the camp 'Wilson's death trap'.

On Tuesday the 14th, the mounted infantry patrols reported that the Boers in small parties were approaching Estcourt from the directions of Weenen and Colenso, and Colonel Long made a reconnaissance in force to ascertain what strength lay behind the advanced scouts. The reconnaissance, which was marked only by an exchange of shots between the patrols, revealed little, but it was generally believed that a considerable portion of the army investing Ladysmith was moving, or was about to move, southwards to attack Estcourt and endeavour to strike at Pietermartzburg. The movement that we had awaited for ten days impended. Accordingly certain military preparations, which I need not now specify, were made to guard against all contingencies, and at daylight on Wednesday morning another spray of patrols was flung out towards the north and north-west, and the Estcourt armoured train was ordered to reconnoitre as far as Chieveley. The train was composed as follows: an ordinary truck, in which was a 7-pounder muzzle-loading gun, served by four sailors from the *Tartar*; an armoured car fitted with loopholes and held by three sections of a company of the Dublin

[1] Also headlined 'With Headquarters.'

Fusiliers; the engine and tender, two more armoured cars containing the fourth section of the Fusilier company, one company of the Durban Light Infantry (volunteers), and a small civilian breakdown gang; lastly, another ordinary truck with the tools and materials for repairing the road; in all five waggons, the locomotive, one small gun and 120 men. Captain Haldane, DSO,[1] whom I had formerly known on Sir William Lockhart's staff in the Tirah Expedition, and who was lately recovered from his wound at Elandslaagte, commanded.

We started at half-past five and, observing all the usual precautions, reached Frere Station in about an hour. Here a small patrol of the Natal Police reported that there were no enemy within the next few miles, and that all seemed quiet in the neighbourhood. It was the silence before the storm. Captain Haldane decided to push on cautiously as far as Chieveley, near which place an extensive view of the country could be obtained. Not a sign of the Boers could be seen. The rolling, grassy country looked as peaceful and deserted as on former occasions, and we little thought that behind the green undulations scarcely three miles away the leading commandos of a powerful force were riding swiftly forward on their invading path.

All was clear as far as Chieveley, but as the train reached the station I saw about a hundred Boer horsemen cantering southwards about a mile from the railway. Beyond Chieveley a long hill was lined with a row of black spots, showing that our further advance would be disputed. The telegraphist who accompanied the train wired back to Estcourt reporting our safe arrival and that parties of Boers were to be seen at no great distance, and Colonel Long replied by ordering the train to return to Frere and to remain there in observation during the day, watching its safe retreat at nightfall. We proceeded to obey and were about a mile and three-quarters from Frere when on rounding a corner we saw that a hill which commanded the line at a distance of 600 yards was occupied by the enemy. So after all there would be a fight, for we could not pass this point without coming under fire. The four sailors loaded their gun— an antiquated toy—the soldiers charged their magazines, and the train, which was now in the reverse of the order in which it had started, moved slowly towards the hill.

[1] Aylmer Lowthorpe Haldane (1862–1950). Served with Churchill in India and South Africa and was officer in command of the armoured train. KCB 1918.

The moment approached; but no one was much concerned, for the cars were proof against rifle fire, and this ridge could at the worst be occupied only by some daring patrol or perhaps a score of men. 'Besides,' we said to ourselves, 'they little think we have a gun on board. That will be a nice surprise.'

The Boers held their fire until the train reached that part of the track nearest to their position. Standing on a box in the rear armoured truck I had an excellent view through my glasses. The long brown rattling serpent with the rifles bristling from its spotted sides crawled closer to the rocky hillock on which the scattered black figures of the enemy showed clearly. Suddenly three-wheeled things appeared on the crest, and within a second a bright flash of light—like a heliograph, but much yellower—open and shut ten or twelve times. Then two much larger flashes; no smoke nor yet any sound, and a bustle and a stir among the little figures. So much for the hill. Immediately over the rear truck of the train a huge white ball of smoke sprang into being and tore out into a cone like a comet. Then came the explosions of the near guns and the nearer shell. The iron sides of the truck tanged with the patter of bullets. There was a crash from the front of the train and half a dozen sharp reports. The Boers had opened fire on us at 600 yards with two field guns, a Maxim[1] firing small shells in a stream, and from riflemen lying on the ridge. I got down from my box into the cover of the armoured sides of the car without forming any clear thought. Equally involuntarily it seems that the driver put on full steam. The train leapt forward, ran the gauntlet of the guns, which now filled the air with explosions, swung round the curve of the hill, ran down a steep gradient, and dashed into a huge stone which awaited it on the line at a convenient spot.

To those who were in the rear truck there was only a great shock, a tremendous crash and a sudden full stop. What happened to the trucks in front of the engine is more interesting. The first, which contained the materials and tools of the breakdown gang and the guard who was watching the line, was flung into the air and fell bottom upwards on the embankment. (I do not know what befell the guard, but it seems probable that he was killed.) The next, an armoured car crowded with the Durban Light Infantry, was carried on twenty yards and thrown over on its side, scattering its occupants

[1] A 1.425 calibre automatic cannon firing half-kilo shells, and fed by a belt containing 25 rounds.

in a shower on the ground. The third wedged itself across the track, half on and half off the rails. The rest of the train kept to the metals.

We are not long left in the comparative peace and safety of a railway accident. The Boer guns, swiftly changing their position, reopened from a distance of 1,300 yards before anyone had got out of the stage of exclamations. The tapping rifle fire spread along the hillsides until it encircled the wreckage on three sides, and a third field gun came into action from some high ground on the opposite side of the line.

The armoured truck gave some protection from the bullets, but since any direct shell must pierce it like paper and kill everyone it seemed almost safer outside and, wishing to see the extent and nature of the damage, I clambered over the iron shield and, dropping to the ground, ran along the line to the front of the train. As I passed the engine another shrapnel shell burst immediately, as it seemed, over-head, hurling its contents with a rasping rush through the air. The driver[1] at once sprang out of the cab and ran to the shelter of the overturned trucks. His face was cut open by a splinter, and he complained in bitter futile indignation. He was a civilian. What did they think he was paid for? To be killed by bombshells? Not he. He would not stay another minute. It looked as if his excitement and misery would prevent him from working the engine further, and as only he understood the machinery all chances of escape seemed to be cut off. Yet when this man, who certainly exhibited lively symptoms of terror, was told that if he continued to stay at his post he would be mentioned for distinguished gallantry in action he pulled himself together, wiped the blood off his face, climbed back into the cab of his engine, and thereafter during the one-sided combat did his duty bravely and faithfully—so strong is the desire for honour and repute in the human breast. I reached the overturned portion of the train uninjured. The volunteers who, though severely shaken, were mostly unhurt, were lying down under such cover as the damaged cars and the gutters of the railway line afforded. It was a very grievous sight to see these citizen soldiers, most of whom were the fathers of families, in such a perilous position. They bore themselves well, though greatly troubled, and their major, whose name I have not learned, directed their fire on the enemy; but since these, lying behind

---

[1] Charles Wagner. He was finally awarded the Albert Medal in 1910 when Churchill, as Home Secretary, raised his case. The fireman, Alexander Stewart, also received the Albert Medal.

the crests of the surrounding hills, were almost invisible I did not expect that it would be very effective.

Efforts were now made to clear the line completely of the wrecked trucks so that the engine and the two cars which still remained on the rails might escape. Meanwhile Captain Haldane endeavoured to keep down the enemy's artillery fire by the musketry of the infantry in the rear armoured truck. The task of clearing the line would not perhaps, in ordinary circumstances, have been a very difficult one. But the breakdown gang and their tools were scattered to the winds, and several had fled along the track or across the fields. Moreover, the enemy's artillery fire was pitiless, continuous and distracting. The affair had, however, to be carried through.

The first thing to be done was to detach the truck half off the rails from the one completely so. To do this the engine had to be moved to slacken the strain on the twisted couplings. When these had been released the next step was to drag the partly-derailed truck backwards along the line until it was clear of the other wreckage and then to throw it bodily off the line. This may seem very simple, but the dead weight of the iron truck half on the sleepers was enormous and the engine wheels skidded vainly several times before any hauling power was obtained. At last the truck was sufficiently far back, and volunteers were called for to overturn it from the side while the engine pushed it from the end. It was very evident that these men would be exposed to considerable danger. Twenty were called for, and there was an immediate response. But only nine, including the major of volunteers, and four or five of the Dublin Fusiliers actually stepped out into the open. The attempt was nevertheless successful. The truck heeled further over under their pushing and, the engine giving a shove at the right moment, it fell off the line and the track was clear. Safety and success appeared in sight together, but disappointment overtook them.

The engine was about six inches wider than the tender, and the corner of its footplate would not pass the corner of the newly over-turned truck. It did not seem safe to push very hard lest the engine itself should be derailed. So time after time the engine moved back a yard or two and shoved forward at the obstruction, and each time it moved a little. But soon it was evident that complications had set in. The newly derailed truck became jammed with that originally off the line, and the more the engine pushed the greater became the block. Volunteers were again called on to assist, but even though seven men, two of whom, I think, were wounded, did their best the attempt was a failure.

Perseverance, however, is a virtue. If the trucks only jammed the tighter for the forward pushing they might be loosened by pulling backwards. But now a new difficulty arose. The coupling chains of the engine would not reach by five or six inches those of the overturned truck. Search was now made for a spare link. By a solitary gleam of good luck, one was found. The engine hauled at the wreckage, and before the chains parted, pulled it about a yard backwards. Now, certainly, at last the line was clear. But again the corner of the foot-plate jammed with the corner of the truck, and again we came to a jarring halt.

I have had, in the last four years, the advantage, if it be an advantage, of many strange and varied experiences, from which the student of realities might draw profit and instruction. But nothing was so thrilling as this: to wait and struggle among those clanging, rending iron boxes, with the repeated explosion of the shells and the artillery, the noise of the projectiles striking the ears, the hiss as they passed in the air, the grunting and pulling of the engine—poor, tortured thing, hammered by at least a dozen shells, any one of which, by penetrating the boiler, might have made an end to all—the expectation of destruction, the realisation of powerlessness, and the alternations of hope and despair—all this for seventy minutes by the clock with only four inches of twisted iron work to make the difference between danger, captivity and shame on the one hand—safety, freedom and triumph on the other.

Nothing remained but to continue pounding at the obstructing corner in the hopes that the ironwork would gradually be twisted and torn, and thus give free passage. As we pounded so did the enemy. The driver was adjured to be patient and to push gently, for it did not seem right to imperil the slender chance of escape by running the risk of throwing the engine off the line. But after a dozen pushes had been given with apparently little result a shell struck the front of the engine, setting fire to the woodwork, and he therefore turned on more steam, and with considerable momentum we struck the obstacle once more. There was a grinding crash; the engine staggered, checked, shore forward again, until with a clanging, tearing sound it broke past the point of interception, and nothing but the smooth line lay between us and home.

Brilliant success now seemed won, for I thought that the rear and gun trucks were following the locomotive, and that all might squeeze into them, and so make an honourable escape. But the longed-for cup was dashed aside. Looking backward, I saw that the couplings had parted, or been severed by a shell, and that the trucks still lay on the wrong side of the obstruction, separated by it from the engine. No one dared to risk imprisoning the engine again by making it go back for the trucks, so an attempt was made to drag the trucks up to the engine. Owing chiefly to the fire of the enemy this failed completely, and Captain Haldane determined to be content with saving the locomotive. He accordingly permitted the driver to retire along the line slowly, so that the infantry might get as much shelter from the ironwork of the engine as possible, and the further idea was to get into some houses near the station, which were about 800 yards away, and there hold out while the engine went for assistance.

As many wounded as possible were piled on to the engine, standing in the cab, lying on the tender, or clinging to the cowcatcher. And all this time the shells fell into the wet earth throwing up white clouds, burst with terrifying detonations overhead, or actually struck the engine and the iron wreckage. Besides the three field guns, which proved to be 15-pounders, the shell-firing Maxim continued its work, and its little shells, discharged with an ugly thud, thud, thud, exploded with startling bangs on all sides. One I remember struck the footplate of the engine scarcely a yard from my face, lit up into a bright yellow flash, and left me wondering why I was still alive. Another hit the coals, hurling a black shower into the air. A third—this also I saw—struck the arm of a private in the Dublin Fusiliers. The whole arm was smashed to a horrid pulp—bones, muscles, blood and uniform all mixed together. At the bottom hung the hand, unhurt, but swelled instantly to three times its ordinary size. The engine was soon crowded and began to steam homewards—a mournful, sorely-battered locomotive—with the woodwork of the firebox in flames and the water spouting from its pierced tanks. The infantrymen straggled along beside it at the double.

Seeing the engine escaping the Boers increased their fire and the troops, hitherto somewhat protected by the iron trucks began to suffer. The major of volunteers fell shot through the thigh. Here and there men dropped to the ground, several screamed—this is very rare in war—and cried for help. About a quarter of the force was very soon killed or wounded. The shells which pursued the retreating soldiers scattered them all along the track. Order and control vanished.

The engine, increasing its pace, drew out from the thin crowd of fugitives and was soon in safety. The infantry continued to run down the line in the direction of the houses and, in spite of their disorder, I honestly consider that they were capable of making further resistance when some natural shelter should be reached. But at this moment one of those incidents—much too frequent in this war—occurred.

A private soldier who was wounded, in direct disobedience of the positive orders that no surrender was to be made, took it on himself to wave a pocket handkerchief. The Boers immediately ceased firing, and with equal daring and humanity a dozen horsemen galloped from the hills into the scattered fugitives, scarcely any of whom had seen the white flag, and several of whom were still firing, and called loudly on them to surrender. Most of the soldiers then halted, gave up their arms and became prisoners of war. Those further away from the horsemen continued to run and were shot or hunted down in twos and threes and some made good their escape.

For my part I found myself on the engine when the obstruction was at last passed and remained there jammed in the cab next to the man with the shattered arm. In this way I travelled some 500 yards, and passed through the fugitives, noticing particularly a young officer, Lieutenant H. Frankland[1] who, with a happy, confident smile was endeavouring to rally his men. As I thought that only the wounded should be carried by the engine and that sound men should run, I jumped on to the line, and hence the address from which this letter is written, for scarcely had the locomotive left me that I found myself alone in a shallow cutting and none of our soldiers to be seen. Then suddenly there appeared on the line at the end of the cutting two men not in uniform. 'Platelayers,' I said to myself, and then with a surge of realisation, 'Boers'. My mind retains a momentary impression of these tall figures, full of animated movement, clad in dark flapping clothes, with slouch, storm-driven hats, poising on their rifles hardly a hundred yards away. I turned and ran between the rails of the tracks, and the only thought I achieved was this, 'Boer marksmanship'. Two bullets passed, both within a foot, one on either side. I flung myself against the banks of the cutting. But they gave no cover. Another glance at the figures; one was now kneeling to aim. Again I

[1] Thomas Hugh Colville Frankland (1879–1915). One of Churchill's fellow prisoners of war at Pretoria. Extracts from his diary were printed in *Ian Hamilton's March*. He was killed at Gallipoli while serving as Brigade Major.

darted forward. Movement seemed the only chance. Again two soft kisses sucked in the air, but nothing struck me. This could not endure. I must get out of the cutting—that damnable corridor. I scrambled up the bank. The earth sprang up beside me, and something touched my hand, but outside the cutting was a tiny depression. I crouched in this, struggling to get my wind. On the other side of the railway a horseman galloped up, shouting to me and waving his hand. He was scarcely forty yards off. With a rifle I could have killed him easily. I knew nothing of white flags, and the bullets had made me savage. But I was a press correspondent without arms of any kind. There was a wire fence between me and the horseman. Should I continue to fly? The idea of another shot at such a short range decided me. Death stood before, grim sullen Death without his light-hearted companion, Chance. So I held up my hand and, like Mr Jorrocks's foxes, cried 'Capivy'. Then I was herded with the other prisoners in a miserable group and about the same time I noticed that my hand was bleeding, and it began to pour with rain.

Two days before I had written to an officer in high command at home, whose friendship I have the honour to enjoy: 'There has been a great deal too much surrendering in this war, and I hope people who do so will not be encouraged.' Fate had intervened, yet though her tone was full of irony she seemed to say, as I think Ruskin once said, 'It matters very little whether your judgments of people are true or untrue, and very much whether they are kind or unkind,' and repeating that I will make an end.

1 January, 1900

4

PRETORIA, 20 November

The position of a prisoner of war is painful and humiliating. A man tries his best to kill another, and finding that he cannot succeed asks his enemy for mercy. The laws of war demand that this should be accorded, but it is impossible not to feel a sense of humbling obligation to the captor from whose hand we take our lives. All military pride, all independence of spirit must be put aside. These may be carried to the grave, but not into captivity. We must prepare ouselves to submit, to obey, to endure certain things—sufficient food and water and protection during good behaviour—the victor must supply or be a savage, but beyond these all else is favour. Favours must be accepted from those with whom we have a long and bitter quarrel, from those who feel fiercely that we seek to do them cruel injustice. The dog who has been whipped must be thankful for the bone that is flung to him.

When the prisoners captured after the destruction of the armoured train had been disarmed and collected in a group we found that there were fifty-six unwounded or slightly wounded men, besides the more serious cases lying on the scene of the fight. The Boers crowded round looking curiously at their prize, and we ate a little chocolate that by good fortune—for we had had no breakfast—was in our pockets, and sat down on the muddy ground to think. The rain streamed down from a dark leaden sky, and the coats of the horses steamed in the damp. 'Voorwärts,' said a voice and, forming in a miserable procession, two wretched officers, a bare-headed, tattered correspondent, four sailors with straw hats and 'HMS Tartar' in gold letters on the ribbon—ill-timed jauntiness—some fifty soldiers and volunteers, and two or three railwaymen, we started, surrounded by the active Boer horsemen. Yet as we climbed the low hills that surrounded the place of combat I looked back and saw the engine steaming swiftly away beyond Frere Station. Something at least was saved from the ruin, information would be carried to the troops at

Estcourt, some of the wounded would escape, the locomotive was itself of value, and perhaps in saving all these things some little honour had been saved as well.

'You need not walk fast,' said a Boer in excellent English, 'take your time.' Then another, seeing me hatless in the downpour, threw me a soldier's cap—one of the Irish Fusilier caps, taken, probably, near Ladysmith. So they were not cruel men, these enemy. That was a great surprise to me, for I had read much of the literature of this land of lies, and fully expected every hardship and indignity. At length we reached the guns which had played on us for so many minutes—two strangely long barrels sitting very low on the axles of the wheels. They looked offensively modern, and I wondered why our army had not got field artillery with fixed ammunition and 8,000 yards range. Some officers and men of the Staats Artillerie, dressed in a drab uniform with blue facings, approached us. The commandant, Adjutant Roos—as he introduced himself—made a polite salute. He regretted the unfortunate circumstances of our meeting; he complimented the officers on their defence—of course, it was hopeless from the first; above all he wanted to know how the engine had been able to get away and how the line could have been cleared under his guns. In fact he behaved as a good professional soldier should, and his manner impressed me. We waited here near the guns for half an hour, and meanwhile the Boers searched among the wreckage for dead and wounded. A few of the wounded were brought to where we were, and laid on the ground, but most of them were placed in the shelter of one of the overturned trucks. As I write I do not know with any certainty what the total losses were, but the Boers say they buried five dead, sent ten seriously wounded into Ladysmith and kept three severely wounded in their field ambulances. Besides this we are told that fifteen severely wounded escaped on the engine, and we have with the prisoners seven men, including myself, slightly wounded by splinters or injured in the derailment. If this be approximately correct it seems that the casualties in the hour and a half of fighting were between 35 and 40; not many, perhaps, considering the fire, but out of 120 enough at least.

After a while we were ordered to march on, and looking over the crest of the hill a strange and impressive sight met the eye. Only about 300 men had attacked the train, and I had thought that this was the enterprise of such a separate detachment, but as the view extended I saw that this was only a small part of the large, powerful forces marching south, under the personal direction of General Joubert,[1] to attack Estcourt. Behind every hill, thinly veiled by driving rain, masses of mounted men, arranged in an orderly disorder, were halted, and from the rear long columns of horsemen rode steadily forward. Certainly I did not see less than three thousand, and I did not see nearly all. Evidently an important operation was in progress, and a collision either at Estcourt or Mooi River impended.

Our captors conducted us to a rough tent which had been set up in a hollow in one of the hills, and which we concluded was General Joubert's headquarters. Here we were formed into a line, and soon surrounded by a bearded crowd of Boers cloaked in mackintosh. I explained that I was a special correspondent and a non-combatant, and asked to see General Joubert. But in the throng it was impossible to tell who were the superiors. My credentials were taken from me by a man who said he was a field cornet, and who promised that they should be laid before the general forthwith. Meanwhile we waited in the rain, and the Boers questioned us. My certificate as a correspondent bore a name better known than liked in the Transvaal. Moreover, some of the private soldiers had been talking. 'You are the son of Lord Randolph Churchill?' said a Scottish Boer abruptly. I did not deny the fact. Immediately there was much talking, and all crowded round me, looking and pointing, while I heard my name repeated on every side. 'I am a newspaper correspondent,' I said, 'and you ought not to hold me prisoner.' The Scottish Boer laughed. 'Oh,' he said, 'we do not catch lords' sons every day.' Whereat they all chuckled, and began to explain that I should be allowed to play football at Pretoria.

All this time I was expecting to be brought before General Joubert, from whom I did not doubt I should obtain assurances that my character as a non-combatant would be respected. But suddenly a mounted man rode up and ordered the prisoners to march away towards Colenso. The escort, twenty horsemen, closed round us. I addressed their leader and demanded either that I should be taken before the general, or that my credentials should be given back. But the so-called field cornet was not to be seen. The only response was 'Voorwärts,' and as it seemed useless, undignified and even dangerous to discuss the matter further with these people I turned and marched off with the rest.

[1] Petrus Jacobus Joubert (1834–1900). Boer Commandant from 1881. Commanded Boer forces at the battle of Majuba Hill.

We tramped for six hours across sloppy fields and along tracks deep and slippery with mud, while the rain fell in a steady downpour and soaked everyone to the skin. The Boer escort told us several times not to hurry and to go our own pace, and once they allowed us to halt for a few moments. But we had neither food nor water, and it was with a feeling of utter weariness that I saw the tin roofs of Colenso rise in the distance. We were put into a corrugated iron shed near the station, the floors of which were four inches deep with torn railway forms and account books. Here we flung ourselves down exhausted, and what with the shame, the disappointment, the excitement of the morning, the misery of the present and physical weakness, it seemed that love of life was gone, and I thought almost with envy of a soldier I had seen during the fight lying quite still on the embankment secure in the calm philosophy of death from 'the slings and arrows of outrageous fortune.'

After the Boers had lit two fires they opened one of the doors of the shed and told us we might come forth and dry ourselves. A newly-slaughtered ox lay on the ground, and strips of his flesh were given to us. These we toasted on sticks over the fire and ate greedily, though since the animal had been alive five minutes before one felt a kind of cannibal. Other Boers besides our escort who were occupying Colenso came to look at us. With two of these who were brothers, English by race, Afrikanders by birth, Boers by choice, I had some conversation. The war, they said, was going well. Of course, it was a great matter to face the power and might of the British Empire, still they were resolved. They would drive the English out of South Africa for ever or else fight to the last man. I said, 'You attempt the impossible. Pretoria will be taken by the middle of March. What hope have you of withstanding a hundred thousand soldiers?' 'If I thought,' said the younger of the two brothers vehemently, 'that the Dutchman would give in because Pretoria was taken I would smash my rifle on those metals this very moment. We will fight for ever.' And I could only reply, 'Wait and see how you feel when the tide is running the other way. It does not seem so easy to die when death is near.' The man said, 'I will wait.' Then we made friends. I told him that I hoped he would come safely through the war and live to see a happier and a nobler South Africa under the flag of his fathers; and he took off his blanket—which he was wearing with a hole in the middle like a cloak—and gave it to me to sleep in. So we parted, and presently, as night fell, the field cornet who had us in charge bade us carry a little forage into the shed to sleep on, and then locked us up in the dark, soldiers, sailors, officers and correspondent—a broken-spirited jumble.

I could not sleep. Vexation of spirit, a cold night and wet clothes withheld sweet oblivion. The rights and wrongs of the quarrel, the fortunes and chances of the war, forced themselves on my mind. What men they were, these Boers! I thought of them as I had seen them in the morning riding forward through the rain—thousands of independent riflemen, thinking for themselves, possessed of beautiful weapons, led with skill, living as they rode without commissariat or transport or ammunition column, moving like the wind, and supported by iron constitutions and a stern, hard, Old Testament God who should surely smite the Amalekite hip and thigh. And then, above the rain storm that beat loudly on the corrugated iron, I heard the sound of a chaunt. The Boers were singing their evening psalm, and the menacing notes—more full of indignant war than love and mercy—struck a chill into my heart, so that I thought after all that the war was unjust, that the Boers were better men than we, that Heaven was against us, that Ladysmith, Mafeking and Kimberley would fall, that the Estcourt garrison would perish, that foreign powers would intervene, that we should lose South Africa, and that that would be the beginning of the end. So for the time I despaired of the Empire, nor was it till the morning sun—all the brighter after the rain storms, all the warmer after the chills—struck in through the windows that things reassumed their true colours and proportions.

1 January, 1900

5

[Written on board the steamer INDUNA, 21–23 December, 1899]

How unhappy is that poor man who loses his liberty! What can the wide world give him in exchange? No degree of material comfort, no consciousness of correct behaviour, can balance the hateful degradation of imprisonment. Before I had been an hour in captivity I resolved to escape. Many plans suggested themselves, were examined and rejected. For a month I thought of nothing else. But the peril and difficulty restrained action. I think that it was the news of the British defeat at Stormberg that clinched the matter. All the news we heard in Pretoria was derived from Boer sources, and was hideously exaggerated and distorted. Every day we read in the *Volksstem*—probably the most amazing tissue of lies ever presented to the public under the name of a newspaper—of Boer victories and of the huge slaughters and shameful flights of the British. However much one might doubt and discount these tales they made a deep impression. A month's feeding on such literary garbage weakens the constitution of the mind. We wretched prisoners lost heart. Perhaps Great Britain would not persevere; perhaps foreign powers would intervene; perhaps there would be another disgraceful, cowardly peace. At the best the war and our confinement would be prolonged for many months. I do not pretend that impatience at being locked up was not the foundation of my determination; but I should never have screwed up my courage to make the attempt without the earnest desire to do something, however small, to help the British cause. Of course, I am a man of peace. I do not fight. But swords are not the only weapons in the world. Something may be done with a pen. So I determined to take all hazards; and, indeed, the affair was one of very great danger and difficulty.

The State Model Schools, the building in which we were confined, is a brick structure standing in the midst of a gravel quadrangle and surrounded on two sides by an iron grille and on two by a corrugated

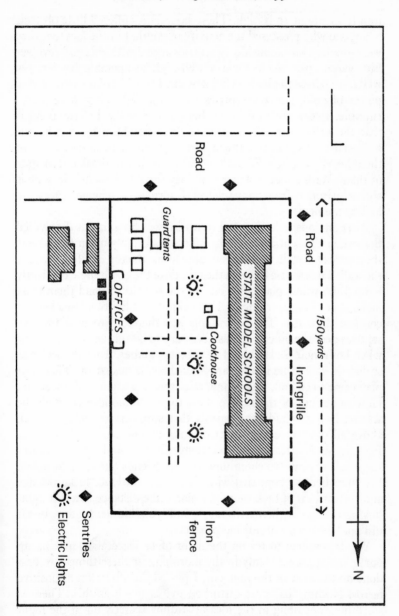

The State Model Schools, Pretoria

iron fence about 10 ft high. These boundaries offered little obstacle to anyone who possessed the activity of youth, but the fact that they were guarded on the inside by sentries armed with rifle and revolver fifty yards apart made them a well-nigh insuperable barrier. No walls are so hard to pierce as living walls. I thought of the penetrating power of gold, and the sentries were sounded. They were incorruptible. I seek not to deprive them of the credit, but the truth is that the bribery market in this country has been spoiled by the millionaires. I could not afford with my slender resources to insult them heavily enough. So nothing remained but to break out in spite of them. With another officer who may for the present—since he is still a prisoner—remain nameless I formed a scheme. Please to look at the plan.

After anxious reflection and continual watching, it was discovered that when the sentries near the offices walked about on their beats they were at certain moments unable to see the top of a few yards of the wall. The electric lights in the middle of the quadrangle brilliantly lighted the whole place, but cut off the sentries beyond them from looking at the eastern wall. For behind the lights all seemed by contrast darkness. The first thing was therefore to pass the two sentries near the offices. It was necessary to hit off the exact moment when both their backs should be turned together. After the wall was scaled we should be in the garden of the villa next door. There our plan came to an end. Everything after this was vague and uncertain. How to get out of the garden, how to pass unnoticed through the streets, how to evade the patrols that surrounded the town and, above all, how to cover the two hundred and eighty miles to the Portuguese frontiers, were questions which would arise at a later stage. All attempts to communicate with friends outside had failed. We cherished the hope that with chocolate, a little Kaffir knowledge and a great deal of luck we might march the distance in a fortnight, buying mealies at the native kraals and lying hidden by day. But it did not look a very promising prospect.

We determined to try on the night of 11 December, making up our minds quite suddenly in the morning, for these things are best done on the spur of the moment. I passed the afternoon in positive terror. Nothing has ever disturbed me as much as this. There is something appalling in the idea of stealing secretly off in the night like a guilty thief. The fear of detection has a pang of its own. Besides, we knew quite well that on occasion, even on excuse, the sentries—

they were armed police—would fire. Fifteen yards is a short range. And beyond the immediate danger lay a prospect of severe hardship and suffering, only faint hopes of success, and the probability at the best of five months in Pretoria Gaol.

The afternoon dragged tediously away. I tried to read Mr Lecky's *History of England*, but for the first time in my life that wise writer wearied me. I played chess and was hopelessly beaten. At last it grew dark. At seven o'clock the bell for dinner rang and the officers trooped off. Now was the time. But the sentries gave us no chance. They did not walk about. One of them stood exactly opposite the only practicable part of the wall. We waited for two hours, but the attempt was plainly impossible, and so with a most unsatisfactory feeling of relief to bed.

Tuesday, the 12th! Another day of fear, but fear crystallising more and more into desperation. Anything was better than further suspense. Night came again. Again the dinner bell sounded. Choosing my opportunity I strolled across the quadrangle and secreted myself in one of the offices. Through a chink I watched the sentries. For half an hour they remained stolid and obstructive. Then all of a sudden one turned and walked up to his comrade and they began to talk. Their backs were turned. Now or never. I darted out of my hiding-place and ran to the wall, seized the top with my hands and drew myself up. Twice I let myself down again in sickly hesitation, and then with a third resolve scrambled up. The top was flat. Lying on it I had one parting glimpse of the sentries, still talking, still with their backs turned; but, I repeat, fifteen yards away. Then I lowered myself silently down into the adjoining garden and crouched among the shrubs. I was free. The first step had been taken and it was irrevocable.

It now remained to await the arrival of my comrade. The bushes of the garden gave a good deal of cover, and in the moonlight their shadows lay black on the ground. Twenty yards away was the house, and I had not been five minutes in hiding before I perceived that it was full of people; the windows revealed brightly-lighted rooms, and within I could see figures moving about. This was a fresh complication. We had always thought the house unoccupied. Presently—how long afterwards I do not know, for the ordinary measures of time, hours, minutes and seconds, are quite meaningless on such occasions —a man came out of the door and walked across the garden in my direction. Scarcely ten yards away he stopped and stood still, looking steadily towards me. I cannot describe the surge of panic which nearly overwhelmed me. I must be discovered. I dared not stir an inch. But amid a tumult of emotion, reason, seated firmly on her throne, whispered, 'Trust to the dark background'. I remained absolutely motionless. For a long time the man and I remained opposite each other, and every instant I expected him to spring forward. A vague idea crossed my mind that I might silence him. 'Hush, I am a detective. We expect that an officer will break out here tonight. I am waiting to catch him.' Reason—scornful this time— replied: 'Surely a Transvaal detective would speak Dutch. Trust to the shadow.' So I trusted, and after a spell another man came out of the house, lighted a cigar, and both he and the other walked off together. No sooner had they turned than a cat pursued by a dog rushed into the bushes and collided into me. The startled animal uttered a 'miaul' of alarm and darted back again making a horrible rustling. Both men stopped at once. But it was only the cat, and they passed out of the garden gate into the town.

I looked at my watch. An hour had passed since I climbed the wall. Where was my comrade? Suddenly I heard a voice from within the quadrangle say quite loud 'All up.' I crawled back to the wall. Two officers were walking up and down the other side jabbering Latin words, laughing and talking all manner of nonsense—amid which I caught my name. I risked a cough. One of the officers immediately began to chatter alone. The other said slowly and clearly: '. . . cannot get out. The sentry suspects. It's all up. Can you get back again?' But now all my fears fell from me at once. To go back was impossible. I could not hope to climb the wall unnoticed. Fate pointed onwards. Besides, I said to myself, 'Of course, I shall be recaptured, but I will at least have a run for my money.' I said to the officers: 'I shall go on alone.'

Now, I was in the right mood for these undertakings—that is to say that, thinking failure almost certain, no odds against success affected me. All risks were less than the certainty. A glance at the plan will show that the gate which led into the road was only a few yards from another sentry. I said to myself, '*Toujours l'audace*': put my hat on my head, strode out into the middle of the garden, walked past the windows of the house without any attempt at concealment, and so went through the gate and turned to the left. I passed the sentry at less than five yards. Most of them knew me by sight. Whether he looked at me or not I do not know, for I never turned my head. But after walking a hundred yards I knew that the second obstacle had been surmounted. I was at large in Pretoria.

I walked on leisurely through the night humming a tune and choosing the middle of the road. The streets were full of burghers, but they paid no attention to me. Gradually I reached the suburbs, and on a little bridge I sat down to reflect and consider. I was in the heart of the enemy's country. I knew no one to whom I could apply for succour. Nearly three hundred miles stretched between me and Delagoa Bay. My escape must be known at dawn. Pursuit would be immediate. Yet all exits were barred. The town was picketed, the country was patrolled, the trains were searched, the line was guarded. I had £75 in my pocket and four slabs of chocolate, but the compass and the map which might have guided me, the opium tablets and meat lozenges which should have sustained me, were in my friend's pockets in the State Model School. Worst of all, I could not speak a word of Dutch or Kaffir, and how was I to get food or direction?

But when hope had departed, fear had gone as well. I formed a plan. I would find the Delagoa Bay railway. Without map or compass I must follow that in spite of the pickets. I looked at the stars. Orion shone brightly. Scarcely a year ago he had guided me when lost in the desert to the bank of the Nile. He had given me water. Now he should lead me to freedom. I could not endure the want of either.

After walking south for half a mile I struck the railroad. Was it the line to Delagoa Bay or the Pietersburg branch? If it were the former it should run east. But as far as I could see this line ran northwards. Still, it might be only winding its way out among the hills. I resolved to follow it. The night was delicious. A cool breeze fanned my face and a wild feeling of exhilaration took hold of me. At any rate I was free, if only for an hour. That was something. The fascination of the adventure grew. Unless the stars in their courses fought for me I could not escape. Where was the need for caution? I marched briskly along the line. Here and there the lights of a picket fire gleamed. Every bridge had its watchers. But I passed them all, making very short detours at the dangerous places, and really taking scarcely any precautions.

As I walked I extended my plan. I could not march three hundred miles to the frontier. I would go by train. I would board a train in motion and hide under the seats, on the roof, on the couplings— anywhere. What train should I take? The first, of course. After walking for two hours I perceived the signal lights of a station. I left the line and, circling round it, hid in the ditch by the track about 200 yards beyond it. I argued that the train would stop at the station and that it would not have got up too much speed by the time it reached me. An hour passed. I began to grow impatient. Suddenly I heard the whistle and the approaching rattle. Then the great yellow headlights of the engine flashed into view. The train waited five minutes at the station and started again with much noise and steaming. I crouched by the track. I rehearsed the act in my mind. I must wait until the engine had passed, otherwise I should be seen. Then I must make a dash for the carriages.

The train started slowly but gathered speed sooner than I had expected. The flaring lights drew swiftly near. The rattle grew into a roar. The dark mass hung for a second above me. The engine driver silhouetted against his furnace glow, the black profile of the engine, the clouds of steam rushed past. Then I hurled myself on the trucks, clutched at something, missed, clutched again, missed again, grasped some sort of handhold, was swung off my feet—my toes bumping on the line, and with a struggle seated myself on the couplings of the fifth truck from the front of the train. It was a goods train, and the trucks were full of sacks, soft sacks covered with coal dust. I crawled on top and burrowed in among them. In five minutes I was completely buried. The sacks were warm and comfortable. Perhaps the engine driver had seen me rush up to the train and would give the alarm at the next station; on the other hand, perhaps not. Where was the train going to? Where would it be unloaded? Would it be searched? Was it on the Delagoa Bay line? What should I do in the morning? Ah, never mind that. Sufficient for the day was the luck thereof. Fresh plans for fresh contingencies. I resolved to sleep, nor can I imagine a more pleasing lullaby than the clatter of the train that carries you at twenty miles an hour away from the enemy's capital.

How long I slept I do not know, but I woke up suddenly with all feelings of exhilaration gone, and only the consciousness of oppressive difficulties heavy on me. I must leave the train before daybreak, so that I could drink at a pool and find some hiding place while it was still dark. Another night I would board another train. I crawled from my cosy hiding place among the sacks and sat again on the couplings. The train was running at a fair speed, but I felt it was time to leave it. I took hold of the iron handle at the back of the truck, pulled strongly with my left hand, and sprang. My feet struck the ground in two gigantic strides, and the next instant I was sprawling in the ditch considerably shaken but unhurt. The train, my faithful ally of the night, hurried on its journey.

It was still dark. I was in the middle of a wide valley, surrounded by low hills and carpeted with high grass drenched in dew. I searched for water in the nearest gully and soon found a clear pool. I was very thirsty, but long after I had quenched my thirst I continued to drink that I might have sufficient for the whole day.

Presently the dawn began to break, and the sky to the east grew yellow and red, slashed across with heavy black clouds. I saw with relief that the railway ran steadily towards the sunrise. I had taken the right line after all.

Having drunk my fill, I set out for the hills, among which I hoped to find some hiding-place, and as it became broad daylight I entered a small group of trees which grew on the side of a deep ravine. Here I resolved to wait till dusk. I had one consolation: no one in the world knew where I was—I did not know myself. It was now four o'clock. Fourteen hours lay between me and the night. My impatience to proceed doubled their length. At first it was terribly cold, but by degrees the sun gained power, and by ten o'clock the heat was oppressive. My sole companion was a gigantic vulture, who manifested an extravagant interest in my condition, and made hideous and ominous gurglings from time to time. From my lofty position I commanded a view of the whole valley. A little tin-roofed town lay three miles to the westward. Scattered farmsteads, each with a clump of trees, relieved the monotony of the undulating ground. At the foot of the hill stood a Kaffir kraal, and the figures of its inhabitants dotted the patches of cultivation or surrounded the droves of goats and cows which fed on the pasture. The railway ran through the middle of the valley, and I could watch the passage of the various trains. I counted four passing each way, and from this I drew the conclusion that the same number would run at night. I marked a steep gradient up which they climbed very slowly, and determined at nightfall to make another attempt to board one of these. During the day I ate one slab of chocolate which, with the heat, produced a violent thirst. The pool was hardly half a mile away, but I dared not leave the shelter of the little wood, for I could see the figures of white men riding or walking occasionally across the valley, and once a Boer came and fired two shots at birds close to my hiding place. But no one discovered me.

185

The elation and the excitement of the previous night had burnt away, and a chilling reaction followed. I was very hungry, for I had had no dinner before starting, and chocolate though it sustains does not satisfy. I had scarcely slept, but yet my heart beat so fiercely and I was so nervous and perplexed about the future that I could not rest. I thought of all the chances that lay against me; I dreaded and detested more than words can express the prospect of being caught and dragged back to Pretoria. I do not mean that I would rather have died than have been retaken, but I have often feared death for much less. I found no comfort in any of the philosophical ideas that some men parade in their hours of ease and strength and safety. They seemed only fair weather friends. I realised with awful force that no exercise of my own feeble wit and strength could save me from my enemies, and that without the assistance of that High Power which interferes more often than we are always prone to admit in the eternal sequence of causes and effects, I could never succeed. I prayed long and earnestly for help and guidance. My prayer, as it seems to me, was swiftly and wonderfully answered. I cannot now relate the strange circumstances which followed, and which changed my nearly hopeless position into one of superior advantage. But after the war is over I shall hope to lengthen this account, and so remarkable will the addition be that I cannot believe the reader will complain.

The long day reached its close at last. The western clouds flushed into fire; the shadows of the hills stretched out across the valley. A ponderous Boer waggon, with its long team, crawled slowly along the track towards the town. The Kaffirs collected their herds and drew around their kraal. The daylight died, and soon it was quite dark. Then, and not till then, I set forth. I hurried to the railway line, pausing on my way to drink at a stream of sweet, cold water. I waited for sometime at the top of the steep gradient in the hope of catching a train. But none came, and I gradually guessed, and I have since found out that I guessed right, that the train I had already travelled in was the only one that ran at night. At last I resolved to walk on and make, at any rate, twenty miles of my journey. I walked for about six hours. How far I travelled I do not know, but I do not expect it was very many miles in the direct line. Every bridge was guarded by armed men; every few miles were gangers' huts; at intervals there were stations with villages clustering round them. All the veldt was bathed in the bright rays of the full moon, and to avoid these dangerous places I had to make wide circuits and often to creep along the ground. Leaving the railroad I fell into bogs and swamps, and brushed through high grass dripping with dew, and so I was drenched to the waist. I had been able to take little exercise during my month's imprisonment, and I was soon tired out with walking, as well as from want of food and sleep. I felt very miserable when I looked around and saw here and there the lights of houses, and thought of the warmth and comfort within them, but knew that they only meant danger to me. After six or seven hours of walking I thought it unwise to go further lest I should exhaust myself, so I lay down in a ditch to sleep. I was nearly at the end of my tether. Nevertheless, by the will of God, I was enabled to sustain myself during the next few days, obtaining food at great risk here and there, resting in concealment by day and walking only at night. On the fifth day I was beyond Middleburg, as far as I could tell, for I dared not inquire nor as yet approach the stations near enough to read the names. In a secure hiding place I waited for a suitable train, knowing that there is a through service between Middleburg and Lourenço Marques.

Meanwhile there had been excitement in the State Model Schools, temporarily converted into a military prison. Early on Wednesday morning—barely twelve hours after I had escaped—my absence was discovered—I think by Doctor Gunning, an amiable Hollander who used often to come and argue with me the rights and wrongs of the war. The alarm was given. Telegrams with my description at great length were despatched along all the railways. A warrant was issued for my immediate arrest. Every train was strictly searched. Everyone was on the watch. The newspapers made so much of the affair that my humble fortunes and my whereabouts were discussed in long columns of print, and even in the crash of the war I became to the Boers a topic all to myself. The rumours in part amused me. It was certain, said the *Standard and Digger's News*, that I had escaped disguised as a woman. The next day I was reported captured at Komati Poort dressed as a Transvaal policeman. There was great delight at this, which was only changed to doubt when other telegrams said that I had been arrested at Bragsbank, at Middleburg and at Bronkerspruit. But the captives proved to be harmless people after all. Finally it was agreed that I had never left Pretoria. I had—it appeared—changed clothes with a waiter, and was now in hiding at the house of some British sympathiser in the capital. On the strength of this all the houses of suspected persons were searched from top to bottom, and these unfortunate people were, I fear, put to a great deal of inconvenience. A special commission was also appointed to investigate 'stringently' (a most hateful adjective in such a connection) the causes 'which had rendered it possible for the war correspondent of the *Morning Post* to escape.'

The *Volksstem* noticed as a significant fact that I had recently become a subscriber to the State Library, and had selected Mill's essay *On Liberty*. It apparently desired to gravely deprecate prisoners having access to such inflammatory literature. The idea will, perhaps, amuse those who have read the work in question.

All these things may provoke a smile of indifference; perhaps even of triumph after the danger is past; but during the days when I was lying up in holes and corners waiting for a good chance to board a train, the causes that had led to them preyed more than I knew on my nerves. To be an outcast, to be hunted, to be under a warrant for arrest, to fear every man, to have imprisonment—not necessarily military confinement either—hanging overhead, to fly the light, to doubt the shadows—all these things ate into my soul and have left an impression that will not perhaps be easily effaced.

On the sixth day the chance I had patiently waited for came. I found a convenient train duly labelled to Lourenço Marques standing in a siding. I withdrew to a suitable spot for boarding it—for I dared not make the attempt in the station—and, filling a bottle with water to drink on the way, I prepared for the last stage of my journey.

The truck in which I ensconced myself was laden with great sacks of some soft merchandise, and I found among them holes and crevices by means of which I managed to work my way into the inmost recess. The hard floor of the truck was littered with gritty coal dust, and made a most uncomfortable bed. The heat was almost stifling. I was resolved, however, that nothing should lure or compel me from my hiding place until I reached Portuguese territory. I expected the journey to take thirty-six hours; it dragged out into two and a half days. I hardly dared sleep for fear of snoring.

I feared lest the trucks should be searched at Komati Poort, and my anxiety as the train approached this neighbourhood was very great. To prolong it we were shunted on to a siding for eighteen hours either at Komati Poort or the station beyond it. Once indeed they began to search my truck, but luckily did not search deep enough so that, providentially protected, I reached Delagoa Bay at last, and crawled forth from my place of refuge and of punishment, weary, dirty, hungry but free once more.

'Induna', *21–23 December, 1899*

Thereafter everything smiled. I found my way to the British Consul, Mr Ross,[1] who at first mistook me for a fireman off one of the ships in the harbour, but soon welcomed me with enthusiasm. I bought clothes, I washed, I sat down to dinner with a real tablecloth and real glasses; and fortune, determined not to overlook the smallest detail, had arranged that the steamer *Induna* should leave that very night for Durban. It is from the cabin of this little vessel, as she coasts along the sandy shores of Africa, that I write these lines, and the reader who may persevere through this hurried account will perhaps understand why I write them with a feeling of triumph, and better than triumph, a feeling of pure joy.

24 January, 1900

[1] Alexander Carnegie Ross (1859–1940). Served as British Consul at Lourenço Marques 1898–1900. CB 1900.

6

FRERE CAMP, NATAL, 24 December

The voyage of the *Induna* from Delagoa Bay to Durban was speedy and prosperous, and on the afternoon of the 23rd we approached our port, and saw the bold headland that shields it rising above the horizon to the southward. An hour's steaming brought us to the roads. More than twenty great transports and supply vessels lay at anchor, while three others, crowded from end to end with soldiery, circled impatiently as they waited for pilots to take them into the harbour. Our small vessel was not long in reaching the jetty, and I perceived that a very considerable crowd had gathered to receive us. But it was not until I stepped on shore that I realised that I was myself the object of this honourable welcome. I will not chronicle the details of what followed. It is sufficient to say that many hundreds of the people of Durban took occasion to express their joy at my tiny pinch of triumph over the Boers, and that their enthusiasm was another sincere demonstration of their devotion to the Imperial cause, and their resolve to carry the war to an indisputable conclusion.

After an hour of turmoil, which I frankly admit I enjoyed extremely, I escaped to the train, and the journey to Pietermaritzburg passed very quickly in the absorbing occupation of devouring a month's newspapers and clearing my palate from the evil taste of the exaggerations of Pretoria by a liberal dose of our own views. I rested a day at Government House and enjoyed long conversations with Sir Walter Hely-Hutchinson—the Governor under whose wise administration Natal has become the most patriotic province of the Empire. Moreover, I was fortunate in meeting Colonel Hime, the Prime Minister of the Colony, a tall, grey, keen-eyed man who talked only of the importance of fighting this quarrel out to the end, and of the obstinate determination of the people he represented to stand by the Queen's Government through all the changing moods of fortune. I received a great number of telegrams from all sorts of people concerning my escape—some serious, some jocular, but mostly congratulatory. Among the exceptions was the following, which I cannot resist quoting:

'London, December 30th—Best friends here hope you won't go on making further ass of yourself. McNeill.'

I hope the publicity thus given to this amiable communication will result in my learning something more of my correspondent. A gentleman who is so unrestricted by poverty or intelligence that he will spend three pounds in cabling impertinences seven thousand miles to a perfect stranger is a human curiosity who should not remain unknown to his generation.

I found time to visit the hospitals—long barracks which before the war were full of healthy men, and are now crammed with sick and wounded. Everything seemed beautifully arranged, and what money could buy and care provide was at the service of those who had sustained hurt in the public contention. But for all that I left with a feeling of relief. Grim sights and grimmer suggestions were at every corner. Beneath a verandah a dozen wounded officers, profusely swathed in bandages, clustered in a silent brooding group. Nurses waited quietly by shut doors that none might disturb more serious cases. Doctors hurried with solemn faces from one building to another. Here and there men pushed stretchers on rubber-tyred wheels about the paths, stretchers on which motionless forms lay shrouded in blankets. One, concerning whom I asked, had just had part of his skull trepanned; another had suffered amputation. And all this pruning and patching-up of broken men to win them a few more years of crippled life caught one's throat like the penetrating smell of the iodoform. Nor was I sorry to hasten away by the night mail northwards to the camps. It was still dark as we passed Estcourt, but morning had broken when the train reached Frere, and I got out and walked along the line inquiring for my tent and found it pitched by the side of the very same cutting down which I had fled for my life from the Boer marksmen, and only fifty yards from the spot on which I had surrendered myself prisoner. So after much trouble and adventure I came safely home again to the wars. Six weeks had passed since the armoured train had been destroyed. Many changes had taken place. The hills which I had last seen black with the figures of the Boer riflemen were crowned with British pickets. The valley in which we had laid exposed to their artillery fire was crowded with the white tents of a numerous army. In the hollows and on the middle slopes canvas villages gleamed like patches of snowdrops. The iron bridge across the Blue Krantz River lay in a tangle of crimson painted wreckage across the bottom of the ravine, and the railway ran over an unpretentious but substantial wooden structure. All along the line near the station fresh sidings had been built, and many trains concerned in the business of supply occupied them. When I had last looked on the landscape it meant fierce and overpowering danger with the enemy on all sides. Now I was in the midst of a friendly host. But though much was altered some things remained the same. The Boers still held Colenso. Their forces still occupied the free soil of Natal. It was true that thousands of troops had arrived to make all efforts to change the situation. It was true that the British army had even advanced ten miles. But Ladysmith was still locked in the strong grip of the invader, and as I listened I heard the distant booming of the same bombardment which I had heard two months before, and which all the time I was wandering had been remorselessly maintained and patiently borne.

Looking backwards over the events of the last two months it is impossible not to admire the Boer strategy. From the beginning they have aimed at two main objects: to exclude the war from their own territories, and to confine it to rocky and broken regions suited to their tactics. Up to the present time they have been entirely successful. Though the line of advance northwards through the Free State lay through flat open country, and they could spare few men to guard it, no British force has assailed this weak point. The 'farmers' have selected their own ground and compelled the generals to fight them on it. No part of the earth's surface is better adapted to Boer tactics than northern Natal, yet observe how we have been gradually but steadily drawn into it, until the mountains have swallowed up the greater part of the whole army corps. By degrees we have learned the power of our adversary. Before the war began men said: 'Let them come into Natal and attack us if they dare. They will go back quicker than they would come.' So the Boers came and fierce fighting took place, but it was the British who retired. Then it was said: 'Never mind. The forces were not concentrated. Now that all the Natal Field Force is massed at Ladysmith there will be no mistake.' But still, in spite of Elandslaagte, concerning which the President remarked, 'The foolhardy shall be punished', the Dutch advance continued. The concentrated Ladysmith force, 20 squadrons, six batteries and eleven battalions, sallied out to meet them. The staff said: 'By tomorrow night there will not be a Boer within twenty miles of Ladysmith.' But by the evening of 30 October the whole of Sir George White's[1] command had been flung back into the town with three hundred men killed and wounded and nearly a thousand prisoners. Then everyone said: 'But now we have touched bottom. The Ladysmith position is the *ne plus ultra*. So far they have gone; but no further!' Then it appeared that the Boers were reaching out round the flanks. What was their design? To blockade Ladysmith! Ridiculous and impossible! However, send a battalion to Colenso to keep the communications open, and make assurance doubly sure. So the Dublin Fusiliers were tailed southwards, and entrenched themselves at Colenso. Two days later the Boers cut the railway south of Ladysmith at Pieters, shelled the small garrison out of Colenso, shut and locked the gate on the Ladysmith force, and established themselves in the almost impregnable positions north of the Tugela. Still there was no realisation of the meaning of the investment. It would last a week, they said, and all the clever correspondents laughed at the veteran Bennet Burleigh for his hurry to get south before the door was shut. Only a week of isolation! Two months have passed. But all the time we have said: 'Never mind; wait till our army comes. We will soon put a stop to the siege—for it soon became more than a blockade—of Ladysmith.' Then the army began to come. Its commander, knowing the disadvantageous nature of the country, would have preferred to strike northwards through the Free State and relieve Ladysmith at Bloemfontein. But the pressure from home was strong. First two brigades, then four, the artillery of two divisions and a large mounted force were diverted from the Cape Colony and drawn into Natal. Finally Sir Redvers Buller[2] had to follow the bulk of his army. Then the action of Colenso was fought, and in that unsatisfactory engagement the British leaders learned that the blockade of Ladysmith was no unstable curtain that could be brushed aside, but a solid wall. Another division is hurried to the mountains, battery follows battery, until the present moment the South Natal Field Force numbers two cavalry and six

---

[1] George Stuart White (1835–1912). Commanded army in Natal 1899. Commanded Ladysmith garrison 2 November, 1899 to 1 March, 1900. VC 1880. KCB 1886, GCMG, GCVO, GCIE, GCB, GCSI, OM 1903. Field-Marshal 1903.

[2] Redvers Henry Buller (1839–1908). Commander in chief, South Africa, 1899. VC, 1897. KCMG 1882, KCB 1885, GCB 1894, GCMG 1900.

infantry brigades and nearly sixty guns. It is with this force that we hope to break through the lines of Boers who surround Ladysmith. The army is numerous, powerful and high-spirited. But the task before it is one which no man can regard without serious misgivings.

Whoever selected Ladysmith as a military centre must sleep uneasily at night. I remember hearing the question of a possible war with the Boers discussed by several officers of high rank. The general impression was that Ladysmith was a tremendous strategic position, and dominated the lines of approach both into the Transvaal and the Orange Free State, whereas of course it does nothing of the sort. The fact that it stands at the junction of the railways may have encouraged the belief, but both lines of advance are barred by a broken and tangled country abounding in positions of extraordinary strength. Tactically Ladysmith may be strongly defensible, but for strategic purposes it is absolutely worthless. It is worse. It is a regular trap. The town and cantonment stand in a huge circle of hills which enclasp it on all sides like the arms of a giant, and though so great is the circle that only guns of the heavier class can reach the town from the heights, once an enemy has established himself on these heights it is beyond the power of the garrison to dislodge him, or perhaps even to break out. Not only do the surrounding hills keep the garrison in, they also form a formidable barrier to the advance of a relieving force. Thus it is that the ten thousand troops in Ladysmith are at this moment actually an encumbrance. To extricate them—I write advisedly to endeavour to extricate them—brigades and divisions must be diverted from all the other easy lines of advance, and Sir Redvers Buller, who had always deprecated any attempt to hold Natal north of Tugela, is compelled to attack the enemy on their own terms and their own ground.

What are those terms? The northern side of the Tugela River at nearly every point commands the southern bank. Ranges of high hills strewn with boulders and dotted with trees rise abruptly from the water, forming a mighty rampart for the enemy. Before this the river, a broad torrent with few and narrow fords and often precipitous banks, flows rapidly—a great moat. And before the river again, on our side stretches a smooth, undulating, grassy country—a regular glacis. To defend the rampart and sweep the glacis are gathered, according to my information derived in Pretoria, seven thousand, according to the Intelligence Branch ten thousand, of the best riflemen in the world armed with beautiful magazine rifles supplied with an inexhaustible store of ammunition, and supported by fifteen or twenty excellent quick-firing guns, all artfully entrenched and concealed. The drifts of the river across which our columns must force their way are all surrounded with trenches and rifle-pits, from which a converging fire may be directed, and the actual bottom of the river is doubtless obstructed by entanglements of barbed wire and other devices. But when all these difficulties have been overcome the task is by no means finished. Nearly twenty miles of broken country, ridge rising beyond ridge, kopje above kopje, all probably already prepared for defence, intervene between the relieving army and the besieged garrison. Such is the situation, and so serious are the dangers and difficulties that I have heard it said in the camp that on strict military grounds Ladysmith should be left to its fate; that a division should remain to hold this fine open country south of the Tugela and protect Natal; and that the rest should be hurried off to the true line of advance into the Free State from the south. Though I recognise all this and its unanswerable force I rejoice that the strategically unwise decision has been taken. It is not possible to abandon a brave garrison without striking a blow to rescue them. The attempt will cost several thousand lives, and may even fail, but it must be made on the grounds of honour, if not on those of policy.

We are going to try almost immediately, for there is no time to be lost. 'The sands,' to quote Mr Chamberlain on another subject, 'are running down in the glass.' Ladysmith has stood two months' siege and bombardment. Food and ammunition stores are dwindling. Disease is daily increasing. The strain on the garrison has, in spite of their pluck and stamina, been a severe one. How long can they hold out? It is difficult to say precisely, because after the ordinary rations are exhausted determined men will eat horses and rats and beetles and such-like odds and ends and so continue the defence. But another month must be the limit of their endurance, and then if no help comes Sir George White will have to fire off all his ammunition, blow up his heavy guns, burn all waggons and equipment, and sally out with his whole force in a fierce endeavour to escape southwards. Perhaps half might succeed in reaching our lines, but the rest, less the killed and wounded, would be sent to occupy the new camp at Waterfall which has already been laid out—such is the intelligent anticipation of the enemy—for their accommodation.

So we are going to try to force the Tugela within the week, and I daresay my next letter will give you some account of our fortunes.

195

8

Meanwhile all is very quiet in the camps. From Chieveley, where there are two brigades of infantry, a thousand horse of sorts, including the 13th Hussars and a dozen naval guns, it is quite possible to see the Boer positions, and the outposts live within range of each other's rifles. Yesterday I rode out to watch the evening bombardment which we make on their entrenchments with the 4.7 guns. From the low hill on which the battery is established the whole scene is laid bare. The Boer lines run in a great crescent along the hills. Tier above tier of trenches have been scored along their sides, and the brown streaks run across the grass of the open country south of the river. After tea in the captain's cabin—I should say tent—Commander Lampus of the *Terrible* kindly invited me to look through the telescope and mark the fall of the shots. The glass was one of great power, and I could plainly see the figures of the Boers walking about in two's and three's, sitting on the embankments or shovelling away to heighten them. We selected one particular group near a kraal, whose range had been carefully noted, and the great guns were slowly brought to bear on the unsuspecting target. I looked through the spyhole at the tiny picture—three dirty beehives for the kraal, a long breastwork of newly-thrown-up soil, six or seven miniature men gathered into a little bunch, two others skylarking on the grass behind the trench, apparently engaged in a boxing match. Then I turned to the guns. A naval officer craned along the seventeen foot barrel, peering through the telescopic sights. Another was pencilling some calculations as to wind and light and other intricate details. The crew stood attentive around. At last all was done. I looked back to the enemy. The group was still intact. The boxers were still playing—one had pushed the other down. A solitary horseman had also come into the picture and was riding slowly across. The desire of murder rose in my heart. Now for a bag! Bang! I jumped at least a foot, disarranging the telescope, but there was plenty of time to reset it while the shell was hissing and roaring its way through nearly five miles of air. I found the kraal again, the group still there, but all motionless and alert, like startled rabbits. Then they began to bob into the earth, one after the other. Suddenly, in the middle of the kraal, there appeared a huge flash, a billowy ball of smoke and clouds of dust. Bang! I jumped again; the second gun had fired. But before the shell could reach the trenches a dozen little figures scampered away, scattering in all directions. Evidently the first had not been without effect. But when I turned the glass to another part of the defences the Boers were working away stolidly, and only those near the explosion showed any signs of disturbance.

The bombardment continued for half an hour, the shells being flung sometimes into the trenches, sometimes among the houses of Colenso, and always directed with marvellous accuracy. At last the guns were covered up again in their tarpaulins, the crowd of military spectators broke up and dispersed amid the tents, and soon it became night.

27 January, 1900

7

CAMP, VENTER SPRUIT, 22 January

On Thursday, 11 January, Sir Redvers Buller began his operations for forcing the Tugela and relieving Ladysmith. Barton's[1] brigade entrenched itself at Chieveley, guarding the line of railway communication. Hildyard's[2] brigade marched westward six miles to Pretorius's Farm, where they were joined by the cavalry, the naval guns, three batteries field artillery and Hart's[3] brigade from Frere. The infantry and two batteries remained and encamped, making Clery's[4] division, while the mounted forces under Dundonald[5] moved forward to take the bridge across the Little Tugela at Springfield and, finding this unoccupied, pushed on and seized the heights overlooking Potgieter's Drift on the Tugela. On the 12th Warren's[6] division, comprising the brigades of Lyttelton[7] and Woodgate,[8] with

[1] Geoffrey Barton (1844–1923). Major-General commanding Fusilier Brigade in South Africa. Knighted 1906.

[2] Henry John Thornton Hildyard (1846–1916). Commanded 5th Division in South Africa. General and KCB 1900. GCB 1911.

[3] Arthur Fitzroy Hart (1844–1910). Commanded Irish Brigade in South Africa. Mentioned in despatches during the relief of Ladysmith. CB 1889, CMG 1900.

[4] Cornelius Francis Clery (1838–1926). Commanded 2nd Division in South Africa. CB 1884, KCB 1899, KCMG 1900. An eccentric officer, who dyed his side-whiskers blue, and rode into action in flared trousers (his varicose veins prevented his wearing the tight cavalry breeches), soft boots and gold spurs.

[5] Douglas Mackinnon Baillie Hamilton, 12th Earl of Dundonald (1852–1935). Baronet, KCB, KCVO. Lieutenant-General 1907.

[6] Charles Warren (1840–1927) Commanded 5th Division in South Africa. General 1904. KCB, GCMG, KCMG. Chief Commissioner of Police 1886–8, during which period he had the habit of issuing his orders in rhyme.

[7] Neville Lyttelton (1845–1931). Chief of General Staff 1904–8.

[8] Edward Woodgate (1845–1900). CB.

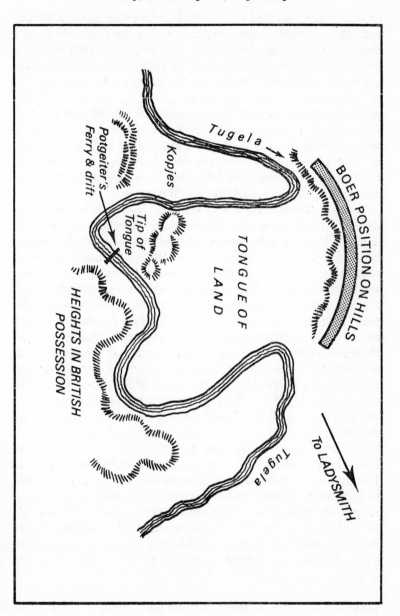

Potgeiter's Ferry

three batteries, marched to Springfield, where they camped. On the 13th the mounted troops, holding the heights above Potgieter's Drift, were strengthened by the arrival of two battalions of Lyttleton's brigade from Springfield. Sir Redvers Buller established his headquarters in this camp. On the 14th the rest of the brigade followed, and the same day the corps troops, consisting of Coke's brigade, one howitzer and one field battery, reached Springfield. On the 15th Coke moved to the position before Potgieter's, and the naval guns were established on the heights commanding the ford. All this while the Boers contented themselves with fortifying their horseshoe position which enclosed the debouches from Potgieter's Drift, and only picket firing disturbed the general peace.

Such was the situation when I wrote my last letter. It was soon to develop, though in a most leisurely and deliberate manner. The mounted forces, who had arrived at Spearman's Hill, as the position before Potgieter's was called, on the 11th, passed nearly a week of expectation. Daily we watched the enemy fortifying his position, and observed the long lines of trenches which grew and spread along the face of the opposite hills. Daily we made reconnoitring expeditions both east and west along the Tugela, expeditions always attended with incident, sometimes with adventure. One day Colonel Byng crawled with two squadrons to the summit of a high hill which overlooked the road from Colenso to Potgieter's, and a long and patient vigil was rewarded by the arrival of five Boer ox waggons toiling sluggishly along with supplies, on which we directed a rapid and effective fire till they found some refuge in a cutting. Another day we strengthened ourselves with two guns and, marching nearly to the junction of the Tugelas, gave the Boers camped there an honest hour's shelling, and extricated a patrol of Bethune's Mounted Infantry from a rather disagreeable position, so that they were able to bring off a wounded trooper. Nightly the cavalry camp went to sleep in the belief that a general attack would open on the enemy's position at dawn. Day after day the expected did not happen. Buller had other resources than to butt his head against the tremendous entrenchments which were springing up before him. Everyone discussed every conceivable alternative, and in the meanwhile it was always 'battle tomorrow' but never 'battle today.' And so it continues until this moment, and the great event—the main trial of strength—remains a future event.

But though there has been but little powder burned the situation has materially altered, and its alteration has been entirely to our advantage. We have crossed the Tugela. The river which for two months has barred the advance of the relieving army lies behind us now. The enemy entrenched and entrenching in a strong position still confronts us, but the British forces are across the Tugela, and have deployed on the northern bank. With hardly any loss Sir Redvers Buller has gained a splendid advantage. The old inequality of ground has been swept away, and the strongest army yet moved under one hand in South Africa stands face to face with the Boers on the ordinary terms of attack and defence. Let me describe the steps by which this result has been obtained.

On the afternoon of the 16th, as we were sitting down to luncheon, we noticed a change in the appearance of the infantry camps on the reverse slopes of Spearman's Hill. There was a busy bustling of men; the tents began to look baggy, then they all subsided together; the white disappeared, and the camping grounds became simply brown patches of moving soldiery. Lyttelton's brigade had received orders to march at once. Whither? It was another hour before this part of the secret transpired. They were to cross the river and seize the nearest kopjes beyond Potgieter's Drift. Orders for the cavalry and guns to move arrived in quick succession; the entire cavalry force, excepting only Bethune's Mounted Infantry, to march at 5.30 p.m., with five days' rations, one hundred and fifty rounds per man, and what they stood up in—tents, blankets, waterproof sheets, picketing gear, all to be left behind. Our camp was to remain standing. The infantry had struck theirs. I puzzled over this for some time, in fact until an officer pointed out that our camp was in full view of the Boer outposts on Spion Kop, while the infantry camps were hidden by a turn of the hill. Evidently a complex and deeply-laid scheme was in progress.

In the interval, while the South African Light Horse were preparing for the march, I rode up to Gun Hill to watch the operation of seizing the near kopjes, which stood on the tongue of land across the river, and as nearly as possible in the centre of the horseshoe position of the enemy. The sailors were hauling their two great guns to the crest of the hill ready to come into action to support the infantry attack. Far below, the four battalions crept through the scrub at the foot of the hills towards the ferry. As they arrived at the edge of the open ground the long winding columns dissolved into sprays of skirmishers, line behind line of tiny dashes, visible only as shadows on the smooth face of the veldt, strange formations, the result of bitter practical experience. Presently the first line—a very thin line—men twenty paces apart—reached the ferry punt and the approaches to the Waggon Drift, and scrambled down to the brim of the river. A single man began to wade and swim across, carrying a line. Two or three others followed. Then a long chain of men, with arms locked—a sort of human caterpillar—entered the water, struggled slowly across and formed up under the shelter of the further bank. All the time the Boers, manning their trenches and guns, remained silent. The infantry of the two leading battalions were thus filtering uneventfully across when the time for the cavalry column to start arrived.

There was a subdued flutter of excitement as we paraded, for though both our destination and object were unknown it was clearly understood that the hour for action had arrived. Everything was moving. A long cloud of dust rose up in the direction of Springfield. A column of infantry—Coke's brigade—curled out of its camp near Spearman's Hill and wound down towards the ferry at Potgieter's. Eight curiously-proportioned guns (naval 12-pounders), with tiny wheels and thin, elongated barrels were passed in a string each tied to the tail of a waggon drawn by 20 oxen. The howitzer battery hurried to follow; its short and squat pieces, suggesting a row of venomous toads, made a striking contrast. As the darkness fell the cavalry column started. On all sides men were marching through the night; much important business was toward, which the reader may easily understand by studying the map, but cannot without such attention.

Having placed his army within striking distance of the various passages across the Tugela, Sir Redvers Buller's next object was to cross and debouch. To this end his plan appears to have been—for information is scarcely yet properly codified—something as follows: Lyttelton's brigade, the corps troops forming Coke's brigade, the ten naval guns, the battery of howitzers, one field battery and Bethune's Mounted Infantry to demonstrate in front of the Potgieter position, keeping the Boers holding the horseshoe in expectation of a frontal attack and masking their main position; Sir Charles Warren to march by night from Springfield with the brigades of Hart, Woodgate and Hildyard, the Royal Dragoons, six batteries of artillery and the pontoon train to a point about five miles west of Spearman's Hill, and opposite Triegard's Drift on the Tugela.

Here he was to meet the mounted forces from Spearman's Hill, and with these troops he was next day, the 17th, to throw bridges, force the passage of the river and operate at leisure and discretion against the right flank of the enemy's horseshoe before Potgieter's, resting on Spion Kop, a commanding mountain, ultimately joining hands with the frontal force from Spearman's Hill at a point on the Acton Homes—Ladysmith road. To sum up briefly, seven battalions, twenty-two guns and three hundred horse under Lyttelton to mask the Potgieter position; twelve battalions, thirty-six guns and sixteen hundred horse to cross five miles to the westward, and make a turning movement against the enemy's right. The Boer covering army was to be swept back on Ladysmith by a powerful left arm, the pivoting shoulder of which was at Potgieter's, the elbow at Triegard's Drift, and the enveloping hand—the cavalry under Lord Dundonald —stretching out towards Acton Homes.

So much for the plan; now for its execution or modifications. One main feature has characterised the whole undertaking—its amazing deliberation. There was to be absolutely no hurry of any kind whatsoever. Let the enemy entrench and fortify. If necessary, we were prepared to sap up to his fortifications. Let him discover where the attack impended. Even then all his resistance should be over-borne. And it seems now that this same deliberation which was so punctiliously observed when speed appeared an essential to success, baffled the enemy almost as much as it mystified the troops. However, the event is not yet decided.

After about two hours' easy marching the cavalry reached the point of rendezvous among the hills opposite Triegard's Drift, and here we halted and awaited developments in the blackness. An hour passed. Then there arrived Sir Charles Warren and staff. 'Move the cavalry out of the way—fifteen thousand men marching along this road tonight.' So we moved accordingly and waited again. Presently the army began to come. I remember that it poured with rain, and there was very little to look at in the gloom but, nevertheless, it was not possible to stand and watch the ceaseless living stream—miles of stern-looking men marching in fours so quickly that they often had to run to keep up, of artillery, ammunition columns, supply columns, baggage, slaughter cattle, thirty great pontoons, white-hooded, red-crossed ambulance waggons, all the accessories of an army hurrying forward under the cover of night—and before them a guiding star, the red gleam of war.

Camp, Venter Spruit, *22 January*

We all made sure that the bridges would be built during the night, so that with the dawn the infantry could begin to cross and make an immediate onfall. But when morning broke the whole force was revealed spread about the hills overlooking the drift and no sound of artillery proclaimed the beginning of an action. Of course, since a lightning blow had been expected we all wondered what was the cause of the delay. Some said folly, others incapacity, others even actual laziness. But so far as the operations have proceeded I am not inclined to think that we have lost anything by not hurrying on this occasion. As I write all is going well, and it would have been a terrible demand to make of infantry that they should attack, after a long night march, such a position as lay and still lies in part before us. In fact it was utterly impossible to do anything worth doing that day beyond the transportation; so that, though the Boers were preparing redoubts and entrenchments with frantic energy, we might just as well take our time.

At about eight o'clock a patrol of the Imperial Light Horse, under Captain Bridges, having ascertained that only a few Dutch scouts were moving in range on the further bank, the passage of the river began. Two battalions of Hildyard's brigade, the West Yorkshires and the Devons, moved towards the drift in the usual open formation, occupied the houses, and began to entrench themselves in the fields. Six batteries came into action from the wooded heights commanding the passage. The pontoons advanced. Two were launched, and in them the West Yorkshire Regiment began to cross, accumulating gradually in the shelter of the further bank. Then the sappers began to build the bridges. Half a dozen Boers fired a few shots at long range, and one unfortunate soldier in the Devons was killed. The batteries opened on the farms, woods and kopjes beyond the river, shelling them assiduously, though there was not an enemy to be seen, and searching out the ground with great thoroughness. I watched this proceeding of making 'sicker' from the heights. The drift was approached from the ground where we had bivouacked by a long, steep, descending valley. At nine o'clock the whole of Hart's brigade poured down this great gutter and extended near the water. The bridge was growing fast—span after span of pontoons sprang out at the ends as it lay along the bank. Very soon it would be long enough to tow into position across the flood. Moreover, the infantry of the West Yorks and Devons had mostly been ferried across, and were already occupying the lately shelled farms and woods. At eleven o'clock the bridge was finished, the transported infantry were spreading up the hills, and Woodgate's brigade moved forward down the valley.

It soon became time for the cavalry to cross, but they were not accommodated, as were the infantry, with a convenient bridge. About a quarter of a mile downstream from Triegard's Drift there is a deep and rather dangerous ford, called the Waggon Drift. Across this at noon the mounted men began to make their way, and what with the uneven bottom and the strong current there were a good many duckings. The Royal Dragoons mounted on their great horses, indeed, passed without much difficulty, but the ponies of the Light Horse and mounted infantry were often swept off their feet, and the ridiculous spectacle of officers and men floundering in the torrent or rising indignantly from the shallows provided a large crowd of spectators—who had crossed by the bridge—with a comedy. Tragedy was not, however, altogether excluded, for a trooper of the 13th Hussars was drowned, and Captain Tremayne, of the same regiment, who made a gallant attempt to rescue him, was taken from the water insensible.

During the afternoon the busy engineers built a second bridge across the river, and by this and the first the artillery, the ammunition columns and the rest of the mass of wheeled transport defiled. All that day and through the night this monotonous business of passing the waggons across continued. The cavalry had bivouacked—all tents and even waterproofs were left behind—within the infantry picket lines, and we awoke at the break of day expecting to hear the boom of the first gun. 'Quite right to wait until there was a whole day to make the attack in. Suppose that was the reason we did not hurry yesterday.' But no guns fired near Triegard's Drift, and only the frontal force at Potgieter's began its usual bombardment. Sir Charles Warren, moreover, said that his artillery had not finished crossing— one battery still to cross—and that there was no hurry. Deliberation was the order of the day. So again everyone was puzzled, and not a few were critical, for in modern times everyone thinks, and even a native camp follower has his views on tactics and strategy.

A very complete consolation awaited the cavalry. All that Warren did with his infantry on this day, the 18th, was to creep cautiously forward about two miles towards the Boer position, which with its left resting on Spion Kop stretched along the edge and crest of a lofty plateau, from which long gently-sloping spurs and arêtes ran down to the river. For us, however, there was more diverting employment. 'The mounted brigade will guard the left flank of the infantry.' Such was the order; and is not offence the surest defence? Accordingly, all the irregular cavalry moved in a considerable column westward across the front of the Boer position, endeavouring to find where its flank rested, and prying with inquisitive patrols at every object of interest. The order of march was as follows: First, the Composite Regiment (one squadron of Imperial Light Horse, the 6oth Rifles, mounted infantry and one squadron of Natal Carbineers), 350 of the very best; next four squadrons of the South African Light Horse, good-shooting, high-class colonial volunteers with officers of experience; then Thorneycroft's[1] Mounted Infantry. 'Lived in Natal all our lives! Know every inch of it, sir!' And behind these alert mounted riflemen moved the ponderous and terrible regulars, 13th Hussars and Royals, with the dreaded *arme blanche*. 'Wait till we get among them.' Altogether a formidable brigade.

There were many halts, and no one hurried, so that at two o'clock the whole cavalry formed a line of observation along the lower kopjes by the river about five miles long. The Composite Regiment was not, however, to be seen. Major Graham, who commanded it, had been seen trotting off to the westward. Two hundred Boers had also been reported moving in that direction. Presently came the sound of distant musketry—not so very distant either. Everyone pricked up his ears. Two miles away to the left was a green hill broken by rocky kopjes. Looking through my glasses I could see ten or twelve riderless horses grazing. A mile further on a group of Boers sheltering behind a kopje from the continual fire was visible. Suddenly one galloped away madly, and even at the distance it was possible to see the cloud of dust from pursuing bullets. A straggling column of Boers was trekking away across the plain back to their main position. Then came reports and rumours. 'Ambuscaded the Dutchmen—shot 'em to bits—some of them cut off—come and bag the lot.' Behind the rumours Barnes, adjutant of the Imperial Light Horse, joyful, with a breathless horse, had seen two hundred Boers running towards distant hills, to make sure of their line of retreat by the Acton Homes road into the Free State; galloped to cut them off; reached the hills first, commanded the road, and waited.

The Boers admitted afterwards that they thought that visible on

[1] Alexander Whitelaw Thorneycroft (1859–1931). Retired as Major-General. CB 1900.

the other hills two miles back were the head of our column, and they also blamed their scouts, particularly one, an Austrian. 'It all comes of trusting these cursed foreigners! If we had only had a veldt Boer out we should never have been caught.' Caught, however, they undoubtedly were. The Carbineers and the Imperial Light Horse held their fire until the scouts walked into their midst, and then let drive at the main body, 300 yards range, mounted men, smooth open grass plain. There was a sudden furious, snapping fusillade. The Boer column stopped, paralysed; then they broke and rushed for cover. The greater number galloped fast from the field; some remained on the ground dead or wounded. Others took refuge among the rocks of the kopjes and apparently proposed to hold out until dark, and hence the arrival of Lieutenant Barnes demanding reinforcements, 60th Rifles, mounted infantry and anything else, so as to attack these fellows in flank and 'bag the lot.' Meanwhile Lord Dundonald had arrived on our hill. 'Certainly, every man we can spare.' Off gallops the mounted infantry and one squadron of the South African Light Horse, and later on some of Thorneycroft's, and later still the brigadier himself. I arrived in time to see the end. The Boers—how many we could not tell—were tenaciously holding the black rocks of a kopje and were quite invisible. The British riflemen curved round them in a half-moon, firing continually at the rocks. The squadron of South African Light Horse had worked almost behind the enemy, and every Dutchman who dared make a dash for liberty ran a terrible gauntlet. Still the surrender did not come. The white flag flickered for a moment above the rocks, but neither side stopped firing. Evidently a difference of opinion among the enemy. What do we care for that? Night is coming on. Let us rush them with the bayonet and settle the matter. This from the Rifles—nobody else had bayonets. So a section pushed forward against the rocks, crawling along the ground. Anxious to see the surrender, I followed on my pony, but on the instant there broke out a savage fire from the kopje, and I with difficulty found shelter in a donga. Here were two of the Natal Carbineers—one a bearded young man of the well-to-do farmer class, the other a young fair-haired gentleman—both privates, both as cool as ice. 'Vewy astonishing outburst of fire,' said the younger man in a delicate voice. 'I would recommend your remaining here with your horse for the present.' Accordingly we lay still on the grass slope and awaited developments. The young gentleman put his helmet over the crest on the end of his rifle, and was much diverted to hear bullets whistle round it. At intervals he substituted his head for the helmet and reported the state of the game. 'Bai Jove, the Rifles are in a hot place.' I peered cautiously. A hundred yards away the mounted infantry section were extended. The dust spurts rose round the men, who remained pinned to the earth, scarcely able to raise their heads to fire. Whatever passed over them came whizzing in our direction. The Natal volunteer, however, was much too interested in the proceedings to forego his view. 'Deah, deah, they've fixed bayonets! Why, they're coming back. They've had someone hurt.' I looked again for a moment. The line of riflemen was certainly retiring, wriggling backwards slowly on their bellies. Two brown forms lay still and hunched in the abandoned position. Then suddenly the retiring riflemen jumped and ran for shelter in our donga. One lad jumped right in among us laughing and panting, and the whole party turned at once and lined the bank. First-class infantry can afford to retire at the double, sure that they will stop at a word. 'We got to within fifty yards of the Dutchmen,' they said; 'but it was too hot to go further. They've shot two fellows through the head.' Eventually we all retired to the main position on the ridge above us. Lord Dundonald and his staff had just arrived.

'There! there's the white flag again. Shoot the devils,' cried a soldier, and the musketry crashed out fiercely. 'What's to be done, sir?' said the captain, turning to the brigadier; 'the white flag has been up off and on for the last half hour, but they don't stop firing, and they've just killed two of my men.' 'Give them one more chance.' 'Cease fire—cease fire there, will you,' for the men were very angry, and so at last the musketry died away, and there was silence. Then from among the rocks three dark figures stood up holding up their hands and at this tangible evidence of surrender we got on our horses and galloped towards them waving pocket-handkerchieves and signalling flags to show them that their surrender was accepted. Altogether there were twenty-four prisoners—all Boers of the most formidable type—a splendid haul, and I thought with delight of my poor friends the prisoners at Pretoria. This might redeem a few. Then we searched the ground, finding ten dead or dying and twenty loose horses, ten dead and eight badly wounded men. The soldiers crowded round these last, covering them up with blankets or mackintoshes, propping their heads with saddles for pillows, and giving them water and biscuits from their bottles and haversacks. Anger had turned to pity in an instant. The desire to kill was gone.

The desire to comfort replaced it. A little alert officer came up to me. Two minutes before his eyes were bright and joyous with the excitement of the manhunt. He had galloped a mile—mostly under fire—to bring the reinforcements to surround the Boers. 'Bag the lot, you know.' Now he was very sad. 'There's a poor boy dying up there—only a boy, and so cold—who's got a blanket?' So the soldiers recovered the Boer wounded, and we told the prisoners that they would be shown courtesy and kindness worthy of brave men and a famous quarrel. The Boer dead were collected and a flag of truce was sent to the enemy's lines to invite a burying and identification party at dawn. I have often seen dead men, killed in war—thousands at Omdurman—scores elsewhere, black and white, but the Boer dead aroused the most painful emotions. Here by the rock under which he had fought lay the field cornet of Heilbronn, Mr de Mentz—a gray-haired man of over sixty years, with firm aquiline features and a short beard. The stony face was grimly calm, but it bore the stamp of unalterable resolve; the look of a man who had thought it all out, and was quite certain that his cause was just, and such as a sober citizen might give his life for. Nor was I surprised when the Boer prisoners told me that Mentz had refused all suggestions of surrender, and that when his left leg was smashed by a bullet had continued to load and fire until he bled to death; and they found him, pale and bloodless, holding his wife's letter in his hand. Beside him was a boy of about seventeen shot through the heart. Further on lay our own two poor riflemen with their heads smashed like eggshells; and I suppose they had mothers or wives far away at the end of the deep-sea cables. Ah, horrible war, amazing medley of the glorious and the squalid, the pitiful and the sublime, if modern men of light and leading saw your face closer simple folk would see it hardly ever.

It could not be denied that the cavalry had scored a brilliant success. We had captured 24, killed 10 and wounded eight—total, 42. Moreover, we had seen the retreating Boers dragging and supporting their injured friends from the field, and might fairly claim 15 knocked out of time, besides those in our hands, total 57; a fine bag, for which we had had to pay scarcely anything. Two soldiers of the mounted infantry killed, one trooper of the Imperial Light Horse slightly, and one officer, Captain Shore—the twenty-third officer of this regiment hit during the last three months, severely wounded.

17 February, 1900

8

CAVALRY CAMP, VENTER SPRUIT, 23 January

It is the remarkable characteristic of strong races, as of honourable men, to keep tempers in the face of disappointment, and never to lose a just sense of proportion; and it is, moreover, the duty of every citizen in times of trouble to do or say or even to think nothing that can weaken or discourage the energies of the state. Sir Redvers Buller's army has met with another serious check in the attempt to relieve Ladysmith. We have approached, tested and assailed the Boer positions beyond the Tugela, fighting more or less continuously for five days, and the result is that we find they cannot be pierced from the direction of Triegard's Drift any more than at Colenso. With the loss of more than two thousand men out of a small army, we find it necessary to recross the river and seek for some other line of attack; and meanwhile the long and brave resistance of Ladysmith must be drawing to a close. Indeed, it is the opinion of many good judges that further efforts to relieve the town will only be attended with further loss. As to this I do not pronounce, but I am certain of one thing—that further efforts must be made, without regard to the loss of life which will attend them.

I have seen and heard a good deal of what has passed here. I have often been blamed for the freedom with which I have written of other operations and criticised their commanders. I respectfully submit that I am as venomous an amateur strategist as exists at this time. It is very easy—and much more easy than profitable—when freed from all responsibility to make daring suggestions and express decided opinions. I assert that I would not hesitate to criticise mercilessly if I was not myself sobered by the full appreciation of the extraordinary difficulties which the relief of Ladysmith presents, and if there be anyone who has not confidence in my desire to write the truth I appeal to him to be patient and calm, to recognise that perhaps the task before Sir Redvers Buller and Sir Charles Warren is an actual impossibility, that if these generals are not capable men—among the best that our times produce—it is difficult to know where and how others may be obtained, and finally to brutally face the fact that Sir George White and his heroic garrison may be forced to become the prisoners of the Boers, remembering always that nothing that happens, either victory or defeat, in northern Natal can affect the ultimate result of the war. In a word, let no one despair of the Empire because a few thousand soldiers are killed, wounded or captured. Now for the story as plainly and briefly as possible.

When Buller had arrived at Potgieter's he found himself confronted by a horseshoe position of great strength, enclosing and closing the debouches from the ford where he had secured a practical bridgehead. He therefore masked Potgieter's with seven battalions and 24 guns, and sent Warren with 12 battalions and 36 guns to turn the right, which rested on the lofty hill—almost mountain—of Spion Kop. The Boers, to meet this turning movement, extended their line westwards along the heights of the Tugela valley almost as far as Acton Homes. Their whole position was, therefore, shaped like a note of interrogation laid on its side, —⌒, the curve in front of General Lyttelton, the straight line before Sir Charles Warren. At the angle formed by the junction of the curve and the line stands Spion Kop—'look-out hill'. The curved position in front of General Lyttelton has already been described in a previous letter. The straight position in front of Sir Charles Warren ran in two lines along the edge and crest of a plateau which rises steeply two miles from the river, but is approachable by numerous long arêtes and dongas. These letters have completed the chronicle down to the evening of the 18th, when the successful cavalry action was fought on the extreme left.

I do not know why nothing was done on the 19th, but it does not appear that anything was lost by the delay. The enemy's entrenchments were already complete, and neither his numbers nor the strength of his position could increase.

On the 20th Warren, having crept up the arêtes and dongas, began his attack. The brigades of Generals Woodgate and Hart pushed forward on the right, and the Lancashire and Irish Regiments, fighting with the usual gallantry of Her Majesty's troops, succeeded, in spite of a heavy fire of rifles and artillery, in effecting lodgements at various points along the edge of the plateau, capturing some portions of the enemy's first line of entrenchments. On the extreme left the cavalry under Lord Dundonald demonstrated effectively, and the

South African Light Horse under Colonel Byng actually took and held without artillery support of any kind a high hill, called henceforward 'Bastion Hill', between the Dutch right and centre. Major Childe, the officer whose squadron performed this daring exploit, was killed on the summit by the shell-fire to which the successful assailants were subjected by the Boers. In the evening infantry reinforcements of Hildyard's brigade arrived, and at dawn the cavalry handed over the hill to their charge. The losses during the day did not exceed 350 officers and men wounded—with a fortunate small proportion of killed—and fell mainly on the Lancashire Fusiliers, the Dublin Fusiliers (always in the front) and the Royal Lancaster Regiment. They were not disproportioned to the apparent advantage gained.

On the 21st the action was renewed. Hart's and Woodgate's brigades on the right made good and extended their lodgements, capturing all the Boer trenches of their first defensive line along the edge of the plateau. To the east of 'Bastion Hill' there runs a deep re-entrant, which appeared to open a cleft between the right and centre of the Boer position. The tendency of General Hildyard's action, with five battalions and two batteries, on the British left this day was to drive a wedge of infantry into this cleft and so split the Boer position in two. But as the action developed the great strength of the second line of defence gradually revealed itself. It ran along the crest of the plateau, which rises about a thousand yards from the edge in a series of smooth grassy slopes of concave surface, forming veritable glacis for the musketry of the defence to sweep; and it consisted of a line of low rock and earth redoubts and shelter trenches, apparently provided with overhead cover, and cleverly arranged to command all approaches with fire—often with cross fire, sometimes with converging fire. Throughout the 21st, as during the 20th, the British artillery, consisting of six field batteries and four howitzers, the latter of apparently tremendous power, bombarded the whole Boer position ceaselessly, firing on each occasion nearly 3,000 shells. They claim to have inflicted considerable loss on the enemy, and must have inflicted some, but failed utterly and painfully to silence the musketry, to clear the trenches, or reach and overpower the Dutch artillery, which did not number more than seven or eight guns and two Maxim shell guns, but which were better served and manoeuvred and of superior quality. The losses in the action of the 20th were about 130 officers and men killed and wounded, but this must be regarded as severe in the face of the fact that no serious collision or even contact took place.

During the 22nd and 23rd the troops held the positions they had won, and the infantry were subjected to a harassing shell fire from the Boer guns which, playing from either flank, searched the re-entrants in which the battalions sheltered, and which, though they did not cause a greater loss than 40 men on the 22nd and 25 on the 23rd, nevertheless made the position extremely uncomfortable. It was quite evident that the troops could not be fairly required to endure this bombardment, against which there was no protection, indefinitely. Nor was any good object, but on the contrary, to be gained by waiting.

Three alternatives presented themselves to the Council of War held on the 22nd. First, to frontally attack the second Boer position along the crest by moonlight. This would involve a great slaughter and a terrible risk. Secondly, to withdraw again beyond the Tugela and look elsewhere for a passage; a moral defeat and a further delay in the relief of Ladysmith; and thirdly, to attack by night the mountain of Spion Kop, and thence to enfilade and command the Boer entrenchments. Sir Redvers Buller, who has always disdained effect, was for the second course—unpalatable as it must have been to a fearless man; miserable as it is to call off infantry after they have made sacrifices and won positions, and to call them off a second time. The discussion was an informal one, and no votes were taken, but the general yielded to the entreaties of his subordinates, rightly, I hold, because now at least we know the strength of the enemy's position, whereas before we only dreaded it; and knowledge is a better reason for action than apprehension.

It was therefore decided to attack Spion Kop by night, rush the Boer trenches with the bayonet, entrench as far as possible before dawn, hold on during the day, drag guns up at night, and thus dominate the Boer lines. There is, of course, no possible doubt that Spion Kop is the key of the whole position, and the reader has only to think of the horizontal note of interrogation, and remember that the mountain at the angle divides, commands and enfilades the enemy's lines, to appreciate this fact. The questions to be proved were whether the troops could hold out during the day, and whether the place could be converted into a fort proof against shell fire and armed with guns during the following night. Fate has now decided both.

General Woodgate was entrusted with the command, and Colonel

Thorneycroft with much of the arrangement and direction of the night attack. It does not seem that anything but good resulted from this too soon broken co-operation. Thorneycroft declined to attack on the night of the 22nd because the ground had not been reconnoitred, and he wanted to be sure of his way. The infantry therefore had another day's shelling on the 23rd. Good reconnaissances were, however, made; Lyttelton was strengthened by two Fusilier battalions from Chieveley, Warren was reinforced by Talbot Coke's brigade and the Imperial Light Infantry, and at one o'clock on the morning of 24 January General Woodgate started from his camp with the Lancashire Fusiliers, the Royal Lancaster Regiment, two companies of the South Lancashires, and Thorneycroft's Mounted Infantry. Guided by Colonel Thorneycroft the force made its way successfully up the southern spur of the mountain, over most difficult and dangerous ground, and surprised the Boers guarding the entrenchments on the summit. At three o'clock those listening in the plain heard the sudden outburst of musketry, followed by the loud cheers of the troops, and knew that the position had been carried. Ten soldiers were killed and wounded in the firing. Six Boers perished by the bayonet. The force then proceeded to fortify itself, but the surface of the hill was extremely unsuited to defence. The rocks which covered the summit made digging an impossibility, and were themselves mostly too large to be built into sangars. Such cover, however, as had been made by the Boers was utilised and improved.

Morning broke, and with it the attack. The enemy, realising the vital importance of the position, concentrated every man and every gun at his disposal for its recapture. A fierce and furious shell fire was opened forthwith on the summit, causing immediate and continual loss. General Woodgate was wounded, and the command devolved on a regimental officer who, at half-past six, applied for reinforcements in a letter which scarcely displayed that composure and determination necessary in such a bloody debate.

Sir Redvers Buller then took the extreme step of appointing Major Thorneycroft—already only a local Lieutenant-Colonel—local brigadier-general commanding on the summit of Spion Kop. The Imperial Light Infantry, the Middlesex Regiment, and a little later the Somersets, from General Talbot Coke's brigade, were ordered to reinforce the defence, but General Coke was directed to remain below the summit of the hill, so that the fight might still be conducted by the brave men who were fighting.

The Boers followed, and accompanied their shells by a vigorous rifle attack on the hill, and about half-past eight the position became most critical. The troops were driven almost entirely off the main plateau and the Boers succeeded in re-occupying some of their trenches. A frightful disaster was narrowly averted. About twenty men in one of the captured trenches abandoned their resistance, threw up their hands and called out that they would surrender. Colonel Thorneycroft, whose great stature made him everywhere conspicuous, and who was from dawn to dusk in the first firing line, rushed to the spot. The Boers advancing to take the prisoners—as at Nicholson Nek—were scarcely thirty yards away. Thorneycroft shouted to the Boer leader: 'You may go to hell. I command on this hill and allow no surrender. Go on with your firing.' Which latter they did with terrible effect, killing many. The survivors, with the rest of the firing line, fled two hundred yards, were rallied by their indomitable commander and, being reinforced by two brave companies of the Middlesex Regiment, charged back, recovering all lost ground, and the position was maintained until nightfall. No words in these days of extravagant expression can do justice to the glorious endurance which the English regiments—for they were all English—displayed throughout the long dragging hours of hell fire. Between three and four o'clock the shells were falling on the hill from both sides, as I counted, at the rate of seven a minute, and the strange discharge of the Maxim shell guns—the 'pom-poms' as these terrible engines are called for want of a correct name—lacerated the hillsides with dotted chains of smoke and dust. A thick and continual stream of wounded flowed rearwards. A village of ambulance waggons grew up at the foot of the mountain. The dead and injured, smashed and broken by the shells, littered the summit till it was a bloody, reeking shambles. Thirst tormented the soldiers, for though water was at hand the fight was too close and furious to give even a moment's breathing space. But nothing could weaken the stubborn vigour of the defence. The Dorset Regiment—the last of Talbot Coke's brigade—was ordered to support the struggling troops. The gallant Lyttelton of his own accord sent the Scottish Rifles and the 3rd King's Royal Rifles from Potgieter's to aid them. But though these troops, with the exception of the Scottish Rifles, did not arrive in time to join in the main action; though the British artillery, unable to find or reach the enemy's guns, could only tear up the ground in impotent fury; though the shell fire and rifle fire never ceased for an instant—the magnificent infantry maintained the defence, and night closed in with the British still in possession of the hill.

I find it convenient, and perhaps the reader will allow me, to break into a more personal account of what followed. It drove us all mad to watch idly in camp the horrible shelling that was directed on the captured position, and at about four o'clock I rode with Captain R. Brooke, 7th Hussars, to Spion Kop, to find out what the true situation was. We passed through the ambulance village and, leaving our horses, climbed up the spur. Streams of wounded met us and obstructed our path. Men were staggering along alone, or supported by comrades, or crawling on hands and knees, or carried on stretchers. Corpses lay here and there. Many of the wounds were of a horrible nature. The splinters and fragments of the shell had torn and mutilated in the most ghastly manner. I passed about two hundred while I was climbing up. There was, moreover, a small but steady leakage of unwounded men of all corps. Some of these cursed and swore. Others were utterly exhausted and fell on the hillside in a stupor. Others again seemed drunk, though they had had no liquor. Scores were sleeping heavily. Fighting was still proceeding, and stray bullets struck all over the ground, while the Maxim shell guns scourged the flanks of the hill and the sheltering infantry at regular intervals of a minute. The 3rd King's Royal Rifles were out of reach. The Dorset Regiment was the only battalion not thrown into the fight, and intact as an effective unit. General Talbot Coke and his staff were sitting on the spur.

I had seen some service and Captain Brooke has been through more fighting than any other officer of late years. We were so profoundly impressed by the spectacle and situation that we resolved to go and tell Sir Charles Warren what we had seen. The fight had been so close that no proper reports had been sent to the general, so he listened with great patience and attention. One thing was quite clear—unless good and efficient cover could be made during the night, and unless guns could be dragged to the summit of the hill to match the Boer artillery the infantry could not, perhaps would not, endure another day. The human machine will not stand certain strains for long.

The questions were: could guns be brought up the hill and, if so, could the troops maintain themselves. The artillery officers had examined the track. They said 'No' and that even if they could reach the top of the hill they would only be shot out of action. Two long-range naval 12-pounders, much heavier than the field guns, had arrived. The naval lieutenant in charge said he could go anywhere, or would have a try anyway. He was quite sure that if he could get on top of the hill he would knock out the Boer guns or be knocked out by them, and that was what he wanted to make sure. I do not believe that the attempt would have succeeded, or that the guns could have been in position by daylight, but the contrast in spirit was very refreshing.

Another informal council of war was called. Sir Charles Warren wanted to know Colonel Thorneycroft's views. I was sent to obtain them. The darkness was intense. The track stony and uneven. It was hopelessly congested with ambulances, stragglers and wounded men. I soon had to leave my horse, and then toiled upwards, finding everywhere streams of men winding about the almost precipitous sides of the mountain, and desultory crackle of musketry at the top. Only one solid battalion remained—the Dorsets. All the others were intermingled. Officers had collected little parties, companies and half-companies; here and there larger bodies had formed, but there was no possibility, in the darkness, of gripping anybody or anything. Yet it must not be imagined that the infantry were demoralised. Stragglers and weaklings there were in plenty. But the mass of soldiers were determined men. One man I found dragging down a box of ammunition quite by himself, 'To do something,' he said. A sergeant with twenty men formed up was inquiring what troops were to hold the position. Regimental officers everywhere cool and cheery, each with a little group of men around him, all full of fight and energy. But the darkness and the broken ground paralysed everyone.

I found Colonel Thorneycroft at the top of the mountain. Everyone seemed to know, even in the confusion, where he was. He was sitting on the ground surrounded by the remnants of the regiment he had raised, who had fought for him like lions and followed him like dogs. I explained the situation as I had been told and as I thought. Naval guns were prepared to try, sappers and working parties were already on the road with thousands of sandbags. What did he think? But the decision had already been taken. He had never received any messages from the general, had not had time to write any. Messages had been sent him, he had wanted to send others himself. The fight had been too hot, too close, too interlaced for him to attend to anything, but to support this company, clear those rocks, or line that trench. So, having heard nothing and expecting no guns, he had decided to

217

retire. As he put it tersely: 'Better six good battalions safely down the hill than a mop up in the morning.' Then we came home, drawing down our rearguard after us very slowly and carefully, and as the ground grew more level the regiments began to form again into their old solid blocks.

Such was the fifth of the series of actions called the Battle of Spion Kop. It is an event which the British people may regard with feelings of equal pride and sadness. It redounds to the honour of the soldiers, though not greatly to that of the generals. But when all that will be written about this has been written, and all the bitter words have been said by the people who never do anything themselves, the wise and just citizen will remember that these same generals are, after all, brave, capable, noble English gentlemen, trying their best to carry through a task which may prove to be impossible, and is certainly the hardest ever set to men.

The Lancashire Fusiliers, the Imperial Light Infantry—whose baptism of fire it was—Thorneycroft's, and the Middlesex Regiment sustained the greater part of the losses.

We will have another try and, if it please God, do better next time.

17 February, 1900

9

Camp, Venter Spruit, 25 January

The importance of giving a general and comprehensive account of the late actions around and on Spion Kop prevented me from describing its scenes and incidents. Events, like gentlemen at a levee, in these exciting days tread so closely on each other's heels that many pass unnoticed, and most can only claim the scantiest attention. But I will pick from the hurrying procession a few—distinguished for no other reason than that they have caught my eye—and from their quality the reader may judge of the rest.

The morning of the 20th discovered the cavalry still encamped behind the hills near the Acton Homes road, on which they had surprised the Boers two days before. The loud and repeated discharge of the artillery advised us that the long-expected general action had begun. What part were the cavalry to play? No orders had been sent to Lord Dundonald except that he was to cover the left flank of the infantry. But the cavalry commander, no less than his brigade, proposed to interpret these instructions freely. Accordingly, at about half-past nine, the South African Light Horse, two squadrons of the 13th Hussars and a battery of four machine guns moved forward towards the line of heights along the edge and crest of which ran the Boer position with the intention of demonstrating against them, and the daring idea—somewhere in the background—of attacking and seizing one prominent feature which jutted out into the plain and which, from its boldness and shape, we had christened 'Bastion Hill'. The Composite Regiment, who watched the extreme left, were directed to support us if all was clear in their front at one o'clock, and Thorneycroft's Mounted Infantry, who kept touch between the main cavalry force and the infantry left flank, had similar orders to co-operate.

At ten o'clock Lord Dundonald ordered the South African Light Horse to advance against Bastion Hill. If the resistance was severe they were not to press the attack, but to content themselves with a musketry demonstration. If, however, they found it convenient to get on they were to do so as far as they liked. Colonel Byng thereon sent two squadrons under Major Childe to advance, dismounted frontally on the hill, and proposed to cover their movements by the fire of the other two squadrons, who were to gallop to the shelter of a wood and creep thence up the various dongas to within effective range.

Major Childe accepted his orders with alacrity, and started forth on what seemed, as I watched from a grassy ridge, a most desperate enterprise. The dark brown mass of Bastion Hill appeared to dominate the plain. On its crest the figures of the Boers could be seen frequently moving about. Other spurs to either flanks looked as if they afforded facilities for cross fire. And to capture this formidable position we could dismount only about a hundred and fifty men; and had, moreover, no artillery support of any kind. Yet as one examined the hill it became evident that its strength was apparent rather than real. Its slopes were so steep that they presented no good field of fire. Its crest was a convex curve, over and down which the defenders must advance before they could command the approaches, and when so advanced they would be exposed without shelter of any kind to the fire of the covering troops. The salient was so prominent and jutted out so far from the general line of hills, and was besides shaped like a blunted redan, that its front face was secure from flanking fire. In fact there was plenty of dead ground in its approaches and, moreover, dongas—which are the same as nullahs in India or gullies in Australia —ran agreeably to our wishes towards the hill in all directions. When first we had seen the hill three days before we had selected it as a weak point in the Dutch line. It afterwards proved that the Boers had no illusions as to its strength and had made their arrangements accordingly.

So soon as the dismounted squadrons had begun their advance, Colonel Byng led the two who were to cover it forward. The wood we were to reach and find shelter in was about a thousand yards distant, and had been reported unoccupied by the Boers, who indeed confined themselves strictly to the hills after their rough handling on the 18th by the cavalry. We moved off at a walk, spreading into a wide open order, as wise colonial cavalry always do. And it was fortunate that our formation was a dispersed one, for no sooner had we moved into the open ground than there was the flash of a gun far away among the hills to the westward. I had had some experience of artillery fire in the armoured train episode, but there the guns were firing at such close quarters that the report of the discharge and the explosion of the shell were almost simultaneous. Nor had I ever heard the menacing hissing roar which heralds the approach of a long-range projectile. It came swiftly, passed overhead with a sound like the rending of thin sheets of iron, and burst with a rather dull explosion in the ground a hundred yards behind the squadron, throwing up smoke and clods of earth. We broke into a gallop, and moved in a curving course towards the wood. I suppose we were a target a hundred yards broad by a hundred and fifty deep. The range was not less than seven thousand yards, and we were at the gallop. Think of this, Inspector-General of Artillery; the Boer gunners fired ten or eleven shells, every one of which fell among or within a hundred yards of our ranks. Between us and the wood ran a deep donga with a river only fordable in places flowing through it. Some confusion occurred in crossing this, but at last the whole regiment was across, and found shelter from the terrible gun—perhaps there were two— on the further bank. Thanks to our dispersed formation only two horses had been killed, and it was possible to admire without having to deplore the skill of the artillerists who could make such beautiful practice at such a range.

Colonel Byng thought it advisable to leave the horses in the cover of the protecting river bank, and we therefore pushed on, dismounted, and, straggling through the high maize crop without presenting any target to the guns, reached the wood safely. Through this we hurried as far as its further edge. Here the riflemen on the hill opened with long-range fire. It was only a hundred yards into the donga, and the troopers immediately began running across in two's and three's. In the irregular corps all appearances are sacrificed to the main object of getting where you want to without being hurt. No one was hurt.

Colonel Byng made his way along the donga to within about twelve or fourteen hundred yards, and from excellent cover opened fire on the Boers holding the summit of the hill. A long musketry duel ensued without any loss to our side, and with probably no more to the enemy. The colonial troopers, as wary as the Dutch, showed very little to shoot at, so that, though there were plenty of bullets, there was no bloodshed. Regular infantry would probably have lost thirty or forty men.

I went back for machine guns, and about half an hour later they were brought into action at the edge of the wood. Boers on the skyline at 2,000 yards—tat-tat-tat-tat-tat half a dozen times repeated; Boers galloping to cover; one—yes, by Jupiter—one on his back in the grass; after that no more targets to shoot at; continuous searching of the skyline, however, on the chance of killing some one and, in any case, to support the frontal attack. We had altogether three guns— the 13th Hussars' Maxim under Lieutenant Clutterbuck, detached from the 4th Hussars; one of Lord Dundonald's battery of Colts under Mr Hill, who is a Member of Parliament, and guides the majestic course of Empire besides managing machine guns; and our own Maxim, all under Major Villiers.

These three machines set up a most exhilarating splutter, flaring and crackling all along the edge of the wood and even attracted the attention of the Boers. All of a sudden there was a furious rush and roar overhead; two or three little casuarina trees and a shower of branches fell to the ground. What on earth could this be? The main action was crashing away on the right. Evidently a shell had passed a few feet over our heads, but was it from our guns shelling the hills in front, or from the enemy? In another minute the question was answered by another shell. It was our old friend the gun to the westward who, irritated by the noisy Maxims, had resolved to put his foot down. Whizz! Bang! came a third shot, exploding among the branches just behind the Colt gun, to the great delight of Mr Hill, who secured a large fragment, which I have advised him to lay on the table in the smoking room of the House for the gratification, instruction and diversion of other honourable members. The next shell smashed through the roof of a farmhouse which stood at the corner of the wood, and near which two troops of the 13th Hussars, who were escorting the Maxims and watching the flanks, had left their led horses. The next, in quick succession, fell right among them, killing one but luckily, very luckily, failed to burst. The officer then decided to move the horses to a safer place. The two troops mounted and galloped off. They were a tiny target, only a moving speck across the plain. But the Boer gunners threw a shell within a yard of the first troop leader. All this at 7,000 yards! English artillery experts please note and if possible copy.

While these things were passing, the advancing squadrons had begun to climb the hill, and found to their astonishment that they were scarcely fired at. It was a great importance, however, that the

Boers should be cleared from the summit by the Maxim fire, and lest this should be diverted on our own men by mistake I left the wood for the purpose of signalling back how far the advance had proceeded and up to what point the guns could safely fire. The ground was broken; the distance considerable. Before I reached the hill the situation had changed. The enemy's artillery had persuaded the Maxims that they would do better to be quiet—at any rate until they could see something to shoot at. Major Childe had reached the top of the hill, one man of his squadron ten minutes in front of anyone else, waving his hat on his rifle at the summit to the admiration of thousands of the infantry, all of whom saw this act of conspicuous recklessness and rejoiced. Lord Dundonald had galloped up to support the attack with Thorneycroft's Mounted Infantry and the rest of the 13th Hussars. We, the South African Light Horse, had taken Bastion Hill.

To advance further forward, however, proved quite impossible. The Boers had withdrawn to a second position a thousand yards in rear of the top of the hill. From this they directed a most accurate and damnable fire on all who showed themselves on the plateau. Beneath the crest one sat in safety and listened to the swish of the bullets passing overhead. Above the men were content to lie quite still underneath the rocks and wait for darkness. I had a message for Major Childe and I found him sitting on this dangerous ground, partly sheltered by a larger rock—a serene old gentleman, exhausted with his climb, justly proud of its brilliant success.

I found no reason to remain very long on the plateau, and had just returned to the brigadier when the Boer guns began to shell the tip of the hill. The first two or three projectiles skimmed over the surface and roared harmlessly away. But the Boers were not long in striking their mark. Two percussion shells burst on the exposed side of the hill, and then a well-exploded shrapnel searched its summit, searched and found what it sought. Major Childe was instantly killed by a fragment that entered his brain, and half a dozen troopers were more or less seriously wounded. After that, as if satisfied, the enemy's gun turned its attention elsewhere.

I think this death of Major Childe was a very sad event even among the inevitable incidents of war. He had served many years ago in the Blues, and since then a connection with the Turf had made him not unknown and well liked in sporting circles. Old and grey as he was, the call to arms had drawn him from home and wife and comfort, as it is drawing many of all ages and fortunes now. And so he was killed in his first fight against the Boers after he had performed an exploit—his first and last in war—which would most certainly have brought him honourable distinction. He had a queer presentiment of impending fate, for he had spoken a good deal to us of the chances of death, and had even selected his own epitaph, so that on the little wooden cross which stands at the foot of Bastion Hill—the hill he took himself and held—there is written: 'Is it well with the child? It is well.'

The coign of vantage which I found on the side of the hill was not only to a great extent sheltered from the bullets, but afforded an extensive view of the general action, and for the rest of the day I remained with Lord Dundonald watching its development. But a modern action is very disappointing as a spectacle. There is no smoke except that of the bursting shells. The combatants are scattered, spread over a great expanse of ground, concealed wherever possible, clad in neutral tint.

All the pomp and magnificence of Omdurman, the solid lines of infantry, the mighty Dervish array, bright with flashing spears and waving flags, were excluded. Rows of tiny dots hurried forward a few yards and vanished into the brown of the earth. Bunches and clusters of brown things huddled among the rocks or in sheltered spots. The six batteries of artillery unlimbered and the horses, hidden in some safe place, were scarcely visible.

Once I saw in miniature through glasses a great wave of infantry surge forward along a spur and disappear beyond a crest line. The patter of the Mauser rifles swelled into a continuous rumbling like a train of waggons passing over a pontoon bridge, and presently the wave recoiled; the minute figures that composed it squeezed themselves into cover among some rocks, a great many groups of men began carrying away black objects. A trickle of independent dots dispersed itself. Then we groaned. There had been a check. The distant drama continued. The huddling figures began to move again —lithe, active forms moved about re-arranging things—officers, we knew, even at the distance. Then the whole wave started again full of impetus—started—went forward, and never came back. And at this we were all delighted, and praised the valour of our unequalled infantry, and wished we were near enough to give them a cheer.

So we watched until nightfall, when some companies of the Queen's, from General Hildyard's brigade, arrived and took over the charge of our hill from us, and we descended to find the horses and, perhaps, some food, finding, by good luck, all we wanted, and lay down on the ground to sleep, quite contented with ourselves and the general progress of the army.

The action of the 21st had begun before I awoke, and a brisk fusillade was going on all along the line. This day the right attack stood still, or nearly so, and the activity was confined to the left, where General Hildyard, with five battalions and two batteries, skilfully felt and tested the enemy's positions and found them most unpleasantly strong. The main difficulty was that our guns could not come into action to smash the enemy in his trenches without coming under his rifle fire, because the edge of the plateau was only a thousand yards from the second and main Boer position, and unless the guns were on the edge of the plateau they could see very little and do less. The cavalry guarded the left flank passively, and I remember no particular incident except that our own artillery flung the fragments of two premature shells among us and wounded a soldier in the Devonshire Regiment. The following fact, however, is instructive. Captain Stewart's squadron of the South African Light Horse dismounted, held an advanced kopje all day long under a heavy fire, and never lost a man. Two hundred yards further back was another kopje held by two companies of regular infantry under equal fire. The infantry had more than 20 men hit.

On the 22nd the action languished and the generals consulted. The infantry had made themselves masters of all the edge of the plateau, and the regiments clustered in the steep re-entrants like flies on the side of a wall. The Boers endeavoured to reach them with shells, and a desultory musketry also proceeded.

During the afternoon I went with Captain Brooke to visit some of the battalions in General Hart's brigade and see what sort of punishment they were receiving. As we rode up the water-course which marks the bottom of the valley a shrapnel shell cleared the western crest line and exploded among one of the battalions. At first it seemed to have done no harm, but as we climbed higher and nearer we met a stretcher carried by six soldiers. On it lay a body with a handkerchief thrown across the face. The soldiers bearing the stretcher were all covered with blood.

We proceeded and soon reached the battalions. A company of the Dublin Fusiliers were among those captured in the armoured train, and I have the pleasure of knowing most of the officers of this regiment. So we visited them first—a dozen gentlemen—begrimed, unwashed, unshaven, sitting on the hillside behind a two-foot wall of rough stones and near a wooden box, which they called: 'The Officers' Mess.' They were in capital spirits in spite of every abominable circumstance.

'What did you lose in the action?'

'Oh, about fifty. Poor Hensley was killed, you know; that was the worst of it.'

Captain Hensley was one of the smallest and bravest men in the army, and the Dublin Fusiliers, who should be good judges, regarded him as their very best officer for all military affairs, whether attack, retreat or reconnaissance. Each had lost a friend, but collectively as a regiment they had lost a powerful weapon.

'Very few of us left now,' said the colonel, surveying his regiment with pride.

'How many?'

'About four hundred and fifty.'

'Out of a thousand?'

'Well, out of about nine hundred.'

This war has fallen heavily on some regiments. Scarcely any has suffered more severely, none has won greater distinction, than the Dublin Fusiliers—everywhere at the front—Dundee, Lombard's Kop, Colenso, Chieveley, Colenso again, and even here at Spion Kop. Half the regiment, more than half the officers killed or wounded or prisoners.

But the survivors were as cheery as ever.

'Do these shells catch anyone?'

'Only two or three an hour. They don't come always; every half hour we get half a dozen. That last one killed an officer in the next regiment. Rather bad luck, picking an officer out of all those men—only one killed today so far, a dozen wounded.'

I inquired how much more time remained before the next consignment of shells was due. They said about ten minutes. I thought that would just suit me, and bade them good morning, for I have a horror of being killed when not on duty, but Captain Brooke was anxious to climb to the top and examine the Boer position, and since we had come so far it was perhaps worthwhile going on. So we did, and with great punctuality the shells arrived.

We were talking to the officers of another regiment when they began. Two came in quick succession over the eastern wall of the valley and then one over the western. All three burst—two on impact, one in the air. A fourth ripped along a stone shelter behind which skirmishers were firing. A fifth missed the valley altogether and screeched away into the plain clear of the hills. The officers and men were quite callous. They scarcely troubled to look up. The soldiers went on smoking or playing cards or sleeping as if nothing had happened. Personally I felt no inclination for any of these pursuits, and I thought to sit and wait indefinitely, for the caprice of one of these shrieking iron devils would be most trying to anyone. But apparently you can get accustomed to anything. The regiment where the officer had been killed a few minutes before was less cheerful and callous. The little group of officers crouching in the scanty shelter had seen one of their number plucked out of their midst and slain— uselessly as it seemed. They advised us to take cover, which we would gladly have done had there been any worth speaking of; for at this moment the Boers discharged their Maxim-Vickers gun—the 'pom- pom'—and I have never heard such an extraordinary noise. Seven or eight bangs, a rattle, an amazing cluttering and whistling overhead, then the explosions of the little shells, which scarred the opposite hill in a long row of puffs of brown dust and blue-white smoke, suggesting a lash from a knotted scourge.

'Look out,' we were told, 'they always follow that with a shell.' And so they did, but it passed overhead without harming anyone. Again the Maxim-Vickers flung its covey of projectiles. Again we crouched for the following shell; but this time it did not come— immediately. I had seen quite enough, however, so we bade our friends good luck—never goodbye on active service—and hurried, slowly, on account of appearances, from this unhealthy valley. As we reached our horses I saw another shell burst among the infantry. After that there was another interval. Further on we met a group of soldiers returning to their regiment. One lad of about nineteen was munching a biscuit. His right trouser leg was soaked with blood. I asked whether he was wounded. 'No, sir, it's only blood from an officer's head,' he answered, and went on—eating his biscuit. Such were the fortunes for four days of the two brigades forming Warren's left attack.

I have already written a general account of the final action of Spion Kop on 24 January, and have little to add. As soon as the news spread through the camps that the British troops were occupying the top of the mountain I hurried to Gun Hill, where the batteries were arrayed, and watched the fight from a flank. The spectacle was inconsiderable but significant. It was like a shadow peep-show. Along the mighty profile of the hill a fringe of little black crotchets advanced. Then there were brown and red smudges of dust from shells striking the ground and white puffs from shrapnel bursting in the air—variations from the black and white. Presently a stretcher borne by five tiny figures jerks slowly forward, silhouetted on the skyline; more shells; back goes the stretcher laden, a thicker horizontal line than before. Then—a rush of crotchets rearward—one leading two mules, mules terrified, jibbing, hanging back—all in silhouette one moment, the next all smudged with dust cloud; God help the driver; shadows clear again; driver still dragging mules—no, only one mule now; other figures still running rearwards. Suddenly reinforcements arrive, hundreds of them, the whole skyline bristles with crotchets moving swiftly along it, bending forward almost double, as if driving through a hailstorm. Thank Heaven for that— only just in time too—and then more smudges on the shadow screen.

Sir Charles Warren was standing near me with his staff. One of his officers came up and told me that they had been disturbed at breakfast by a Boer shell, which had crashed through their waggon, killing a servant and horse. Presently the general himself saw me. I inquired about the situation, and learned for the first time of General Woodgate's wound—death it was then reported—and that Thorney-croft had been appointed brigadier-general. 'We have put what we think is the best fighting man in command regardless of seniority. We shall support him as he may request. We can do no more.'

I will only relate one other incident—a miserable one. The day before the attack on Spion Kop I had chanced to ride across the pontoon bridge. I heard my name called, and saw the cheery face of a boy I had known at Harrow—a smart, clean-looking young gentleman —quite the rough material for irregular horse. He had just arrived and pushed his way to the front; hoped, so he said, 'to get a job.' This morning they told me that an unauthorised press correspondent had been found among the killed on the summit. At least they thought at first it was a press correspondent, for no one seemed to know him. A man had been found leaning forward on his rifle, dead. A broken pair of field-glasses, shattered by the same shell that had killed their owner, bore the name 'McCorquodale'. The name and the face flew together in my mind. It was the last joined subaltern of Thorney-croft's Mounted Infantry, joined in the evening, shot at dawn.

Poor gallant young Englishman; he had soon 'got his job'. The great sacrifice had been required of the Queen's latest recruit.

27 February, 1900

CAMP, SPEARMAN'S HILL, 4 February

The first gleams of daylight crept underneath the waggon, and the sleepers, closely packed for shelter from the rain showers, awoke. Those who live under the conditions of a civilised city, who lie abed till nine and ten of the clock in artificially darkened rooms, gain luxury at the expense of joy. But the soldier, who fares simply, sleeps soundly and rises with the morning star, wakes in an elation of body and spirit without an effort and with scarcely a yawn. There is no more delicious moment in the day than this, when we light the fire and, while the kettle boils, watch the dark shadows of the hills take form, perspective and finally colour, knowing that there is another whole day begun, bright with chance and interest, and free from all cares. All cares—for who can be worried about the little matters of humdrum life when he may be dead before the night? Such a one was with us yesterday—see, there is a spare mug for coffee in the mess—but now gone for ever. And so it may with us tomorrow. What does it matter that this or that is misunderstood or perverted; that So-and-so is envious and spiteful; that heavy difficulties obstruct the larger schemes of life, clogging nimble aspiration with the mud of matters of fact? Here life itself, life at its best and healthiest, awaits the caprice of a bullet. Let us see the development of the day. All else may stand over, perhaps for ever. Existence is never so sweet as when it is at hazard. The bright butterfly flutters in the sunshine, the expression of the philosophy of Omar Khayyam, without the potations.

But we awoke on the morning of the 25th in most gloomy spirits. I had seen the evacuation of Spion Kop during the night, and I did not doubt that it would be followed by the abandonment of all efforts to turn the Boer left from the passage of the Tugela at and near Triegard's Drift. Nor were those forebodings wrong. Before the sun was fairly risen orders arrived: 'All baggage to move east of Venter's

Spruit immediately. Troops to be ready to turn out at thirty minutes notice'. General retreat, that was their meaning. Buller was withdrawing his train as a preliminary to disengaging, if he could, the fighting brigades, and retiring across the river. Buller! So it was no longer Warren! The commander-in-chief had arrived, in the hour of misfortune, to take all responsibility for what had befallen the army, to extricate it, if possible, from its position of peril, to encourage the soldiers, now a second time defeated without being beaten, to bear the disappointment. Everyone knows how all this, that looked so difficult, was successfully accomplished.

The army was irritated by the feeling it had made sacrifices for nothing. It was puzzled and disappointed by failure which it did not admit nor understand. The enemy were flushed with success. The opposing lines in many places were scarcely 1,000 yards apart. As the infantry retired the enemy would have commanding ground to assail them from at every point. Behind flowed the Tugela, a deep, rapid, occasionally fordable river, 85 yards broad, with precipitous banks. We all prepared ourselves for a bloody and even disastrous rearguard action. But now, I repeat, when things had come to this pass, Buller took personal command. He arrived on the field calm, cheerful, inscrutable as ever, rode hither and thither with a weary staff and a huge notebook, gripped the whole business in his strong hands, and so shook it into shape that we crossed the river in safety, comfort and good order, with most remarkable mechanical precision, and without the loss of a single man or a pound of stores.

The fighting troops stood fast for two days, while the train of waggons streamed back over the bridges and parked in huge black squares on the southern bank. Then on the night of the 26th the retreat began. It was pitch dark, and a driving rain veiled all lights. The ground was broken. The enemy near. It is scarcely possible to imagine a more difficult operation. But it was performed with amazing ease. Buller himself—not Buller by proxy or Buller at the end of a heliograph—Buller himself managed it. He was the man who gave orders, the man whom the soldiers looked to. He had already transported his train. At dusk he passed the Royals over the ford. By ten o'clock all his cavalry and guns were across the pontoon bridges. At ten he began disengaging his infantry, and by daylight the army stood in order on the southern bank. While the sappers began to take the bridges to pieces the Boers, who must have been astonished by the unusual rapidity of the movement, fired

231

their first shell at the crossing. We were over the river none too soon.

A successful retreat is a poor thing for a relieving army to boast of when their gallant friends are hard pressed and worn out. But this withdrawal showed that this force possesses both a leader and machinery of organisation, and it is this, and this alone, that has preserved our confidence. We believe that Buller has gauged the capacity of one subordinate at Colenso, or another at Spion Kop, and that now he will do things himself, as he was meant to do. I know not why he has waited so long. Probably some pedantic principle of military etiquette: 'Commander-in-chief should occupy a central position, turning movements should be directed by subordinates.' But the army believes that this is all over now, and that for the future Buller will trust no one but himself in great matters; and it is because they believe this that the soldiers are looking forward with confidence and eagerness to the third and last attempt—for the sands at Ladysmith have run down very low—to shatter the Boer lines.

We have waited a week in the camp behind Spearman's Hill. The general has addressed the troops himself. He has promised that we shall be in Ladysmith soon. To replace the 1,600 killed and wounded in the late actions drafts of 2,400 men have arrived. A mountain battery, A Battery RHA, and two great fortress guns have strengthened the artillery. Two squadrons of the 14th Hussars have been added to the cavalry, so that we are actually today numerically stronger by more than 1,000 men than when we fought at Spion Kop, while the Boers are at least 500 weaker—attrition versus recuperation. Everyone has been well fed, reinforced and inspirited, and all are prepared for a supreme effort, in which we shall either reach Ladysmith or be flung back truly beaten with a loss of 6,000 or 7,000 men.

I will not try to foreshadow the line of attack, though certain movements appear to indicate where it will be directed. But it is generally believed that we fight tomorrow at dawn, and as I write this letter seventy guns are drawing up in line on the hills to open the preparatory bombardment.

It is a solemn Sunday, and the camp, with its white tents looking snug and peaceful in the sunlight, holds its breath that the beating of its heart may not be heard. On such a day as this the services of religion would appeal with passionate force to thousands. I attended a church parade this morning. What a chance this was for a man of great soul who feared God. On every side were drawn up deep masses of soldiery, rank behind rank—perhaps, in all, 5,000. In the hollow square stood the general, the man on whom everything depended. All round were the men who within the week had been face to face with Death, and were going to face him again in a few hours. Life seemed very precarious, in spite of the sunlit landscape. What was it all for? What was the good of human effort? How should it befall a man who died in a quarrel he did not understand? All the anxious questionings of weak spirits. It was one of those occasions when a fine preacher might have given comfort and strength where both were sorely needed, and have printed on many minds a permanent impression. The bridegroom opportunity had come. But the Church had her lamp untrimmed. A chaplain with a raucous voice discoursed on the details of 'The siege and surrender of Jericho.' The soldiers froze into apathy, and after a while the formal perfunctory service reached its welcome conclusion.

As I marched home an officer said to me: 'Why is it, when the Church spends so much on missionary work among heathens, she does not take the trouble to send good men to preach in time of war. The medical profession is represented by some of its greatest exponents. Why are men's wounded souls left to the care of a village practitioner?' Nor could I answer; but I remembered the venerable figure and noble character of Father Brindle[1] in the River War, and wondered whether Rome was again seizing the opportunity which Canterbury disdained—the opportunity of telling the glad tidings to soldiers about to die.

5 March, 1900

---

[1] Rt. Rev. Robert Brindle (1837–1916). Chaplain-General holding the rank of Major-General. DSO 1898. Roman Catholic Bishop of Nottingham 1901–1916.

II

General Buller's Headquarters, 13 February

When Sir Redvers Buller broke off the combat of Vaal Krantz, and for the third time ordered his unbeaten troops to retreat, it was clearly understood that another attempt to penetrate the Boer lines was to be made without delay.

The army has moved from Spearman's and Springfield to Chieveley. General Lyttelton, who has succeeded Sir Francis Clery, in command of the 2nd Division and 4th Brigade, marching via Pretorius's Farm on the 9th and 10th, Sir Charles Warren covering the withdrawal of the supplies and transport and following on the 10th and 11th. The regular cavalry brigade, under Burn-Murdoch,[1] was left with two battalions to hold the bridge at Springfield, beyond which place the Boers, who had crossed the Tugela in some strength at Potgieter's, were reported to be showing considerable activity. The left flank of the marching infantry columns was covered by Dundonald's brigade of light horse, and the operations were performed without interruption from the enemy.

On the 12th orders were issued to reconnoitre Hussar Hill, a grassy and wooded eminence four miles to the east of Chieveley, and the direction of the next attack was revealed. The reader of the accounts of this war is probably familiar with the Colenso position and understands its great strength. The proper left of this position rests on the rocky scrub-covered hill of Hlangwani, which rises on the British side of the Tugela. If this hill can be captured and artillery placed on it, and if it can be secured from cross fire, then all the trenches of Fort Wylie and along the river bank will be completely enfiladed, and the Colenso position will become untenable, so that Hlangwani is the key of the Colenso position. In order, however, to guard this key carefully the Boers have extended their left—as at

[1] John Francis Burn-Murdoch (1859-1931). Commanded 1st Royal Dragoons in South Africa. CB 1900, CMG 1918, CBE 1919, KCVO 1925.

234

Triegard's Drift they extended their right—until it occupies a very lofty range of mountains four or five miles to the east of Hlangwani, and all along this front works have been constructed on a judicious system of defence. The long delays have given ample time to the enemy to complete his fortifications, and these trenches here are more like forts than field works, being provided with overhead cover against shells and carefully made loopholes. In front of them stretches a bare slope, on either side rise formidable hills from which long-range guns can make a continual cross fire. Behind this position, again, are others of great strength. But there are also encouraging considerations. We are to make—at least in spite of disappointments we hope and believe we are to make—a supreme effort to relieve Ladysmith. At the same time we are the army for the defence of south Natal. If we had put the matter to the test at Potgieter's and failed our line of communications might have been cut behind us, and the whole army, weakened by the inevitable heavy losses of attacking these great positions, might have been captured or dispersed. Here we have the railway behind us. We are not, as we were at Potgieter's, 'formed to a flank'. We derive an accession of strength from the fact that the troops holding Railhead are now available for the general action.

Besides these inducements this road is the shortest way. Buller, therefore, has elected to lose his men and risk defeat—without which risk no victory can be won—on this line. Whether he will succeed or not were foolish to prophesy, but it is the common belief that this line offers as good a chance as any other and that at last the army will be given a fair run, and permitted to begin a general engagement and fight it out to the end. If Buller goes in and wins he will have accomplished a wonderful feat of arms, and will gain the lasting honour and gratitude of his country. If he is beaten he will deserve the respect and sympathy of all these soldiers as a man who has tried to the best of his ability to perform a task for which his resources were inadequate. I hasten to return to the chronicle. Hussar Hill—so-called because a small post of the 13th Hussars was surprised on it six weeks ago and lost two men killed—is the high ground opposite Hlangwani and the mountainous ridges called Monte Cristo and Cingolo, on which the artillery must be posted to prepare the attack. Hence the reconnaissance of the 12th.

At eight o'clock—we never get up early in this war—Lord Dundonald started from the cavalry camp near Stuart's Farm with the South African Light Horse, the Composite Regiment, Thorney-croft's Mounted Infantry, the Colt battery, one battalion of infantry, the Royal Welsh Fusiliers and a battery of field artillery. The irregular horse were familiar with the ground, and we soon occupied Hussar Hill, driving back a small Boer patrol which was watching it and wounding two of the enemy. A strong picket line was thrown out all round the captured ground and a dropping musketry fire began at long range with the Boers, who lay hidden in the surrounding dongas. At noon Sir Redvers Buller arrived, and made a prolonged reconnaissance of the ground with his telescope. At one o'clock we were ordered to withdraw, and the difficult task of extricating the advanced pickets from close contact with the enemy was performed under a sharp fire, fortunately without the loss of a man.

After you leave Hussar Hill on the way back to Chieveley camp it is necessary to cross a wide dip of ground. We had withdrawn several miles in careful rearguard fashion, the guns and the battalion had gone back, and the last two squadrons were walking across this dip towards the ridge on the homeward side. Perhaps we had not curled in our tail quite quick enough, or perhaps the enemy had grown more enterprising of late, but in any case just as we were reaching the ridge a single shot was fired from Hussar Hill, and then without more ado a loud crackle of musketry burst forth. The distance was nearly 2,000 yards, but the squadrons in close formation were a good target. Everybody walked for about twenty yards, and then without the necessity of an order broke into a brisk canter, opening the ranks to a dispersed formation at the same time. It was very dry weather, and the bullets striking between the horsemen raised large spurts of dust, so that it seemed that many men must surely be hit. Moreover, the fire had swelled to a menacing roar. I chanced to be riding with Colonel Byng in rear, and looking round saw that we had good luck. For though bullets fell among the troopers quite thickly enough, the ground two hundred yards further back was all alive with jumping dust. The Boers were shooting short.

We reached the ridge and cover in a minute, and it was very pretty to see these irregular soldiers stop their horses and dismount with their carbines at once without any hesitation. Along the ridge Captain Hill's Colt battery was drawn up in line, and as soon as the front was clear the four little pink guns began spluttering furiously. The whole of the South African Light Horse dismounted and, lining the ridge, opened fire with their rifles. Thorneycroft's Mounted

Infantry came into line on our left flank, and brought two tripod Maxims into action with them. Lord Dundonald sent back word to the battery to halt and fire over our heads, and Major Gough's regiment and the Royal Welsh Fusiliers, who had almost reached cover, turned round of their own accord and hurried eagerly in the direction of the firing, which had become very loud on both sides.

There now ensued a strange little skirmish, which would have been a bloody rifle duel but for the great distance which separated the combatants and for the cleverness with which friends and foes concealed and sheltered themselves. Not less than four hundred men on either side were firing as fast as modern rifles will allow. Between us stretched the smooth green dip of ground. Beyond there rose the sharper outlines of Hussar Hill, two or three sheds and a few trees. That was where the Boers were. But they were quite invisible to the naked eye, and no smoke betrayed their positions. With a telescope they could be seen—a long row of heads above the grass. We were equally hidden. Yet their bullets—a proportion of their bullets—found us, and I earnestly trust that some of ours found them. Indeed, there was a very hot fire, in spite of the range. Yet no one was hit. Ah, yes, there was one, a tall trooper turned sharply on his side, and two of his comrades carried him quickly back behind a little house, shot through the thigh. A little further along the firing line another was being helped to the rear. The Colt battery drew the cream of the fire, and Mr Garrett, one of the experts sent out by the firm, was shot through the ankle, but he continued to work his gun. Captain Hill walked up and down his battery exposing himself with great delight, and showing that he was a very worthy representative of an Irish constituency.

I happened to pass along the line on some duty or other when I noticed my younger brother,[1] whose keen desire to take some part in the public quarrel had led me, in spite of some misgivings, to procure him a lieutenancy, lying on the ground, with his troop. As I approached I saw him start in the quick, peculiar manner of a stricken man. I asked him at once whether he was hurt, and he said something—he thought it must be a bullet—had struck him on the gaiter and numbed his leg. He was quite sure it had not gone in, but when we carried him away we found—as I expected—that he was shot through the leg. The wound was not serious, but the doctors declared he

[1] John Strange Spencer-Churchill (1880–1947). Mentioned in despatches, South Africa. Served at Gallipoli.

would be a month in hospital. It was his baptism of fire, and I have since wondered at the strange caprice which strikes one man down in his first skirmish and protects another time after time. But I suppose all pitchers will get broken in the end. Outwardly I sympathised with my brother in his misfortune which he mourned bitterly, since it prevented him from taking part in the impending battle, but secretly I confess myself well content that this young gentleman should be honourably out of harm's way for a month.

It was neither our business nor our pleasure to remain and continue this long-range duel with the Boers. Our work for the day was over, and all were anxious to get home to luncheon. Accordingly, as soon as the battery had come into action to cover our withdrawal we commenced withdrawing squadron by squadron, and finally broke off the engagement, for the Boers were not inclined to follow further. At about three o'clock our loss in this interesting affair was one officer, Lieutenant John Churchill, and seven men of the South African Light Horse wounded and a few horses. Thorneycroft's Mounted Infantry also had two casualities, and there were two more in the Colt detachments. The Boers were throughout invisible, but two days later when the ground was revisited we found one dead burgher—so that at any rate they lost heavier than we. The Colt guns worked very well, and the effect of the fire of a whole battery of these weapons was a marked diminution in the enemy's musketry. They were mounted on the light carriage patented by Lord Dundonald, and the advantage of these in enabling the guns to be run back by hand so as to avoid exposing the horses was very obvious.

I shall leave the great operation which has already, as I write, begun to another letter, but since gaiety has its value in the troublous times let the reader pay attention to the story of General Hart and the third-class shot. Major-General Hart, who commands the Irish Brigade, is a man of intrepid personal courage, and to his complete contempt for danger the heavy losses among his battalions, and particularly in the Dublin Fusiliers, must be to some extent attributed. After Colenso there were bitter things said on this account. But the reckless courage of the general was so remarkable in subsequent actions that, being brave men themselves, they forgave him everything for the sake of his daring. During the first day at Spion Kop General Hart discovered a soldier sitting safely behind a rock and a long way behind the firing line.

'Good afternoon, my man,' he said in his most nervous, apologetic voice; 'what are you doing here?'

'Sir,' replied the soldier, 'an officer told me to stop here, sir.'

'Oh! Why?'

'I'm a third-class shot, sir.'

'Dear me,' said the general after some reflection, 'that's an awful pity, because you see you'll have to get quite close to the Boers to do any good. Come along with me and I'll find you a nice place,' and a mournful procession trailed off towards the most advanced skirmishers.

19 March, 1900

12

Camp, Cingolo Neck, 19 February

Not since I wrote the tale of my escape from Pretoria have I taken up my pen with such feelings of satisfaction and contentment as I do tonight. The period of doubt and hesitation is over. We have grasped the nettle firmly, and shrewdly as firmly, and have taken no hurt. It remains only to pluck it. For heaven's sake no more over-confidence or premature elation; but there is really good hope that Sir Redvers Buller has solved the Riddle of the Tugela—at last. At last! I expect there will be some who will inquire—'Why not "at first?" ' All I can answer is this: there is certainly no more capable soldier of high rank in all the army in Natal than Sir Redvers Buller. For three months he has been trying his best to pierce the Boer lines and the barrier of mountain and river which separates Ladysmith from food and friends; trying with an army—magnificent in everything but numbers, and not inconsiderable even in that respect—trying at a heavy price of blood in Africa, of anxiety at home. Now, for the first time, it seems that he may succeed. Knowing the general and the difficulties, I am inclined to ask not whether he might have succeeded sooner, but rather whether anyone else would have succeeded at all. But to the chronicle!

Anyone who stands on Gun Hill near Chieveley can see the whole of the Boer position about Colenso sweeping before him in a wide curve. The mountain wall looks perfectly unbroken. The river lies everywhere buried in its gorge, and is quite invisible. To the observer there is only a smooth green bay of land sloping gently downwards, and embraced by the rocky scrub-covered hills. Along this crescent of high ground runs—or rather, by God's grace, ran—the Boer line, strong in its natural features, and entrenched from end to end. When the map is consulted, however, it is seen that the Tugela does not flow uniformly along the foot of the hills as might be expected, but that after passing Colenso village, which is about the centre of the position, it plunges into the mountainous country, and bends sharply northward; so that, though the left of the Boer line might appear as strong as the right, there was this difference, that the Boer right had the river on its front, the Boer left had it in its rear.

The attack of 15 December had been directed against the Boer right, because after reconnaissance Sir Redvers Buller deemed that, in spite of the river advantage, the right was actually the weaker of the two flanks. The attack of the 15th was repulsed with heavy loss. It might, therefore, seem that little promise of success attended an attack on the Boer left. The situation, however, was entirely altered by the great reinforcements in heavy artillery which had reached the army, and a position, which formerly appeared unassailable, now looked less formidable.

Let us now consider the Boer left by itself. It ran in a chain of sangars, trenches and rifle pits from Colenso village, through the scrub by the river, over the rugged hill of Hlangwani, along a smooth grass ridge we called 'The Green Hill', and was extended to guard against a turning movement on to the lofty wooded ridges of Monte Cristo and Cingolo and the neck joining these two features. Sir Redvers Buller's determination was to turn this widely extended position on its extreme left, and to endeavour to crumple it from left to right. As it were, a gigantic right arm was to reach out to the westward, its shoulder at Gun Hill, its elbow on Hussar Hill, its hand on Cingolo, its fingers the irregular cavalry brigade, actually behind Cingolo.

On 12 February a reconnaissance in force of Hussar Hill was made by Lord Dundonald. On the 14th the army moved east from Chieveley to occupy this ground. General Hart with one brigade held Gun Hill and Railhead. The 1st Cavalry Brigade watched the left flank at Springfield, but with these exceptions the whole force marched for Hussar Hill. The irregular cavalry covered the front, and the South Africa Light Horse, thrown out far in advance, secured the position by half-past eight, just in time to forestall a force of Boers which had been despatched so soon as the general movement of the British was evident, to resist the capture of the hill. A short sharp skirmish followed, in which we lost a few horses and men, and claim to have killed six Boers, and which was terminated after half an hour by the arrival of the leading infantry battalion—the Royal Welch Fusiliers. During the day the occupation was completed, and the brigades of Generals Wynne, Coke and Barton, then joining Warren's division with the artillery, entrenched themselves strongly and bivouacked on the hill. Meanwhile Lyttelton's division marched from its camp in the Blue Krantz Valley, east of Chieveley, along the valley to a position short of the eastern spurs of Hussar Hill. These spurs are more thickly wooded and broken than the rest of the hill, and about four o'clock in the afternoon about a hundred Boers established themselves among the rocks and opened a sharp fire. They were, however, expelled from their position by the artillery and by the fire of the advanced battalions of Lyttelton's division operating from the Blue Krantz Valley.

During the 15th and 16th Sir Redvers Buller resolved to plunge, and orders were issued for a general advance at dawn. Colonel Sandbach, under whose supervision the Intelligence Department has attained a new and refreshing standard of efficiency, made comprehensive and, as was afterwards proved, accurate reports of the enemy's strength and spirit, and strongly recommended the attack on the left flank. Two hours before dawn the army was on the move. Hart's brigade, the 6-inch and other great guns at Chieveley, guarded Railhead. Hlangwani Hill and the long line of entrenchments rimming the Green Hill were masked and fronted by the display of the field and siege batteries, whose strength in guns was as follows:

	Guns
4 5-inch siege guns	4
6 naval 12-pounder long-range guns	6
2 4.7-inch naval guns	2
1 battery howitzers	6
1 battery Corps artillery (RFA)	6
2 brigade divisions RFA	36
1 mountain battery	6
	—
	66

and which were also able to prepare and support the attack on Cingolo Neck and Monte Cristo Ridge. Cingolo Ridge itself, however, was almost beyond their reach. Lyttelton's division with Wynne's fusiliers brigade was to stretch out to the eastward and, by a wide turning movement pivoting on the guns and Barton's brigade, attack the Cingolo Ridge. Dundonald's cavalry brigade was to make a far wider detour and climb up the end of the ridge, thus making absolutely certain of finding the enemy's left flank at last.

By daybreak all were moving, and as the irregular cavalry forded the Blue Krantz stream on their enveloping march we heard the boom of the first gun. The usual leisurely bombardment had begun, and I counted only thirty shells in the first ten minutes, which was not very hard work for the gunners considering that nearly seventy guns were in action. But the artillery never hurry themselves, and indeed I do not remember to have heard in this war a really good cannonade, such as we had at Omdurman, except for a few minutes at Vaal Krantz.

The cavalry brigade marched ten miles eastward through most broken and difficult country, all rock, high grass and dense thickets which made it imperative to move in single file, and the sound of the general action grew fainter and fainter. Gradually, however, we began to turn again towards it. The slope of the ground rose against us. The scrub became more dense. Riding further was impossible. We dismounted and led our horses, who scrambled and blundered painfully among the trees and boulders. So scattered was our formation that I did not care to imagine what would have happened had the enemy put in an appearance. But our safety lay in these same natural difficulties. The Boers doubtless reflected: 'No one will ever try to go through such ground as that,' besides which war cannot be made without running risks. The soldier must chance his life.

The general must not be afraid to brave disaster. But how tolerant the armchair critics should be of men who try daring coups and fail. You must put your head into the lion's mouth if the performance is to be a success. And then I remembered the attacks on the brave and capable General Gatacre after Stormberg, and wondered what would be said of us if we were caught 'dismounted and scattered in a wood'.

At length we reached the foot of the hill and halted to reconnoitre the slopes as far as was possible. After half an hour, since nothing could be seen, the advance was resumed up the side of a precipice and through a jungle so thick that we had to cut our road. It was eleven o'clock before we reached the summit of the ridge and emerged into a more or less open plateau, diversified with patches of wood and heaps of great boulders. Two squadrons had reformed on the top and had deployed to cover the others. The troopers of the remaining seven squadrons were working their way up about four to the minute. It would take at least two hours before the command was complete; and meanwhile! Suddenly there was a rifle shot. Then another, then a regular splutter of musketry. Bullets began to whizz overhead. The Boers had discovered us.

Now came the crisis. There might be a hundred Boers on the hill, in which case all was well. On the other hand there might be a thousand, in which case . . .! and retreat down the precipice was, of course, quite out of the question. Luckily there were only about a hundred, and after a skirmish, in which one of the Natal Carbineers was unhappily killed, they fell back and we completed our deployment on the top of the hill.

The squadron of Imperial Light Horse and the Natal Carbineers now advanced slowly along the ridge, clearing it of the enemy, slaying and retrieving one field cornet and two burghers, and capturing ten horses. Halfway along the Queen's, the right battalion of Hildyard's attack which, having made a smaller detour, had now rushed to the top, came into line and supported the dismounted men. The rest of the cavalry descended into the plain on the other side of the ridge, outflanking and even threatening the retreat of its defenders, so that in the end the Boers, who were very weak in numbers, were hunted off the ridge altogether, and Cingolo was ours. Cingolo and Monte Cristo are joined together by a beck of ground from which both heights rise steeply. On either side of Monte Cristo and Cingolo long spurs run at right angles to the main hill.

By the operations of the 17th the Boer line had been twisted off Cingolo and turned back along the subsidiary spurs of Monte Cristo, and the British forces had placed themselves diagonally across the left of the Boer position. [See diagram opposite].

The advantages of this situation were to be enjoyed on the morrow.

Finding our further advance barred by the turned-back position the enemy had adopted, and which we could only attack frontally, the cavalry threw out a line of outposts which were soon engaged in a long-range rifle duel, and prepared to bivouac for the night. Cingolo Ridge was meanwhile strongly occupied by the infantry, whose line ran from its highest peak slantwise across the valley of the Gomba Stream to Hussar Hill, where it found its pivot in Barton's brigade and the artillery. The Boers, who were much disconcerted by the change in the situation, showed themselves ostentatiously on the turned-back ridge of their position as if to make themselves appear in great strength, and derisively hoisted white flags on their guns. The colonial and American troopers (for in the South African Light Horse we have a great many Americans, and one even who served under Sheridan) made some exceedingly good practice at the extreme range. So the afternoon passed, and the night came in comparative quiet.

At dawn the artillery began on both sides, and we were ourselves awakened by Creusot shells bursting in our bivouac. The enemy's fire was chiefly directed on the company of the Queen's which was holding the top of Cingolo, and only the good cover which the great rocks afforded prevented serious losses. As it was several men were

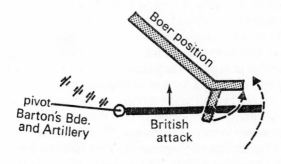

Monte Cristo: The Turning of the Boer Flank

injured. But we knew that we held the best cards; and so did the Boers. At eight o'clock Hildyard's brigade advanced against the peak of the Monte Cristo ridge which lay beyond the neck. The West Yorks led, the Queen's and East Surreys supported. The musketry swelled into a constant crackle like the noise of a good fire roaring up the chimney but, in spite of more than a hundred casualties, the advance never checked for an instant, and by half-past ten o'clock the bayonets of the attacking infantry began to glitter among the trees of the summit. The Boers, who were lining a hastily-dug trench halfway along the ridge, threatened in front with an over-whelming force and assailed in flank by the long-range fire of the cavalry, began to fall back. By eleven o'clock the fight on the part of the enemy resolved itself into a rearguard action.

Under the pressure of the advancing and enveloping army this degenerated very rapidly. When the Dutchman makes up his mind to go he throws all dignity to the winds, and I have never seen an enemy leave the field in such a hurry as did these valiant Boers who found their flank turned, and remembered for the first time that there was a deep river behind them. Shortly after twelve o'clock the summit of the ridge of Monte Cristo was in our hands. The spurs which started at right angles from it were, of course, now enfiladed and commanded. The Boers evacuated both in great haste. The eastern spur was what I have called the 'turned-back' position. The cavalry under Dundonald galloped forward and seized it as soon as the enemy were seen to be in motion, and from this advantageous standpoint we fired heavily into their line of retreat. They scarcely waited to fire back, and we had only two men and a few horses wounded.

The spur on the Colenso or western side was none other than the Green Hill itself, and judging rightly that its frowning entrench-ments were now empty of defenders, Sir Redvers Buller ordered a general advance frontally against it. Two miles of trenches were taken with scarcely any loss. The enemy fled in disorder across the river. A few prisoners, some wounded, several cartloads of ammuni-tion and stores, five camps with all kinds of Boer material and, last of all, and compared to which all else was insignificant, the dominat-ing Monte Cristo ridge stretching northward to within an easy spring of Bulwana Hill, were the prize of victory. The soldiers, delighted at the change of fortune, slept in the Boer tents—or would have done had these not been disgustingly foul and stinking.

From the captured ridge we could look right down into Ladysmith, and at the first opportunity I climbed up to see it for myself. Only eight miles away stood the poor little persecuted town, with whose fate there is wrapt up the honour of the Empire, and for whose sake so many hundred good soldiers have given life or limb—a twenty-acre patch of tin houses and blue gum trees, but famous to the uttermost ends of the earth.

The victory of Monte Cristo has revolutionised the situation in Natal. It has laid open a practicable road to Ladysmith. Great difficulties and heavy opposition have yet to be encountered and

246

Camp, Cingolo Neck, *19 February*

overcome, but the word 'impossible' must no longer be—should, perhaps, never have been used. The success was won at the cost of less than two hundred men killed and wounded, and surely no army more than the army of Natal deserves a cheaply-bought triumph.

27 March, 1900

13

Hospital Ship 'Maine,' 5 March

At half-past twelve on the 23rd General Hart ordered his brigade to advance. The battalions, which were sheltering among stone walls and other hastily-constructed cover on the reverse slope of the kopje immediately in front of that on which we stood, rose up one by one and formed in rank. They then moved off in a single file along the railroad, the Inniskilling Fusiliers leading, the Connaught Rangers, Dublin Fusiliers and the Imperial Light Infantry following in succession. At the same time the Durham Light Infantry and the 2nd Rifle Brigade began to march to take the place of the assaulting brigade on the advanced kopje.

Wishing to have a nearer view of the attack, I descended the wooded hill, cantered along the railway—down which the procession of laden stretchers, now hardly interrupted for three days, was still moving—and, dismounting, climbed the rocky sides of the advanced kopje. On the top, in a little half-circle of stones, I found General Lyttelton, who received me kindly, and together we watched the development of the operation. Nearly a mile of the railway was visible, and along it the stream of infantry flowed steadily. The telescope showed the soldiers walking quite slowly with their rifles at the slope. Thus far, at least, they were not under fire. The low kopjes which were held by the other brigades shielded the movement. A mile away the river and railway turned sharply to the right; the river plunged into a deep gorge, and the railway was lost in a cutting. There was certainly plenty of cover; but just before the cutting was reached the iron bridge across the Onderbrook Spruit had to be crossed, and this was evidently commanded by the enemy's riflemen. Beyond the railway and the moving trickle of men the brown dark face of Inniskilling Hill, crowned with sangars and entrenchments, rose up gloomily and, as yet, silent.

The patter of musketry along the left of the army, which reached

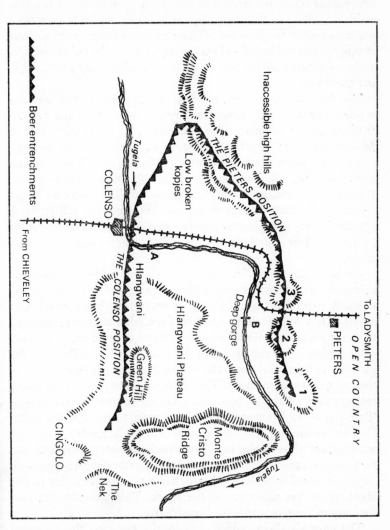

The Battle of Pieters: general position

back from the advanced kopjes to Colenso village, the boom of the heavy guns across the river, and the ceaseless thudding of the field artillery making a leisurely preparation, were an almost unnoticed accompaniment to the scene. Before us the infantry were moving steadily nearer to the hill and the open ground by the railway bridge, and we listened amid the comparatively peaceful din for the impending fire storm.

The head of the column reached the exposed ground, and the soldiers began to walk across it. Then at once above the average fusillade and cannonade rose the extraordinary rattling roll of Mauser musketry in great volume. If the reader wishes to know exactly what this is like he must drum the fingers of both his hands on a wooden table, one after the other as quickly and as hard as he can. I turned my telescope on the Dutch defences. They were no longer deserted. All along the rim of the trenches, clear-cut and jet black against the sky stood a crowded line of slouch-hatted men, visible as far as their shoulders and wielding what looked like thin sticks.

Far below, by the red ironwork of the railway bridge—2,000 yards at least from the trenches—the surface of the ground was blurred and dusty. Across the bridge the infantry were still moving, but no longer slowly—they were running for their lives. Man after man emerged from the sheltered railroad, which ran like a covered way across the enemy's front, into the open and the driving hail of bullets, ran the gauntlet and dropped down the embankment on the further side of the bridge into safety again. The range was great, but a good many soldiers were hit and lay scattered about the ironwork of the bridge. 'Pom-pom-pom,' 'pom-pom-pom,' and so on, twenty times went the Boer automatic gun, and the flights of little shells spotted the bridge with puffs of white smoke. But the advancing infantry never hesitated for a moment, and continued to scamper across the dangerous ground, paying their toll accordingly. More than sixty men were shot in this short space. Yet this was not the attack. This was only the preliminary movement across the enemy's front.

The enemy's shells, which occasionally burst on the advanced kopje, and a whistle of stray bullets from the left, advised us to change our position, and we moved a little further down the slope towards the river. Here the bridge was no longer visible. I looked towards the hilltop, whence the roar of musketry was ceaselessly proceeding. The artillery had seen the slouch hats too, and forgetting their usual apathy in the joy of a live target, concentrated a most hellish and terrible fire on the trenches.

Meanwhile the afternoon had been passing. The infantry had filed steadily across the front, and the two leading battalions had already accumulated on the eastern spurs of Inniskilling Hill. At four o'clock General Hart ordered the attack, and the troops forthwith began to climb the slopes. The broken ground delayed their progress, and it was nearly sunset by the time they had reached the furthest position which could be gained under cover. The Boer entrenchments were about 400 yards away. The arête by which the Inniskillings had advanced was bare, and swept by a dreadful frontal fire from the works on the summit and a still more terrible flanking fire from the other hills. It was so narrow that, though only four companies were arranged in the firing line, there was scarcely room for two to deploy. There was not, however, the slightest hesitation, and as we watched with straining eyes we could see the leading companies rise up together and run swiftly forward on the enemy's works with inspiring dash and enthusiasm.

But if the attack was superb, the defence was magnificent; nor could the devoted heroism of the Irish soldiers surpass the stout endurance of the Dutch. The artillery redoubled their efforts. The whole summit of the hill was alive with shell. Shrapnel flashed into being above the crests, and the ground sprang up into dust whipped by the showers of bullets and splinters. Again and again whole sections of the entrenchments vanished in an awful uprush of black earth and smoke, smothering the fierce blaze of the lyddite shells from the howitzers and heavy artillery. The cannonade grew to a tremendous thundering hum. Not less than 60 guns were firing continuously on the Boer trenches. But the musketry was never subdued for an instant. Amid the smoke and the dust the slouch hats could still be seen. The Dutch, firm and undaunted, stood to their parapets and plied their rifles with deadly effect.

The terrible power of the Mauser rifle was displayed. As the charging companies met the storm of bullets they were swept away. Officers and men fell by scores on the narrow ridge. Though assailed in front and flank by the hideous whispering Death, the survivors hurried obstinately onward, until their own artillery were forced to cease firing, and it seemed that, in spite of bullets, flesh and blood would prevail. But at the last supreme moment the weakness of the attack was shown. The Inniskillings had almost reached their goal.

They were too few to effect their purpose; and when the Boers saw that the attack had withered they shot all the straighter, and several of the boldest leapt out from their trenches and, running forward to meet the soldiers, discharged their magazines at the closest range. It was a frantic scene of blood and fury.

Thus confronted, the Irish perished rather than retire. A few men, indeed, ran back down the slope to the nearest cover, and there savagely turned to bay, but the greater part of the front line was shot down. Other companies, some from the Connaught Rangers, some headed by the brave Colonel Sitwell, from the Dublin Fusiliers, advanced to renew—it was already too late to support—the attack, and as the light faded another fierce and bloody assault was delivered and was repulsed. Yet the Irish soldiers would not leave the hill and, persuaded at length that they could not advance further, they lay down on the ground they had won, and began to build walls and shelters, from behind which they opened a revengeful fire on the exulting Boers. In the two attacks both colonels, three majors, 20 officers and 600 men had fallen out of an engaged force of scarcely 1,200. Then darkness pulled down the curtain, and the tragedy came to an end for the day.

All through the night of the 23rd a heavy rifle fire was maintained by both sides. Stray bullets whistled about the bivouacs, and the South African Light Horse, who had selected a most sheltered spot to sleep in, had a trooper hit. There was a certain number of casualties along the whole front. As soon as it was daylight I rode out with Captain Brooke to find out what had happened in the night. We knew that the hill had not been carried before dusk but hoped, since the combatants were so close together, that in the darkness the bayonet would have settled the matter.

We had just reached the hollow behind the advanced kopje from which I had watched the attack on the previous evening, when suddenly a shrapnel shell burst in the air above our heads with a sharp, startling bang. The hollow and slope of the hill were crowded with infantry battalions lying down in quarter column. The bullets and splinters of the shell smote the ground on all sides. We were both mounted and in the centre of the cone of dispersion. I was immediately conscious that nothing had happened to me, though the dust around my horse was flicked up, and I concluded that everyone had enjoyed equally good fortune. Indeed, I turned to Brooke, and was about to elaborate my theory when I saw some stir and turmoil and no less than eight men were picked up killed or wounded by this explosion. I have only once before seen in war such a successful shell, and on that occasion I was studying the effect from the other side.

My respect for modern artillery was mightily increased by this example of its power. Two more shells followed in quick succession. The first struck down four men and broke in two the leg of an infantry officer's charger, so that the poor beast galloped about in a circle, preventing his rider from dismounting for some time; the second shore along the howitzer battery killing one soldier and wounding an officer, five soldiers and three horses. All this occurred in the space of about two minutes, and the three shells between them accounted for nineteen men and four horses. And then the gun, which was firing 'on spec' and could not see the effect of its fire, turned its attention elsewhere; but the thought forced itself on me, 'Fancy if there had been a battery.' The crowded infantry waiting in support would certainly have been driven out of the re-entrant with a frightful slaughter. Yet in European war there would have been not one, but three or four batteries. I do not see how troops can be handled in masses under such conditions, even when in support and on reverse slopes. Future warfare must depend on the individual.

We climbed on to the top of the kopje, which was sprinkled with staff officers and others—all much interested in the exhibition of shell fire, which they discussed as a purely scientific question. Inniskilling Hill was still crowned with the enemy, though they no longer showed above their trenches. Its slopes were scored with numerous brown lines, the stone walls built by the attacking brigade during the night, and behind these the telescope showed the infantry clustering thickly. The Boers on their part had made some new trenches in advance of those on the crest of the hill, so that the opposing firing lines were scarcely 300 yards apart, which meant that everyone in them must lie still or run grave risks. Thus they remained all day, firing at each other continually, while on the bare ground between them the dead and wounded lay thickly scattered, the dead mixed with the living, the wounded untended, without dressings, food or water, and harassed by the fire from both sides and from our artillery. It was a very painful thing to watch these poor fellows moving about feebly and trying to wriggle themselves into some position of safety, and it reminded me of the wounded Dervishes after Omdurman—only these were our own countrymen.

It seems that a misunderstanding of the rights and wrongs, of which the reader shall be himself a judge, arose with the enemy. When day broke, the Boers, who were much nearer to the wounded than were our own troops, came out of their trenches with a Red Cross flag, and the firing thereupon ceased locally. Our people ought then to have been ready to come forward with another Red Cross flag, and an informal truce might easily have been arranged for an hour or two. Unfortunately, however, there was some delay on our part. The Boers therefore picked up their own wounded, of whom there were a few, gave some of our men a little water, and took away their rifles. All this was quite correct, but the Boers then proceeded to strip and despoil the dead and wounded, taking off their boots and turning out their pockets, and this so infuriated the watching soldiers behind the wall that they forthwith fired on the Boers, Red Cross flags notwithstanding. This, of course, was the signal for fighting to recommence fiercely, and during the day neither side would hear of parley. The Boers behaved cruelly in various instances, and several wounded men who tried to crawl away were deliberately destroyed by being shot at close quarters with many bullets.

During the 24th there was heavy firing on both sides, but no movement of infantry on either. The army suffered some loss from the Boer artillery, particularly the automatic guns, which were well served, and which enfiladed many of our positions on the slopes of the low kopjes. In this way Colonel Thorold, of the Royal Welch Fusiliers, and other officers met their deaths. The casualties were principally in Hildyard's English and Kitchener's Lancashire brigades. Hart's six battalions found good cover in the gorge of the Tugela.

Sir Redvers Buller now saw that his plan of filing his army round the angle of the river and across the enemy's front would, in any case, be very costly, and was perhaps impossible. He therefore determined to get back to the Hlangwani plateau, and try the extreme left of the enemy's position. He had the strategic advantage of being on interior lines, and was consequently able to move his troops with great ease from one flank to the other. His new plan was to pass the brigades of his left and centre across the pontoon bridge from the left to the right, so that Hart, who was formerly the extreme right, would now become almost the extreme left and, having thus extended his right arm, to cross the river where it flowed east and west, and make a still wider swoop on the enemy's flank.

The first thing to do was to move the heavy guns, and this, with certain redistributions of the cavalry, occupied the whole day. A long-range four gun naval battery was established on the western slopes of the Monte Cristo ridge. Another similar battery was placed on the spurs of Hlangwani. The 4.7 inch naval guns and the 5 inch fortress battery were brought into line in the centre of the Hlangwani plateau. All this was good. The big guns were getting back on to the big hills. The firing, which continued all day, swelled into a roar towards night as the Boers made vigorous attempts to drive Hart's brigade from its lodgements. The general had thought fit to dispense with several ordinary precautions, and had not these omissions been repaired by an officer on General Lyttelton's staff a serious situation might have been created. As it was, however, four companies of the 2nd Rifle Brigade watched the flanks of the command, and the Boers were foiled in their endeavour to squeeze in between the troops and the river.

The battalions who were attacked frontally lay down with fixed bayonets and prayed that the Boers might be encouraged by their silence to make an assault. The latter, however, were fully aware of the eagerness of the soldiers for personal collision, and kept their distance. The firing on both sides was unaimed and very little harm was done. No one, however, had much sleep. The condition of the wounded, still lying sore and thirsty on the bare hillside, was now so shocking that Sir Redvers Buller was forced, much against his inclination, at dawn on the 25th to send in a flag of truce to the Boer commander and ask for an armistice. This the Boers formally refused, but agreed that if we would not fire on their positions during the day they would not prevent our bearer companies from removing the wounded and burying the dead.

The arrangement worked well; the enemy were polite to our medical officers, and by noon all the wounded had been brought down and the dead buried. The neglect and exposure for 48 hours had much aggravated the case of the former, and the bodies of the dead, swollen, blackened and torn by the terrible wounds of the expansive bullets, now so generally used by the enemy, were ugly things to see. The fact that no regular armistice was agreed on was an advantage, as we were not thereby debarred from making military movements. The Boers improved their entrenchments, and Sir Redvers Buller employed the day in withdrawing his train across the river. This movement, seeming to foreshadow another retreat, sorely disquieted the troops, who were only reassured by the promise of a general onslaught from the other flank at no distant time.

The strange quiet of this Sunday, the first day since the 14th of the month unbroken by musketry and cannonade, was terminated at nine o'clock at night.

The Boers had seen the waggons passing back over the bridge and were anxious to find out whether or not the infantry were following, and if the low kopjes were evacuated. They therefore opened a tremendous magazine fire at long range on the brigades holding the line from Colenso village to the angle of the river. The fusillade was returned, and for ten minutes the musketry was louder than any other time in this campaign. Very few casualties occurred, however, and after a while the Boers, having learned that the positions were still occupied, ceased firing, and the British soon imitated them, so that, except for the ceaseless 'sniping', silence was restored.

At dawn on the 26th the artillery reopened on both sides, and during the day a constant bombardment was maintained, in which we, having more guns, fired the greater number of shells, and the Dutch, having larger targets, hit a greater number of men. The losses were not, however, severe, except in view of the fact that they had to be endured by the infantry idly and passively.

Considerable movements of troops were made. Colenso and the kopjes about Fort Wylie were converted into a bridgehead, garrisoned by Talbot Coke's brigade. A new line of communications was opened around the foot of Hlangwani. A pontoon bridge (B) was arranged ready to be thrown below the falls of the river, not far from the still intact Boer bridge. Hildyard's English brigade stood fast on the advanced low kopjes forming the extreme left of the line. Hart's command held its position about the slopes of Inniskilling Hill and in the gorge of the river. Barton's fusilier brigade, Kitchener's Lancashire Regiment and the two remaining battalions of Norcott's[1] (formerly Lyttelton's) brigade crossed the old bridge to the Hlangwani plateau.

All was now ready for the final attack on the left of the Pieters position, and in spite of the high quality of the infantry it was generally recognised throughout the army that the fate of Ladysmith must depend on the success of the next day's operations. The spirit of the army was still undaunted, but they had suffered much from losses, exposure and disappointment.

Since 11 January, a period of more than six weeks, the troops had been continuously fighting and bivouacking. The peaceful intervals

[1] Charles Hawtrey Brice Norcott (1849–1931). CMG 1900.

of a few days had merely been in order to replenish stores and ammunition. During this time the only reinforcements to reach the army had been a few drafts, a cavalry regiment, a horse battery and some heavy guns. Exclusive of the 1,100 casualties suffered at Colenso in December, the force, rarely more than 20,000 men, had had more than 3,500 killed and wounded, had never had a single gleam of success, and had hardly seen the enemy who hit them so hard.

Colenso, Spion Kop, Vaal Krantz and the third day at Pieters were not inspiring memories, and though everyone was cheered by the good news of the entanglement of Cronje's[1] army on the western side, yet it was felt that the attempt to be made on the morrow would be the last effort the Natal Field Force would be asked or allowed to make. And oppressed by these reflections we went anxiously to rest on the eve of Majuba Day.

10 April, 1900

---

[1] Piet Cronje. Boer General. Surrendered to Lord Roberts after the battle of Paardeburg, 1900.

14

Commandant's Office, Durban, 6 March

Day broke behind a cloudy sky, and the bang of an early gun reminded us that a great business was on hand. The bivouac of the irregular cavalry which, since they had recrossed the river, had been set at the neck between Monte Cristo and Cingolo, was soon astir. We arose—for all had slept in their boots and had no need to dress—drank some coffee and rejoiced that the day promised to be cool. It would help the infantry, and on the infantry all depended.

At half-past six Dundonald's brigade marched towards the northern end of the Hlangwani plateau, where we were to take up positions on the spurs of Monte Cristo and along the bluffs of the south bank of the Tugela, from which we might assist the infantry attack, and particularly the attack of Barton's brigade, by long-range rifle fire, and by our Colt battery and Maxim guns. While we marched the artillery fire grew more rapid, as battery after battery joined in the bombardment, and when we reached the high wooded ridge which we were ordered to line, I could see our shells bursting merrily in the enemy's trenches.

The position which had been assigned to the South African Light Horse afforded a close yet extensive view of the whole scene. Deep in its gorge below our feet flowed the Tugela, with the new pontoon bridge visible to the left, just below a fine waterfall. Behind us, on a rounded spur of Monte Cristo, one of the long-ranged batteries was firing away busily. Before us, across the river, there rose from the water's edge first a yellow strip of sandy foreshore, then steep, scrub-covered banks, and then smooth, brown slopes, terminating in the three hills which were to be successively assaulted, and which were surmounted by the dark lines of the Boer forts and trenches.

It was like a stage scene viewed from the dress circle. Moreover, we were very comfortable. There were large convenient rocks to sit behind in case of bullets, or to rest a telescope on, and the small trees which sparsely covered the ridge gave a partial shade from the sun. Opposite our front a considerable valley, thickly wooded, ran back from the river, and it was our easy and pleasant task to 'fan' this, as an American officer would say, by scattering a ceaseless shower of rifle and machine-gun bullets throughout its length. In these satisfactory circumstances I watched the battle.

It developed very slowly and with the deliberation which characterises all our manoeuvres. The guns gradually worked themselves into a stage of excitement, and what with our musketry, supplemented by that of the Border Regiment and the Composite Battalion, whose duties were the same as ours, and the machine guns puffing like steam engines, we soon had a capital loud noise, which I think is a most invigorating element in an attack. Besides this, the enemy's sharpshooters were curiously subdued. They found an unexpected amount of random bullets flying about and, as they confessed afterwards, it puzzled and disturbed them.

The spectacle of 2,000 men firing for half a day at nothing may provoke the comment 'shocking waste of ammunition'. Very likely there was waste. But all war is waste, and cartridges are the cheapest item on the bill. At any rate, we made it too hot for the 'snipers' to show their heads, which was certainly worth fifty men to the assaulting brigades. This method of preparing an attack by a great volume of unaimed—not undirected—rifle fire is worthy of the closest attention. I have only once before noticed its employment, and that was when Sir Bindon Blood attacked and took the Tanga Pass. Then, as now, it was most effective.

While we were thus occupied the infantry of Barton's brigade were marching across the pontoon bridge, turning to the right and filing along the sandy foreshore. The plan of attack to which Sir Redvers Buller had finally committed himself was as follows: Hildyard's brigade to hold its positions on the low kopjes; Barton's brigade to cross the new pontoon bridge opposite to the left of the enemy's position, and assault the hill marked '3' on my diagram, and hereinafter called Barton's Hill. Next Kitchener's brigade was to cross, covered by Barton's fire, to assault the centre hill marked '2', and called Railway Hill. Lastly, Norcott's two untouched battalions were to join the rest of their brigade, and supported by General Hart's brigade to attack Inniskilling Hill.

In brief we were to stretch out our right arm, reach round the enemy's flank, and pivoting on Hildyard's brigade crumple him from (his) left to right. It was the same plan as before, only that we now had our right hand on the Monte Cristo ridge, from which commanding position our long-range guns could enfilade and even take in reverse some of the enemy's trenches.

The leading brigade was across the river by nine o'clock, and by ten had reached its position ready for attacking at the foot of Barton's Hill. The advance was begun forthwith and the figures of the infantry could be seen swarming up the steep slopes of the river gorge. The Boers did very little to stop the attack. They knew their weakness. One side of Barton's Hill was swept and commanded by the guns on Monte Cristo. The other side, at the back of which was the donga we were 'fanning', was raked by the heavy artillery on the Hlangwani spur and by the field batteries arranged along the south side of the river. Observe the influence of the Monte Cristo ridge! It made Barton's Hill untenable by the Boers; and Barton's Hill prepared the way for an attack on Railway Hill, and Railway Hill—but I must not anticipate. Indeed, next to Monte Cristo, Barton's Hill was the key of the Boer position, and so unfortunate was the enemy's situation that he could not hold this all-important feature once he had lost Monte Cristo ridge.

What was tactically possible and safe—for the Boer is a cautious warrior—was done. Knowing that his left would be turned he extended a sort of false left in the air beyond the end of the Monte Cristo ridge, and here he brought a gun into action, which worried us among other people but did not, of course, prevent any military movement.

By noon the whole of Barton's Hill was in the possession of his brigade, without, as it seemed to us, any serious opposition. The artillery then turned its attention to the other objectives of the attack. The Boer detached left was, however, of considerable strength, and as soon as Barton had occupied this hill (which proved, moreover, far more extensive than had been expected), he was heavily attacked by rifle fire from its under features and from a network of dongas to the eastward, and as the artillery were busy preparing the attack on Railway Hill, the brigade, particularly the Scots and Irish Fusiliers, soon became severely engaged and suffered grievous loss.

The fact that Barton's Hill was in our possession made the Boers on Railway and Inniskilling Hills very insecure. A powerful infantry force was holding the left of their position, and though it was itself being actively attacked on the eastern face, it could spare at least a

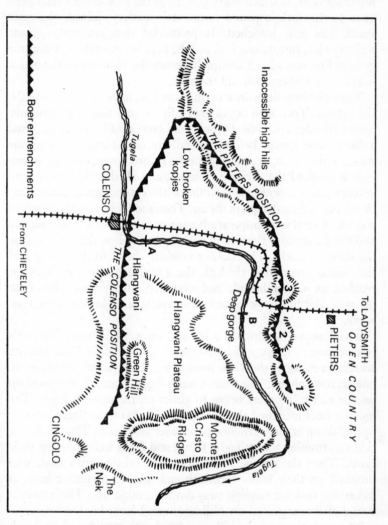

The Battle of Pieters; general position

battalion to assail their flank and threaten their rear. Covered by this flanking fire, by the long-range musketry, and by a tremendous bombardment, in which every gun, from the lumbering 5 inch siege guns to the little 9 pounder mountain battery, joined, the main attack was now launched. It proceeded simultaneously against Railway Hill, Inniskilling Hill and the neck between them, but as the general line was placed obliquely across the Boer front, the attack fell first on Railway Hill and the neck.

The right battalions drew up in many long lines on the sides of the river gorge. Then men began gradually to work their way upwards, until all the dead patches of ground and every scrap of cover sheltered a fierce little group. Behind the railway embankment, among the rocks, in the scrub, in a cutting, near a ruined house, clusters of men eagerly awaited the decisive moment; and all this time more than seventy guns concentrated their fire on the entrenchments, scattering the stones and earth high in the air. Then suddenly, shortly after four o'clock, all further attempts at advancing under cover were abandoned and the Lancashire Brigade marched proudly into the open and on the enemy's works. The Mauser musketry burst forth at once, and the bullets, humming through the assaulting waves of infantry, reached us on our hillside and wounded a trooper in spite of the distance. But bullets or no bullets we could not take our eyes off the scene.

The Lancashire Brigade advanced on a wide front. Norcott's riflemen were already prolonging their line to the right. The Boer fire was dispersed along the whole front of attack instead of converging on one narrow column. The assault was going to succeed. We stood up on our rocks. Bayonets began to glitter on the distant slopes. The moving lines increased their pace. The heads of the Boers bobbing up and down in their trenches grew fewer and fewer. They knew the tide was running too strongly. Death and flight were thinning their ranks. Then the skyline of Railway Hill bristled with men, who dropped on their knees forthwith and fired in particular haste at something that was running away down the other side. There was the sound of cheering. Railway Hill was ours. I looked to the left.

The neck between the hills was lined with trenches. The South Lancashire Regiment had halted, pinned to the ground by the Boer fire. Were they going to lose the day for us when it was already won? The question was soon answered. In an instant there appeared on the left of the Boer trench a dozen—only a dozen—violent forms rushing forward. A small party had worked their way to the flank, and were at close quarters with cold steel. And then—by contrast to their former courage—the valiant burghers fled in all directions, and others held out their rifles and bandoliers and begged for mercy, which was sometimes generously given, so that by the time the whole attack had charged forward into the trenches there was a nice string of thirty-two prisoners winding down the hill; at which token of certain victory we shouted loudly.

Inniskilling Hill alone remained, and that was almost in our hands. Its slopes were on three sides alive with the active figures of the Light Brigade, and the bayonets sparkled. The hill ran into a peak. Many of the trenches were already deserted, but the stone breastwork at the summit still contained defenders. There, painted against the evening sky, were the slouch hats and moving rifles. Shell after shell exploded among them; overhead, in their faces, in the trench itself, behind them, before them, around them. Sometimes five or six shells were bursting on the very apex at the same instant. Showers of rock and splinters fell on all sides.

Yet they held their ground and stayed in greater peril than was ever mortal man before. But the infantry were drawing very near. At last the Dutchmen fled. One, a huge fellow in a brown jersey, tarried to spring on the parapet and empty his magazine once more into the approaching ranks, and while he did so a 50 lb lyddite shell burst, as it seemed, in the midst of him, and the last defender of Inniskilling Hill vanished.

Then the artillery put up their sights and began to throw their shells over the crest of hill and ridge, so that they might overtake fugitives. The valleys behind fumed and stewed. Wreaths of dust and smoke curled upward. The infantry crowned the trenches all along the line, some firing their rifles at the flying enemy, others beckoning to nearer folk to surrender, and they all cheered in the triumph of successful attack till the glorious sound came down to us who watched, so that the whole army took up the shout, and all men knew that the battle of Pieters was won.

Forthwith came orders for the cavalry to cross the river, and we mounted in high expectation, knowing that behind the captured hill lay an open plain stretching almost to the foot of Bulwana. We galloped swiftly down to the pontoon bridge, and were about to pass over it when the general-in-chief met us. He had ridden to the other bank to see for himself and us. The Boer artillery were firing heavily to cover the retreat of their riflemen. He would not allow us to go across that night lest we lose heavily in horses. So the brigade returned disappointed to its former position, watered horses and selected a bivouac. I was sent to warn the naval battery that a heavy counterstroke would probably be made on the right of Barton's brigade during the night, and climbing the spur of Monte Cristo, on which the guns were placed, had a commanding view of the field.

In the gathering darkness the Boer artillery, invisible all day, was betrayed by his flashes. Two 'pom-poms' flickered away steadily from the direction of Doornkloof, making a regular succession of small bright flame-points. Two more guns were firing from the hills to our left. Another was in action far away on our right. There may have been more, but even so it was not much artillery to oppose our eleven batteries. But it is almost an open question whether it is better to have many guns to shoot at very little, or few guns to shoot at a great deal; hundreds of shells tearing up the ground or a dozen plunging into masses of men. Personally, I am convinced that future warfare will be to the few, by which I mean that to escape annihilation soldiers will have to fight in widely dispersed formations, when they will have to think for themselves, and when each must be to a great extent his own general; and with regard to artillery it appears that advantages of defensive action, range, concealment and individual initiative may easily counterbalance numbers and discipline. The night fell on these reflections, and I hastened to rejoin the cavalry.

On the way I passed through Sir Charles Warren's camp, and there I found a gang of prisoners—forty-eight of them—all in a row, almost the same number that the Boers had taken in the armoured train. Looking at these very ordinary people, who grinned and chattered without dignity, and who might from their appearance have been a knot of loafers round a public house, it was difficult to understand what qualities made them such a terrible foe.

'Only forty-eight, sir,' said a private soldier, who was guarding them, 'and there wouldn't have been so many as that if the officers hadn't stopped us from giving them the bayonet. I never saw such cowards in my life; shoot at you till you come up to them and then beg for mercy. I'd teach 'em.' With which remark he turned to the prisoners, who had just been issued rations of beef and biscuit, but who were also very thirsty, and began giving them water to drink from his own canteen, and so left me wondering at the opposite and contradictory sides of human nature as shown by Briton as well as Boer.

We got neither food nor blankets that night, and slept in our waterproofs on the ground, but we had at last that which was better than feast or couch, for which we had hungered and longed through many weary weeks, which had been thrice forbidden us, and which was all the more splendid since it had been so long delayed—victory.

11 April, 1900

15

COMMANDANT'S OFFICE, DURBAN, 9 March

The successful action of the 27th had given Sir Redvers Buller possession of the whole of the left and centre of the Pieters position, and in consequence of these large sections of their entrenchments having fallen into British hands, the Boers evacuated the remainder and retreated westward on to the high hills and northward towards Bulwana Mountain.

About ninety prisoners were captured in the assault and more than a hundred bodies were counted in the trenches. After making allowances for the fact that these men were for the most part killed by shell fire, and that therefore the proportion of killed to wounded would necessarily be higher than if the loss were caused by bullets, it seems probable that not less than three hundred wounded were removed. Forty were collected by British ambulance parties. Of the Boers who were killed in the retreat no accurate estimate can be formed, but the dongas and kopjes beyond the position were strewn with occasional corpses. Undoubtedly the enemy was hard hit in personnel, and the fact that we had taken two miles of entrenchments as well as considerable stores of ammunition proved that a very definite and substantial success had been won.

But we were not prepared for the complete results that followed the operations of the 27th. Neither the general nor his army expected to enter Ladysmith without another action. Before us a smooth plain, apparently unobstructed, ran to the foot of Bulwana, but from this forbidding feature a line of ridges and kopjes was drawn to the high hills of Doornkloof, and seemed to interpose another serious barrier. It was true that this last position was within range, or almost within range, of Sir George White's guns, so that its defenders might be caught between two fires, but we knew, and thought the Boers knew, that the Ladysmith garrison was too feeble from want of food and other privations to count for very much. So

Sir Redvers Buller, facing the least satisfactory assumption, determined to rest his army on the 28th, and attack Bulwana Hill on the 1st of March.

He accordingly sent a message by heliograph into Ladysmith to say that he had beaten the enemy thoroughly, and was sending on his cavalry to reconnoitre. Ladysmith had informed herself, however, of the state of the game. Captain Tilney, from his balloon, observed all that passed in the enemy's lines on the morning of the 28th. At first, when he heard no artillery fire, he was depressed and feared lest the relieving army had retreated again. Then, as it became day, he was sure that this was not so, for the infantry in crowds were occupying the Boer position, and the mounted patrols pricked forward into the plain. Presently he saw the Boers rounding up their cattle and driving off to the north. Next they caught and began to saddle their horses. The great white tilted waggons of the various laagers filed along the road round the eastern end of Bulwana. Lastly, up went a pair of shears over 'Long Tom', and at this he descended to earth with the good news that the enemy were off at last.

The garrison, however, had been mocked by false hopes before, and all steeled themselves to await 'at least another ten days'.

Meanwhile, since there was no fire from the enemy's side, our cavalry and artillery were rapidly and safely crossing the river. There was a considerable block at the bridge when the South African Light Horse arrived, and we had full leisure to examine the traffic. Guns, men, horses and mules were hurrying across to the northern bank, and an opposing stream of wounded flowed steadily back to the south. I watched these with interest.

First came a young officer riding a pony and smoking a cigarette, but very pale and with his left arm covered in bloody bandages. Brooke greeted him and asked, 'Bone?' 'Yes,' replied the subaltern laconically, 'shoulder smashed up.' We expressed our sympathy. 'Oh, that's all right; good show, wasn't it? The men are awfully pleased;' and he rode on slowly up the hill—the type of an unyielding race—and stoical besides; for wounds, especially shattered bones, grow painful after twelve or fourteen hours. A string of wounded passed by on stretchers, some lying quite still, others sitting up and looking about them; one, also an officer, a dark, black-moustached captain, whose eyes were covered with a bandage, kept his bearers busy with continual impatient questions. 'Yes, but what I want to know is this, did they get into them with the bayonet ?' The volunteer stretcher-bearers could make no satisfactory reply, but said, 'Yes, they give 'em 'ell, sir.' 'Where, on the left of Railway Hill,' 'Oh, everywhere, sir.' The group passed by and the last thing I heard was, 'How much of the artillery has crossed ? Are they sending the cavalry over ? What the. . . .'

Presently came stretchers with wounded Boers. Most of these poor creatures were fearfully shattered. One tall man with a great fierce beard and fine features had a fragment of rock or iron driven through his liver. He was, moreover, stained bright yellow with lyddite, but did not seem in much pain, for he looked very calm and stolid. The less seriously injured among the soldiers hobbled back alone or assisted by their comrades.

I asked a smart-looking sergeant of the Dublin Fusiliers, who was limping along with a broken foot, whether the regiment had been again heavily engaged. Of course they had.

'Sure, we're always in the thick of it, sorr. Mr . . . was hit; no, not badly; only his wrist, but there's not many of the officers left; only two now who were at Talana.'

At last the time came for the cavalry to cross the bridge, and as we filed on to the floating roadway we were amused to see a large finger-post at the entrance, on which the engineers had neatly painted 'To Ladysmith'. The brigade passed over the neck between Railway and Inniskilling Hills, and we massed in a suitable place on the descending slopes beyond. We looked at the country before us, and saw that it was good. Here at last was ground cavalry could work on at some speed. Ladysmith was still hidden by the remaining ridges, but we thought that somehow, and with a little luck, we might have a look at it before night.

Under Bulwana the waggons of the Boers and several hundred horsemen could be seen hurrying away. It was clearly our duty to try to intercept them unless they had made good covering dispositions. Patrols were sent out in all directions, and a squadron of Thorneycroft's Mounted Infantry proceeded to Pieters Station, where a complete train of about twenty trucks had been abandoned by the enemy. While this reconnaissance was going on I climbed up Inniskilling Hill to examine the trenches. It was occupied by the East Surrey Regiment, and the soldiers were very eager to do the honours. They had several things to show: 'Come along here, sir; there's a bloke without a head; took clean off, sir;' and were mightily disappointed that I would not let them remove the blanket which covered the grisly shape.

The trench was cut deep in the ground and, unlike our trenches, there was scarcely any parapet. A few great stones had been laid in front, but evidently the Boer believed in getting well into the ground. The bottom was knee deep in cartridge cases, and every few yards there was an enormous heap of Mauser ammunition, thousands of rounds, all fastened neatly, five at a time, in clips. A large proportion were covered with bright green slime, which the soldiers declared to be poison, but which on analysis may prove to be wax, used to preserve the bullet.

The Boers, however, were not so guiltless of other charges. A field officer of the East Surreys, recognising me, came up and showed me an expansive bullet of a particularly cruel pattern. The tip had been cut off, exposing the soft core, and four slits were scored down the side. Whole boxes of this ammunition had been found. An officer who had been making calculations told me that the proportion of illegal bullets was nearly one in five. I would not myself have thought it was so large, but certainly the improper bullets were very numerous. I have a specimen of this particular kind by me as I write, and I am informed by people who shoot big game that it is the most severe bullet of its kind yet invented. Five other sorts have been collected by the medical officers, who have also tried to classify the wounds they respectively produce.

I cannot be accused of having written unfairly about the enemy; indeed, I have only cared to write what I thought was the truth about everybody. I have tried to do justice to the patriotic virtues of the Boers, and it is now necessary to observe that the character of these people reveals in stress a dark and spiteful underside. A man, I use the word in its fullest sense, does not wish to lacerate his foe, however earnestly he may desire his death.

The popping of musketry fire made me hasten to rejoin my regiment. The squadron of mounted infantry had reached Pieters Railway Station, only to be heavily fired on from a low hill to the westward, and they now came scampering back with half a dozen riderless horses. Happily, the riders mostly arrived on foot after a few minutes. But it was evidently necessary to push forward very carefully. Indeed, it is hard to imagine how pursuits will occur in future war. A hundred bold men with magazine rifles on a ridge can delay a whole army. The cavalry must reconnoitre and retire.

Infantry and guns must push forward. Meanwhile the beaten troops are moving steadily to safety. In a little while—to revert to the narrative—the horse artillery battery came up, and the offending hill was conscientiously shelled for an hour. Then the patrols crept forward again, but progress was necessarily slow. We were still six miles from Ladysmith by three o'clock.

At this hour the Boer ambulances had been invited to come for such of their wounded as could be moved, for since the enemy returned our wounded from Spion Kop, we have followed the practice of sending back theirs on all occasions should they prefer it.

Anxious to find out the impression produced on the Boers by the late actions, I hastened to meet the ambulances which, preceded by three horsemen carrying a large white flag, were now coming from the direction of Bulwana. They were stopped at our cavalry picket line, and a report of their arrival was sent back to the nearest brigadier. Their leader was a fine old fellow of the genuine veldt Boer type. He spoke English fluently, and we were soon in conversation.

Cronje's surrender had been officially announced to us on the previous day, and I inquired whether he had heard of it. He replied that he knew Cronje was in difficulties, but understood he had managed to escape with his army. As for the surrender, it might be true or it might be false. 'We are told so many lies that we believe nothing.'

But his next remark showed that he realised that the tide had begun to turn. 'I don't know what we poor Afrikanders have done that England won't let us be a nation.' I would have replied that I remembered having heard something about 'driving the English into the sea,' but I had been over this ground before in every sense, and knew the futility of any discussion. Indeed, when the debate is being conducted with shells, bullets and bayonets, words are feeble weapons. So I said with an irony which was quite lost on him, 'It must be all those damned capitalists,' and this, of course, won his complete agreement, so that he confided that losing the position we had taken on the 28th was 'a sore and bitter blow'.

It happened that two squadrons of the 13th Hussars had ridden forward beyond us towards Bulwana, and at this moment the Boer artillery began to shell them rather heavily. We watched the proceedings for a few minutes, and the Boer was much astonished to see soldiers riding leisurely forward in regular though open order without paying the slightest attention to the shrapnel. Then several more squadrons were odered to support the reconnaissance. A great company of horsemen jingled past the halted ambulances and cantered off in the direction of the firing. My companion regarded these steadfastly, then he said:

'Why do they all look so pleased?'

'Because they think they are going to fight; but they will not be allowed to. It is only desired to draw your fire and reconnoitre.'

The whole plain was now occupied by clouds of cavalry, both brigades being on the move.

'Little did we think a week ago,' said the Boer, 'that we should see such a sight as this, here in this plain.'

'Didn't you think we would get through?'

'No, we didn't believe it possible.'

'And you find the soldiers brave?'

'They do not care for life.'

'And Ladysmith?'

'Ah,' his eye brightened, 'there's pluck, if you like. Wonderful!'

Then we agreed that it was a sad and terrible war, and whoever won we would make the gold mines pay, so that 'the damned capitalists' should not think they had scored, and thus parted.

I afterwards learned that the Boer ambulances removed 27 of their wounded. The condition of the others was too serious to allow of their being moved, and in spite of every attention they all died while in our hands.

When I rejoined the South African Light Horse, the irregular brigade had begun to advance again. Major Gough's Composite Regiment had scouted the distant ridge and found it unoccupied. Now Dundonald moved his whole command thither, and with his staff climbed to the top. But to our disappointment Ladysmith was not to be seen. Two or three other ridges hung like curtains before us. The afternoon had passed, and it was already after six o'clock. The Boer artillery was still firing, and it seemed rash to attempt to reconnoitre further when the ground was broken and the light fading.

The order was given to retire, and the movement had actually begun when a messenger came back from Gough with the news that the last ridge between us and the town was unoccupied by the enemy, that he could see Ladysmith, and that there was, for the moment, a clear run in. Dundonald immediately determined to go on himself into the town with the two squadrons who were scouting in front, and send the rest of the brigade back to camp. He invited me to accompany him, and without delay we started at a gallop.

Never shall I forget that ride. The evening was deliciously cool. My horse was strong and fresh, for I had changed him at midday. The ground was rough with many stones, but we cared little for that. Beyond the next ridge, or the rise beyond that, or around the corner of the hill, was Ladysmith—the goal of all our hopes and ambitions during weeks of ceaseless fighting. Ladysmith, the centre of the world's attention, the scene of famous deeds, the cause of mighty efforts. Ladysmith was within our reach at last. We were going to be inside the town within an hour. The excitement of the moment was increased by the exhilaration of our gallop. Onward wildly, recklessly, up and down hill, over the boulders, through the scrub. Hubert Gough with his two squadrons, Mackenzie's Natal Carbineers and the Imperial Light Horse, was clear of the ridges already. We turned the shoulder of a hill, and there before us lay the tin houses and dark trees we had come so far to see and save.

The British guns on Caesar's Camp were firing steadily in spite of the twilight. What was happening? Never mind, we were nearly through the dangerous ground. Now we were all on the flat. Brigadier, staff and troops let their horses go. We raced through the thorn bushes by Intombi Spruit.

Suddenly there was a challenge. 'Halt, who goes there?' 'The Ladysmith Relief Column,' and thereat from out of trenches and rifle pits artfully concealed in the scrub a score of tattered men came running, cheering feebly, and some were crying. In the half-light they looked ghastly pale and thin. A poor, white-faced officer waved his helmet to and fro, and laughed foolishly, and the tall, strong colonial horsemen, standing up in their stirrups, raised a loud resounding cheer, for we then knew we had reached the Ladysmith picket line.

Presently we arranged ourselves in military order, Natal Carbineers and Imperial Light Horse riding two and two abreast so that there might be no question about precedence, and with Gough, the youngest regimental commander in the army, at the head of the column, we forded the Klip River and rode into the town.

That night I dined with Sir George White, who had held the town for four months against all comers, and was placed next to Hamilton, who won the fight at Elandslaagte and beat the Boers off at Waggon Hill, and next but one to Hunter, whom everyone said was the finest man in the world. Never before had I sat in such brave company nor stood so close to a great event. As the war drives slowly to its close more substantial triumphs, larger battles, wherein the enemy suffers heavier loss, the capture of towns, and the surrender of armies may mark its progress. But whatever victories the future may have in store, the defence and relief of Ladysmith, because they afford, perhaps, the most remarkable examples of national tenacity and perseverance which our later history contains, will not be soon forgotten by the British people, whether at home or in the colonies.

12 April, 1900

16

DURBAN, 10 March

Since the road by which Dundonald's squadrons had entered the town was never again closed by the enemy, the siege of Ladysmith may be said to have ended on the last day of February. During the night the heavy guns fired at intervals, using up the carefully husbanded ammunition in order to prevent the Boers from removing their artillery.

On 1 March the garrison reverted to a full half-ration of biscuits and horseflesh, and an attempt was made to harass the Boers who were in full retreat towards the Biggarsberg. Sir George White had made careful inquiries among the regiments for men who would undertake to walk five miles and fight at the end of the march. But so reduced were the soldiers through want of food that, though many volunteered, only two thousand men were considered fit out of the whole garrison. These were, however, formed into a column, under Colonel Knox, consisting of two batteries of artillery, two squadrons of the 19th Hussars and 5th Lancers, 'all that was left of them', with horses and detachments, each about two hundred and fifty strong, from the Manchester, Liverpool and Devon Regiments, the 60th Rifles and the Gordon Highlanders, and this force moved out of Ladysmith at dawn on the 1st to attack the Boers on Pepworth's Hill, in the hope of interfering with their entrainment at Modderspruit Station.

The Dutch, however, had left a small rearguard sufficient to hold in check so small a force, and it was two o'clock before Pepworth's Hill was occupied. The batteries then shelled Modderspruit Station, and very nearly caught three crowded trains, which just managed to steam out of range in time. The whole force of men and horses was by this time quite exhausted. The men could scarcely carry their rifles. In the squadron of 19th Hussars nine horses out of sixty fell down and died, and Colonel Knox therefore ordered the withdrawal into the town.

Only about a dozen men were killed or wounded in this affair, but the fact that the garrison was capable of making any offensive movement after their privations is a manifest of their soldierly spirit and excellent discipline.

On the same morning Sir Redvers Buller advanced on Bulwana Hill. Down from the comanding positions which they had won by their courage and endurance marched the incomparable infantry, and by two o'clock the plain of Pieters was thickly occupied by successive lines of men in extended order, with long columns of guns and transport trailing behind them. Shortly before noon it was ascertained that Bulwana Hill was abandoned by the enemy, and the army was thereupon ordered to camp in the plain, no further fighting being necessary.

The failure to pursue the retreating Boers when two fine cavalry brigades were standing idle and eager must be noticed. It is probable that the Boer rearguard would have been sufficiently strong to require both infantry and guns to drive it back. It is certain that sharp fighting must have attended the effort. Nevertheless the opinion generally expressed was that it should have been made. My personal impression is that Sir Redvers Buller was deeply moved by the heavy losses the troops had suffered, and was reluctant to demand further sacrifices from them at this time. Indeed, the price of victory had been a high one.

In the fortnight's fighting, from 14 to 28 February, two generals, six colonels commanding regiments, a hundred and five other officers, and one thousand five hundred and eleven soldiers had been killed or wounded out of an engaged force of about eighteen thousand men; a proportion of slightly under 10 per cent.

In the whole series of operations for the relief of Ladysmith the losses amounted to three hundred officers and more than five thousand men out of a total engaged force of about twenty-three thousand, a proportion of rather more than 20 per cent. Nor had this loss been inflicted in a single day's victorious battle, but it was spread over twenty-five days of general action in a period of ten weeks; and until the last week no decided success had cheered the troops.

The stress of the campaign, moreover, had fallen with peculiar force on certain regiments: the Lancashire Fusiliers sustained losses of over 35 per cent, the Inniskillings of 40 per cent, and the Dublin Fusiliers of over 60 per cent. It was very remarkable that the fighting efficiency of these regiments was in no way impaired by such serious reductions. The casualties among the officers maintained their usual glorious disproportion, six or seven regiments in the army having less than eight officers left alive and unwounded. Among the cavalry the heaviest losses occurred in Dundonald's brigade, the South African Light Horse, Thorneycroft's Mounted Infantry, and the squadron of the Imperial Light Horse, each losing a little less than a quarter of their strength.

The ceaseless marching and fighting had worn out the clothes and boots of the army, and a certain number of the guns of the field artillery were unserviceable through constant firing. The troops, besides clothes, needed fresh meat, an exclusive diet of tinned food being unwholesome if unduly prolonged. Sir Redvers Buller's estimate that a week's rest was needed does not seem excessive by the light of such facts, but still one more effort might have saved much trouble later on.

On 3 March the relieving army made its triumphal entry into Ladysmith, and passing through the town encamped on the plain beyond. The scene was solemn and stirring, and only the most phlegmatic were able to conceal their emotions. The streets were lined with the brave defenders, looking very smart and clean in their best clothes, but pale, thin and wasp-waisted—their belts several holes tighter than was satisfactory.

Before the little Town Hall, the tower of which, sorely battered, yet unyielding, seemed to symbolise the spirit of the garrison, Sir George White and his staff sat on their skeleton horses. Opposite to them were drawn up the pipers of the Gordon Highlanders. The townsfolk, hollow-eyed but jubilant, crowded the pavement and the windows of the houses. Everyone who could find a flag had hung it out, but we needed no bright colours to raise our spirits.

At eleven o'clock precisely the relieving army began to march into the town. First of all rode Sir Redvers Buller with his headquarters staff and an escort of the Royal Dragoons. The infantry and artillery followed by brigades, but in front of all, as a special recognition of their devoted valour, marched the Dublin Fusiliers, few but proud. Many of the soldiers, remembering their emerald island, had fastened sprigs of green in their helmets, and all marched with a swing that was wonderful to watch. Their colonel and their four officers looked as happy as kings are thought to be. As the regiments passed Sir George White, the men recognised their former general and, disdaining the rules of the service, waved their helmets and rifles, and cheered him with intense enthusiasm. Some even broke from the ranks. Seeing this, the Gordon Highlanders began to cheer the Dublins, and after that the noise of cheering was continual, every regiment as it passed giving and receiving fresh ovations.

All through the morning and on into the afternoon the long stream of men and guns flowed through the streets of Ladysmith and all marvelled to see what manner of men these were—dirty, war-worn, travel-stained, tanned, their uniforms in tatters, their boots falling to pieces, their helmets dinted and broken, but nevertheless magnificent soldiers, striding along, deep-chested and broad-shouldered, with the light of triumph in their eyes and the blood of fighting ancestors in their veins. It was a procession of lions. And presently when the two battalions of Devons met—both full of honours—and old friends breaking from the ranks gripped each other's hands and shouted, everyone was carried away, and I waved my feathered hat, and cheered and cheered until I could cheer no longer for the joy that I had lived to see the day.

At length all was over. The last dust-brown battalion had passed away and the roadway was again clear. Yet the ceremony was incomplete. Before the staff could ride away the Mayor of Ladysmith advanced and requested Sir George White to receive an address which the townspeople had prepared, and were anxious to present to him. The general dismounted from his horse, and standing on the steps of the Town Hall, in the midst of the inhabitants whom he had ruled so rigorously during the hard months of the siege, listened while their Town Clerk read their earnest grateful thanks to him for saving their town from the hands of the enemy. The general replied briefly, complimented them on their behaviour during the siege, thanked them for the way in which they had borne their many hardships and submitted to the most severe restrictions which the circumstances of war had brought on them, and rejoiced with them that they had been enabled by their devotion and by the bravery of the soldiers to keep the Queen's flag flying over Ladysmith. And then everybody cheered everybody else, and so, very tired and very happy, we all went home to our belated luncheons.

Walking through the streets it was difficult to see many signs of the bombardment. The tower of the Town Hall was smashed and chipped, several houses showed large holes in their walls, and heaps of broken brickwork lay here and there. But on the whole the impression produced was one of surprise that the Boers had done so little

277

damage with the sixteen thousand shells they had fired during the siege.

On entering the houses, however, the effect was more apparent. In one the floor was ripped up, in another the daylight gleamed through the corrugated iron roof, and in some houses the inner walls had been completely destroyed, and only heaps of rubbish lay on the floor.

The fortifications which the troops had built, though of a very strong and effective character, were neither imposing nor conspicuous; indeed, being composed of heaps of stone, they were visible only as dark lines on the rugged kopjes, and if the fame of the town were to depend on relics of war it would not long survive the siege.

But memories dwell among the tin houses and on the stony hills that will keep the name of Ladysmith fresh and full of meaning in the hearts of our countrymen. Every trench, every mound has its own tale to tell, some of them sad, but not one shameful. Here and there, scattered through the scrub by the river or on the hills of red stones almost red-hot in the sun blaze, rise the wooden crosses which mark the graves of British soldiers. Near the iron bridge a considerable granite pyramid records the spot where Dick-Cunynghame, Colonel of the Gordons—what prouder office could a man hold?—fell mortally wounded on 6 January. Another monument is being built on Waggon Hill to commemorate the brave men of the Imperial Light Horse who lost their lives but saved the day. The place is also marked where the gallant Ava fell.

But there was one who found, to use his own words, 'a strange sideway out of Ladysmith,' whose memory many English-speaking people will preserve. I do not write of Steevens[1] as a journalist, nor as a master of a popular and pleasing style, but as a man.

I knew him, though I had met him rarely. A dinner up the Nile, a chance meeting at an Indian junction, five days on a Mediterranean steamer, two in a continental express, and a long Sunday at his house near Merton—it was a scanty acquaintance, but sufficient to be quite sure that in all the varied circumstances and conditions to which men are subjected Steevens rang true. Modest yet proud, wise as well as witty, cynical but above all things sincere, he combined the characters of a charming companion and a good comrade.

[1] George Warrington Steevens (1869–1900). Special correspondent of the *Daily Mail*. He had earlier been a Press colleague of Churchill during the Sudan campaign.

His conversation and his private letters sparkled like his books and articles. Original expressions, just similitudes, striking phrases, quaint or drill ideas welled in his mind without the slightest effort. He was always at his best. I have never met a man who talked so well, so easily. His wit was the genuine article—absolutely natural and spontaneous.

I once heard him describe an incident in the Nile campaign, and the description amused me so much that I was impatient to hear it again, and when a suitable occasion offered I asked him to tell his tale to the others. But he told it quite differently, and left me wondering which version was the better. He could not repeat himself if he tried, whereas most of the renowned talkers I have met will go over the old impression with the certainty of a phonograph.

But enough of his words. He was not a soldier, but he walked into the Atbara zareba with the leading company of the Seaforth Highlanders. He wrote a vivid account of the attack, but there was nothing in it about himself.

When the investment of Ladysmith shut the door on soldiers and war correspondents alike, Steevens set to work to do his share of keeping up the good spirits of the garrison and of relieving the monotony of the long days. Through the first three months of the siege no local event was awaited with more interest than the publication of a *Ladysmith Lyre*, and the weary defenders had many a good laugh at its witticisms.

Sun, stink and sickness harassed the beleaguered. The bombardment was perpetual, the relief always delayed; hope again and again deferred. But nothing daunted Steevens, depressed his courage or curbed his wit. What such a man is worth in gloomy days those may appreciate who have seen the effect of public misfortunes on a modern community.

At last he was himself stricken down by enteric fever. When it seemed that the worst was over there came a fatal relapse, and the brightest intellect yet sacrificed by this war perished; nor among all the stubborn garrison of Ladysmith was there a stouter heart or a more enduring spirit.

Dismal scenes were to be found at the hospital camp by Intombi Spruit. Here in a town of white tents under the shadow of Bulwana were collected upwards of two thousand sick and wounded—a fifth of the entire garrison. They were spared the shells, but exposed to all the privations of the siege.

Officers and men, doctors and patients, presented alike a most melancholy and even ghastly appearance. Men had been wounded, had been cured of their wounds, and had died simply because there was no nourishing food to restore their strength. Others had become convalescent from fever, but had succumbed from depression and lack of medical comforts. Hundreds required milk and brandy, but there was only water to give them. The weak died; at one time the death rate averaged fifteen a day. Nearly a tenth of the whole garrison died of disease. A forest of crosses marking the graves of six hundred men sprang up behind the camp.

It was a painful thing to watch the hungry patients, so haggard and worn that their friends would scarcely recognise them; and after a visit to Intombi I sat and gloated for an hour at the long train of waggons filled with all kinds of necessary comforts which crawled along the roads, and the relief of Ladysmith seemed more than ever worth the heavy price we had paid.

On the evening after Buller's victorious army had entered the town I went to see Sir George White, and was so fortunate as to find him alone and disengaged. The general received me in a room the windows of which gave a wide view of the defences. Bulwana, Caesar's Camp, Waggon Hill lay before us, and beneath—for the house stood on high ground—spread the blue roofs of Ladysmith. From the conversation that followed, and from my own knowledge of events, I shall endeavour to explain so far as it is at present possible the course of the campaign in Natal; and I will ask the reader to observe that only the remarks actually quoted should be attributed to the various officers.

Sir George White told me how he had reached Natal less than a week before the declaration of war. He found certain arrangements in progress to meet a swiftly approaching emergency, and he had to choose between upsetting all these plans and entirely reconstructing the scheme of defence, or of accepting what was already done as the groundwork of his operations.

Sir Penn Symons, who had been commanding in the colony, and who was presumably best qualified to form an opinion on the military necessities, extravagantly underrated the Boer fighting power. Some of his calculations of the force necessary to hold various places seem incredible in the light of recent events. But everyone was wrong about the Boers, and the more they knew the worse they erred. Symons laughed at the Boer military strength, and laboured to impress his opinions on Sir George White, who having Hamilton's South African experience to fall back on, however, took a much more serious view of the situation, and was particularly disturbed at the advanced position of the troops at Dundee. He wanted to withdraw them. Symons urged the opposite considerations vehemently. He was a man of great personal force, and his manner carried people with him. 'Besides,' said the general, with a kindling eye and extraordinary emphasis, 'he was a good, brave fighting man, and you know how much that is worth in war.'

In spite of Symons's confidence and enthusiasm White hated to leave troops at Dundee, and Sir Archibald Hunter,[1] his chief of staff, agreed with him. But not to occupy a place is one thing; to abandon it after it has been occupied is another.

They decided to ask Sir Walter Hely-Hutchinson what consequences would in his opinion follow a withdrawal. They visited him at ten o'clock at night and put the question straightly. Thus appealed to, the Governor declared that in that event 'loyalists would be disgusted and discouraged; the results as regards the Dutch would be grave, many, if not most, would very likely rise, believing us to be afraid . . . and the effect on the natives, of whom there are some 750,000 in Natal and Zululand, might be disastrous.'

On hearing this opinion expressed by a man of the Governor's ability and local knowledge Sir Archibald Hunter said that it was a question 'of balancing drawbacks,' and advised that the troops be retained at Glencoe. So the matter was clinched, 'and,' said Sir George, 'when I made up my mind to let Symons stay I shared and shared alike with him in the matter of troops, giving him three batteries, a regiment and an infantry brigade, and keeping the same myself.'

For his share in this discussion the Governor was at one time subjected to a considerable volume of abuse in the public press, it being charged against him that he had 'interfered' with the military arrangements.

Sir Walter Hely-Hutchinson, with whom I have had many pleasant talks, makes this invariable reply: 'I never said a word to Sir George White until I was asked. When my opinion was called for I gave it according to the best of my judgment.'

In the actual event Dundee had to be abandoned, nor was this a

[1] Archibald Hunter (1856–1936). Commanded 10th Division in South Africa. Governor of Dongola Province 1895-9. Knighted 1898.

deliberate evacuation arising out of any regular military policy, but a swift retreat without stores or wounded, compelled by the force of the enemy.

It is, therefore, worthwhile considering how far the Governor's judgment has been vindicated by events. Undoubtedly loyalists throughout the colony were disgusted, and that they were not discouraged was mainly due to the fact that with the Anglo-Saxon peoples anger at the injury usually overcomes dismay. The effect on the Dutch was grave, but was considerably modified by the electrical influence of the victory of Elandslaagte, and the spectacle of Boer prisoners marching southwards.

The whole of the Klip River county, however, rose, and many prominent Natal Dutch farmers joined the enemy. The loyalty of the natives alone exceeded the Governor's anticipations, and their belief in the British power and preference for British rule were found to stand more knocking about than those best able to judge expected. We have reaped a rich reward in this dark season for having consistently pursued a kindly and humane policy towards the Bantu races; and the Boers have paid a heavy penalty for their cruelty and harshness.

On the subject of holding Ladysmith Sir George White was quite clear. 'I never wanted to abandon Ladysmith; I considered it a place of primary importance to hold. It was on Ladysmith that both Republics concentrated their first efforts. Here, where the railways join, the armies of the Free State and Transvaal were to unite, and the capture of the town was to seal their union.'

It is now certain that Ladysmith was an essential to the carefully thought out Boer plan of campaign. To make quite sure of victory they directed twenty-five thousand of their best men on it under the commandant-general himself. Flushed with the spirit of invasion, they scarcely reckoned on a fortnight's resistance; nor in their wildest nightmares did they conceive a four months' siege terminating in the furious inroad of a relieving army.

Exasperated at unexpected opposition—for they underrated us even more than we underrated them—they sacrificed around Ladysmith their chances of taking Pietermaritzburg and raiding all Natal; and it is moreover incontestable that in their resolve to take the town, on which they had set their hearts, they were provoked into close fighting with Sir Redvers Buller's army, and even to make an actual assault on the defences of Ladysmith, and so suffered far heavier losses than could otherwise have been inflicted on so elusive an enemy in such broken country.

'Besides,' said the general, 'I had no choice in the matter. I did not want to leave Ladysmith, but even if I had wanted it would have been impossible.'

He then explained how not only the moral value, the political significance of Ladysmith and the great magazines accumulated there rendered it desirable to hold the town, but that the shortness of time, the necessity of evacuating the civil population, and of helping in the Dundee garrison, made its retention actually obligatory.

Passing to the actual siege of the town, Sir George White said that he had decided to make an active defence in order to keep the enemy's attention fixed on his force, and so prevent them from invading south Natal before the reinforcements could arrive. With that object he had fought the action of 30 October, which had turned out so disastrously. After that he fell back on his entrenchments, and the blockade began.

'The experience we had gained of the long-range guns possessed by the enemy,' said Sir George, 'made it necessary for me to occupy a very large area of ground, and I had to extend my lines accordingly. My lines are now nearly fourteen miles in circumference. If I had taken up a smaller position we should have been pounded to death.'

He said that the fact that they had plenty of room alone enabled them to live, for the shell fire was thus spread over a large area and, as it were, diluted. Besides this the cattle were enabled to find grazing, but these extended lines were also a source of weakness. At one time on several sections of the defences the garrison could only provide two hundred men to the mile.

'That is scarcely the prescribed proportion. I would like to have occupied Bulwana, in which case we should have been quite comfortable, but I did not dare extend my lines any further. It was better to endure the bombardment than to run the risk of being stormed. Because my lines were so extended I was compelled to keep all the cavalry in Ladysmith.'

Until they began to eat instead of feed the horses this powerful mounted force, upwards of three thousand strong, had been his mobile, almost his only reserve. Used in conjunction with an elaborate system of telephones the cavalry from their central position could powerfully reinforce any threatened section.

The value of this was proved on 6 January. The general thought that the fierce assault delivered by the enemy that day vindicated his policy in not occupying Bulwana and in keeping his cavalry within the town, on both of which points he had been much criticised.

He spoke with some bitterness of the attacks which had been made on him in the newspapers, and of the attempts of the War Office to supersede him, attempts which Sir Redvers Buller had prevented. He had always begged that the relieving operations should not be compromised by any hurry on his account, and he said, with earnestness, 'It is not fair to charge me with all the loss of life they have involved.' He concluded by saying deliberately: 'I regret Nicholson's Nek; perhaps I was rash then, but it was my only chance of striking a heavy blow. I regret nothing else. It may be that I am an obstinate man to say so, but if I had the last five months to live over again I would not—with that exception—do otherwise than I have done.'

And then I came away and thought of the cheers of the relieving troops. Never before had I heard soldiers cheer like that. There was not much doubt about the verdict of the army on Sir George White's conduct of the defence, and it is one which the nation may gracefully accept.

But I am anxious also to discuss the Ladysmith episode from Sir Redvers Buller's point of view. This officer reached Capetown on the very day that White was driven back on Ladysmith. His army, which would not arrive for several weeks, was calcuated to be strong enough to overcome the utmost resistance the Boer Republics could offer.

To what extent he was responsible for the estimates of the number of troops necessary is not known. It is certain, however, that everyone —ministers, generals, colonists and intelligence officers—concurred in making a most remarkable miscalculation.

It reminds me of Jules Verne's story of the men who planned to shift the axis of the earth by the discharge of a great cannon. Everything was arranged. The calculations were exact to the most minute fraction. The world stood aghast at the impending explosion. But the men of science whose figures were otherwise so accurate had left out a nought, and their whole plan came to nothing. So it was with the British. Their original design of a containing division in Natal and an invading army of three divisions in the Free State would have been excellent if only they had written 'army corps' instead of 'division.'

Buller found himself confronted with an alarming and critical situation in Natal. Practically the whole force which had been deemed sufficient to protect the colony was locked up in Ladysmith, and only a few line of communication troops stood between the enemy and the capital or even the seaport. Plainly, therefore, strong reinforcements—at least a division—must be hurried to Natal without an hour's unnecessary delay.

When these troops were subtracted from the forces in the Cape Colony all prospect of pursuing the original plan of invading the Free State was destroyed. It was evident that the war would assume dimensions which no one had ever contemplated.

The first thing to be done therefore was to grapple with the immediate emergencies, and await the arrival of the necessary troops to carry on the war on an altogether larger scale. Natal was the most acute situation. But there were others scarcely less serious and critical. The Cape Colony was quivering with rebellion. The Republican forces were everywhere advancing. Kimberley and Mafeking were isolated. A small British garrison held a dangerous position at Orange River bridge. Nearly all the other bridges had been seized or destroyed by rebels or invaders.

From every quarter came clamourings for troops. Soldiers were wanted with vital need at Stormberg, at Rosemead Junction, at Colesberg, at De Aar, but most of all they were wanted in Natal—Natal, which had been promised protection 'with the whole force of the Empire,' and which was already half-overrun and the rest almost defenceless. So the army corps, which was to have marched irresistibly to Bloemfontein and Pretoria, had to be hurled into the country—each unit as it arrived—wherever the need was greatest where all was great.

Sir Redvers Buller, thus assailed by the unforeseen and pressed on every side, had to make up his mind quickly. He looked to Natal. It was there that the fiercest fighting was in progress and that the strength and vigour of the enemy was apparently most formidable. He had always regarded the line of the Tugela as the only defensive line which British forces would be strong enough to hold, and had recorded his opinion against placing any troops north of that river.

In spite of this warning Ladysmith had been made a great military depot, and had consequently come to be considered a place of primary importance. It was again a question of balancing drawbacks. Buller therefore telegraphed to White asking him whether he could entrench and maintain himself pending the arrival of reinforcements.

White replied that he was prepared to make a prolonged defence of Ladysmith. To this proposal the general-in-chief assented, observing only 'but the line of the Tugela is very tempting.'

General Buller's plan now seems to have been briefly as follows: first, to establish a *modus vivendi* in the Cape Colony, with sufficient troops to stand strictly on the defensive; secondly, to send a strong force to Natal, and either restore the situation there or, failing that, extricate Sir George White so that his troops would be again available for the defence of the southern portion of the colony; thirdly, with what was left of the army corps—no longer strong enough to invade the Free State—to relieve Kimberley; fourthly, after settling Natal to return with such troops as could be spared and form with reinforcements from home a fresh army to carry out the original scheme of invading the Free State.

The defect in this plan was that there were not enough troops to carry it out. As we had underestimated the offensive vigour which the enemy was able to develop before the army could reach South Africa, so now we altogether miscalculated his extraordinary strength on the defensive. But it is impossible to see what else could have been done, and at any rate no one appreciated the magnitude of the difficulties more correctly than Sir Redvers Buller. He knew northern Natal and understood the advantages that the Boers enjoyed among its mountains and kopjes.

On one occasion he even went so far as to describe the operation he had proposed as a 'forlorn hope,' so dark and gloomy was the situation in South Africa during the first fortnight in November. It was stated that the general was ordered by the War Office to go to Natal, and went there against his own will and judgment. This, however, was not true; and when I asked him he replied: 'It was the most difficult business of all. I knew what it meant, and that it was doubtful whether we should get through to Ladysmith. I had not the nerve to order a subordinate to do it. I was the big man. I had to go myself.'

What followed, with the exception of the battle of Colenso, our first experience of the Boer behind entrenchments, has been to some extent described in these letters. Viewed in the light of after-knowledge it does not appear that the holding of Ladysmith was an unfortunate act.

The flower of the Boer army was occupied and exhausted in futile efforts to take the town and stave off the relieving forces. Four precious months were wasted by the enemy in a vain enterprise. Fierce and bloody fighting raged for several weeks with heavy losses to both sides but without shame to either. In the end the British were completely victorious. Not only did their garrison endure famine, disease and bombardment with constancy and composure and repel all assaults, but the soldiers of the relief column sustained undismayed repeated disappointments and reverses, and finally triumphed because through thick and thin they were loyal to their commander and more stubborn even than the stubborn Dutch.

In spite of, perhaps because of, some mistakes and many misfortunes the defence and relief of Ladysmith will not make a bad page in British history. Indeed, it seems to me very likely that in future times our countrymen will think that we were most fortunate to find after a prolonged peace leaders of quality and courage, who were moreover honourable gentlemen, to carry our military affairs through all kinds of difficulties to a prosperous issue; and whatever may be said of the generals it is certain that all will praise the enduring courage of the regimental officer and the private soldier.

16 April, 1900

17

CAMP BEFORE DEWETSDORP, 22 April

Whether I am to see the white cliffs of Dover again I know not, nor will I attempt to predict. But it seems that my fortunes in this land are to be a succession of adventures and escapes, which—I write with all reserve—are beyond and beside the ordinary perils of war, and any one of which would suffice for a personal experience of the campaign.

I acquit myself of all desire to seek for these. Indeed, since I have severed my connection with the 'Cockyolibirds' and am again only a 'curse of modern armies' (to quote Lord Wolseley), I have zealously tried to avoid all danger except what must attend a war correspondent's precarious existence. This I recognise as a necessary evil, for the lot of the writer in the field is a hard and heavy one.

'All the danger of war and one-half per cent the glory': such is our motto, and that is the reason we expect large salaries. But these hazards swoop on me out of a cloudless sky, and that I have hitherto come unscathed through them, while it fills my heart with thankfulness to God for His mercies, makes me wonder why I must be so often thrust to the brink and then withdrawn.

However, I will tell the tale of the doings of the Army, and what happened to me shall fill its proper place, so that the reader may himself be the judge of the matter.

The night of the 20th passed quietly, but the Boers were awake with the sunrise and saluted us with discharges of the 'pom-pom' which, as far as I could see, did no harm to anyone. We could not press the attack on the previous day because the infantry were tired out and the enemy's position of sufficient natural strength to make an assault a serious business.

In the night the Dutchmen had been busy, and the black lines of entrenchments marked the hillsides. When I inquired whether there would be a battle or not that day staff officers pointed over the veldt to a column of dust which was coming slowly nearer.

General Campbell, with three battalions (including two of Her Majesty's Guards) and a battery, was marching to join the main column. It was necessary, in view of the entrenchments and the approaching reinforcements, to wait until the force was complete.

The event would be decided on the morrow, and meanwhile Brabazon[1] and the mounted troops—cavalry, I shall call them—were to make a reconnaissance of the Boer left.

The brigade, which included the mounted infantry and was about a thousand strong, moved southward behind the outpost line, and making a rapid and wide circuit soon came on the enemy's left flank. Here we waited while patrols were pushed out and while Brabazon was clearing his own right by a still wider turning movement.

The patrols soon drew the fire of the Boer pickets, and the rifle shots began to ring out in the clear cool air of the morning. Presently a party of a dozen Boers appeared in the distance galloping down towards a farm whence they might fire on the gradually advancing cavalry.

The general asked the subaltern in charge of our two guns whether they were within range. The young officer was anxious to try. We watched the experiment with attention.

The practice was extremely good. The first shell burst in the middle of the Boer horsemen, who at once spread into a looser formation. The next exploded in front of them, and all the seven shells that were fired fell within measurable distance of someone.

For the first time in this war I saw the Boers show what I consider cowardice; for without anyone being killed or wounded the whole party turned back and, abandoning their intention or duty, scurried away to cover behind the long swell of ground over which they had come. The Boer Army in Natal was not thus easily dissuaded from its objects.

Meanwhile the flanking movement was in progress, and as the ground to our right was gradually made good and secured by Colonel Sitwell, Brabazon pushed his centre forward until McNeill's[2] Scouts

---

[1] John Palmer Brabazon (1843–1922). Commanded 4th Hussars from 1893 and was Churchill's first commanding officer. Commanded 2nd Cavalry Brigade in South Africa. Retired as Major-General. KCB 1911.

[2] Angus McNeill (1874–1950). An old schoolmate of Churchill, he commanded Montmorency's Scouts in South Africa, and served as Brigadier-General during the 1914–18 war. *The River War* included his illustrations.

were cantering all over the slopes where the Boers had just been shelled, and hunting such of the enemy as tarried to safer and more remote positions.

At last we arrived at the edge of the swell of ground. It fell steeply towards a flat basin, from the middle of which rose a most prominent and peculiar kopje. Invisible behind this was Dewetsdorp. Round it stood Boers, some mounted, some on foot, to the number of about two hundred.

Our rapid advance, almost into the heart of their position, had disturbed and alarmed them. They were doubtful whether this was reconnaissance or actual attack. They determined to make certain by making an attempt to outflank the outflanking cavalry; and no sooner had our long range rifle fire compelled them to take cover behind the hill than a new force, as it seemed, of two hundred rode into the open and, passing across our front at a distance of, perhaps, 2,000 yards, made for a white stone kopje on our right.

Angus McNeill ran up to the general. 'Sir, may we cut them off? I think we can just do it.' The Scouts pricked up their ears. The general reflected. 'All right,' he said, 'you may try.'

'Mount, mount, mount, the Scouts,' cried their impetuous officer, scrambling into his saddle. Then to me, 'Come with us, we'll give you a show now—first-class.'

A few days before, in an unguarded moment, I had promised to follow the fortunes of the Scouts for a day. I looked at the Boers, they were nearer to the white stone kopje than we but, on the other hand, they had the hill to climb, and were probably worse mounted.

It might be done, and if it were done—I thought of the affair of Acton Homes—how dearly they would have to pay in that open plain. So in the interests of the *Morning Post* I got on my horse and we all started—forty or fifty Scouts, McNeill and I, as fast as we could, by hard spurring, make the horses go.

It was from the very beginning a race, and recognised as such by both sides. As we converged I saw the five leading Boers, better mounted than their comrades, outpacing the others in a desperate resolve to secure the coign of vantage.

I said, 'We cannot do it', but no one would admit defeat or leave the matter undecided. The rest is exceedingly simple.

We arrived at a wire fence 100 yards—to be accurate 120 yards—from the crest of the kopje, dismounted and, cutting the wire, were about to seize the precious rocks when—as I had seen them in the railway at Frere cutting, grim, hairy and terrible—the heads and shoulders of a dozen Boers appeared; and how many more must be close behind them.

There was a queer, almost inexplicable pause, or perhaps there was no pause at all, but I seem to remember much happening. First the Boers—one fellow with a long, drooping, black beard and a chocolate-coloured coat, another with a red scarf round his neck. Two Scouts cutting the wire fence stupidly. One man taking aim across his horse, and McNeill's voice quite steady. 'Too late; back to the other kopje. Gallop!'

Then the musketry crashed out, and 'swish' and 'whirr' of the bullets filled the air.

I put my foot in the stirrup. The horse, terrified at the firing, plunged wildly. I tried to spring into the saddle. It turned under the animal's belly. He broke away and galloped madly off.

Most of the Scouts were already 200 yards off. I was alone, dismounted, within the closest range, and a mile at least from cover of any kind.

One consolation I had—my pistol. I could not be hunted down unarmed in the open as I had been before. But a disabling wound was the brightest prospect.

I turned and, for the second time in this war, ran for my life on foot from the Boer marksmen, and I thought to myself, 'Here at last I take it.'

Suddenly, as I ran, I saw a Scout. He came from the left across my front; a tall man, with skull and crossbones, on a pale horse. Death in Revelations, but life to me.

I shouted to him as he passed; 'Give me a stirrup.' To my surprise he stopped at once. 'Yes,' he said shortly. I ran up to him, did not bungle the business of mounting, and in a moment found myself behind him on the saddle.

Then we rode. I put my arms round him to catch a grip of the mane. My hand became soaked with blood. The horse was hard hit; but, gallant beast, he extended himself nobly. The pursuing bullets piped and whistled—for the range was growing longer—overhead.

'Don't be frightened,' said my rescuer, 'they won't hit you.' Then, as I did not reply, 'My poor horse, oh, my poor horse; shot with an explosive bullet. The devils! But their hour will come. Oh, my poor horse!'

I said, 'Never mind, you've saved my life.' 'Ah,' he rejoined,

291

'but it's the horse I'm thinking about.' That was the whole of our conversation.

Judging from the number of bullets I heard I did not expect to be hit after the first 500 yards were covered, for a galloping horse is a difficult target, and the Boers were breathless and excited. But it was with a feeling of relief that I turned the corner of the further kopje and found I had thrown double sixes again.

The result of the race had been watched with strained attention by the rest of the troops, and from their position they knew that we were beaten before we ever reached the wire fence. They had heard the sudden fierce crackle of musketry and had seen what had passed.

All the officers were agreed that the man who pulled up in such a situation to help another was worthy of some honourable distinction. Indeed, I have heard that Trooper Roberts[1]—note the name, which seems familiar in this connection—is to have his claims considered for the Victoria Cross. As to this I will not pronounce, for I feel some diffidence in writing impartially of a man who certainly saved me from a great danger.

Well satisfied with my brief experience with the Scouts, I returned to General Brabazon. While we had been advancing deeply into the Boer flank they had not been idle, and now suddenly from the side of the solitary kopje behind which they had collected three guns came into action against us.

For ten minutes the shell fire was really hot, and as these guns were firing with black powder, the smoke springing out in a thick white cloud from the muzzle warned us whenever a projectile was on its way and, I think, added to the strain on the nerves.

You could watch the distant artillery. There was the gun again; four or five seconds to wonder whether the shell would hit you in the face; the approaching hiss rushing into a rending shriek; safe over; bang! right among the horses 100 yards behind.

Here comes the next—two guns fired together this time. Altogether, the Boers fired nearly thirty shells—several of which were shrapnel—on this small space of ground.

But fate was in a merciful mood that day, for we had but one man killed and five or six—including the general's orderly—wounded by them.

[1] Clement Roberts of Montmorency's Scouts. He was not awarded the Victoria Cross, and six years later wrote to Churchill, who sent him £10. In 1907 he was finally awarded the DCM.

It was, however, evident that this could not endure. Brabazon had not cared to bring his own two guns into such an advanced position, because they were not horse guns, and might not be able to get away safely if the Boers should make a strong counter-attack.

Indeed, so long as the loss of guns is considered a national disaster instead of only an ordinary incident of war, cavalry officers will regard them rather as sources of anxiety than as powerful weapons.

Without guns it was useless to stay and as, moreover, Sir Leslie Rundle's[1] orders were that the cavalry were not to be severely engaged, Brabazon decided to withdraw the reconnaissance, and did so most successfully, after a little instructive rearguard action.

He had penetrated far into the enemy's position; had compelled him to move his guns and disturb his frontal dispositions; had reconnoitred the ground, located the laagers, and come safely away with the loss of little more than a dozen men. Had there been on this day an infantry support behind the cavalry we should have hustled the enemy out of his whole position and slept triumphantly in Dewetsdorp.

Sir Leslie Rundle was much impressed by the vigour and success of the cavalry, whose fortunes were watched from the plateau, and as evening came the report spread through the camp that a general engagement would be fought on the next day.

He also decided to entrust the direction of the actual turning attack to General Brabazon who, besides his cavalry force, was to have twelve guns and an infantry brigade under his command.

With every feeling of confidence in the issue, the Army went to bed, impatient for the dawn. But in the dead of night a telegram arrived from Lord Roberts,[2] instructing Rundle not to press his attack until he was in touch with Pole-Carew[3] and other reinforcements, and it thus became evident that the operations had grown to an altogether larger scale.

28 May, 1900

[1] Leslie Rundle (1856–1934). Adjutant-General of Egyptian Army. Governor of Malta 1909–1915. KCB 1898.

[2] Frederick Sleigh Roberts, 1st Earl (1832–1914). Staff Officer to Sir Neville Chamberlain during the Indian Mutiny. VC 1858. Commander in chief, India, 1885–1893. Field-Marshal and Commander in chief, Ireland 1895–1899. Supreme Commander in South Africa 1899.

[3] Reginald Pole-Carew (1849–1924). Commanded 11th Division in South Africa. Retired as Major-General. Knighted 1900.

18

WINBURG, 8 May

The general's[1] orders were to march north from Thabanchu on Winburg by the Jacobsrust road, and he was expected, if no opposition was encountered, to reach his destination by 7 May. The column with which he started from Thabanchu was composed of Smith-Dorrien's[2] 19th Infantry Brigade, Ridley's Mounted Infantry Brigade, and two batteries of artillery; but at Jacobsrust he would receive a strong reinforcement consisting of Bruce-Hamilton's[3] 21st Brigade of Infantry, Broadwood's[4] Cavalry Brigade, two batteries of field and one of horse artillery, and two 5 in. guns. This accession would raise his force to a total of 7,500 infantry, 4,000 mounted men and thirty-two guns, an imposing command for an officer who had not yet had time to take the badges of a colonel off his shoulders. The first thing, however, was to reach Jacobsrust and effect the junction with Bruce-Hamilton's force.

The Thabanchu column started at daybreak on 30 April, and when it was within three or four miles of Houtnek Poort the enemy suddenly unmasked field guns and 'pom-poms' and opened a long range fire with them from the east on the right flank of the marching troops. Colonel Bambridge, with the 7th Corps of Mounted Infantry,

[1] Ian Standish Monteith Hamilton (1853–1947). Commanded 3rd Brigade, Tirah Expeditionary Force, 1898. Served South Africa 1899–1901. Wounded at Majuba Hill. Commanded Mediterranean Expeditionary Force at Gallipoli, 1915. KCB 1900. General 1905.

[2] Horace Lockwood Smith-Dorrien (1858–1930). Served on Kitchener's staff at Omdurman. Governor of Gibraltar 1918–1923. Knighted 1904.

[3] Bruce Meade Hamilton (1857–1936). AAG 2nd Division and CO 21st Brigade in South Africa. KCB 1902, KCVO 1911, GCB 1915.

[4] Robert George Broadwood (1862–1917). Commanded the Egyptian cavalry during the Sudan campaign. Later served in South Africa and South China.

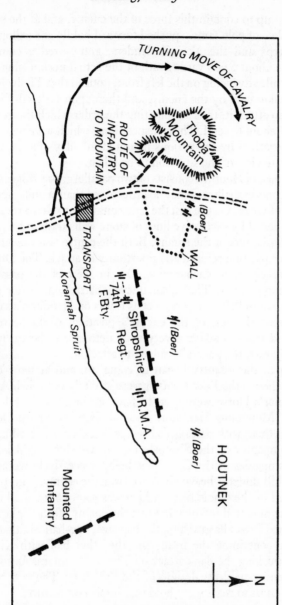

TURNING MOVE OF CAVALRY

Thoba Mountain

ROUTE OF INFANTRY TO MOUNTAIN

(Boer)

WALL

TRANSPORT

Korannah Spruit

74th F.Bty.

Shropshire Regt.

(Boer)

R.M.A.

(Boer)

HOUTNEK

Mounted Infantry

N

The Action at Houtnek

wheeled up to contain this force of the enemy, and at the same time De Lisle—of polo fame—pushed forward boldly at a gallop with the 6th Corps and the New Zealanders, and seized a commanding position about 2,000 yards south of the actual neck. Colonel Legge, meanwhile advancing on the left front, noticed that Thoba Mountain was weakly held by the enemy, and thereupon ordered Kitchener's Horse to attack it, thus anticipating the order which the general was himself about to send. These dispositions, which were made on their own initiatives by the various mounted infantry officers, enabled a deliberate view of the situation to be taken.

The pass of Houtnek consists of two parallel grassy ridges separated by a smooth shallow valley a little more than a mile across, and devoid of cover. On the east the pass runs up into sharp rocky kopjes, strengthened by successive lines of stone walls trailing away towards the main laagers of the enemy. Both the centre and the left flank of the Boer position refused all opportunity of attack. The Dutch right was scarcely more encouraging. On the west of the pass rose the great mountain of Thoba, an uneven battlefield, better suited to Boers than to British troops. Yet as it was on Hamilton's safer flank, dominated the rest of the enemy's position, could be turned by mounted troops making a very wide detour, and being, moreover, the only way, the general resolved to attack it.

At 9.30 the infantry began to come up, and at ten o'clock the approaches to the Boer position were strongly occupied. As soon as Kitchener's Horse were seen to have made good their footing on Thoba Mountain, Hamilton ordered General Smith-Dorrien to support them with part of his brigade, which was accordingly done, two companies of the Shropshires, the Gordon Highlanders, and four companies of the Canadians being successively worked up on to the hill under a heavy shell fire from the enemy. This practically disposed of the whole force, which was soon engaged all along the line, the mounted infantry holding the enemy off the right and right rear, the Cornwalls guarding the baggage, one-half Smith-Dorrien's brigade containing the front, and the other half with Kitchener's Horse pushing the flank attack on Thoba Mountain. As soon as the Boers understood the designs of the British on Thoba they made a strong effort to regain and hold that important feature.

At first the troops made good progress, but as the enemy received continual reinforcements their resistance became more severe, until presently, far from gaining ground, they began to lose it. At last

Winburg, *8 May*

about two o'clock some one hundred and fifty of the German corps
of the Boer force advanced from the northern point of Thoba in four
lines across the table top to drive the British off the hill. So regular
was their order that it was not until their levelled rifles were seen
pointing south that they were recognised as foes and artillery opened
on them. In spite of an accurate shell-fire they continued to advance
boldly against the highest part of the hill, and meanwhile, cloaked by
a swell of the ground, Captain Towse, of the Gordon Highlanders,
with twelve of his own regiment and ten of Kitchener's Horse, was
steadily moving towards them. The scene on the broad stage of the
Thoba plateau was intensely dramatic. The whole army were the
witnesses.

The two forces, strangely disproportionate, drew near to each
other. Neither was visible to the other. The unexpected collision
impended. From every point field glasses were turned on the spectacle,
and even hardened soldiers held their breath. At last, with suddenness,
both parties came face to face at fifty yards' distance. The Germans,
who had already made six prisoners, called loudly on Captain Towse
and his little band to surrender. What answer was returned is not
recorded, but a furious splutter of musketry broke out at once, and
in less than a minute the long lines of the enemy recoiled in confusion,
and the top of the hill was secured to the British. Among the foreigners
wounded in the encounter was Colonel Maximoff.

Captain Towse for his conspicuous gallantry and for the extraordinary results which attended it has been recommended for the
Victoria Cross; but in gaining what is above all things precious to a
soldier he lost what is necessary to a happy life, for in the moment
when his military career was assured by a brilliant feat of arms it was
terminated by a bullet which, striking him sideways, blinded him in
both eyes. Thus do misery and joy walk hand in hand on the field of
war.

All this time the rifle and gun fire along the whole front had been
continuous, and as the day wore on without the British making good
their hold on Thoba Mountain the enemy gathered in a more and
more threatening attitude on the right of the column, and by four
o'clock at least fifteen hundred men were collected, with guns and
'pom-poms', which threw shell into the rearguard and transport.
Hamilton, however, was determined to fight the matter out. He
therefore directed that all troops should post guards on their front,
lie down wherever darkness found them, and prepare to renew the

action at daybreak. He then telegraphed to General French[1] for some assistance, the need of more mounted men being painfully felt.

At dawn on May Day fighting recommenced, and soon after six o'clock parties of the Gordons and Canadians succeeded in gaining possession of the two peaks of Thoba Mountain. Besides this, half a company of the Shropshires, under Colour-Sergeant Sconse, managed to seize the neck between them, and though subjected to a severe crossfire, which caused in this small party ten casualties out of forty, maintained themselves stubbornly for four hours. The points which dominate the flat top of the mountain were thus gained.

Meanwhile reinforcements, consisting of the 8th Hussars, a composite Lancer regiment, the East Yorkshire, and a field battery, had arrived from Thabanchu, and the approach of Bruce-Hamilton's force from the direction of Kranz Kraal was also felt. General Ian Hamilton now ordered Colonel Clowes, commanding the cavalry, to move right round Thoba Mountain and threaten the Boer line of retreat as a preliminary and accompaniment of the main infantry assault, which had now become inevitable. Clowes's force was strengthened by the addition of a horse battery. The newly-arrived infantry and the battery had to be diverted to support the right and right rear, where the pressure was now very strong.

At about eight o'clock General Smith-Dorrien had himself gone up to the top of Thoba Mountain to direct personally the decisive movement when the time should come. A little before one o'clock, the progress of the cavalry being satisfactory, he determined to settle the matter, so that if successful the force might get its baggage over the pass before dark. He therefore formed a line of infantry right across the plateau, two companies of Shropshires in the centre, and one and a half companies of the Gordons on either flank. The advance was sounded.

The troops moved forward with alacrity. For a few moments the fire was heavy, but the Boers knew themselves 'bested', and on the soldiers raising the cheer that precedes the actual assault they rushed to their horses, and the whole of Thoba Mountain was won. The rest of the positions became untenable, and the enemy to the number of four thousand, promptly evacuated it, galloping swiftly back in the direction of Jacobsrust.

[1] John Denton Pinkstone French (1852–1925). Commanded cavalry division in South Africa. Commander in chief, British Expeditionary Force, 1914–15. 1st Earl of Ypres.

The 8th Hussars alone got near enough to charge, and half a dozen Dutchmen were sabred. The Boers who were making the attack on the right retreated at the same time as their comrades, and the transport, no longer molested, passed safely over the pass and parked for the night on the northern side. No trustworthy estimate can be formed of the enemy's loss, but a score of prisoners were taken and an equal number of bodies were found on the position.

The British casualties were fortunately slight considering the fire and its duration, and did not exceed a hundred officers and men.

The next day the junction between the columns was effected, and Ian Hamilton's force formed, with reference to the main advance, the army of the right flank, composed as follows:

Infantry	19th Brigade	Smith-Dorrien
	21st Brigade	Bruce-Hamilton
Cavalry	2nd Cavalry Regiment	Broadwood
Artillery	3 Batteries F.A.	
	2 Batteries H.A.	Waldron
	2 5 in. guns	

This force was supported by the Highland Brigade and two 4.7 naval guns, under General Colvile, who was directed to follow the leading column at a distance of ten miles. Hamilton proposed to march forward on 2 May, but an order from headquarters enjoined a halt; nor was it until the afternoon of the 3rd that the force reached Jacobsrust, as it is called by the inhabitants, Isabellasfontein, as our maps record. A little cavalry skirmishing in the neighbourhood of the camp resulted in the death of one Lancer.

On 4 May the whole army moved forward again, Lord Roberts passing through Brandfort towards Smaldeel, Hamilton continuing his march on Winburg. This day did not pass without fighting for scarcely had the troops left camp when a patter of musketry warned the general that his cavalry had become engaged.

Riding forward, he was the witness of a very dashing cavalry exploit. Across the line of advance was drawn up a strong force of the enemy, estimated at 4,000 men and 13 guns. These in a good position along a range of wooded bluffs promised a sufficient task for the troops during the day. But now suddenly, from the direction of Brandfort, a new army of Boers began to appear, riding swiftly down to join hands with their comrades athwart the road and fall on the left flank of the column.

The thing was urgent, and perhaps vital. But between the fast converging Boer forces at the angle where they would meet ran a long ridge of indefinite extent. General Broadwood at once, without a moment's delay, galloped forward, and with two squadrons of the Guards' Cavalry and two of the 10th Hussars seized it. The Boers were already scrambling up its lower slopes. A sharp fight immediately opened. Kitchener's Horse, hurrying up in support, occupied a further point of the ridge and the Dutch, after a determined but futile attempt to clear the hill, fell back. The junction of the two Boer columns was prevented. It seems that the whole of their plan for the day was based on this first condition, and in an army where every individual soldier must have the details of any plan explained to him it is not easy to make fresh dispositions in the field.

Indeed, a sort of panic seems to have taken hold of the enemy, for without waiting for the infantry attack to develop they fled forthwith at great speed, galloping madly across the drift. As the British proprietor of Welcome Farm told me—horsemen and guns, pell-mell, in downright rout, pursued, so swift was their departure, only by the shells of the horse artillery.

The losses in this brief affair were not large, and almost entirely among the cavalry. In those few minutes of firing about a dozen troopers had been hit. Lord Airlie was slightly wounded in the arm, and Lieutenant Ross, Royal Horse Guards, was killed. He had been sent forward to see what lay beyond the further crest of the hill, and found that deadly riflemen lay there waiting for a certain victim. He fell pierced by several bullets and lived only for half an hour.

The officer was a most zealous soldier. Though possessed of private means which would have enabled him to lead a life of ease and pleasure, he had for several years devoted himself assiduously to the military profession. He went to India as a volunteer during the Tirah campaign, and served with distinction on Sir Penn Symon's staff—general and aide-de-camp both vanished now, as the foam fades in the wake of a fast ship! From India he hastened to West Africa, and in that vile and pestilential region won a considerable reputation; indeed, he was to have received the Distinguished Service Order for his part in recent operations had not another war intervened. He arrived at the Cape scarcely a month ago full of hope and energy. This is the end, and while it is one which a soldier must be ready to meet, deep sympathy will be felt for the father, from whom the public necessities have now required two gallant sons.

Though the disorderly and demoralised nature of the Boer flight through Welcome Farm was known throughout the British army, it was not expected that so strong a position as the bluffs behind the Vet River would be yielded without a shot fired. This, nevertheless, proved to be the case, for when, on the morning of the 6th, Hamilton resumed his advance he found that no force of the enemy stood between him and Winburg.

He therefore sent shortly after noon a staff officer, Captain Balfour to wit, under a flag of truce, with a letter to the mayor of the town summoning him forthwith to surrender the town and all stores therein, and promising that if this were done he would use every effort to protect private property and that whatever foodstuffs were required by the troops would be paid for. This message, which was duly heralded by the sound of a trumpet, concluded by saying that unless an acceptance was received within two hours the general would understand that his offer had been declined.

Thus accredited Captain Balfour made his way into the town and was soon the centre of an anxious and excited crowd of burghers and others who filled the market square. The mayor, the landdrost, other prominent persons, indeed, all the inhabitants, were eager to avail themselves of the good terms, and a satisfactory settlement was almost arranged when, arriving swiftly from the north-east, Philip Botha[1] and a commando of five hundred men, mostly Germans and Hollanders, all very truculent since they were as yet unbeaten, entered the town.

A violent and passionate scene ensued. Botha declared he would never surrender Winburg without a fight. Dissatisfied with the attentions paid him by Captain Balfour, he turned furiously on him and rated him soundly. Several of the Free Staters had asked what would be done to them if they laid down their arms. Balfour had replied that they would be permitted to return to their farms, unless actually captured on the field. This Botha held to be a breach of the laws of war, and he thereupon charged the officer with attempting to suborn his burghers. What had he to say that he should not be made a prisoner? 'I ask favours of no Dutchman' replied Balfour sternly.

'Arrest that man,' shouted Botha in a fury. 'I shall begin shooting soon.' At these shameful words a great commotion arose. The women screamed, the mayor and landdrost rushed forward in the hopes of

[1] One of the brothers of Louis Botha, he led a Boer commando for most of the war before he was killed in action.

averting bloodshed. The Boers raised their rifles in menance, and the unarmed British envoy flourished his white flag indignantly.

For several minutes it seemed that an actual scuffle, possibly a tragedy, would occur. But the influence of the town-folk, who knew that their liberty and property lay in the hands of the Imperial general, and that the great siege guns were even then being dragged into effective range, prevailed, and Philip Botha, followed by his men, galloped furiously from the square towards the north.

That afternoon General Ian Hamilton entered Winburg at the head of his troops. Under a shady tree outside the town the mayor and landdrost tendered their submission and two large silver keys. The Union Jack was hoisted in the market-place amid the cheers of the British section of the inhabitants, and as each battalion marching through the streets saw the famous emblem of pride and power, bright in the rays of the setting sun, these feeble or interested plaudits were drowned in the loud acclamations of the victorious invaders.

Hamilton was expected to arrive on the 7th, if no opposition was encountered. He had fought nearly every day, and reached the town on the evening of the 6th.

25 June, 1900

19

Heilbron, 23 May

Heilbron lies in a deep valley. About it on every side rolls the grassy upland country of the Free State, one smooth grey-green surge beyond another like the after swell of a great gale at sea; and here in the trough of the waves, hidden almost entirely from view, is the town itself, white stone houses amid dark trees all clustering at the foot of a tall church spire. It is a quiet, sleepy little place, with a few good buildings and pretty rose gardens, half a dozen large stores, a hotel and a branch line of its own.

For a few days it had been capital of the Free State. Christian de Wet appeared with sixty waggons, five guns and a thousand burghers, very weary, having trekked all night from the direction of Kroonstad, and glad to find a place of rest and refreshment. 'What of the English?' inquired the newcomers, and the Heilbron folk replied that the English were coming, and so was Christmas, and that the country to the southward was all clear for ten miles. Thereat the war-worn commando outspanned their oxen and settled themselves to coffee. Forty minutes later the leading patrols of Broadwood's brigade began to appear on the hills to the south of the town.

Looked at from any point of view the British force was a formidable array: Household Cavalry, 12th Lancers and 10th Hussars, with P and Q Batteries, Royal Horse Artillery (you must mind your P's and Q's with them), two 'pom-poms', and two galloping Maxims; and hurrying up behind them light horse, mounted infantry, 19th and 21st Brigades, thirty field guns, more 'pom-poms', two great 5 in. guns, ox-drawn siege pieces ('cow guns', the army calls them), and Ian Hamilton. It was an army formidable to any foe, but to those who now stared upwards from the little town and saw the dark swift-moving masses on the hills—an avalanche of armed men and destructive engines about to fall on them—terrible beyond words. 'And then', as the poet observes, 'there was mounting in hot haste,' saddling up of weary ponies, frantic inspanning of hungry oxen cheated of their well-earned rest and feed, cracking of long whips, kicking of frightened Kaffirs; and so pell-mell out of the town and away to the northward hurried the commando of Christian de Wet.

The cavalry halted on the hills for a while, the general being desirous of obtaining the formal surrender of Heilbron, and so preventing street-fighting or bombardment. An officer was despatched with a flag of truce and a trumpeter; message most urgent, answer to be given within twenty minutes, or heaven knows what would happen; but all these things take time. Flags of truce prescribe the customs of war—must approach the enemy's picket line at a walk; a mile and a half at a walk—twenty minutes, add twenty for the answer, ten for the return journey, and nearly an hour is gone. So we wait impatiently watching the solitary figures with a white speck above them draw nearer to the Boer lines; 'and', says the brigadier, 'bring two guns up and have the ranges taken.'

There was just a chance that while all were thus intent on the town, the convoy and commando might have escaped unharmed, for it happened that the northern road runs for some distance eastward along the bottom of the valley, concealed from view. But the clouds of dust betrayed them.

'Hullo! what the deuce is that?' cried an officer.

'What?' said everyone else.

'Why, that! Look at the dust. There they go. It's a Boer convoy. Gone away.'

And with this holloa the chase began. Never have I seen anything in war so like a fox hunt. At first the scent was uncertain and the pace was slow with many checks.

Before us rose a long smooth slope of grass, and along the crest the figures of horsemen could be plainly seen. The tail of the waggon train was just disappearing. But who could say how many rifles lined that ridge? Besides, there were several barbed wire fences which, as anyone knows, will spoil the best country.

Broadwood began giving all kinds of orders—Household Cavalry to advance slowly in the centre; 12th Lancers to slip forward on the right, skirting the town, and try to look behind the ridge, and with them a battery of horse guns; 10th Hussars, to make a cast to the left, and the rest of the guns to walk forward steadily.

Slowly at first and silently besides, but soon the hounds gave tongue. Pop, pop, pop—the advanced squadron—Blues—had found something to fire at, and something that fired back, too; pip-pop, pip-pop came the double reports of the Boer rifles. Bang—the artillery opened on the crestline with shrapnel, and at the first few shells it was evident that the enemy would not abide the attack. The horsemen vanished over the skyline.

The leading squadron pushed cautiously forward—every movement at a walk so far. Infantry brigadiers and others, inclined to impatience, ground their teeth, and thinking there would be no sport that day went home criticising the master. The leading squadron reached the crest, and we could see them dismount and begin to fire.

We were over the first big fence, and now the scent improved. Beyond the first ridge was another, and behind this, much nearer now, dust clouds high and thick. The general galloped forward himself to the newly-captured position and took a comprehensive view. 'Tell the brigade to come here at once—sharp.'

A galloper shot away to the rear. Behind arose the rattle of trotting batteries. The excitement grew. Already the patrols were skirting the second ridge. The Boer musketry, fitful for a few minutes, died away. They were abandoning their second position. 'Forward, then.' And forward we went accordingly at a healthy trot.

In front of the jingling squadrons two little galloping Maxims darted out, and almost before the ridge was ours they were spluttering angrily at the retreating enemy, so that four burghers, as I saw myself, departed amid a perfect hail of bullets, which peppered the ground on all sides.

But now the whole hunt swung northward towards a line of rather ugly-looking heights. Broadwood looked at them sourly. 'Four guns to watch those hills, in case they bring artillery against us from them.' Scarcely were the words spoken when there was a flash and a brown blur on the side of one of the hills, and with a rasping sound a shell passed overhead and burst among the advancing cavalry. The four guns were on the target without a moment's delay.

The Boer artillerists managed to fire five shots, and then the place grew too hot for them—indeed, after Natal, I may write, even for them. They had to expose themselves a great deal to remove their gun, and the limber and its six horses showed very plainly on the hillside, so that we all hoped to smash a wheel or kill a horse, and thus capture a real prize. But at the critical moment our 'pom-poms' disgraced themselves. They knew the range, they saw the target. They fired four shots. The aim was not bad.

But four shots—four miserable shots! Just pom-pom, pom-pom. That was all. Whereas, if the Boers had had such a chance, they would have rattled through the whole belt and sent eighteen or twenty shells in a regular shower. So we all saw with pain how a weapon, which is so terrible in the hands of the enemy, may become feeble and ineffective when used on our side by our own gunners.

After the menace of the Boer artillery was removed from our right flank, the advance became still more rapid. Batteries and squadrons were urged into a gallop. Broadwood himself hurried forward, till he was hard on the tail of the leading dog. We topped a final rise.

Then at last we viewed the vermin. There, crawling up the opposite slope, clear-cut on a white road, was a long line of waggons—ox-waggons and mule-waggons—and behind everything a small cart drawn by two horses. All were struggling with frantic energy to escape from their pursuers. But in vain.

The batteries spun round and unlimbered. Eager gunners ran forward with ammunition and some with belts for the 'pom-poms'. There was a momentary pause while ranges were taken and sights aligned, and then—! Shell after shell crashed among the convoys. Some exploded on the ground, others, bursting in the air, whipped up the dust all round mules and men.

The 'pom-poms', roused at last from their apathy by this delicious target and some pointed observations of the general, thudded out strings of little bombs. For a few minutes the waggons persevered manfully. Then one by one they came to a standstill. The drivers fled to the nearest shelter and the animals strayed off the road or stood quiet in stolid ignorance of their danger.

And now at this culminating moment I must, with all apologies to 'Brooksby', change the metaphor, because the end of the chase was scarcely like a fox hunt. The guns had killed the quarry, and the cavalry dashed forward to secure it. It was a fine bag—to wit, fifteen laden waggons and seventeen prisoners. Such was the affair of Heilbron, and it was none the less joyous and exciting, because so far as we could learn, no man on either side was killed, and only one trooper and five horses wounded. Then we turned homewards.

On the way back to the town I found, near a fine farmhouse with deep verandahs and a pretty garden, Boer ambulance waggons, two German doctors and a dozen bearded men. They inquired the issue of the pursuit: how many prisoners had we taken. We replied by other questions. 'How much longer will the war last?'

'It is not a war any more,' said one of the Red Cross men. 'The poor devils haven't got a chance against your numbers.'

'Nevertheless,' interposed another, 'they will fight to the end.'

I looked towards the last speaker. He was evidently of a different class to the rest.

'Are you,' I asked, 'connected with the ambulance?'

'No, I am the military chaplain to the Dutch forces.'

'And you think the Free State will continue to resist?'

'We will go down fighting. What else is there to do? History and Europe will do us justice.'

'It is easy for you to say that, who do not fight; but what of the poor farmers and peasants you have dragged into this war. They do not tell us that they wish to fight. They think they have been made a catspaw for the Transvaal.'

'Ah,' he rejoined warmly, 'they have no business to say that now. They did not say so before the war. They wanted to fight. It was a solemn pledge. We were bound to help the Transvaalers; what would have happened to us after they were conquered?'

'But surely you, and men like you, knew the strength of the antagonist you challenged. Why did you urge these simple people to their ruin?'

'We had had enough of English methods here. We knew our independence was threatened. It had to come. We did not deceive them. We told them. I told my flock often that it would not be child's play.'

'Didn't you tell them it was hopeless?'

'It was not hopeless,' he said. 'There were many chances.'

'All gone now.'

'Not quite all. Besides, chances or no chances, we must go down fighting.'

'You preach a strange Gospel of Peace.'

'And you English,' he rejoined, 'have strange ideas of liberty.'

So we parted without more words, and I rode on my way into the town. Heilbron had one memory for me, and it was one which was now to be revived. In the hotel—a regular country inn—I found various British subjects who had been assisting the Boer ambulances —possibly with rifles. It is not my purpose to discuss here the propriety of their conduct. They had been placed in situations which do not come to men in quiet times, and for the rest they were mean-spirited creatures.

307

While the Republican cause seemed triumphant they had worked for the Dutch, had doubtless spoken of 'damned rooineks' and other similar phrases; so soon as the Imperial arms predominated they had changed their note; had refused to go on commando in any capacity, proclaimed that Britons never should be slaves, and dared the crumbling organism of Federal Government to do its worst.

We talked about the fighting in Natal which they had seen from the other side. The Acton Homes affair cropped up. You will remember that we of the irregular brigade plumed ourselves immensely on the ambuscading of the Boers—the one undoubted score we ever made against them on the Tugela.

'Yes,' purred my renegades, 'you caught the damned Dutchmen fairly then. We were delighted, but of course we dared not show it.' (Pause.) 'That was where De Mentz was killed.'

De Mentz! The name recalled a vivid scene—the old field-cornet lying forward, grey and grim, in a pool of blood and a litter of empty cartridge cases, with his wife's letter clasped firmly in his stiffening fingers. He had 'gone down fighting', had had no doubts what course to steer. I knew when I saw his face that he had thought the whole thing out. Now they told me that there was no man in all Heilbron more bitterly intent on war, and that his letter in the *Volksstem* calling on the Afrikanders to drive the English scum from the land had produced a deep impression.

'Let them,' thus it ran, 'bring fifty thousand men, or eighty thousand men, or even'—it was a wild possibility—'a hundred thousand, yet we will overcome them.' But they brought two hundred thousand, so all his calculations were disproved, and he himself was killed with the responsibility on his shoulders of leading his men into an ambush which, with ordinary precautions, might have been avoided. Such are war's revenges. His widow, a very poor woman, lived next door to the hotel, nursing her son who had been shot through the lungs during the same action. Let us hope he will recover, for he had a gallant sire.

I can write no more about Heilbron, for with Hamilton's column we march so fast and so far that neither energy nor leisure help the pen. Indeed, I have not been able to give you any account of the passage of the Sand River on 10 May, of the concentration at Kroonstad, the forced march to Lindley, or the rearguard action north of that town, or of the passage of the Rhenoster, all of which events were full of interest and worthy of record. Nor can I hope to retrieve the neglect for, as I write, the orders come to march again at dawn eastward towards the main army. But the reader must not complain, for there are as many fine adventures in the sea of the future as have ever been drawn out on to the dry lands of the past.

12 July, 1900

20

PRETORIA, 8 June

The Commander-in-Chief had good reasons for wishing to push on at once to the enemy's capital, without waiting at Johannesburg. But the fatigue of the troops and the necessities of supply imposed a two days' halt. On the 3rd of June the advance was resumed. The army marched in three columns. The left, which, thrown forward in echelon, consisted of the cavalry division under French; the centre was formed by Ian Hamilton's force; and the right or main column nearest the railway comprised the Seventh and Eleventh Dvisions (less one brigade left to hold Johannesburg), Gordon's cavalry brigade and the corps troops under the personal command of the Field-Marshal.

The long forward stride of the 3rd was, except for a small action against French, unchecked or unopposed by the Boers, and all the information which the Intelligence Department could collect seemed to promise a bloodless entry into the capital. So strong was the evidence that at dawn on the 4th of June Hamilton's column was diverted from its prescribed line of march on Elandsfontein and drawn in towards the main army, with orders to bivouac on Pretoria green, west of the town. French, whom the change of orders did not reach, pursued his wide turning movement.

At ten o'clock it was reported that Colonel Henry, with the corps of mounted infantry in advance of the main column, was actually in the suburbs of Pretoria without opposition. The force continued to converge, and Ian Hamilton had almost joined Lord Roberts's force when the booming of guns warned us that our anticipations were too sanguine. The army had just crossed a difficult spruit, and Colonel Henry with the mounted infantry had obtained a lodgement on the heights beyond. But here they were sharply checked. The Boers, apparently in some force, were holding a wooded ridge and several high hills along the general line of the southern Pretoria forts.

Determined to hold what he had obtained, Lord Roberts thrust his artillery well forward and ordered Ian Hamilton to support Colonel Henry immediately with all mounted troops. This was speedily done. The horsemen galloped forward and, scrambling up the steep hillsides reinforced the thin firing line along the ridge. The artillery of the Seventh Division came into action in front of the British centre. The Boers replied with a brisk rifle fire, which reached all three batteries, and drew from them a very vigorous cannonade.

Meanwhile the infantry deployment was proceeding. The 14th Brigade extended for attack. Half an hour later Pole-Carew's batteries prolonged the line of guns to the right, and about half-past two the corps and heavy artillery opened in further prolongation. By three o'clock fifty guns were in action in front of the main army, and both the Seventh and Eleventh Divisions had assumed preparatory formations. The balloon ascended and remained hanging in the air for an hour—a storm signal.

During this time Hamilton was pushing swiftly forward, and Smith-Dorrien's 19th Infantry Brigade occupied the line of heights, and thus set free the mounted troops for a turning movement. The 21st Brigade supported. The heights were so steep in front of Hamilton that his artillery could not come into action, and only one gun and one 'pom-pom' could, by great exertion, be dragged and manhandled into position. The fire of these pieces, however, caught the Boers holding the wooded ridge in enfilade, and was by no means ineffective.

So soon as Hamilton had collected the mounted troops he sent them to reinforce Broadwood, whom he directed to move round the enemy's right flank. The ground favoured the movement, and by half-past four the cavalry were seen debouching into the plain beyond the Boer position, enveloping their flank and compromising their retreat.

Colonel de Lisle's corps of mounted infantry, composed mainly of Australians, made a much shorter circuit, and reaching the level ground before the cavalry espied a Boer Maxim retreating towards the town. To this they immediately gave chase, and the strong Waler horses were urged to their utmost speed. The appearance of this clattering swarm of horsemen must have been formidable to those below. But we who watched from the heights saw what looked like a charge of infuriated mice, streaming across the brown veldt; so great are the distances in modern war.

Towards four o'clock the cannonade all along the front had died away, and only the heavy artillery on the right of Pole-Carew's division continued to fire, shelling the forts, whose profile showed plainly on the skyline and even hurling their projectiles right over the hills into Pretoria itself. So heavy had the artillery been that the Boers did not endure, and alarmed as well by the flank movement they retreated in haste through the town; so that before dusk their whole position was occupied by the infantry without much loss. Night, which falls at this season as early as half-past five, then shut down on the scene and the action—in which practically the whole Army Corps had been engaged—ended.

The fact that the forts had not replied to the British batteries, showed that their guns had been removed and that the Boers had no serious intention of defending their capital. The field-marshal's orders for the morrow were, therefore, that the army should advance at daybreak on Pretoria, which it was believed would then be formally surrendered. Meanwhile, however, Colonel de Lisle, with the infuriated mice—in other words, the Australians—was pressing hotly on, and at about six o'clock, having captured the flying Maxim, he seized a position within rifle shot of the town. From here he could see the Boers galloping in disorder through the streets, and encouraged by the confusion that apparently prevailed, he sent an officer under flag of truce to demand the surrender. This the panic-stricken civil authorities, with the consent of Commandant Botha, obeyed, and though no British troops entered the town until the next day, Pretoria actually fell before midnight on 4 June.

As soon as the light allowed the army moved forward. The Guards were directed on the railway station. Ian Hamilton's force swept round the western side. Wishing to enter among the first of the victorious soldiers the town I had crept away from as a fugitive six months before, I hurried forward and, with the Duke of Marlborough, soon overtook General Pole-Carew who, with his staff, was advancing towards the railway station. We passed through a narrow cleft in the southern wall of mountains, and Pretoria lay before us: a picturesque little town with red or blue roofs peeping out among masses of trees, and here and there an occasional spire or factory chimney. Scarcely 200 yards away stood the railway station.

Arrived at this point General Pole-Carew was compelled to wait to let his infantry catch him up; and while we were delayed a locomotive whistle sounded loudly and, to our astonishment—for had not the town surrendered?—a train drawn by two engines steamed out of the station on the Delagoa Bay line. For a moment we stared at this insolent breach of the customs of war, and a dozen staff officers, aides-de-camp, and orderlies (no mounted troops being at hand) started off at a furious gallop in the hopes of compelling the train to stop, or at least of shooting the engine-driver, and so sending it to its destruction. But wire fences and the gardens of the houses impeded the pursuers, and in spite of all their efforts the train escaped, carrying with it ten trucks of horses, which might have been very useful, and one truck-load of Hollanders. Three engines with steam up and several trains, however, remained in the station, and the leading company of Grenadiers doubling forward captured them and their occupants. These Boers attempted to resist the troops with pistols but surrendered after two volleys had been fired, no one fortunately being hurt in the scrimmage.

After a further delay the Guards, fixing bayonets, began to enter the town, marching through the main street, which was crowded with people, towards the central square, and posting sentries and pickets as they went. We were naturally very anxious to know what had befallen our comrades held prisoner all these long months. Rumour said they had been removed during the night to Waterfall Boven, two hundred miles down the Delagoa Bay line. But nothing definite was known.

The Duke of Marlborough, however, found a mounted Dutchman who said he knew where all the officers were confined, and who undertook to guide us, and without waiting for the troops who were advancing with all due precautions, we set off at a gallop.

The distance was scarcely three-quarters of a mile, and in a few minutes, turning a corner and crossing a little brook, we saw before us a long tin building surrounded by a dense wire entanglement. Seeing this, and knowing its meaning too well, I raised my hat and cheered. The cry was instantly answered from within. What followed resembled the end of an Adelphi melodrama. The Duke of Marlborough called on the commandant to surrender forthwith. The prisoners rushed out of the house into the yard, some in uniform, some in flannels, hatless or coatless, but all violently excited.

The sentries threw down their rifles. The gates were flung open, and while the rest of the guards—they numbered fifty-two in all—stood uncertain what to do, the long penned-up officers surrounded them and seized their weapons. Someone—Grimshaw of the Irish Fusiliers—produced a Union Jack (made during imprisonment out of a Vierkleur). The Transvaal emblem was torn down, and amid wild cheers, the first British flag was hoisted over Pretoria. Time 8.47, 5 June.

The commandant then made formal surrender to the Duke of Marlborough of a hundred and twenty officers and thirty-nine soldiers whom he had in his custody as prisoners of war, and surrendered, besides himself, four corporals and forty-eight Dutchmen. These latter were at once confined within the wire cage and guarded by their late prisoners, but since they had treated the captives well they have now been permitted to take the oath of neutrality and return to their homes. The anxieties which the prisoners had suffered during the last few hours of their confinement were terrible, nor did I wonder when I heard the account why their faces were so white and their manner so excited. But the reader shall learn the tale from one of their number, nor will I anticipate.

At two o'clock Lord Roberts, the staff and the foreign attaches entered the town and proceeded to the central square, wherein the Town Hall, the Parliament House and other public buildings are situated. The British flag was hoisted over the Parliament House amid some cheers. The victorious army then began to parade past it, Pole-Carew's division, with the Guards leading, coming from the south, and Ian Hamilton's force from the west. For three hours the broad river of steel and khaki flowed unceasingly, and the town-folk gazed in awe and wonder at these majestic soldiers, whose discipline neither perils nor hardships had disturbed, whose relentless march no obstacles could prevent.

With such pomp and the rolling of drums the new order of things was ushered in. The former Government had ended without dignity. One thought to find the President[1]—stolid old Dutchman—seated on his stoep reading his Bible and smoking a sullen pipe. But he chose a different course. On the Friday preceding the British occupation he left the capital and withdrew to Lydenburg, taking with him a million pounds in gold, and leaving behind him a crowd of officials clamouring for pay, and far from satisfied with the worthless cheques they had received, and Mrs Kruger, concerning whose health the British people need not further concern themselves.

It were premature and foolish to imagine that because the Republics have vanished the war is at, or even near, its end. Indeed, with our communications cut behind us we are unpleasantly reminded of its

[1] (Stephen John) Paul Kruger (1825–1904). President of the Transvaal Republic.

continuance. But it has certainly entered on a different phase. British soil is freed from the invader. Both hostile capitals are in our hands. We hold the greater part of his railroads and telegraphs, and have secured his arsenals, his factories, most of his stores, and the gold mines whence he drew his strength. There still remain fighting fiercely, and still a dangerous foe, the wild Boers of the north, the patriots and the hired scum of Europe, and with these two we must presently deal according to their deserts, always remembering that unless we make it easy for them to give in the war will continue indefinitely.

I cannot end this letter without recalling for one moment the grave risks Lord Roberts bravely faced in order to strike the decisive blow and seize Pretoria. When he decided to advance from Vereeniging without waiting for more supplies, and so profit by the enemy's disorder, he played for a great stake. He won, and it is very easy now to forget the adverse chances. But the facts stand out in glaring outline: that if the Boers had defended Pretoria with their forts and guns they could have checked us for several weeks; and if, while we were trying to push our investment, the line had been cut behind us, as it has since been cut, nothing would have remained but starvation or an immediate retreat on Johannesburg, perhaps on the Vaal. Even now our position is not thoroughly secure, and the difficulties of subjugating a vast country, though sparsely populated, are such that the troops in South Africa are scarcely sufficient. But the question of supplies is for the present solved. The stores of Johannesburg, and still more of Pretoria, will feed the army for something over a fortnight, and in the meanwhile we can reopen our communications, and perhaps do much more. But what a lucky nation we are to have found, at a time of sore need and trouble, a general great enough to take all risks and overcome all dangers.

17 July, 1900

21

PRETORIA, 14 June

The feeble resistance which the Boers offered to our advance from Bloemfontein favoured the hope that with the fall of Pretoria they would sue for peace, and after the almost bloodless capture of the town there was a very general tendency to regard the war as practically over. The troops who had been marching for so many days with Pretoria as their goal not unnaturally hoped that when that goal was achieved a period of rest and refreshment would be given them. But the imperious necessities of war demanded fresh efforts.

The successes gained in the Free State by the redoubtable Christian de Wet and the cutting of the communications near Rhenoster awoke everyone to the fact that further exertions were required. Though the Boers under Botha had made but a poor resistance in front of their capital, they were encouraged by the news from the Free State to adopt a more defiant attitude and to make what we hope has been a final effort. As to that I will not be sanguine, but it is certain that whereas on the 7th and 8th of June the Boer leaders in the Transvaal were contemplating surrender, on the 9th and 10th they were making all kinds of bold schemes to harass and even entrap the British army.

On the 7th the news ran through the camp that Mrs Botha had come through the lines with some mission on her husband's behalf, and General Schoeman had himself made very decided overtures. On the 8th, therefore, an armistice was observed by both sides, and a conference on Zwartskop, where Lord Roberts was to meet the Republican generals, was arranged for the 9th; but when the 9th came circumstances had changed. The field-marshal had actually his foot in the stirrup ready to ride to the meeting-place, when a messenger arrived from Botha declining, unless Lord Roberts had some new proposal to make, to enter into any negotiations. The consequence of this was an immediate resumption of active operations.

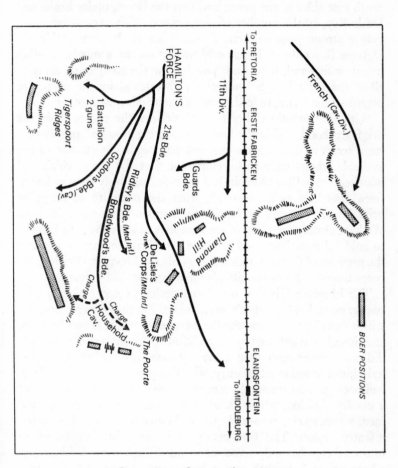

Operations of 11–13 June, 1900

The military situation was, briefly, that Lord Roberts's army was spread around and in Pretoria in various convenient camping grounds, with the greater part of its force displayed on the east and north-east sides of the town; and that the Boers, under Botha and De la Rey, to the number of about 7,000, with twenty-five guns, held a strong position some fifteen miles to the east astride the Delagoa Bay railway. It was evident that on any grounds, whether moral or material, it was not possible for the conquering army to allow the capital to be perpetually threatened by the enemy in organised force and, indeed, to be in a state of semi-siege.

With the intention, therefore, of driving the enemy from the neighbourhood, and in the hope of capturing guns and prisoners, a large series of combined operations was begun. Practically all the available troops were to be employed. But the army which had marched from Bloemfontein had dwindled seriously from sickness, from casualties and, above all, from the necessity of dropping brigades and battalions behind it to maintain the communications. We have already seen how it was necessary to leave the 14th Brigade to hold Johannesburg, and now the 18th Brigade became perforce the garrison of Pretoria, thus leaving only the Eleventh Division, the corps troops and Ian Hamilton's force free for field operations.

The Eleventh Division numbered perhaps 6,000 bayonets with twenty guns. Ian Hamilton's force had lost Smith-Dorrien's Brigade, which was disposed along the line between Kroonstad and Pretoria, and though strengthened by the addition of Gordon's cavalry brigade did not number more than 3,000 bayonets, 1,000 sabres and 2,000 light horse or mounted infantry, with thirty guns. But the shrinkage had been greatest among the mounted troops. French's command of a cavalry division, which should have been some 6,000 mounted men, was scarcely, even with part of Hutton's brigade of mounted infantry, 2,000. The two cavalry brigades with Ian Hamilton mustered together only 1,100 men, and Ridley's mounted infantry, whose nominal strength was at least 4,000, was scarcely half that number in actuality. Brigades, therefore, were scarcely as strong as regiments, regiments only a little stronger than squadrons, and the pitiful—absurd if it had not been so serious—spectacle of troops of eight and ten men were everywhere to be seen. It must, therefore, be remembered that though the imposing names of divisions and brigades might seem to indicate a great and powerful force the army at Lord Roberts's disposal was really a very small one.

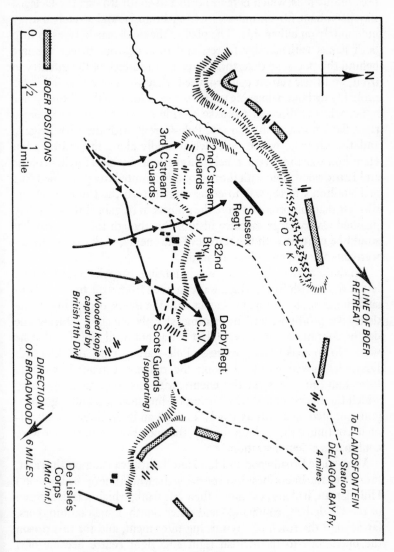

The Action at Diamond Hill, 11–12 June, 1900

The enemy's position ran along a high line of steep and often precipitous hills, which extend north and south athwart the Delagoa Bay line about fifteen miles east from Pretoria, and stretched away indefinitely on either side. The plan of the field-marshal was to turn both flanks with cavalry forces, and to endeavour to cut the line behind the Boers, so that, threatened by the attack of the infantry in front, and their retreat compromised, they would have to fall back, probably without being able to save some, at least, of their heavy guns.

French was directed to make a wide sweep round the enemy's right flank north of the railway, Pole-Carew, with the 18th Brigade and the Guards, was to advance frontally along the railway; Ian Hamilton was to move parallel to him about six miles further south; and Broadwood, who with the rest of the mounted troops formed part of Hamilton's force, was to endeavour to turn the enemy's left. It was felt that important as were the objects to be gained they scarcely justified a very large sacrifice of life. But though the field-marshal would be content with the retreat of the enemy, both cavalry forces were intended to press hard inward.

On the 11th the whole army was in motion. French on the extreme left of the British front, which was extended from flank to flank about sixteen miles, soon came in contact with the Boers, occupying strong defensive positions, and he became sharply engaged. During the day he continued to persevere, but it was not until nightfall that he was able to make any progress. Pole-Carew, with the Eleventh Division, moved eastward along the railway, extended in battle formation, and engaged the enemy with his long-range guns, to which the Boers replied with corresponding pieces, including a 6 in. gun mounted on a railway truck. Though an intermittent bombardment continued throughout the day, the operations in the centre were confined to a demonstration.

Meanwhile Broadwood and Ian Hamilton, advancing on the right, found that the Boers, besides occupying the whole line of the Diamond Hill plateau, had also extended their left flank, which was composed of the Heidelberg commando and other South Transvaal burghers, far beyond the reach of any turning movement, and for this reason the operations to the British right and right centre became of a piercing rather than of an enveloping nature. Hamilton endeavoured to hold off the enemy's unduly extended left by detaching a battalion, two field guns and Gordon's cavalry with its horse battery in the direction of Tigerspoort ridges. Ridley's brigade of mounted infantry curved inwards towards the railway, and while these two forces struck out, like the arms of a swimmer, Broadwood's brigade was extended to push through the gap thus made.

A dropping musketry and artillery fire began shortly after eight o'clock along the front of the force engaged in containing the Boers near Tigerspoort, and half an hour later Ridley's brigade was engaged along the southern slopes of Diamond Hill. Meanwhile Broadwood was advancing steadily to the eastward, and crossing a difficult spruit debouched into a wide, smooth grass plain, surrounded by hills of varying height, at the eastern end of which was a narrow gap. Through this the line of march to the railway lay. He became immediately engaged with the Boers round the whole three-quarters of a circle, and a scattered action, presenting to a distant observer no picturesque features, and yet abounding in striking incidents, began. The Boers brought seven guns, so far as we could observe, against him, and since the fire of these pieces was of a converging nature, the cavalry was soon exposed to a heavy bombardment.

In spite of this Broadwood continued to push on. The country was well suited for cavalry action, and the gap, or 'poort', as it is called in this country, plainly visible along the hills to the eastward, encouraged him to try to break through. Accordingly, at about eleven o'clock, he brought two horse guns under Lieutenant Conolly into a very forward position with the design of clearing his road by their fire. The Boers, however, fought with a stubbornness and dash which had long been absent from their tactics. They were in this part of the field largely composed of Germans and other foreigners, of colonial rebels, and of various types of irreconcilables.

No sooner had these two guns come into action than a very ugly attack was made on them. The ridge from which they were firing was one of those gentle swells of ground which, curving everywhere, nowhere allows a very extended view; and the Boers, about two hundred strong, dashed forward with the greatest boldness in the hope of bringing a close musketry fire to bear on the gunners and of capturing their pieces. So sudden was the attack that their heads were seen appearing over the grass scarcely 300 yards away. In these circumstances the guns fired case shot, but though they prevented the Boers from coming nearer, it was evident that the position was still critical. Broadwood was compelled, therefore, to ask the 18th Lancers to charge.

The continual shrapnel fire of the last few hours had in spite of their disturbed formation caused a good deal of loss among the horses of the brigade. The Earl of Airlie, who was riding with the brigadier, had had his horse shot under him, and had gone away to find another. He returned to place himself at the head of his regiment just as it was moving forward to the attack, and perhaps unacquainted with the latest development of the action he gave a direction to the charge, which was slightly more mortherly than that which Broadwood had intended; so that in advancing the regiment gradually came under the fire of the enemy holding the lower slopes of Diamond Hill, instead of falling on those who were directly threatening the guns. But it was a fine, gallant manoeuvre, executed with a spring and an elasticity wonderful and admirable in any troops, still more in troops who have been engaged for eight months in continual fighting with an elusive enemy, and who must have regarded any action, subsequent to the capture of Pretoria, rather in the nature of an anticlimax.

Its effect was instantaneous. Though the regiment scarcely numbered one hundred and fifty men, the Boers fled before them, those who were threatening the guns towards the south and those immediately in the line of the charge eastward and northwards, towards Diamond Hill. Had the horses been fresh and strong a very severe punishment would have been administered to the enemy, but with weary and jaded animals—many of them miserable Argentines, and all worn out with hard work and scanty food—they were unable to overtake the mass of fugitives who continued to fly before them. A few, however, stood boldly, and one man remained firing his rifle until the charge was close on him, when he shot Lieutenant Wright dead at only a few yards distance, and then holding up his hands claimed quarter. This was, however, most properly refused. Altogether ten Boers perished by the lance, and the moral effect on those who escaped must certainly have been considerable. But now in pursuit the regiment gradually came nearer to the enemy's main position and drew a heavy fire on their left flank.

Seeing this, and having obtained the object with which he had charged—the immediate relief of the guns—Lord Airlie gave the order 'files about', and withdrew his regiment before it became too seriously involved. As he issued this command he was struck by a heavy bullet through the body and died almost immediately. So fell, while directing his regiment in successful action, an officer of high and noble qualities, trusted by his superiors, beloved by his friends, and honoured by the men he led. The scanty squadrons returned in excellent order to the positions they had won, having lost in the charge and mostly in the retirement two officers, seventeen men, including a private of the 10th Hussars, who managed to join in, and about thirty horses.

Meanwhile the pressure on Broadwood's right had become very severe. A large force of Boers who were already engaging the 17th Lancers and the rest of Gordon's brigade, but who were apparently doubtful of attacking, now swooped down and occupied a kraal and some grassy ridges whence they could bring a heavy enfilading fire to bear. Broadwood, who throughout these emergencies preserved his usual impassive composure, and whose second horse had been shot under him, ordered the Household Cavalry to 'clear them out.'

The troopers began immediately to dismount with their carbines, and the general had to send a second message to them saying that it was no good firing now, and that they must charge with the sword. Whereupon, delighted at this unlooked-for, unhoped-for opporunity, the Life Guardsmen scrambled back into their saddles, thrust their hated carbines into the buckets and, drawing their long swords, galloped straight at the enemy. The Boers, who in this part of the field considerably outnumbered the cavalry, might very easily have inflicted severe loss on them. But so formidable was the aspect of these tall horsemen cheering and flogging their gaunt horses with the flat of their swords, that they did not abide and, running to their mounts, fled in cowardly haste so that, though eighteen horses were shot, the Household Cavalry sustained no loss in men.

These two charges and the earnest fashion in which they were delivered completely restored the situation, but though Broadwood maintained all the ground he had won he did not feel himself strong enough in the face of the severe opposition evidently to be encountered, to force his way through the poort.

At about noon the field-marshal, who was with the Eleventh Division, observing an apparent movement of the enemy in his front, concluded that they were about to retreat, and not wishing to sacrifice precious lives if the strategic object were obtained without them, sent Ian Hamilton a message not, unless the resistance of the enemy was severe, to weary his men and horses by going too far. Hamilton, however, had seen how closely Broadwood was engaged, and fearing that if he stood idle the enemy would concentrate their whole strength on his cavalry commander, he felt bound to make an attack on the enemy on the lower slopes of Diamond Hill, and so hold out a hand to Broadwood.

He therefore directed Bruce-Hamilton to advance with the 21st Brigade. This officer, bold both as a man and as a general, immediately set his battalions in motion. The enemy occupied a long scrub-covered rocky ridge below the main line of hills, and were in considerable force. Both batteries of artillery and the two 5 in. guns came into action about two o'clock. The Sussex Regiment moving forward established themselves on the northern end of the ridge, which was well prepared by shelling, and while the City Imperial Volunteers and some parts of the mounted infantry, including the Corps of Gillies, held them in front, gradually pressed them out of it by rolling up their right.

There is no doubt that our infantry have profited by the lessons of this war. The widely-extended lines of skirmishers moving forward, almost invisible against the brown grass of the plain, and taking advantage of every scrap of cover, presented no target to the Boer fire. And once they had gained the right of the ridge it was very difficult for the enemy to remain.

Accordingly at 3.30 the Boers in twenties and thirties began to abandon their position. Before they could reach the main hill, however, they had to cross a patch of open ground, and in so doing they were exposed to a heavy rifle fire at 1,200 yards from the troops who were holding the front.

From where I lay, on the left of the Gillies' firing line, I could see the bullets knocking up the dust all round the retreating horsemen, while figures clinging to saddles or supported by their comrades and riderless horses showed that some at least of the bullets had struck better things than earth. So soon as they reached fresh cover, the Dutchmen immediately reopened fire, and two of the Gillies were wounded about this time.

The City Imperial Volunteers then occupied the whole of the wooded ridge. One poor little boy, scarcely fourteen years old, was found shot through the head but still living, and his father, a very respectable-looking man who, in spite of his orders from the field-cornet, had refused to leave his son, was captured; but with those exceptions the Boers had removed their wounded and made good their retreat to the main position. It being now nearly dark the action was broken off and, having strongly picketed the ground they had won, the infantry returned to their waggons for the night.

It was now imperative to carry the matter through, and in view of the unexpected obstinacy of the enemy, the field-marshal directed Pole-Carew to support Hamilton in his attack the next day with the Brigade of Guards.

Early the next morning Hamilton's infantry moved forward and re-occupied the whole of the ground picketed the previous day. On the right De Lisle's corps of mounted infantry prepared to attack; the cavalry maintained their wedge-like position and exchanged shots all along their front with the Boers; but no serious operations were begun during the morning, it being thought better to await the arrival or, at least, the approach of the brigade which had been promised.

During this interval the Boers shelled our batteries heavily with their long-range guns, and General Ian Hamilton, who was sitting on the ground with his staff near the 82nd Field Battery, was struck by a shrapnel bullet on the left shoulder. Fortunately the missile did not penetrate, but only caused a severe bruise with numbness and pain, which did not, however, make it necessary for him to leave the field.

At one o'clock the leading battalion of the Guards was seen to be about four miles off, and Bruce-Hamilton's brigade was therefore directed to attack. The Derbyshire Regiment, which had been briskly engaged during the morning, advanced up a flat tongue of land on the right. The City Imperial Volunteers moved forward in the centre, and the Sussex on the British left. Though this advance was exposed to a disagreeable enfilade fire from the Boer 'pom-pom', the dispersed formations minimised the losses, and lodgements were effected all along the rim of the plateau. But once the troops had arrived here the fight assumed a very different complexion.

The top of the Diamond Hill plateau was swept by fire from a long rocky kopje about 1,800 yards distant from the edge, and was, moreover, partially enfiladed from the enemy's position on the right. The musketry immediately became loud and the fighting severe. The City Imperial Volunteers in the centre began to suffer loss, and had not the surface of the ground been strewn with stones, which afforded good cover, many would have been killed or wounded, though it was not humanly possible to know from below what the ground on the top of the hill was like—we were now being drawn into a regular rat-trap.

It was quite evident that to press the attack to an assault at this point would involve very heavy loss of life and, as the reader will see by looking at the rough plan I have made [See page 319], the troops would have become more and more exposed to enfilade and cross-fire in proportion as they advanced.

After what I had seen in Natal the idea of bringing guns up on to the plateau to support the infantry attack when at so close a range from the enemy's position seemed a very unpleasant one. But General Bruce-Hamilton did not hesitate, and at half-past three the 82nd Field Battery, having been dragged to the summit, came into action against the Boers on the rocky ridge at a distance of only 1,700 yards.

This thrusting forward of the guns undoubtedly settled the action. The result of their fire was immediately apparent. The bullets which had hitherto been whistling through the air at a rate of perhaps fifteen to twenty to the minute, and which had compelled us all to lie close behind the protecting stones, now greatly diminished, and it was possible to walk about with comparative immunity. But the battery which had reduced the fire by keeping the enemy's heads down, drew most of what was left on themselves. Ten horses were shot in the moment of unlimbering, and during the two hours they remained in action, in spite of the protection afforded by the guns and waggons, a quarter of the gunners were hit. Nevertheless, the remainder continued to service their pieces with machine-like precision, and displayed a composure and devotion which won them the unstinted admiration of all who saw the action.

About four o'clock General Ian Hamilton came himself to the top of the plateau, and orders were then given for the Coldstream Guards to prolong the line to the left and for the Scots Guards to come into action in support of the right. Two more batteries were also brought forward, and the British musketry and artillery being now in great volume, the Boer fire was brought under control. Ian Hamilton did not choose to make the great sacrifice which would accompany an assault, however, nor did his brigadier suggest that one should be delivered, and the combatants therefore remained facing each other at the distance of about a mile, both sides firing heavily with musketry and artillery, until the sun sank and darkness set in.

General Pole-Carew, who with the 18th Brigade was still responsible for containing the Boer centre across the railway, now rode over to Hamilton's force, and plans were made for the next day. It must have been a strange experience for these two young commanders, who, fifteen years ago had served together as aides-de-camp on Lord Roberts's staff, to find themselves now under the same chief designing a great action as lieutenant-generals. It was decided that Hamilton's force should move further to the right and attack on the front, which on the 12th had been occupied by De Lisle's Corps of Mounted Infantry, that the Brigade of Guards should take over the ground which the 21st Brigade had won and were picketing, and that the 18th Brigade, which was now to be brought up, should prolong the line to the left. But these expectations of a general action on the morrow were fortunately disappointed. Worsted in the fire fight, with three parts of their position already captured, and with the lodgement effected by Colonel De Lisle's corps on the left threatening their line of retreat, the Boers shrank from renewing the conflict.

During the night they retreated in good order from the whole length of the position which they occupied, and marched eastward along the railway in four long columns. When morning broke and the silence proclaimed the British the victors, Hamilton in order to carry out his original orders marched northward and struck the railway at Elandsfontein station, where he halted. The mounted infantry and cavalry were hurried on in pursuit, but so exhausted were their horses that with one tremendous exception they did not overtake the enemy.

A hundred and fifty Westralians, however, belonging to Colonel De Lisle's corps, pushing their way cautiously forward, came during the afternoon of the 13th to the top of a commanding kopje. Below them at a distance of scarcely 1,000 yards lay the Boer army. Upwards of 4,000 men with guns, hundreds of waggons, and herds of oxen, were littered about the plain, covering several acres of ground, and engaged in crossing—mark the place—Bronkhorst Spruit. There, as they sat on the site of the old battlefield near the grave of the gallant 94th, the Boers overtaken by one of Time's revenges they were surprised, as twenty years before they had surprised the British. If the Westralians and their officers had kept their heads and had sent back for Colonel De Lisle with his 500 men and two 'pom-poms', there is no saying what might have happened. As it was, intoxicated by their target, they lay down forthwith on the ground and fired methodically every cartridge of one hundred and fifty they each carried into the brown of the Boer force. A scene of wild confusion followed; horsemen galloped madly in all directions, some fled in panic, others endeavoured to make some reply to the fire; horses and oxen were shot, waggons were inspanned with furious haste, guns galloped away over the plain with horses dropping down in the teams. At length, however, the ammunition failed. And when they had expended upwards of 2,000 rounds the Westralians, though far from satisfied, returned home rejoicing. What the actual losses of the Boers were is not yet known, but it is certain that they were severe, both in men and horses, and the panic which followed must, by scattering them, tend to diminish still further their number.

Such were the operations of the 11th, 12th and 13th of June, by which, at a cost of about 200 officers and men, the country round Pretoria for forty miles was cleared of the Boers, and a heavy blow dealt to the only powerful force that still keeps the field in Transvaal. We were also cheered by the news of Lord Methuen's victory over Christian de Wet, and the consequent re-opening of the line of communication, and of Sir Redvers Buller's successful passage of Lang's Nek, both of which events must make the prospects of peace nearer and clearer.

20 July, 1900

22

CAPETOWN, 28 June

After the action of Diamond Hill the whole army returned to Pretoria, leaving only a mounted infantry corps to hold the positions they had won to the eastward. French and Pole-Carew, whose troops had marched far and fought often, were given a much-needed rest. Ian Hamilton, whose force had marched further and fought more than either—perhaps more than both—was soon sent off on his travels again. The military exigencies forbade all relaxation, and only three days breathing space was given to the lean infantry and the exhausted horses. By the unbroken success of his strategy Lord Roberts had laid the Boer Republics low. We had taken possession of the Rand, the bowels from which the hostile Government drew nourishment in gold and munitions of war. We had seized the heart at Bloemfontein, the brain at Pretoria. The greater part of the railways, the veins and nerves, that is to say, was in our hands. Yet, though mortally injured, the trunk still quivered convulsively, particularly the left leg which, being heavily booted, had already struck us several painful and unexpected blows.

To make an end two operations were necessary: first to secure the dangerous limb, and secondly, to place a strangling grip on the windpipe somewhere near Komati Poort. The second will perhaps be the business of Sir Redvers Buller and the glorious army of Natal. The first set Hamilton's brigades in motion as part of an intricate and comprehensive scheme, which arranged for the permanent garrisoning of Frankfort, Heilbron, Lindley and Senekal, and directed a simultaneous movement against Christian de Wet by four strong flying columns.

I had determined to return to England; but it was with mixed feelings that I watched the departure of the gallant column in whose good company I had marched so many miles and seen successful fights. Their road led them past Lord Roberts's headquarters, and the old field-marshal came out himself to see them off. First the two cavalry brigades marched past. They were brigades no longer; the Household Cavalry Regiment was scarcely fifty strong; in all there were not a thousand sabres. Then Ridley's fourteen hundred mounted infantry, the remnants of what on paper was a brigade of nearly five thousand; thirty guns dragged by skinny horses; the two trusty 5 in. 'cow guns' behind their teams of toiling oxen; Bruce-Hamilton's infantry brigade, with the City Imperial Volunteers, striding along—weary of war, but cheered by the hopes of peace and quite determined to see the matter out; lastly, miles of transport; all stream by, grow faint in the choking red dust and vanished through the gap in the southern line of hills. May they all come safely home.

Two days later I left Pretoria for Capetown, travelling with the Duke of Westminster, who was going south in charge of Lord Roberts's mails, and who therefore enjoyed many special advantages in the way of carriages, engines and escorts, of which I was very glad, at his invitation, to avail myself. The first day's journey was without incident, nor was it until the next morning that we entered on the dangerous section of the line. It was still dark when we crossed the Vaal, but day had broken before the train passed Vrederfort.

South of the station the advanced guard of a great convoy hove in sight, and we presently ran along the whole column. It was preceded and indeed surrounded by a perfect network of Yeomanry and mounted infantry, who dotted the rolling plains almost to their horizons.

Within this circle came infantry—Highlanders and Linesmen, drafts probably for the regiments at the front—all extended to nearly fifty yards interval between each man and his neighbour. Nearer to the railway were several companies in close order, a couple of Maxims and some artillery.

Through the midst of the troops flowed the line of waggons, perhaps three or four hundred in all, each with its long span of mules or oxen and its little group of Kaffirs and escorting soldiers. It may have carried eight days' supplies for two divisions. Lord Roberts was not relying entirely on the railway.

We rattled on. Convoy and escort disappeared behind us, and soon it was evident that the debatable ground was reached. Kopjes Station takes its name from the rocky hillocks that rise all round it, and make a regular upward step from the Rhenoster River. Its garrison, since it was retaken by Lord Methuen, consists of half a battalion of the Shropshire Regiment, two field guns (one damaged, but can fire another 100 rounds) and a formidable 5 in. gun, all under Colonel Spens. Both infantry and guns are strongly sangared among the rocks and stones of the kopjes, and they are provided with seven days' supplies of food at the very least.

The train descended the step by a watercourse between the kopjes, and slowed down to cross the Rhenoster Bridge. The line here had been destroyed with a thoroughness which excited a mournful admiration. Not only had the bridge over the deep chasm through which the river flows been blown up, but the ordinary permanent way had been scientifically wrecked for more than three miles. A slab of gun cotton had been exploded under every alternate joining place of rails, making the strong iron bars curl into the air like paper before it catches light, and excavating a deep hole in the formation beneath.

The new bridge—the second new bridge, that is to say, for the first had been burned by Christian de Wet—a good piece of timber trestle work, was approached by a long deviation, over which the train moved with much deliberation. Gangs of coolies under the direction of men of the Railway Pioneer Regiment—a corps of brave and skilled Volunteers—were still at work on the foundations of the temporary piers. Their cartridge belts and rifles and the old line with its curling rails leading to the tangled ruins of the old bridge filled the mind with the realisation of war. Other reminders were forthcoming.

Two miles from Rhenoster Bridge is Roodeval Station. When we had marched north a month before this had been quite a pretty little oasis in the great plain. There were trees, a few iron buildings, a well, a watertank, and the stationmaster's house—all standing up amid green grass. Now the eye surveyed a scene of woeful devastation.

For ten days two thousand mailbags, containing the longed-for letters of the army, thousands of warm coats, and all the reserve of heavy ammunition had been confided to the charge of the garrison of Roodeval—eight men strong. On the evening of the 6 June a hundred and fifty more arrived to share their fate. The storm broke with the daybreak, heralded by a Dutchman with a white flag.

'Have fourteen hundred men and four guns,' said the Boer summons. 'Give you ten minutes to surrender.'

But they would not surrender until more than a quarter had been shot and all hope of relief had gone. Then the Boers got to work on

331

their prey. What they needed they took. The rest, together with the building already sorely battered by the shells, they gave to the flames. The enormous lyddite shells for the 9.2 and 5 in. guns formed the foundation of the pyre.

An officer who listened ten miles away told me he thought that a great battle was being fought, so terrific and continuous were the explosions. Sheds, buildings, trees and water tank were blown to the wind. Nothing—absolutely nothing but one bent and battered piece of corrugated iron remained, hanging insecurely to the ruins of a railway truck.

The ground was strewn with splinters of the mighty bombs. On the siding a complete train of trucks stood in skeleton. All the woodwork was consumed, and only the iron frames remained—with iron stancheons bolting air, and rows of funny little nails sticking into nothing. Many of the monstrous projectiles, though curiously stained by the fire and battered by the explosions, were still live and lay in heaps.

For nearly a quarter of a mile the veldt was thickly carpeted with the ashes of the warm coats, a pile of half-charred scraps of paper marked the destruction of the two thousand mail bags. And Christian de Wet cannot be complimented on his chivalry thereon, for it seems a poor and spiteful thing to burn up soldiers' letters, nor can I see how this can benefit the cause of his campaign.

So much for Roodeval, but I do not desire to leave the letters yet. It is necessary to state soberly and solemnly that the administration of the military post office during the war in South Africa has not been good. Letters have usually been delayed; many have been sent to the wrong destinations; a considerable proportion has been lost.

Finally mails which, if dealt with week by week, would have imposed no strain on the transport, have been allowed to accumulate in vast heaps, such as this one at Roodeval. Once they attain these unmanageable dimensions no straining transport can find room for them, and the result is that they lie neglected at the caprice of the enemy.

It must be remembered that the private soldier, and the officer for that matter, regards the deprivations of his letters as little less than a personal insult. In times of war, when life hangs on an uncertain thread, the soldier longs for and clings to the letter from home, which fills his mind with the memory of other scenes and refreshes his love for the country in whose cause he fights.

332

The German army, in which these things are studied, was distinguished during the Franco-Prussian war for the excellence of its postal arrangements in the field. On the Indian frontier, in victory or defeat, letters and newspapers arrive with strict punctuality. But here in South Africa delay and confusion culminate in hopeless irretrievable loss which has caused, and is causing, intense annoyance and distress throughout the army, and perhaps some dissatisfaction at home.

After leaving Roodeval, it being now nearly seven o'clock, we made haste to breakfast, and were soon at a suitable meal of sardines, pickles, and whisky. Suddenly the train came to a standstill, and the servant came into the compartment with the news that the bridge in front of us was burning. Without much thought we jumped out on to the line to see what was the matter.

It was even as the man had said. A culvert about thirty feet broad, temporarily repaired with cribs of railway sleepers and massive longitudinal baulks, was blazing away merrily. My companion with the engine-driver very properly ran on towards the bridge to learn the extent of the damage. They were followed sheep-like by most of the passengers.

Without any precautions whatever, without discipline or order, and quite unarmed, nearly a hundred soldiers and twenty or thirty Kaffirs came scuttling along the track laughing and shouting at the fine joke of a burning bridge, and just as if they had never heard of the word 'war.'

Meanwhile, I could see two dark horsemen cantering away a quarter of a mile to the left and sixty or seventy more approaching along the railway to the north. The dongas on either side of the line afforded excellent cover to any number of riflemen who might happen to be near there. The crowd near the culvert provided them with the best of targets.

I was in the act of climbing back into the train to get my Mauser pistol, from which I have never been separated since that miserable morning at Frere, when a shell skimmed over the engine and exploded in the ditch by the line—some four or five yards away.

Its effect was electrical. Back in comical hurry, with surprise writ large on their faces, scampered the foolish sightseers, and jumped into their trucks. The engine-driver re-entered his cab, and without more ado, the engine whistling loudly, began to retire. The second shell fell wide.

Before the third could come we were out of range. Only the two Boers who had been cantering away to a safe distance dismounted and let fly until their magazines were empty. We replied with a vicious spluttering from pistols and carbines, the noise of which, though it did these gentlemen no more harm than the bullets, had the effect of making their advancing comrades pause and consider.

Now the hardened soldier and even the paceful correspondent may view with composure the spectacle of a burning bridge so long as it be in front of them. But a burning bridge between you and home is quite a different thing. I could not help thinking of armoured trains—and this train was not even armoured. It was therefore a distinct pleasure to see the remains of Roodeval Station once more. Here we learned that the telegraph signal had failed before we started, and that there was no longer any communication with the south. Inevitable incident of war—no doubt.

But—and this is the moral which justifies the tale—in such cases it might be as well to inform the senior officer in the train, so that he can make some sort of preparations for defence. Surely that is a mild criticism. Let me extend it and make it stronger. When we go to war our conceit costs us much in blood and honour. We are always absolutely sure that the enemy will not dare to attack us, and so certain that he will fly at our approach.

I have scarcely seen an action in this war which officers of a certain class have not begun with an incredulous sniff. Never have I shared in a defeat without hearing afterwards that the enemy had actually taken to their heels when we retreated.

It is all due to lack of imaginative power. Our troops are visible. The enemy is unseen. Therefore, it is argued, he cannot be very numerous. Our troops are strong. Therefore, he must be very frightened. Therefore, he will run away, has run away already. Therefore, there is nothing to fear—never was (for who's afraid?)—but nothing to guard against.

So we go on. While there is firing all is well. But let there be three days of peace. The Lancers stick their lances into the ground point foremost to preserve the sharpness. The whole camp wears a bored expression. The infantry officers carry out the precautions which the Drill Book prescribes with a smile of pitying contempt for the nerves of its writer. Everyone concludes that the war is over—forgets that there has ever been a war, and then suddenly—Bang! and another glorious page is added to British military history.

334

Thinking of this, and with plenty of time to spare, now that the Boers have cut the line, I strolled back to the spot where the Derby Militia had met their fate. There was the usual litter of biscuit tins and rubbish which mark a wartime camp. Here and there a few splinters of shell and empty twisted shrapnel cases caught the eye. Round a cluster of graves a colony of tiny brown African foxes—dachshunds with brushes—were playing in the sunlight.

The unfortunate regiment had arrived late in the afternoon and had bivouacked forthwith. Either on the rocky kopjes or near the scarped bed of the Rhenoster River they would have been safe, would at least have had a run for their money, for both were strong defensive positions. River and kopjes were scarcely a mile apart, and if the hour was late, why not stop at the first? The river bed offered water and security. The kopjes security only. They halted midway between the two.

Now here imagination, the torturer of cowards, the protector of brave men, should have intervened; should have peopled the dark rocks with crafty Dutchmen creeping stealthily to the attack; should have flashed on the mental screen the inspiring picture of a small force making a record defence among the deep dongas of a river; should have flashed in vivid colours the appalling spectacle of such a force crowded together in the open, and swiftly destroyed in spite of its gallantry.

'What awful rot. There isn't a Boer within fifty miles.'

'Still,' argues imagination, 'if I were a Boer just at this time I might very possibly attempt something against the communications; and if I did, and got on those kopjes in the dark, and in the morning found you at the bottom, I would smash you to pieces with rifles and artillery without losing a man myself.'

'Good Lord! my dear fellow, you have got the jumps. Come and let's have some dinner.'

Near Rhenoster Bridge we found a force of seventy Westralians and two field guns whose orders were to march to Honing Spruit, but who now had to wait for reinforcements. The mounted infantry detachments were taken out of the train and arranged in companies under such officers as were available. The ammunition was unloaded.

The Westralians threw out patrols in all directions. A message was sent to Colonel Spens on the kopje to explain the situation. The telegraph, moreover, began to click, telling the army two hundred

335

miles away that its communications with the south were cut and urgently requiring guns, men and reconstruction trains.

Presently the mounted patrols came galloping in with their reports: 'Four or five hundred Boers with several guns astride of the railway; frequent explosions along the line; heavy firing from the direction of Honing Spruit Station.' And at this news we backed our train under the protection of the fortified kopjes and the 5 in. gun and waited.

We waited all day long, while contradictory orders succeeded one another, and rumours ran amuck through the bridge-builders' camp. At about four o'clock in the afternoon definite news arrived. Headquarters had received the telegrams from Roodeval, had also received telegrams from Honing Spruit.

How, since the wire was cut? Quite simply, 'via Kroonstad, Bloemfontein, Norval's Point, De Aar, Kimberley, Mafeking, Potchefstroom and Pretoria: clear the line.'

Telegrams said that Honing Spruit was being sharply attacked by a large force of Boers, but that Kroonstad was marching north to help it. In reply to which headquarters ordered all troops at Rhenoster to halt pending reinforcements of the arrival of the general commanding the communications north of Kroonstad, Smith-Dorrien.

The night was bitterly cold, and we retreated thankfully to the shelter of our railway carriage. Provisions were getting rather scanty. Luckily, I had guarded against the chance of delay. The African winter, if it whets the appetite, chills the blood. We shivered under three blankets. The train was shunted several times during the night, and morning revealed us in a wide basin surrounded by the fortified kopjes. I peered about me. The ground gleamed with hoar frost. The air was biting. The sun had not yet risen, and his advancing glow shot a queer, unreal light on the scene, which might, as far as its natural features were concerned, have been laid in Antarctic regions.

The figures of the sentries among the rocks to the east moved black and active against the dull yellow sky. An early cooking fire crackled briskly in the foreground in pleasing contrast. The effects of cutting the railway were apparent. Three great trains had arrived during the night and stood blocked one behind another on the line, their locomotives blowing off immense white clouds of steam. The hindmost train was laden with huge baulks of timber and crowded with men. The reconstruction gangs had arrived.

336

But it was not till evening that they got to work. All the day passed in shunting the other trains out of the way—quite a puzzle on a single line with one siding too few—and in reconnaissance. In the evening General Smith-Dorrien arrived full of spirits and energy, but disgusted at the cutting of his line. It appeared that troops had been moved from the railway on the order of the chief of the staff, without timely notification to the officer responsible for its safety.

There should have been nearly six hundred mounted men at Rhenoster, in which case what would five hundred Boers be doing across the line near Roodeval. There should have been two field guns at Honing Spruit, in which case—but I shall come to Honing Spruit presently. Lord Kitchener had sent the mounted men to join Methuen, and had taken the two guns to reinforce Hamilton, had meant indeed to replace them with another two guns, the same we had seen at Roodeval, but in the interval Christian de Wet struck his blow. Fortunately no great harm was done.

It was arranged that as the Honing Spruit garrison had given a good account of themselves, and the country between that place and Roodeval was now more or less clear, Lord Roberts's mails should be sent through with a small mounted escort at daybreak next morning. (Observe the advantage of travelling with mails.)

Everything and everybody else would wait till the line was repaired, and for aught I know are waiting still. Nevertheless, no one could grudge one night with the reconstruction gangs.

Night had fallen before they began. I had known the officer in charge in Egypt. He was one of the subalterns who built the Desert Railway; had written a book about it besides—a plain record of sterling work told by one of the hardest workers. Now he was a major. I hope he may become a general. He gave us an excellent hot dinner in his little travelling saloon at the end of the train, and then we all proceeded to the bridge.

Two powerful gas flares and a huge fire made from the half-burned sleepers illuminated the scene. Round, dotted about in the velvet blackness, twinkled the picket fires. Above, the frosty sky was bright with stars. The remains of the bridge swarmed with men—swarthy Basutos directed by British engineers—and there arose a clamour of voices and hammering.

The speed at which they worked took hold of one. Already they had pulled away the charred cribs and built new ones of fresh sleepers. Now they were unbolting the rails to pull away the damaged

337

baulks. Such a crowd of weird figures struggling in the firelight to an accompaniment of crashes and creaks!

Presently on the railroad there arose a loud monotonous chant. My companion dragged me back to look. Walking along the line past the engine which waited under steam ready to fly at a moment's notice were some seventy or eighty men—Basutos—carrying an enormous log of wood. Perhaps it was forty feet long, and two feet six inches thickness, and may have weighed, Heaven knows what, but it was very heavy at any rate. The men moving it slowly forward on their shoulders looked as if they were the legs of a colossal black caterpillar; and as they moved a dusky fugleman at the rear sang solemnly:

'Awa chowàchy: ehooka ehowee'

or words to that effect; to which the others chorussed with the most extraordinary earnestness and conviction,

'Azziz
Awa chowàchy: ehooka ehowee:
Azziz'

and so on, remorselessly, until at length they reached the edge of the chasm which their log was to span. Then they set it down carefully— woe to unlucky fingers and feet—and went back for another.

I looked back to the workers under the flare lights. They had stripped the damaged rails from the track and had cleared the half-burnt baulks away. Though it was freezing hard all were wet with perspiration.

'How much longer?' I asked the officer.

'Only three hours, with any luck,' he answered; and then a little bitterly: 'This is the third time we've built this blasted bridge. I wonder if they'll take the trouble to guard it when it's finished?'

The escort—twenty Canadians and fifteen Westralians—waited in the morning. The officer commanding the latter lent me his horse. The Duke fastened his precious despatches to his saddle; we started at a trot in a formation which soon spread out more than a mile in every direction, and in two hours arrived without adventure at Honing Spruit Station. Here a train had been ordered from Kroonstad to meet the mails; but as it had not yet arrived we were compelled to wait, and passed the time, not unprofitably, in learning the story of the fight two days before.

338

General Smith-Dorrien, who after the capture of Pretoria had been entrusted with the charge of the railway between Kroonstad and Pretoria, was dissatisfied with the security of the section south of the Rhenoster River, and particularly with the garrison of Honing Spruit Station. The two guns which should have formed part of the force at this point had been removed by Lord Kitchener's order—because they properly belong to one of Ian Hamilton's batteries.

Smith-Dorrien, therefore, so soon as he was informed, ordered two other guns from Rhenoster to Honing Spruit and railed thither part of the Provisional Battalion formed from the British prisoners released when Pretoria fell. The guns, as I have described, were late, but the men, four hundred strong, under Colonel Bullock of Colenso repute, arrived in the nick of time. The train pulled up at the station, the soldiers got out and proceeded to take stock of their new abode.

While they were doing this someone observed Boers riding slowly along the grassy ridges on both flanks and other Boers tampering with the line a mile to the northward. The next event was the arrival of a flag of truce with a formal demand for surrender.

'No,' said Colonel Bullock with decision, and the poor released prisoners, long starved in Waterfall Cage, added, 'Never again.'

So the Boer envoy departed, and both sides settled down to their work: the Dutch to surround and bombard the station; the British to scratch up what shelters they could. It was a curious fight. The ground was of that undulating character which gives no marked advantage to either, but if anything it favoured the Boers.

Moreover, their enveloping position enabled them to bring a converging fire to bear on the water tank and three tin houses round which the defenders lay. But the greatest disparity was in respect of arms. The Boers had three modern guns and were all armed with Mauser rifles.

The Provisional Battalion were only armed with Martinis, no other rifles being available in Pretoria. In one-third of these obsolete weapons the carbine ammunition supplied jammed or failed to explode owing to weak strikers, and such as would fire revealed by their puff of smoke every man's position. Moreover, their range was lamentably short compared to the Mauser, and the Boers walking about carelessly beyond reach of their enemies struck them down in safety. The British had no guns, and could therefore make no reply to the enemy's artillery.

By good luck the officers, of whom there were nearly twenty, had armed themselves with Mauser carbines, and it was on their fire that the defence mainly relied, keeping their tell-tale black powder for a supreme moment at close quarters. The unequal fight lasted seven hours, and in spite of the widely-extended formation which Colonel Bullock adopted, the fire caused a considerable proportion of casualties.

In the absence of any medical officers or appliances, the wounded were dressed under fire by Mr Cheatle, a London consulting surgeon, who was assisted in his task by the Hon Somers Somerset, the despatch rider of *The Times* newspaper. This gentleman's carbolic tooth powder was the only antiseptic dressing available, and was therefore used in all cases, with what results I recommend the *Lancet* to inquire.

The train standing at the siding was much knocked about by the artillery. The tin houses were pierced from various directions. The enemy, being unused to firing at such short range—two thousand yards—burst most of their shrapnel too close to the target, so that the showers of bullets passed overhead and caused little loss. But to lie exposed hour after hour, armed with useless weapons and unable to reply, was a trying ordeal to men picked haphazard from various regiments and united by no honourable association.

With an exception all behaved with the greatest discipline and fortitude. One mixed company, however, being exposed to the cross shell fire, lost heart, and when two more shells burst among them, though these did little harm, they broke despite the entreaties of the young officer who commanded, and ran southward along the railway in an attempt to escape.

They succeeded desperately in driving away some Boers who tried to intercept them, and meeting the relieving force near Kroonstad, told a wild tale of disaster. Indeed, five men did not stop until they reached Kroonstad itself (twenty miles) where they were promptly arrested and, it is said, are likely to be shot for their conduct. The rest of the battalion held their ground stubbornly.

Towards evening the Boers, apprised of the approach of succour, drew off, and were pursued by Yeomanry and guns, which had arrived on the scene. Their losses in this unequal combat were certainly very small. The Provisional Battalion lost eight killed and seventeen wounded, including among the former Major Hobbs, o the West Yorkshire Regiment, who was taken prisoner at the end of his first engagement, and killed at the beginning of his second.

Capetown, *28 June*

Our train arrived about midday, and without further incidents worthy of record we reached Kroonstad, and so to Capetown. Here, then, I make my bow to the reader, and bring these letters to a conclusion. They have chronicled as faithfully as lay in my power nearly every exciting adventure or military affair it has been my fortune to share or witness during the last nine months. They have been written among many difficulties and often adverse conditions, with pen or pencil as the fates decreed, under a waggon, in the shadow of a rock, by the uncertain light of a lantern, or even sitting on the ground in the rain. They had to hurry home without waiting for second thoughts, and spring into print guided by a strange hand; and for these reasons perhaps I may claim some indulgence for their crudities and imperfections. So far as my memory serves me, and subject to the demands of truth, they have maligned no one, certainly no one who was unfortunate; and if there be anybody who feels himself assailed unjustly here and now I crave his pardon.

Such as it is, the work at least represents the changing moods and forecasts of the camp, and if in this fashion it has helped to bring those who have borne the long anxiety at home into closer sympathy with their soldiers at the wars, I shall be content, and even be bold to ask the reader to dismiss me with a smile.

25 July, 1900

Index

INDEX

Index

Index

347

Index

Kerreri, 95, 98, 99, 101, 104, 105, 108, 118, 124, 146
Khalifa, The, *see* Abdullahi Ibn Sayed Mohammed
Khar, 7, 11, 19, 20
Khartoum, 69, 70, 72, 83, 90, 91, 94, 96, 98, 99, 100, 120, 122, 133, 136, 137, 145
King's Royal Rifles, 3rd, 215, 216
Kitchener, Herbert Horatio, xv, xvi, xvii, 94, 101, 108, 109, 115, 117, 119, 123, 130, 131, 138, 337, 339
Kitchener's Horse, 296, 297, 300
Kohat, 4, 12
Kruger, Paul, 139, 314

Ladysmith, xx, 156, 161, 163, 164, 174, 177, 192-3, 195, 198, 203, 213, 235, 247, 266, 267, 268, 270, 271-3, 274-87
Ladysmith Lyre, 279
Lancashire Fusiliers, 83, 91, 96, 212, 214, 218, 275
Lancaster Regiment, Royal, 212, 214
Lancers, 12th, 112, 303, 304
Lancers, 17th, 323
Lancers, 18th, 321-3
Lancers, 21st, xvi, 83, 84, 99, 100, 101, 104, 106, 107, 108, 109-12, 113, 114, 115, 116, 118, 120, 121, 125, 130, 131-3, 141, 146
Lancers, Bengal, 5, 19, 22, 31, 38, 46, 47, 62, 115
Lewis, General, 108
Liverpool Regiment, 274
Lobengula, 139
Lockhart, Sir William, 165
London to Ladysmith, xxv
Long, Colonel, 164, 165
Lourenço Marques, 187, 188, 189
Lyttelton, Neville, 198, 200, 201, 202, 211, 215, 234, 242, 248, 255, 256

MacDonald, General, 108, 120, 126
McNeill, Angus, 289, 290-1
Madras Infantry, 3
Mahdi, The, *see* Mohammed Ahmed
Mahmoud Wad Ahmed, 83, 92, 136
Malakand, 3, 4, 5, 7, 8, 11, 12
Malakand Field Force, The Story of the, xv, xxv
Manchester Regiment, 274
Marlborough, Duchess of, xxi
Marlborough, Duke of, 312, 313-4
Martin, Rowland Hill, 99, 109, 111, 131-2
Matabele war, 117, 118
Methuen, Lord, 328, 330, 337
Metemmeh, 83, 85, 91, 92, 147
Middlesex Regiment, 214, 215, 218
Milner, Sir Alfred, 156
Mohammed Ahmed, xvii, 99, 102, 103, 117, 134, 136, 137, 138, 139
Mohmand, 6, 8, 12, 15, 18, 21, 22, 31, 34, 35, 43, 44, 48, 49, 51, 52, 53, 57, 58, 61
Molyneux, Richard Frederick, 141-2
Montagu-Stuart-Wortley, Edward James, 96
Montmorency's Scouts, 289-92
Morning Post, xix, xx, 188, 290

Index

Index